Death & Co
WELCOME HOME

Death & Co
WELCOME HOME

———

ALEX DAY • NICK FAUCHALD • DAVID KAPLAN

WITH DEVON TARBY & TYSON BUHLER

PHOTOGRAPHS BY DYLAN + JENI

ILLUSTRATIONS BY TIM TOMKINSON

TEN SPEED PRESS
California | New York

CONTENTS

INTRODUCTION

On New Year's Eve 2006, I opened Death & Co on a quiet side street in Manhattan's East Village. Within our first couple of years of business, our bar had secured its place among the world's leading cocktail bars, and by the time Alex became a partner in 2008, we began planning to open more Death & Co bars around the country—and perhaps one day abroad. It wasn't a matter of *if* we'd open more locations, but *when* and *where*.

The *when*, it turns out, would be more than a decade later. Early negotiations with Death & Co's two other founding partners, Ravi and Craig, went nowhere, so I put our unfinished agreement in a drawer and focused my attention elsewhere. Alex and I started a hospitality consulting company, Proprietors LLC, and we both moved to Los Angeles.

As our new lives and business took off in California, we did our best to put our dreams of opening another Death & Co to rest. We took on numerous projects around L.A., built a proper office and development lab, and expanded our consulting work across the world. As Proprietors LLC grew, so did our ambitions. We formed a partnership with L.A. nightlife impresario Cedd Moses, which allowed us to develop three new bars from the ground up: the downtown cocktail bar and dance club Honeycut, and a pair of bars inside the Normandie Hotel in Koreatown: a lively lounge called the Normandie Club, and an ambitious, omakase-inspired cocktail den called the Walker Inn.

While this partnership helped us build our confidence and competence in opening and operating bars, it did little to help us improve our financial acumen, as the accounting responsibilities fell to Cedd's group. Meanwhile, business at Death & Co was as good as ever, but we were so disconnected from the day-to-day operations at the bar that the culture began to suffer from our lack of oversight. Alex and I decided that it was time to recommit ourselves to our partnership with the other Death & Co founders and pave a path

to opening more bars that would be completely our own. In our previous projects, we'd always felt like the little kids at the grown-ups' table. We decided that the only way forward was to embrace any fears of failure, take control of all the details of running a bar, and build our own fucking table.

So we slowly disentangled ourselves from our three L.A. partnership bars, pulled our unfinished Death & Co agreement out of the drawer, and patched up relationships with Ravi and Craig. We reinserted ourselves into the New York bar, working to tighten up the operations and financials and to revitalize the working culture there. I started reading every business book I could get my hands on, and I joined Acceler8, a coaching program for hospitality owners who want to grow their business. From there we trained ourselves in something called the Entrepreneurial Operating System (EOS) and used it to align our values and vision for the company and its future. EOS was like rocket fuel for our leadership team, and everything was finally starting to gel.

Learning a structured system that we could apply to our company felt liberating. It gave us a framework for many aspects of our operations and also helped us understand the differences in our personalities, responsibilities, and roles—something we had long been missing. It became clear that although Alex and I both love every part of running bars, we excel at very different things. I tend to think like a typical founder, chasing long-term vision and instilling the values and culture that will help lead us there. Alex thrives in problem solving and the details, finding the path from an idea to a finalized product. An example of this rests in your hands—I get to chase the deals for our books while Alex works with Nick to transpose our working worlds to the page.

Around this time we received a short (and mythically serendipitous) email from Ryan Diggins, a Denver-based real-estate developer who was building a hotel, the Ramble, in the city's up-and-coming RiNo (River North Art District) neighborhood. The hotel needed a hospitality partner to operate its food and beverage programs, and he wanted Death & Co to be that partner. When we met Ryan, it quickly became clear that our values and vision were aligned, and while the Denver project would be uncharted territory for our company—we'd be responsible for multiple bars and a central kitchen (almost) twenty-four hours a day, seven days a week—we felt that we were ready, personally and professionally, to finally open another Death & Co.

The process of opening Death & Co Denver was unlike anything we'd done before. But through our many years of opening and running bars, we'd learned from both our successes and our many setbacks, and we had the right mix of experience, confidence, and humility to pull it off. The physical space of Death & Co Denver couldn't be more different than that of our small New York bar: five individual bars comprising some twelve thousand square feet. Our first challenge was to figure out how to make this massive, all-day space still feel like a Death & Co. The culture of our New York bar is largely defined by the intimacy of its space and the smallness of its team, which isn't easy to replicate in a bustling hotel. But when we looked more deeply into what defines our cocktails and approach to hospitality, we identified some core values and qualities that could be planted in our Denver location, and beyond.

Death & Co's approach to cocktails has always been driven by a dual dedication to quality and elegance. Our drinks are rooted in classic cocktails, with honest, direct flavors and compositions. We welcome innovation, of course, but it is not our driving motivation. Most of all, we want our cocktails to elicit a response that's not "Hmm, that's interesting," but "Wow, that's fucking delicious!" As simple as that sounds, "that's fucking delicious" extends far beyond just what's in the glass. Let's zoom out: The temperature of the glass, the coaster on which it rests, and the texture of the marble bar below it all contribute to the enjoyment of that cocktail, as do the engagement and personality of the staff who served it, the guests surrounding you, the music and lighting that fill the space—all of these things contribute to "fucking delicious," and all are essential to the Death & Co experience.

Although the space and staff at Death & Co Denver dwarfed that of our New York bar, we were able to express its ethos in new and additional ways. We hired a staff of wonderful, well-rounded humans; some arrived with experience and technical prowess; others had little or no cocktail chops,

but the drive to learn and develop. We reimagined our approach to cocktail and menu development (more on this in chapter 3), and we forced ourselves to focus on intentional and transparent management rather than the passive maintenance that had adversely affected the culture of our New York bar in the past.

As the Death & Co Denver project was getting off the ground, we signed a lease in L.A.'s Arts District in a building that was around the corner from our longtime office, where all of our projects, prior to Denver, had been incubated. Over the years, we'd become part of the neighborhood's community of artists and entrepreneurs, and we were beyond excited to finally open Death & Co Los Angeles after years of scouting, negotiations, and setbacks. Our new bar was to be located in the basement of a building that had yet to be renovated, so we also had our first opportunity to design a space from the ground up (or rather, from the street level down). Death & Co L.A. would also be the biggest bet we'd ever placed on ourselves, as we were covering all of the costs. The physical space was small(ish) and cavernous, like our New York bar, but we didn't want to simply replicate Death & Co NYC. New York and Los Angeles are very different cities, with different nightlife scenes. It's easy to maneuver around New York City, so our guests tend to bar-hop, especially when they have to wait for a seat at Death & Co. In L.A., you tend to pick a spot and stay there for the night, so we wanted to create an environment that wouldn't have to turn guests away (as we did hundreds of times a night in NYC) and would invite long, lingering evenings. We added a second space to Death & Co L.A., called the Standing Room, where the cocktail menu was succinct, service was swift, and guests could stick around for a drink while they waited for a table in the main lounge. L.A.'s cocktail culture is also more informal, so we wanted to balance the seating-room-only main bar with this more casual adjacency without abandoning our high-touch approach to service.

We opened Death & Co L.A. in mid-December 2019, which is one of the worst times of the year to open a bar, but we quickly outperformed our modest expectations for our first month of business. A few weeks in, we were very proud of what everyone had accomplished: we had a great management team in place, which allowed Alex and me to take a step back from the minutiae of opening a bar and let our talented team drive the bus, a natural evolution of the company that we'd been working toward for years.

At the same time, we were working on opening yet another Death & Co by the end of 2020, this one in Chicago. Chicago was always high on my list of prospective locations, as I was born there, my family is still based there, and bringing Death & Co to the Windy City feels like an important full-circle opportunity. We had been scouting spaces there for some time and had a killer project team in place. By opening Death & Co L.A., we'd proved to ourselves that we could tackle a full-scale bar opening, from design to open doors, without our other bars, businesses, or sanity suffering in the process.

And then there was a global pandemic.

If it had hit a few years earlier, I don't know how we would have proceeded. But because we'd become a more organized and intentional company, we immediately started asking ourselves, and each other, *what can we do?* We realized it was our job to take care of our people as best we could while keeping the company alive, so they'd have a job to return to. We knew we'd have to lay off a significant number of staff, but we didn't know how far down the line it would go. We created multipage models of various scenarios, each with a list of names and when we would have to let them go in order to maximize our chances of survival. It was fucking awful.

Having learned from our past mistakes, we knew it was essential to maintain a level of complete transparency and frank, open, constant communication with our teams. We started an internal newsletter to share daily updates about the state of the business, as well as resources for employees. We found the funds to keep some employees on payroll for a while and to continue paying health insurance for an extra ten weeks for those we had to lay off. We quickly created both a staff fund to help those who needed financial assistance and an employee committee to decide how to distribute the funds. Our industry was already rife with mental health issues, and we knew that the mental health implications of layoffs and a pandemic could be significant, so we covered the cost of a therapist for anyone who wanted one. Our managers, even the ones we'd had to let go, worked hard to keep our culture and sense of community alive by organizing virtual hangouts and socially distanced outdoor meetups.

But as we focused on closing down our businesses and shoring up any funds we could find to stay afloat, we were equally focused on a plan for reopening. Alex and our operations team worked night and day on writing our reopening playbook. It was a massive document, detailing, down to the most granular level, how to reopen and operate each of our venues during, and after, a pandemic. When it was finished, we shared it with our team, and, as per Alex's suggestion, we made it available to the public. Our playbook

quickly made its way around the industry, and the response from our peers was overwhelmingly positive.

To us, the playbook embodied our approach to hospitality and, well, everything. The secret to our success is to have no secrets. We've seen what happens when you spend all of your time and energy trying to protect something you've created, rather than focusing on creating something new and different. Excellence isn't about ownership, but openness—and execution. This isn't true of every industry, but it sure as hell applies to hospitality. This is why we decided, years ago, to share everything we knew about cocktails—and all of our recipes—in our first book. It's one of our core values to endlessly pursue learning and improvement, and to share those learnings along the way—which is why, as we continued to develop the way we think and teach about cocktails, we wrote a second book. And now we've written a third, in which we're sharing all of the new things we've learned (and some we've unlearned) since we published our first book. We've said it before, but it's worth repeating: A cocktail is a blueprint, nothing more than a list of ingredients and instructions on how to assemble them. Likewise, a bar is just a room with some chairs and bottles of booze. But a human is what makes a cocktail come to life, just as many humans, banded together in the name of hospitality, make a bar come to life. We hope you'll take the lessons and recipes in this book and make them come to life.

As 2020 progressed, we were able to put our reopening playbook to work—first in Denver, then in New York, then in Los Angeles. As I write this, we still haven't emerged from the grip of this goddamn pandemic, but I'm very hopeful that, by the time you're reading this, we can welcome you safely into all of our bars, and raise a glass with you to a better future.

—DAVID KAPLAN, OCTOBER 2020

HOW TO USE THIS BOOK

When we wrote our first cocktail book, our intention was to tell the story of a little bar that could, to make every reader simultaneously feel like both a regular and a seasoned Death & Co bartender, and to share everything we'd learned—including the cocktails we'd created along the way. After that book surprised us (and our publisher?) with its success, we realized we had lots more to share about the way we *think* about cocktails—that is, understanding that a handful of fundamental recipes can unlock the secrets to all cocktails. When this somewhat-abstractive exercise, titled *Cocktail Codex*, surprised us again (and *definitely* our publisher this time) with its success, we used it to inform how we continued to rethink and reorganize our approach to cocktails at Death & Co.

By the time we'd decided to write a third book—and our second that focused specifically on Death & Co—a lot had changed. The craft-cocktail industry had evolved: There are more and better ingredients and tools released every year, and more and better cocktail bars opening in every corner of the country. Two of these new bars—Death & Co Denver and Death & Co Los Angeles—belong to us, and our original New York location was consistently doing its best business ever.

Until it wasn't, thanks to the global pandemic. But as devastating as this crisis was for everyone, including the hospitality industry and our own businesses, it gave us the opportunity to look back at how we had turned Death & Co into an ever-evolving brand, and how we grew from one bar to three distinct properties in three very different parts of the country. And because we were spending so much time isolated in our own homes, it gave us a renewed appreciation for all of the enthusiasts, both amateur and professional, who use our books to inform the way they make cocktails at home. So we started to see this book as an opportunity to not only tell the story of Death & Co's evolution, but also bridge the gaps between the bar and the home bar—after all, we all want the same thing in the end: a welcome home, a drink, and a moment of pause.

So here we are. This book traces a path similar to what new members of the Death & Co team follow, as they're introduced to our philosophies on work, hospitality, and, of course, cocktails. If it helps you get into the right mindset, imagine you're a rookie bartender who's just joined our family, and this is your employee handbook. You'll get the most out of the experience if you read the book from cover to cover, as each chapter builds on the previous, but feel free to skip around or just flip to the back and start making drinks—unlike for our actual employees, there won't be a test at the end.

Chapter 1, "Preparation," examines the guiding principles we use to frame and focus our work. If you've ever wondered what it's like to work at one of our bars, this chapter closely follows the way we train our staffs. You'll learn the importance of working with *intention* (a word you'll encounter frequently throughout this book—you've been warned). We'll also walk you through a bunch of hands-on exercises to help you understand your own palate and personal preferences, and we'll outline the tools and techniques you'll need to start making cocktails.

Chapter 2, "Selection," covers the various liquids we use to make our drinks: spirits, modifiers, sweeteners, bitters, and so on. Whereas in our previous books we did a deep dive on specific brands that we frequently use, here we're broadening our focus to help you make more informed decisions (and, if needed, substitutions) in your own cocktails.

Over the past few years, we've radically changed the way we develop and organize our cocktail menus. Chapter 3, "Development," uses the story of a single Death & Co Denver menu to peek behind the curtains of our creative process. We hope you come away from this section armed with new strategies for creating drinks—and perhaps a new or renewed appreciation for spreadsheets.

The biggest surprise that came out of publishing *Death & Co: Modern Classic Cocktails* is how many readers actually make our drinks (as written!) at home. We expected people to learn plenty about cocktails from our first book, but have you seen some of those specs? Who's going to source *so much* esoteric booze, make endless infusions and time-consuming syrups, and crush ice by hand, just to wet their whistle? *You*—that's who. Over the years we've met countless "amateurs" who have fearlessly stirred and shaken their way through hundreds of recipes in *Death & Co* and *Cocktail Codex* in their own homes. Every time we hear about your home-bartending adventures, we're awed by your ambition and enthusiasm—and more dedicated to helping you get more out of your home bar setup, whether it's stocked with three bottles of liquor or three hundred. Chapter 4, "Cocktails at Home," shares all of the secrets and advice we've amassed over years of playing bartender in our own abodes.

Finally, we've packed chapter 5, "Specs," with hundreds of new Death & Co cocktail recipes. While we didn't have room to include every recipe we've created since the writing of our first book, we whittled down a pool of around a thousand prospects to about five hundred of our favorites, with an eye toward specs that are easy (okay, *easier*) to execute at home. We've arranged these specs to mimic how we now organize our menus, which will help guide you to the perfect cocktail to match your drinking mood.

THE NEW DEATH & CO LEXICON

An updated glossary of relevant and irreverent colloquialisms, slang, and inside jokes heard around our bars.

BACK-POCKET SPEC: A new cocktail recipe that is almost complete and saved for the right slot on a future menu.

BIG WEIRD SHOTS: Death & Co NYC doorman Josh Polina's definition of cocktails.

COBBLER SHIT: The customarily lavish garnish on top of a cobbler, usually a combination of berries, citrus, and mint, often dusted with powdered sugar.

COLD CRISPY: A post-shift beer, aka "crispy boi."

DAVE KAPLAN: Staff shorthand for an order of seltzer on ice.

DEATH & COCONUT: Nickname we gave ourselves when we realized we were using Kalani coconut liqueur in an alarming number of drinks.

FLABBY: Our way of calling a cocktail "boring."

FLAT: Used when a drink lacks character or dimension of flavor.

GLOSS AND TOSS: Shorthand for expressing a citrus twist over a drink, then discarding it.

GRIGGS'D: When a bartender creates a drink that isn't very popular because of its excessively nerdy nature, named in honor of Death & Co Denver's Adam Griggs.

HARD BOY: A staff nip of ice-cold brandy during one's shift.

THE HOOK: The element of a cocktail that makes it particularly interesting.

HOT: Used when a drink tastes too boozy or alcoholic.

ICR: Ice cold receptacle, or a well-chilled glass.

KNOLL YOUR STATION: Get your work area organized. Always be knolling (ABK)!

"MAY I?": How we start conversations with coworkers during service.

MIND-MOUTH: Shannon Tebay's term for imagining flavor combinations in one's brain before any actual tasting or development begins.

MUDDY: Used to call out indiscriminate flavors in a cocktail, aka "brown."

"NO RUNNING AT THE POOL!": Coined when a coworker was running through the Death & Co Denver lobby to the restroom. Don't run anywhere at work; the juice is not worth the squeeze.

PRESHIFT: A quick five-minute meeting before we open for the day.

SCUPPER: The name for the perforated metal work surface on top of our bar.

SPICY: See "hot."

STRIKING DISTANCE: Used to signify a new cocktail recipe that's almost there, but needs a tiny tweak or two.

THIN: See "washed out."

TIGHT: A drink that needs more dilution to allow each of the flavors to shine.

TOUGH GUY: See "hard boy."

WASHED OUT: Used when a drink becomes overdiluted in the glass.

WATER SHOT: A brief moment during a busy service when a teammate hands you a shot of water because they know you probably haven't had one in hours. Used as a bonding moment and opportunity to reset and take a breather. Also known as "Shannon's rain delay."

WORK TO CODE: A polite way to tell a coworker to not cut corners; appropriated from our unofficial mentor, Tom Sachs.

PREPARATION

In 2009, American artist Tom Sachs uploaded a YouTube video titled *Ten Bullets*, an art piece in the guise of an employee orientation video that highlights ten key expectations for working at Sachs's studio.

In the video, Sachs and his team detail the artist's meticulous, methodical, and almost maniacal ethos: the sanctity of the studio, the power of a list, an unwavering commitment to thoroughness, and the importance of being on time (something we bartenders struggle with). Each section is a bullet point in a grammatical sense—a lesson for a new assistant in the studio's best practices—but each is also a not-so-subtle threat, a bullet in the physical sense: *Veer away from these expectations, and you'll be done. You'll be done forever.*

While we don't sanction threatening anyone, we, like Sachs, want to create an environment in our bars that balances creativity with order. Halfway through the video, Sachs introduces a bullet that we've adopted as a mantra in our bars: "Always Be Knolling," or "ABK." In photography, "knolling" refers to arranging objects in parallel or 90-degree angles. To Sachs, it means: (1) Scan your environment for tools, materials, and other objects that are not in use. (2) Put away everything not in use.

FAULT LINE, PAGE 252

If you aren't sure, put it away. (3) Group all "like" objects. (4) Align all objects in parallel or 90-degree angles to either the surface they rest on or the studio itself.

Though we use different tools from Sachs—he, soldering irons; we, cocktail shakers and barspoons—we both thrive in environments that benefit from working tidy even in the midst of chaos. For bartenders, a well-knolled work station is essential. But it's not just about efficiency. ABK is not only a physical exercise; it's also a mental and emotional one, a way to organize a chaotic world. Creating a Zen-like space free of clutter is an exercise in conviction, and one of the ways great bars and bartenders set their intention.

ESTABLISHING INTENTION

The word *intention* has been bandied about to the point that it can lose its meaning. You'll hear it paired with other workplace buzzwords: hospitality, quality, execution, consistency. But these words all represent the end of a process, and you can't get there without intention.

Whether your goal is to serve a delicious cocktail, develop a new menu, or build a bar from scratch, it is essential to have a vision of the end result. Intention is the materialization of vision, a way to give focus to a goal and articulate the steps necessary to reach it. At a bar, intention is also a shared understanding of *why* something is done a certain way; not just a rule for rule's sake, but rather a consensus that works toward the larger aspiration of the bar. Without it, common issues with cocktails arise: drinks taste different from one bartender to another (there's no expectation for recipes); a shaken drink lacks texture, or a stirred drink has too much (a lack of understanding of what the target dilution is and why); fizzy drinks are served flat (bubbles are king!); cold drinks are served in warm glassware (*blasphemy*); garnishes are sloppy (the beauty is in the details); and so on.

Bartenders often come to work for us because they want to improve their craft. But we don't begin their education by teaching them new cocktail recipes or techniques. Like Sachs, we start by explaining what matters to us and what we expect of them—that is, we set our collective intention. It's at this stage that we introduce knolling and the mantra "ABK" as a first step: by simply organizing your work area

with rigor, you will begin to understand our expectations in a more global sense and align with our aspirations of excellence. We seek excellence, knowing that it is an unattainable end, that the path toward excellence is the whole point, and that *navigating that path with intention is key to everything we do.*

We don't believe in the idea of the Brilliant Artist, the savant who pulls virtuosity from thin air. All great craftspeople and artists are deeply disciplined. We believe that if you aspire to make great cocktails or to be a confident bartender, you must work diligently toward that goal—often with grueling repetition.

So we return to Sachs's *Ten Bullets* and our mantra of *always be knolling*. If you care deeply about something—even something as simple as arranging objects on a table—the act of caring sets a standard that will impact everything you want to achieve: the jump from simple to complex, from mediocre to excellent.

So, with that intention as our guide, let us begin your path toward excellence in cocktails.

THE PHYSICAL SETUP

Beginning this book with a discussion of *knolling* and philosophical musings about *intention* is our way of bringing you into our world of bartender training. Welcome! Just as we want for any new bartender, we want you to understand the *whys* underlying everything we do. Anyone can teach you a recipe. We want to teach you how to set up your space and mentally organize your thoughts when making or creating cocktails. The ABK mantra weaves its way through everything we do and guides us in decisions both large and small.

ESSENTIAL TOOLS FOR MAKING COCKTAILS

This is not a comprehensive list of all the gear we use behind the bar (we covered that in our first book), but rather a survey of tools, and their intended purposes, that any drink maker needs to make most cocktails. When choosing tools and glassware for a home bar, you don't need to own everything listed here; think about the types of cocktails you most enjoy making, and stock up on the items you'll use most often.

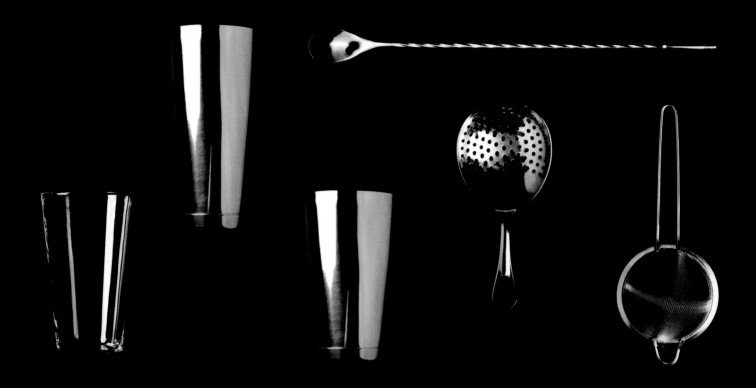

MIXING GLASS

We've always loved the fancy etched Japanese mixing glasses, but over time (and many broken glasses and tears), we've landed on the humble pint glass as our preferred vessel for making stirred drinks. Pint glasses are many times cheaper than their Japanese counterparts, of course, but they also take up a smaller footprint on top of the bar, and we can store more of them in the freezer. It's important to use one made from durable tempered glass, so it will handle the rapid temperature changes that occur when you're working with (and washing) frozen glassware.

SHAKERS

In our early days, most of our bartenders worked with their own shakers during service, which were most commonly a pair of stainless steel tins of varying weights (one smaller, and one larger). Now that we operate several bars, we use "18-28" sets of tins that hold 18 and 28 ounces, respectively. The 18-ounce tin is much larger than most "tin-on-tin" shaker combinations for a very specific reason: with an inward bevel, this larger shaker creates a much better seal while maintaining a good balance between the two tins. This setup is durable and cheap; if you want something

a bit nicer and longer-lasting, look for Koriko or Vollrath brands. A three-piece cobbler shaker is a great alternative to the 18-28 set for the home bar, as it's a handsome piece of equipment and sports a built-in strainer, but we don't use these at the bars for a couple of reasons. First, a vacuum tends to build up inside the cobbler as you shake a drink, which makes removing the cap a real pain, and the shaker's three pieces (versus the 18-28 set's two pieces) means just one more thing to wash between drinks.

STRAINERS

If you have to choose one strainer for using on all styles of drinks, buy a lightweight Hawthorne strainer with a tightly coiled spring and two or four protruding tabs that allow you to adjust the flow of the drink (aka "gate control") as you strain it. A julep strainer is also nice to have for stirred drinks, as liquid will pass through the holes more quickly and fluidly than it would through a Hawthorne strainer, thus maintaining the silky texture of the stirred cocktail. We use both styles, sourced from Cocktail Kingdom. You also need a mesh cone strainer for double straining shaken drinks; at home you can use a cheap kitchen sieve, but we prefer one designed specifically for cocktails, with a deeper cone that will hold an entire drink's worth of liquid.

BARSPOON

Barspoons come in myriad styles, lengths, and metallic finishes, and most will get the job done once you learn how to use them. We've found the best all-around spoon to be about 12 inches in length, with a twisted handle (for a more secure grip) and a teardrop-shaped weight on top that adds a counterbalance that helps you achieve a smooth, steady stirring rhythm. Our house barspoons are made by Barfly or Cocktail Kingdom, though many of our bartenders still use their own, either as a piece of personal flair, or because they prefer a different length of spoon.

ICE CRACKER

This is a generic term for anything that will crack the ice you need for making stirred drinks. In the past we used Tap-Icers, a product built specifically for the task. But their lifespan in a busy bar is short, so we now use a cheap, heavy barspoon (the kind we tell you *not* to use for mixing drinks) to crack ice. At home, the back of a soup spoon will also get the job done.

JIGGERS

Like barspoons, jiggers come in many shapes and styles. We prefer Japanese-style jiggers, which are taller and skinnier than the more common squat, cone-shaped ones you'd find at a kitchen supply store. The smaller diameter of the Japanese-style jigger makes it easier to measure ingredients more accurately, and the longer shape is easier to maneuver around the glass. Whatever style you choose, a set of two jiggers — one that measures 1 and 2 ounces, the other ½ and ¾ ounce (with an interior etching marking ¼ ounce) — will allow you to make any cocktail; any smaller measurement should be tackled with a measuring spoon.

MEASURING SPOONS

Barspoons are both awkward and inaccurate measuring implements, so we always keep ½- and 1-teaspoon kitchen measuring spoons (ours are made by Vollrath) behind the bar for measuring small amounts of ingredients.

MUDDLER

A good muddler should be weighty enough to do most of the work for you. Our longtime favorite is the "Bad Ass" muddler from Cocktail Kingdom; it's made from black food-grade plastic and looks like it could kill you.

VEGETABLE PEELER

Try cutting a few citrus twists with a knife and you'll quickly see the value of a good vegetable peeler. The best style is shaped like a Y, with a sharp, nonserrated blade. Our workhorse peeler is the heavy metal model with a non-slip rubber grip made by OXO.

UTILITY KNIFE

For all other garnishes, we use an inexpensive kitchen utility knife, which falls in size about halfway between a paring knife and a chef's knife. We sharpen ours before every service (on an electric sharpener, which purists will hate).

DASHER BOTTLES

Decanting your bottles of store-bought bitters into elegant glass dasher bottles might seem pretentious, but off-the-shelf bitters bottles are wildly inaccurate, which can really throw off a drink when you're working with an intense seasoning like bitters. If you choose to invest in a set, get some with screw-on caps (versus corks); corks will deteriorate over time, and they tend to pop off if you dash too enthusiastically. However, most home bartenders don't heed our advice and work with off-the-shelf bottles, which is why we write recipes with this in mind. If you're using fancy dasher bottles, double the amount of dashes called for in a recipe.

SETTING UP YOUR STATION

Whether you're making drinks in a bar or in your kitchen, it's good to set up your tools within easy reach before you start making drinks. The photo at left shows how we set up our bar stations, which should be used as a jumping-off point for creating your own configuration. Generally, we like to dedicate an open space for "building" the cocktails—on either a bar mat or a folded kitchen towel—and then surround the area with ingredients and tools. When making a drink, we'll bring our mixing glass or shaker tin into this space, build and finish the cocktail, and then reset all tools and ingredients before moving on. Just remember: Always. Be. Knolling.

GLASSWARE

As our bars have aged, we've streamlined the collection of glassware we use to serve drinks. This helps with economies of scale, sure, but it also helps us stay focused on what goes into the glass, rather than worrying too much about embellishment. The glassware we select for permanent rotation meets a few criteria: it must be (1) affordable but elegant enough to honor the drinks it will serve, (2) versatile (for example, we use double old-fashioned glasses for their namesake cocktail family as well as many drinks served over crushed ice), and (3) durable (dishwashers were invented for a reason). If you're making drinks at home, you can get away with as few as five glassware styles: double old-fashioned, coupe, Nick & Nora, collins, and wine glass.

SINGLE OLD-FASHIONED GLASS

Also known as a Sazerac glass or single rocks glass, we use these to serve both Sazerac-style drinks and Old-Fashioned variations of 2½ ounces or less. Each of our bars stocks a different brand, but they all hold about 10 ounces.

DOUBLE OLD-FASHIONED GLASS

Our "DOF" glasses range from 13 to 15 ounces, and are used for stirred drinks served on a large ice cube, as well as many shaken drinks served over crushed ice.

COUPE

Where once we served both stirred and shaken drinks in coupes, we now use them primarily for the latter. Our coupes are made by Urban Bar and hold 7 ounces of liquid. That leaves plenty of headspace for any of our shaken drinks, which range in volume from 3 to 5 ounces.

NICK & NORA

We serve most of our stirred-and-up drinks in these classic tulip-shaped vessels. There are now several great options on the market; we use the 5.5-ounce Nick & Nora from Steelite's Rona Minners collection.

MARTINI GLASS

A classic Martini deserves a martini glass: ours are on the smaller side (4.5 ounces) and are also made by Urban Bar.

COLLINS GLASS

Collins glasses are slightly larger (about 13 ounces) than highball glasses (10 ounces), which allows us to use one style of glassware for both collins and highball variations.

BEER GLASS

We use two styles of beer glasses for shaken drinks served over ice: a 16-ounce Belgian tulip glass, and a 14-ounce pilsner glass, both made by Spiegelau.

FIZZ GLASS

These slender glasses are used for fizz-style drinks served neat. We splurge on the 10-ounce striped fizz glasses made by the Japanese company Hard Strong.

JULEP TIN

We almost always serve julep-style drinks in the traditional vessel. Ours are silver-plated, hold 12 ounces, and come from Cocktail Kingdom.

WINE GLASSES

For spritzes and other effervescent drinks served on the rocks, we use 13-ounce white wine glasses. For champagne- and other sparkling-wine-based drinks, we no longer use a traditional flute; we use a wine glass with slightly more tapered sides, which is much better for appreciating the aromas and flavors of champagne (and other sparkling wines). Ours hold about 7 ounces, the perfect size to contain most effervescent cocktails served up.

TIKI MUGS

We've parted ways with our vintage (and culturally problematic) tiki mugs—and are distancing ourselves from using the term "tiki" more and more ("tropical" works just fine in most cases), due to the baggage it carries—and are now making our own proprietary mugs that hold about 16 ounces. We also use ceramic coconuts that hold about 14 ounces.

PUNCH BOWL

We served a lot of punch in the early days at the New York bar, but not so much as of late. When we do, we pull out one of our vintage punch bowls and serve the punch alongside some single old-fashioned glasses.

**SINGLE
OLD-FASHIONED
GLASS**

**DOUBLE
OLD-FASHIONED
GLASS**

COUPE

NICK & NORA

MARTINI GLASS

COLLINS GLASS

BEER GLASS

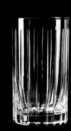

FIZZ GLASS

JULEP TIN

WINE GLASS

WINE GLASS

TIKI MUGS

PUNCH BOWL

Each type of ice we use serves one or more specific purposes: large blocks for serving cocktails in a single or double old-fashioned glass; Kold-Draft ice for both shaking and serving tall cocktails; and pellet ice for chilling down glassware and serving coolers, cobblers, juleps, and tropical cocktails. (For advice on replicating these ice styles for your home bar, see page 34.)

BLOCK ICE

One of the most exciting changes in our industry over the past fifteen years is the increasing availability of "good ice" in cities across the country. In our early days, we made blocks of 2-inch ice cubes using plastic molds in a dedicated freezer; this was a labor-intensive process, and the results were okay—about as good as you could pull off at home. Now there are dedicated craft-ice companies near each of our bars, which allows us to save on labor and source 2½ by 2 by 2-inch blocks of perfectly pellucid ice for stirred (and some shaken) drinks served in old-fashioned glasses.

Another improvement in the ice world is the reliability of cube-ice machines. In New York, our original Kold-Draft machine used to fail on us frequently, and there was exactly one guy who could fix it (and charge you accordingly for his monopoly). Today, we still use Kold-Draft machines at all our bars to make 1¼ by 1¼-inch cubes, but the equipment breaks down much less frequently. We use these cubes for both shaking cocktails and serving drinks in collins glasses.

CRUSHED ICE

Nothing beats the consistent, crunchy nuggets that our dependable Scotsman machines put out for making juleps, tropical drinks, swizzles, and other shaken drinks served over "crushed ice." This is the hardest style of ice to replicate at home, but you can make your crushed ice by filling a clean towel or canvas bag (we keep an unused canvas tote handy at home) with ice cubes and smashing them with a wooden mallet, rolling pin, or small saucepan. The bag will absorb any melted water, leaving you with dry, serviceable crushed ice that's better, in our experience, than what most residential freezers spit out of their ice dispenser.

GARNISHES

We view garnishes as extensions of a cocktail, used to complement and enhance the drink by adding aromatic and/or visual cues. Sight and smell are powerful senses that directly affect how we perceive flavor, so we use garnishes as tools to excite these senses. Garnishes shouldn't be superfluous adornments or outlandish distractions; when selecting a garnish for a new cocktail, we always ask ourselves: *What does this garnish add to the drink?* If a garnish doesn't enhance the drinking experience—which is often the case—we don't use one.

With certain cocktails, garnishes also allow the guest to personalize the drink to his or her liking, such as a lime wedge on a Daiquiri or margarita.

From the simplicity of a citrus twist for an Old-Fashioned or an olive in a Martini to the lavish bouquets of mint in a julep or the mini fruit salads jutting out of a cobbler, we must be thoughtful not only in the choice of garnish but also in how we execute that garnish during service. See the following pages for a visual guide of our most common garnishes.

GARNISH BEST PRACTICES

• Garnishes should be prepared at the last moment, either right before you shake a drink, or after you stir a cocktail but before you pour it into the serving glass.

• Garnishes should always look as if they came from a healthy plant or piece of fruit.

• Lemon, lime, and orange slices should be brightly colored, with shiny, smooth skin and juicy pulp. Use organic and unwaxed fruit whenever possible, and always wash it first.

• Citrus twists should be sturdy enough to squeeze oils on top of a drink without the peel breaking or tearing.

• Herbs such as basil and mint should also be vibrantly colored, with no brown spots, holes, or tears.

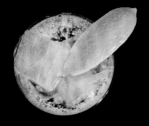

CITRUS WEDGE

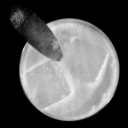

CITRUS WEDGE

CITRUS HALF WHEEL

CITRUS TWIST

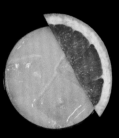

CITRUS HALF WHEEL

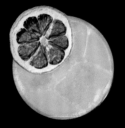

CITRUS DEHYDRATED

RASPBERRIES

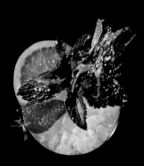

"COBBLER SHIT" WITH
POWDERED SUGAR

PINEAPPLE FRONDS

CUCUMBER RIBBON

OLIVE

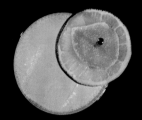

CANDIED GINGER

APPLE FLAG

PINEAPPLE WEDGE

STRAWBERRY

BRANDIED CHERRY

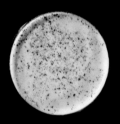

GRATED CINNAMON

MINT BOUQUET

BITTERS STRIPE

BASIL LEAVES

HENRIK STEEN PETERSEN

Henrik Steen Petersen is a cocktail writer and historian based in Copenhagen, Denmark.

I go back and forth between Copenhagen and New York several times a year, spending long stretches in NYC. On one evening in the spring of 2007, I had dinner in the Lower East Side and decided to walk home to my accommodation in Hell's Kitchen. By accident I happened to walk down East Sixth Street, when I saw this strange, almost unwelcoming facade. A man standing outside asked, "Do you want to come in?" and told me it was a new cocktail bar. I entered. I'd been to bars before, but never like this one. The bartender gave me a look like he was genuinely excited to see me, and before I knew it, it was last call. Crazy in a city that never sleeps, but there was only one thing to do: order the last drink of the night and come back for more.

I soon found out what made me come back again and again. The cocktails were intriguing and complex yet simple and clean, well balanced, and served by top-shelf bartenders. But that is not all. Not only the liquors come from the top shelf. Everyone at Death & Co is picked from the same top shelf: the doorman, the hosts, the bartenders, the barbacks, the chefs, the servers. When you go to a nice cocktail bar, you'll have great cocktails, but there's usually a weak link, or bartenders will put all of their attention into making drinks. Not so at Death & Co. The people who work there are so well trained that they can concentrate on their guests having the best time. They understand that "our guests could go anywhere tonight, but they picked us, so let's not let them regret it."

Following that visit I was overflowing with inspiration. I decided to form my own bar family and open Moltke's Bar, which became one of the first bars in Copenhagen to focus entirely on classic cocktails. On top of that, the visit also led to organizing the first bar show in Copenhagen, with David and Alex as the opening presenters.

All over the world there are new bars popping up all the time. Most of them disappear. But to stay around for fifteen years and get better with age, that's an achievement.

DON'T FORGET THE STRUGGLE, DON'T FORGET THE STREETS
Al Sotack, 2015

1 ounce Del Maguey Chichicapa mezcal

1 ounce Nardini amaro

1 ounce Lustau Los Arcos amontillado sherry

Stir all the ingredients over ice, then strain into a chilled Nick & Nora glass. No garnish.

WORKING WITH INTENTION

Now that you've got your tools and glassware all set up and neatly knolled, let's try a couple of exercises to put *working with intention* into practice and better understand the nexus of mental and physical planning.

EXERCISE 1: BUILDING A DRINK

Let's look at an example: a home bartender making a casual predinner Martini. In considering the components of a great Martini—quality gin, fresh vermouth, a frozen mixing glass to chill the cocktail even further, ice, a frozen cocktail glass, and a fresh lemon twist for garnish (if that's your preference, as it is ours)—there is both a physical and mental checklist that will help make the best Martini possible.

1. Select the recipe of your choice, be it dry or wet.

2. At least an hour before making the cocktail, place both the mixing and cocktail glasses in the freezer.

3. Assess your vermouth: if previously opened, has it been stored properly, and is it still fresh? A fresh vermouth will be brightly aromatic, whereas a stale one will be more subdued. It's not the end of the world if your vermouth lacks luster, so long as it hasn't spoiled.

4. Gather the tools and ingredients and arrange on a work surface in an organized way: gin, vermouth, jigger, barspoon, julep strainer, knife, cutting board, and a lemon for the twist (always be knolling!).

5. Pull the mixing glass from the freezer.

6. Accurately measure the ingredients and add to the mixing glass, starting from the smallest to the largest.

7. Add ice to the mixing glass so it fills the glass all the way to the top, stirring to settle the ice and liquid.

8. Prepare the lemon twist garnish.

9. Stir the drink until optimal dilution is reached.

10. Remove the cocktail glass from the freezer.

11. Strain the finished cocktail into the glass.

12. Express the lemon twist over the top of the drink.

Could you make a Martini in a different order of steps? Of course! You may choose to put the ice in the mixing glass first, measure the ingredients in a different order, or prepare the lemon twist before you make the drink. But we contend that the steps just listed, when followed sequentially, produce a fine Martini. More important, by organizing your area before beginning the drink-making process—and keeping that space knolled—you pay better attention to accuracy and technique. Veer off course at any step, and compromises begin to pop up. One compromise leads to another, which leads to a mediocre Martini. And sadness.

Even more important, though, is the mental clarity that comes with having a plan: by organizing your process and seeing it through, you've achieved intention with your cocktail making. Within those steps are purposeful choices that make an objective difference in the quality of the drink. Using frozen glassware or keeping fresh, cold vermouth on hand is very much like having a robust pantry for cooking, where having the right tools and ingredients at the ready make all the difference.

WORKING IN THE ZONES

During service, we add ingredients to cocktails in a specific order. In general, we add the cheapest ingredients and the smallest amounts first; this prevents costly wastage if something goes awry and you need to start over. But following this simple rule isn't always the most efficient way to build a drink. Instead, we group our ingredients into zones on and around each bartender station: bitters and "cheater" bottles atop the bar, juices and syrups in an ice box just below the surface of the bar, and bottles of liquor and batches in the rail. By working from zone to zone, we can build a drink without any superfluous movements. While our cocktail recipes typically list base spirits first, followed by modifiers, fresh juice, syrups, and bitters, you'll actually work backward through the ingredient list when following this method during bar service.

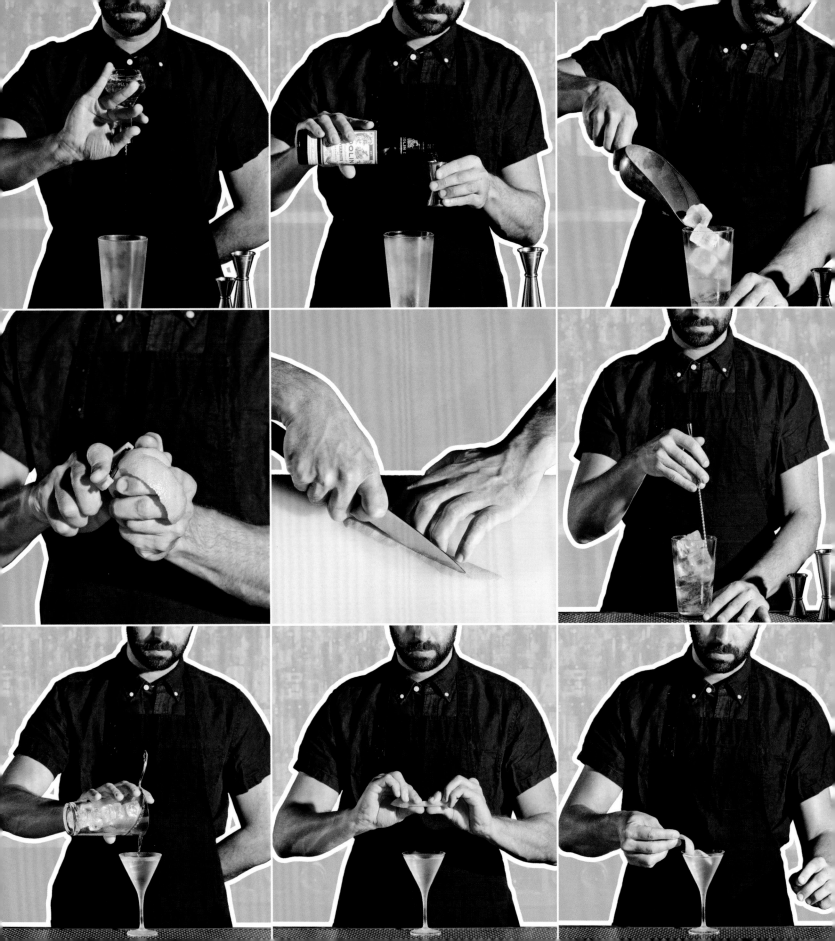

EXERCISE 2: BUILDING A ROUND

What if you are having some friends over and want to showcase your bartending skills? First, you should ask yourself: *What do I want out of the experience?* If your intention is to be mixing drinks all evening, perhaps you curate a small menu of cocktails and have the ingredients ready and organized for easy execution. Or if your intention is to be more social and not shackled to the bar all evening (believe us: your guests will come thirsty!), perhaps you prebatch certain elements of the cocktails to make the process even quicker. And if you really don't want to do much, you can go full-bore batching by making a self-serve punch, prebatching a Manhattan in the freezer, or organizing a DIY cocktail station for your guests to take matters into their own hands (more on these party tricks can be found in chapter 4).

For the professional bartender, assembling a number of cocktails at a time—what we call "round building"—is an essential part of the job. At our bars, our intention is always that a round of cocktails—that is, the full drink order from a group, be it two guests perched on bar stools or a group of six at a table—is prepared and delivered at the same time.

When there's an order of shaken and stirred cocktails—as well as ones with various types of ice, glassware, and garnishes—building a round can become a complicated calculus of execution that requires mental and physical preparation. The bartender must think in terms of a single meta recipe, not a collection of individual recipes.

For example, imagine a bartender who is tasked with preparing cocktails for a trio of guests: a Daiquiri, a Gin Rickey, and a Negroni. One approach is to make each drink from start to finish, one at a time. This may result in drinks that are executed flawlessly but delivered minutes apart from one another. Nobody wants to drink alone.

Another approach is to build each drink in their respective vessels and add ice, stir the Negroni, then shake the Daiquiri and gin rickey, topping the latter with soda water just before serving. This produces drinks that come out at the same time. Success!

But eagle-eyed readers may notice an inefficiency: You'll have picked up and measured a number of the same ingredients (the lime juice, gin, and simple syrup) twice. In a professional cocktail bar, these small inefficiencies will add up over the course of a night. This is why we want you to think of multiple drinks as a single recipe, with certain ingredients and tools spread across several drinks. Here's what a round-building cocktail ninja would do.

1. Ensure all tools and ingredients are within reach.

2. Place two shaker tins and one mixing glass on the bar.

3. Holding one jigger with measurement lines of 2 ounces, 1 ounce, and ¾ ounce, build the round in the following order:

   • Simple syrup: add ¾ ounce to each small shaker tin.

   • Lime juice: add 1 ounce to each shaker tin.

   • Rum: add 2 ounces to the Daiquiri shaker tin.

   • Gin: add 2 ounces to the rickey tin and 1 ounce to the mixing glass for the Negroni.

   • Sweet vermouth: add 1 ounce to the mixing glass.

   • Campari: add 1 ounce to the mixing glass.

4. Add ice to the mixing glass and stir for a few seconds to start chilling the drink.

5. Prepare garnishes:

   • Lime wedges for Daiquiri and gin rickey.

   • Orange half wheel for Negroni.

6. Stir the Negroni for a few more seconds. Taste the drink to gauge the dilution and temperature. When nearing optional temperature and dilution (about three-quarters of the way there), move forward with the round.

7. Place all glassware in front of the mixing vessels: a coupe for the Daiquiri, a collins glass for the rickey, and a double old-fashioned glass for the Negroni (adding one ice block to the double old-fashioned glass).

8. Add ice to the shaker tins, seal tightly, and flip over.

9. Strain the Negroni into the double old-fashioned glass.

10. Shake the Daiquiri and gin rickey for five seconds, then set the gin rickey on the bar and resume shaking the Daiquiri for ten seconds more.

11. Strain the gin rickey into the collins glass, then add 2 ounces of seltzer.

12. Shake the Daiquiri for two seconds (to "wake it up"), then double strain it into the coupe.

13. Add ice cubes to the rickey. Top with seltzer, if needed.

14. Garnish all drinks.

15. Serve.

Among professional bartenders, there will be debate on certain steps. *Should the Negroni be strained before the cocktails are shaken? Is that the right time for the glassware to come from the freezer? Why wouldn't you top the collins at the very end to keep those bubbles alive?!* And while we agree that there's more than one way to execute this round, the point here is less about which approach you take, and more about having an approach at all.

Through repetition and practice, professional bartenders hone their process into one that's more focused and methodical. The home bartender can do the very same thing. Though the stakes may not seem as high in the home, the ability to feel at ease putting together many cocktails at the same time will empower anyone making drinks to enjoy the experience more. The rep a professional bartender earns by making hundreds of cocktails a night has an impact on their physical comfort with the task (shaking Daiquiris is a *workout*) and also the mental clarity that comes with muscle memory. By being vigilant in any cocktail methodology, through repetition you'll make better and better cocktails with increased speed and less mess. Over time, making cocktails will become less stressful and more meditative.

TECHNIQUE

To be a great bartender, you must be both a generalist and a specialist. A truly great bartender is aware of big-picture trends in the world of spirits, is well-versed in thousands of products, has mastered many mixed drinks (and is probably knowledgeable of many, many more), and is comfortable with the professional mechanics of serving guests with various needs and desires.

As cocktail culture has grown up and bartenders have become more skilled, a great cocktail bartender must also be a technician. A fast-paced and high-quality cocktail bar requires bartenders who are coordinated and highly efficient—intellectually and athletically.

From the other side of the bar, it can be mesmerizing to watch a bartender who's trained their movements into fluid motions. To the novice or aspiring bartender, cocktail technique seems intimidating. But every great bartender has learned through practice. At its simplest, developing technique is repeating the same motion over and over again and finding efficiencies (which are often tiny and unnoticeable when they happen) through the repetition.

As noted elsewhere, we're strong proponents of learning by doing—that is, by activating not just your brain, but also your body and senses. We do so in three stages: **comprehension**, **fluency**, and, finally, **speed**. Before you can get good at something, you must first comprehend it, to understand its purpose so you can integrate it into your mind. But you won't be good at it. Only with practice will you gain a fluency in the technique; you need to put it into practice, be bad at it at times, and struggle through repetition. Only then—when you fully understand the technique and can execute it with ease—can you start to fly. Working fast isn't the true marker of mastery; speed is more about how your mind and body are collaborating to utilize the new skill.

COMPREHENSION: SLOW, METHODICAL, MERCILESS ACCURACY

Too many new bartenders obsess over the flashier side of bartending: long, beautiful ribbons of liquid cascading from a bottle held high above a jigger, the flourish of a bottle being twisted to cut the flow of pouring liquid, the juggling of bar tools. These are all fun to watch (and certainly fun to get good at!), but they do not make a great bartender. There is a place for theatrics, but never at the expense of quality and efficiency.

The number-one thing we can teach any novice or professional is the importance of accuracy. With powerful ingredients such as spirits and fresh citrus, small measurements have an incredible impact on the quality of a cocktail. In our view, there is no "good enough" when it comes to cocktail measurement: either it's correct or it's not.

FLUENCY: ISOLATE, THEN COMBINE

We find the best way to teach technique is through a process called "isolate, then combine." Don't start by teaching someone how to make a cocktail from start to finish; rather, teach them to isolate individual movements, improve on them in isolation, then recombine them into a full motion. For example, when learning to stir a cocktail (a shockingly frustrating process for first timers!), we don't begin by filling a mixing glass with liquid and ice. Rather, we isolate the hand holding the spoon, master control of moving that spoon with the hand, then progress to actually stirring.

We use this approach for all our technique training—from how to hold a bottle to jiggering to shaking and straining. By slowing down these motions, we expose the ways that we're moving inefficiently or that will cause harm to our bodies over time through repetitive stress. In moving slowly before we move fast, our motions behind a bar can be purposeful and natural. If a movement is painful or awkward in isolation and at a slow speed, that issue will only compound when moving faster.

SPEED: HOW TO STAND AND MOVE

We think a lot about body positions and fatigue when bartending. There's a way to bartend that is fluid, almost dance-like in its grace, and doesn't leave you achy the next day. There's also a way to bartend that is choppy, disoriented, and painful, which will build over years into chronic pain.

Our fragile bodies are put through the wringer when making hundreds of cocktails a night, but with a few trusted adjustments, you can confer long-lasting benefits on your body, stay in the game of making cocktails, and be more efficient. For the home bartender, this is just as true: there's no reason you shouldn't be mindful about your physical body while making drinks for yourself and your friends.

Through years of messing up our bodies, we've come to conclusions that have helped us protect ourselves when working, informed how we set up our bars, and challenged us to rethink our motions while making cocktails. Beginning with our workspace, we arrange our ingredients and tools so that as many as possible are within a single pivot point (ABK!). This pivot should allow us to reach glassware, tools, spirits, juices, and fresh ingredients, leaving an open area for assembling drinks. We then position ourselves directly in front of this open area. This will be our starting place—our "zero"—for any drink we make, and we will always return to it.

We know from dance and martial arts that it's easier to pull something toward you than to push it away. This is why we emphasize the preparation of space and body positioning so much. In doing so, we are able to draw ingredients toward us through all of our working motions, rather than stretching behind a pivot and throwing ourselves off balance.

Similarly, standing fully upright will allow you to reach ingredients with greater ease, maintain a welcoming body position to guests in front of you, and use your peripheral vision to maintain awareness. While this is less important for the home bartender, it is critical for the pro: keeping your eyes up while making cocktails is essential for being aware of the mood of your guests and the room, and allows for that extra-critical first eye contact with a guest when they walk into a bar—an acknowledgment that sets the tone for the entire experience. When we're hunched over with our eyes down, that opportunity is lost.

RESETTING TO ZERO

The ability to clean one's workspace and "reset to zero"— that is, return everything to its intended place—is just as important as making the actual drink. In trials of different bar setups—be it a traditional bar or one designed specifically for cocktail making with lots of bells and whistles—we've found that a bartender's ability to clean their area and tools and return the setup to its starting place has a far greater impact on bar productivity than any other element. By contrast, at a bar that makes it difficult to clean and reset (a sink ten feet from the ice bin? Yikes!), a bartender may be able to execute a cocktail quickly, but the time it takes to be ready to start making the next round becomes cumbersome.

This may sound a little inside-baseball of us, but anyone making cocktails can benefit from this wisdom. For the home bartender whose time is precious—whether making one cocktail or serving a crowd—the ability to work efficiently can he hugely helpful in enjoying the process. The most critical component for any bartender is to have a sink nearby (preferably a deep one) to collect dirty tools and clean them quickly. Combine this with a work surface that can collect liquid (a rubber mat or a dishtowel), and you'll be well set up to make cocktails and reset to zero.

All drink-makers can also benefit from stepping back and assessing their ambitions relative to their environment. We're prone to making our lives a lot more complicated than they need to be; realizing what about your space will enable you to accomplish with relative ease or what will make the process painful can help you gauge how much you can pull off. With a less-than-ideal setup, it helps to limit the number of drinks you offer. This is why you see short menus of drinks at private events and weddings. Keep it simple.

HOW TO JIGGER

The first step to mixing consistent cocktails is accurately measuring the ingredients. Practice your jiggering technique by filling a liquor bottle with water and placing a mixing glass on top of a piece of paper, which will call out any liquid that misses the glass. Professional bartenders might want to use a speed pourer; home bartenders will likely pour straight from the bottle, which is actually more difficult, but results in fewer dirty dishes.

You might feel like a robot at first when you're following these steps, but with practice, you'll notice a natural flow developing in your jiggering technique. Once you've jiggered an entire bottle of water with one hand (try alternating between measuring 2, 1, ¾, ½, and ¼ ounces), switch hands and pour another bottle with your nondominant hand—we train our bartenders to be ambidextrous. When you're very comfortable jiggering with both hands, feel free to adapt your technique or add your own personal flair. As Picasso said: "Learn the rules like a pro, so you can break them like an artist."

1. Set a mixing glass directly in front of you. If you're right-handed, place a liquor bottle to the right of the mixing glass, and a jigger to the left of it. Lefties should reverse these instructions.

2. Using your left hand, grab the middle of the jigger between your thumb and forefinger and pick it up. Hold the jigger above the glass so its bottom is just above the rim of the glass, orienting it between 9 and 10 o'clock.

3. Using your right hand, grasp the bottle firmly around the middle of its neck. Pick up the bottle and bring it toward the jigger. Slowly pour the liquid into the jigger, keeping the mouth of the bottle as close to the rim of the jigger as possible (without bumping it). Try to keep your wrist "flat" and use your entire arm when pouring. A wristy pouring motion can lead to repetitive motion injury.

4. Stop pouring when the liquid is flat and level with the rim of the jigger. If you're using a speed pourer, you can twist your wrist to "cut" the flow of liquid, but the easiest (and most ergonomic) way to stop pouring is to simply lower the bottom of the bottle. In the past, we taught bartenders to keep pouring until the liquid formed a slightly convex meniscus, or a shallow bubble, above the rim. We've abandoned this practice over the years, as it leads to inconsistency and can slow down the measuring process.

5. Using a steady motion, tilt the jigger toward the mixing glass and pour out the liquid, making sure you don't bang the jigger on the side of the glass. When you've finished pouring, pull the jigger toward your body across the top of the glass, then reset to zero.

HOW TO SHAKE COCKTAILS

Like fingerprints, every bartender has their own unique shaking motion, but we try to instill a process and technique that's as consistent and ergonomic as possible. The following steps illustrate how to use our standard 18-28 shaking tin setup.

If you've read our other two books, you'll notice a shift in the type of ice we use for shaking drinks. In our early years, we shook cocktails using two large blocks of ice. This allowed us to achieve a lot of aeration and a very cold temperature before the drink reached its target dilution. Over time (and many sore shoulders), we realized that despite its advantages, this method was really hard on our bodies and was difficult to perfect—that is, shaking without busting apart the blocks. We then experimented with combining one or two Kold-Draft cubes with a large block. This worked fine as well, but we were still going through hundreds of large blocks a night, which meant we had to spend more time prepping ice. In the *Cocktail Codex*, we advocate shaking

INSIDE THE SHAKER

Our intention when shaking a drink is to move the ice around in the shaker in a circular motion, which will round off the ice's edges, rather than a back-and-forth piston, which will shatter it to pieces (and overdilute your drink before it's cold). Try to "catch" the ice cubes just before they reach either end of the shaker; we train our bartenders to picture a long rectangle inside the shaker, with the goal of the ice hitting all four corners of the rectangle without crashing into the ends of either tin. We practice this technique using ice cubes and no liquid, which is much harder than it sounds.

We've said this before, but it's one of the home-bartending questions we still get asked the most, so it bears repeating. If you're forced to work with ice from your freezer's ice maker, or cubes made in a smaller ice mold, you need to pack the smaller shaking tin with ice, *plus* add ice to the large tin until it's about one-quarter full. If all goes well, all of the ice will fuse into one mass, and you won't hear the individual cubes clanking around in the shaker. Don't shake quite as long as you would with larger ice cubes, as the extra ice will dilute your drink more quickly. And always double strain when shaking with shitty ice.

with one large block (*make up your minds, already!*), which creates a lot of aeration and minimizes ice chops. This technique still works great (especially at home), but for our busy bars, it doesn't eliminate the cost of using big-block ice—which we now purchase, and it ain't cheap. So we've (finally?) landed on what we consider the ideal ice for shaking: Kold-Draft cubes, or something of equivalent size (about 1 inch) that you freeze in a tray. Not only does this method cut down on costs and labor, but after training dozens of new bartenders over the past decade, we've found that it's easier to perfect your shaking technique when using 1-inch ice cubes.

1. Place the 18-ounce tin directly in front of you. Add the cocktail ingredients, beginning with the smallest amounts and least-expensive ingredients.

2. Add 5 to 7 ice cubes (or as many as you can fit) to the 18-ounce tin. Hold the base of the bottom tin in place with your thumb and index finger and set the 28-ounce tin on top, lowering it at a slight angle so one side of the combined shakers forms a straight line. Firmly push the large tin down to form a seal. You shouldn't need to bang the shakers on the bar; this serves only as a distraction. You can test the seal by lifting the top tin; the bottom tin should come with it.

3. When you're ready to shake, place the serving glass (which ideally is waiting in the freezer) and set it in front of you. Make sure you're standing in a strong, balanced stance: feet aligned, about hip-distance apart. Angle yourself slightly to the left or right so you're not shaking directly at an imaginary guest sitting in front of you.

4. Pick up the shakers with the top of the 18-ounce tin facing you. This way should the tin separate while you're shaking, any escaping liquid will fly toward you, not your guests. Place your dominant hand over the 18-ounce tin, with your thumb on the side and your fingers spread out over the tin as if you're gripping a football; your bottom one or two fingertips will rest on the 28-ounce tin. Place your nondominant hand on the 18-ounce shaker, placing your thumb toward the top (where the shakers overlap), with your middle and ring finger tips curling around the bottom. This grip should feel secure; you have fingers at either end of the shakers holding everything together (just in case!), and there's minimal skin-to-tin contact (only the pads of your fingers should be touching the tins). This prevents your palms from warming up the shaker as you work, which will result in an overdiluted drink.

5. Find your center of gravity and bring the shaker up in front of your chest, elbows comfortably away from your body. And away we go! Using a push-and-pull motion that follows a gentle arc, begin your shake slowly, then progressively increase your speed for a few seconds, until you reach one you can comfortably maintain for about 5 seconds. After about 5 seconds at your top speed, begin to slow your shake down, taking slightly less time than you did to speed it up. The total shaking process should take 10 to 15 seconds.

6. Set the shaker down with the 18-ounce tin on top. Squeeze the sides of the 28-ounce tin to break the seal and release the smaller tin; if this doesn't work, pick up the tins and bang the palm of your hand near the top of the larger tin where the gap between the two tins is at its widest. Strain the drink (see page 37) and reset to zero.

OTHER SHAKING STYLES

Depending on the style of drink we're making, we employ a few different shaking styles.

SHORT SHAKE

For drinks that will be served over ice and/or combined with a bubbly ingredient (seltzer, sparkling wine, and the like), we "short shake" the cocktail for about 5 seconds, using the same amount of ice cubes as a regular shake, to slightly chill it and to prevent overdilution in the glass.

WHIP SHAKE

For cocktails served over a lot of crushed ice, we first chill the drink slightly and add aeration by shaking it with 5 to 7 Scotsman pebbles (at home you can use a single ice cube) until we can hear that the ice has completely melted, then dump the liquid into the glass.

DRY SHAKE

When making cocktails that contain egg whites (or egg white alternatives), we first dry shake the liquid ingredients without ice until we can hear the sloshy liquid becoming more homogeneous, then add ice cubes and shake again. This helps break apart the egg white's protein structure and

SHAKING VS. STIRRING

If a cocktail has any fruit (citrus or otherwise), egg, or cream, it should be shaken—vigorously. These ingredients are usually very viscous and must be integrated into the drink with a good deal of effort. Conversely, if a cocktail is mostly spirituous—with vermouth, bitters, or small amounts of sugar or other modifiers—it should be stirred.

Another way to look at it is through the lens of intention. With a shaken drink, you're looking to agitate and "liven up" the ingredients by creating lots of tiny air bubbles, which results in a light layer of froth on top of the drink and a slightly effervescent texture. When stirring a drink, you want to integrate the ingredients without adding any air bubbles, resulting in a texture that's smooth and silky over the tongue.

help it bond around air molecules more easily, resulting in an emulsified cocktail with a beautiful cap of foam floating on top of the surface.

HOW TO STIR COCKTAILS

In our first book, we preached practicing your stirring technique with a barspoon and an empty mixing glass. This is still a great way to develop the motion and muscle control you'll need to stir a cocktail. Once you feel comfortable with your stirring technique, you're ready to make a cocktail, following these steps.

1. Place a mixing glass in front of you. Add the cocktail ingredients, beginning with the smallest amounts and least-expensive ingredients. Make sure you pour the ingredients gently; you don't want to add any air bubbles to the glass.

2. If you're using a pint glass (see page 14), place 1 Kold-Draft (or 1-inch) ice cube in the bottom of the glass, and two more cubes on top of that, forming an upside-down pyramid. Crack 2 ice cubes over the pyramid; the cracked ice will fill in the gaps in the bottom of the glass. Add 2 more ice cubes. If you're using a Japanese-style (or other wider) mixing glass, add enough ice cubes to fill the glass about three-quarters full, layering the ice as tightly as possible.

3. Position the barspoon in your dominant hand between the middle and ring fingers. Depending on the length of your barspoon, your hand should be positioned somewhere on the upper half of the spoon. Insert the spoon into the mixing glass with the rounded side of the spoon resting against the top (12 o'clock) side of the glass.

4. Hold the base of the mixing glass steady between the thumb and forefinger of your nondominant hand. Begin stirring the drink, following a steady rhythm and keeping the curved side of the spoon in contact with the glass at all times. It doesn't matter if you go clockwise or counterclockwise; use whichever direction feels more natural.

5. After about 15 seconds, stop stirring and taste your drink by using a cocktail straw or (less wastefully) spooning a few drops onto the back of your hand. If it isn't cold and/or diluted enough, stir for a few more seconds and taste again. Repeat until you're satisfied with the drink, then strain it (see page 37) and reset to zero.

HOW TO STRAIN STIRRED COCKTAILS

You can strain stirred drinks using either a julep or Hawthorne strainer. The goal is to gently move the drink from mixing glass to serving glass without adding any extra bubbles.

JULEP STRAINER

1. Position the handle of the strainer between your index and middle fingers near the base (where it meets the bowl), with the concave side of the strainer facing up.

2. Rest the strainer opposite of the shaking tin's pour spout (if it has one), and hold the strainer in place by grabbing the mixing glass with your thumb, ring, and pinky fingers.

3. Lower the bowl into the glass, using your index and middle fingers to press the strainer tightly against the ice.

4. Slowly pour the drink from the side, making sure to keep the mixing glass near the serving glass (resist the urge to lift it as you pour; this will only introduce air bubbles to the drink). When most of the liquid is in the serving glass, give the mixing glass a gentle shake to release any remaining liquid.

HAWTHORNE STRAINER

1. Set the strainer on top of the mixing glass, with the handle facing away from the pour spout (if there is one).

2. Grab the mixing glass below the strainer and rest your index finger against the raised tab (if there is one).

3. Slowly pour the drink from the side, giving the glass a gentle shake or two to release any remaining liquid. If you're serving a drink over a large block of ice, strain it directly into the center of the ice cube.

HOW TO STRAIN SHAKEN COCKTAILS

You should always use a Hawthorne strainer when straining shaken drinks. Your goal is to transfer the drink from the shaker to the serving glass as quickly as possible, to retain that perfectly aerated drink you just finished shaking.

1. Set a Hawthorne strainer on top of the large shaking tin.

2. Grab the mixing glass below the strainer, and rest your index finger against the raised tab (if there is one). Use that finger to push the strainer all the way forward until the top of the strainer is in contact with the rim of the shaker (this is called "closing the gate").

3. Pour the drink from the side, giving the glass a few shakes to release any remaining liquid.

HOW TO DOUBLE STRAIN SHAKEN COCKTAILS

We double strain most shaken cocktails served up, when we don't want any tiny ice chips or pieces of muddled herbs or fruit ruining the texture of the drink.

Follow the steps above for straining a shaken drink using a Hawthorne strainer, but instead of pouring the drink straight into the serving glass, hold a mesh cone strainer (see page 14) over the glass, and pour the cocktail into the strainer. To speed up the flow of liquid through the strainer, you can gently knock the side of it with the bottom of the shaking tin after you've emptied its contents.

BRUNO SAD

Bruno Sad is a bartender with New York City's Happy Cooking Hospitality Group.

I went to Death & Co for the first time in 2016, when I was visiting the city from San Antonio. I came by myself on a Tuesday night, thinking it wouldn't be too busy. I sat at the bar in front of Shannon and gave her a very specific drink order: 5 to 1 Blue Gin Martini, dash of orange bitters, lemon twist discarded. I had been barhopping all day and already had a good number of cocktails in me, so I wanted something classic that was executed correctly. I don't order Martinis very often because most people don't take enough care to make them well, so I order them only from people I trust. Shannon served me my drink, and it was perfect. She's super talented, a fucking boss.

Next, I ordered a glass of Aaron Burr cider with a shot of Cyril Zangs 00 apple cider eau-de-vie on the side. Shannon gave me a strange look, like *Who the fuck* are *you*? I told her I was a traveling bartender. Turns out Alex Day was in the bar earlier that evening and had ordered the exact same Martini.

Two years later I moved to New York and became a regular. I usually go by myself after I finish my bartending shift. As a professional, I'm always observing what's going on. Every time I sit at the bar, I learn something new. Now everyone there knows me, so I'll bring burgers from work for the staff. I'm low key, so I want to be a perfect guest. I'm quiet, I tip well, and I get out of there. When I'm at Death & Co I feel like they're hosting me at their home. Death & Co's hospitality is so spot-on, so genuine, so knowledgeable. It's great to see that in a world-class bar.

I love sending people I love to the bar, and they always tell me that "they took such great care of us." That makes me so happy.

BRUNO'S MARTINI

2½ ounces Blue Gin

½ ounce Dolin dry vermouth

1 dash House Orange Bitters (page 298)

Garnish: 1 lemon twist

Stir all the ingredients over ice, then strain into a chilled Nick & Nora glass. Express the lemon twist over the drink, then place it in the drink.

CREATING COCKTAILS WITH INTENTION

So many tiny, precise decisions go into a well-made cocktail: choosing ingredients, deciding how to assemble them, and paying attention to the smallest details with the same vigor as the large ones—the accuracy of a dash, the precision of a manicured lemon twist. Once a bartender is oriented in their workspace and has a baseline for how best to work within it, only then do we teach them about the creative process behind making drinks.

In our last book, *Cocktail Codex*, we dove deep into six "root cocktails" that are the foundation of the entire cocktail canon: the Old-Fashioned, the Martini, the Daiquiri, the Sidecar, the Whiskey Highball, and the Flip. Every cocktail shares DNA with at least one of these drinks.

If you understand the root six—how and why they work—then you can use them as a springboard to innovate and create new drinks.

Mastering the root cocktails is an important part of our *intellectual approach* to cocktails. Drawing inspiration from our personal experiences, cultural references, and flavor preferences is part of our *emotional approach.*

We think all great cocktails must be a marriage between an intellectual understanding of the cocktail—its core architecture, what makes it work from a technical level—and the emotional, the human connections that evoke feeling, provoke thoughts, and ultimately produce more delicious drinks.

EXERCISE 3: CREATING A NEW COCKTAIL

Imagine you are inspired by a recent trip to a Thai market, where you came across some fresh purple basil and can't get its bright anise aroma out of your head. Wanting to make a cocktail that features it, you begin mulling over recipes, homing in on the best possible starting point to celebrate the basil's flavor. Should it be in a boozy drink? The alcoholic punch of an Old-Fashioned may overshadow the delicate herb. A Martini could work, especially if you swapped out dry vermouth for blanc vermouth, which offers a sweeter platform for making a basil infusion. But it was the freshness of the basil that first captivated you, so you gravitate toward a citrusy shaken cocktail.

You pick a classic Daiquiri as your starting point. Fresh herbs are powerful, but they are also delicate. Knowing this, you start simple:

> 6 purple basil leaves
> ¾ ounce simple syrup
> 2 ounces white rum
> 1 ounce fresh lime juice
>
> In a shaking tin, gently muddle the basil into the simple syrup. Add the rum and lime juice, then shake the cocktail with ice and double strain into a coupe.

What results is a tasty enough drink: bright, refreshing, but not terribly complex—what we affectionately refer to as "My First Cocktail." No one's going to kick it out of bed, but neither is anyone going to invite it to Thanksgiving. What's missing? The basil flavor is present, but its vibrancy is numbed by the rum and lime juice. What got us excited about the purple basil was the shock of its anise flavor; how about enhancing that with a couple of dashes of absinthe? And that lime juice is punchy and refreshing, but the basil draws out some of its more astringent qualities. Taking those two changes into account, we try this:

> 6 purple basil leaves
> ¾ ounce simple syrup
> 2 ounces white rum
> ¾ ounce fresh lime juice
> 2 dashes absinthe
>
> In a shaking tin, gently muddle the basil into the simple syrup. Add the remaining ingredients, then shake the cocktail with ice and double strain into a coupe.

There we go! The purple basil now shines through with clarity, and the citrus is in check. You've made a refreshing, focused cocktail that expresses the original idea in a clear way. This is a perfectly acceptable cocktail and could very well be the finish line. But here's the trick in striving toward excellence: You must not stop until you've considered all the variables.

Rum is one of the most diverse categories of any spirit: some white rums are sweet and funky, while others are dry and clean. For this cocktail, we likely wouldn't use the former, as it would distract from the intent of the drink (to showcase the purple basil—don't lose this focus!), nor would we want a rum so restrained in flavor that it wouldn't contribute to the cocktail's overall personality. This is where recipe development goes down to the micro level and we experiment with a number of rums to find the right platform for our idea. After lots of shaking and tasting, we may settle on the following spec:

6 purple basil leaves

¾ ounce simple syrup

2 ounces Plantation 3 Stars white rum

¾ ounce fresh lime juice

2 dashes absinthe

In a shaking tin, gently muddle the basil into the simple syrup. Add the remaining ingredients, then shake the cocktail with ice and double strain into a coupe.

Notice anything missing? There's no garnish! During recipe development we don't generally add garnish until the recipe is near completion. At this near-final stage we would begin asking ourselves what is needed to either contribute aroma (such as a purple basil leaf) or add personalization for the imbiber (a lime wedge to customize the drinker's desired level of tartness). Having already determined that more acid does the cocktail harm, we nix the lime wedge. An aromatic garnish is a great opportunity to reinforce the drink's featured ingredient: a perfectly placed purple basil leaf on top of the finished cocktail will add aromatic complexity, again reinforcing the original intention of the recipe.

The example here is a marriage between intellectual and emotional understandings of cocktails; it also shows our approach to creating new cocktails: starting from a big idea and working down through the small-but-important details, one step at a time. This is a fine-tuning mechanism we find useful in many areas of our work: working from the big picture (macro) to the broad generalities (meso) to the fine details (micro). With this example, we started with a general intention (purple basil!), found a means to express that intention, then sorted through the variables. This simple mental reframing can be incredibly helpful when working through a recipe, helping you figure out what you actually want to accomplish before going too deep into specifics.

TRADITIONALISM VS. ICONOCLASM

It's easy for anyone passionate about cocktails to get caught up in tradition. There's so much history and lore surrounding cocktails, and in our early bar days we found ourselves mesmerized by stories of late nineteenth-century bartenders who lorded over gin palaces and saloons, mixing cocktails while guiding social agendas and changing the world. We were so absorbed in this history that we took their recorded work as gospel without asking the important question: "Do these drinks taste good?" In some cases, the answer was, yes; in others, hell no.

We believe the traditions that have been forged over the years ought to be considered as guideposts, not dogma. Consider the cultural evolutions of taste (we certainly consume more sugar today than at any other time in human history), or the change in agriculture since the birth of mixed drinks (a lime as we know it today is nothing like what was called for in early cocktail books; those old cocktail books used a lime likely much closer to Key lime). Breaking tradition is a necessary avenue in any art form; without it, the medium will never progress. And so, we view cocktails—even longstanding recipes, like the Martini or Old-Fashioned—as being

worthy of both *perfection* and *evolution*. We seek not to make the most historical version of a drink, but to adhere to the spirit of the cocktail while making the best possible version we can.

Take the Negroni. Tradition would dictate that the cocktail comprises equal measures of gin, sweet vermouth, and Campari, served on the rocks with an orange half wheel. Is that the best version? In the earlier years of Death & Co, we thought that recipe lacked clarity, so we upped the gin proportion a bit, poured it into a coupe, and garnished it with an orange twist. This was considered heretical to some and sparked late-night debates with fellow bartenders. We stood on the side of pushing the Negroni toward the palate of the day and the aesthetic of Death & Co in those early years: elegance and simplicity. Interestingly, the more Negronis we drank, the more we appreciated the original intent of the drink as an aperitif, and we have since moved back to a more typical build: equal parts of the ingredients, served on the rocks with an orange wedge.

There are certainly times we feel a recipe requires manipulation. The Blood & Sand is a perfect example, an

equal-parts cocktail made with scotch, Cherry Heering, sweet vermouth, and orange juice. The issue with this recipe is the orange juice: there is very little consistency in oranges. Some oranges have a nicely acidic juice (which puts the richness of sweet vermouth and the Cherry Heering in check). In the dead of winter in the United States, at the height of citrus season, you can expect juicy Valencia oranges bursting with flavor, acidity, and sweetness, the perfect companion for cocktails. But in other times of the year, you may have off-season navel oranges: sweet but lacking flavor, with very little acidity. To find a level of consistency and to create a more drinkable Blood & Sand, we add a teaspoon of fresh lemon juice, just enough to give the cocktail a tart backbone. Match this with a very specific scotch (our preferred whisky for this cocktail is Highland Park 12-year single malt) in a slightly higher proportion than equal parts, and you have a Blood & Sand that is far more focused than its traditional iteration.

Our approach is to question tradition but never shed it altogether. The endurance of these drinks in history says a lot about their integrity. Evolution for evolution's sake can be a slippery slope.

SELECTION

Although we may be charmed by a heart-warming story or well-designed packaging when selecting ingredients to stock at our bars, we strive to be as objective as possible. This means we cannot be swayed by a brand's marketing or origin story; we must taste, taste, taste. First, the ingredient in isolation; then, combined with other ingredients to see how it interacts. A cocktail is a composition, so isolating any individual component is only part of the equation. This chapter begins with a primer on how to taste (and taste, and taste . . .) ingredients to dial in your palate, then several exercises to help you taste cocktails to identify a well-balanced drink.

MOUNTAIN OF LIGHT, PAGE 237

IDENTIFYING YOUR PALATE

For the novice, tasting anything—be it cocktails, spirits, wine, or food—with someone more experienced can be intimidating. The expert seems to know the right words, speak with authority, understand the connections between things; they just *get it*.

But take it from us: It's just a cocktail. You're allowed to like what you like.

The word *palate* is used to describe a person's ability to taste and speak intelligently—or at least intelligibly—about flavor. This word carries a lot of baggage, and it has taken on a wider meaning, often implying one's innate ability to comprehend and describe flavors. You see this manifested in jokes about wine snobs and the alienating language they employ to describe fermented grape juice.

Palate is not something you're born with. Yes, there are those who physiologically have an ability to taste or smell differently from others. But most of us can be comforted to know that palate is, in effect, wisdom. Developing the ability to understand and describe flavor is learned by smelling and tasting and reflecting on the experience (even if it's as simple as *mmm, I like that!*). Many people develop their palate in their daily lives by eating mindfully and discovering what they like and dislike. This means you have to get out of your comfort zone and try new flavors. But once you do, and once you start sharing your preferences, you build a language around those preferences. With this language, the wisdom of your palate comes to life.

In the following exercises, we'll show you how to better understand your own preferences, how to approach flavors you don't know, develop tools to understand them, and feel confident in talking about flavor. This isn't an exercise in changing what you like; rather, it's about broadening your horizons so that you truly know what you like, and why. For all of the exercises in this section, approach each with the perspective of not simply enjoying the drinks (though that'll probably happen), but also taking the time to reflect on the underlying lesson of each.

PALATE LESSON #1: KNOW WHAT YOU KNOW

We begin palate development with a flavor so many of us know well: pear. Our goal with this exercise is to reflect on something we know, using this familiarity to focus on articulating what our nose smells and our tongue tastes. We're establishing a process with tasting and reflection that will allow us to approach new, more challenging flavors in the future. We highly recommend gathering a friend (or friends!) for all of these lessons—talking about what you're tasting will accelerate your learning.

You'll need:

- **Raw pear.** Preferably a ripe Bartlett or Bosc variety so that you're tasting the natural ingredient in its most focused form.

- **Pear cider.** Find a quality alcoholic French-style pear cider, such as Eric Bordelet Poire Authentique or Lamorton Poiré Sparkling Perry. If it's French, made from pears (or mostly pears), and labeled "dry," you're in business. If you can't find either, buy some organic bottled pear juice.

- **Pear brandy.** Look for the clear stuff without any barrel aging. Our favorite bottles include Clear Creek Williams pear brandy, St. George pear brandy, and Massenez Poire Williams.

- **Small wine glasses or single old-fashioned glasses, two per person.** Steer away from snifters or large wine glasses; they concentrate too much of the alcohol. Make sure that you have the same (or *very* similar) glassware for each taster—it's important that you're smelling and tasting the same way.

- **Pen and paper.** Write down your thoughts, draw pictures that represent what you're smelling and tasting, doodle—anything to activate your brain while smelling and tasting.

Prepare the tasting:

- Chill the cider for at least two hours. Serve the brandy at room temperature.

- Wash the pear and cut it into small slices, giving one to each taster.

- Distribute one water and one spit glass for each taster.

- Pour 4 ounces cider into a glass for each taster.

- Pour 2 ounces pear brandy into a glass for each taster.

THE LANGUAGE OF TASTING

There are those who taste and discuss to show off, and those who taste to collaborate. We prefer the latter; tasting with others is advantageous because it allows us to identify impressions that may be on the tip of our tongue, and it broadens our perspective. To this end, we shun esoteric language and instead encourage people to use words that mean something to them. It's less about describing "unicorn tears" and "the whimsical impression of childhood" than it is about "that smell from summer camp when I was a kid."

That summer camp aroma might have been a field (grassy and floral?), or woodsy (pine?) or something entirely different. The point is: memories and personal references are often the first thing that comes to our mind when we taste something—use them to draw out your language for aroma and taste and share them with others.

We emphasize language in tasting because the act of communicating is as powerful as the actual tasting itself. You'll begin by fumbling with the words to adequately describe flavors, unable to trust your own instincts and insecure about the words you're using, but over time, speaking about smells, tastes, and connections to other flavors will give you greater confidence and focus in your thoughts—and, ultimately, contribute to a greater understanding of flavor. This isn't academic; the better your understanding of flavor, the stronger your ability to appreciate and create cocktails.

The goal here is to connect your nose and tongue to your brain. We critically taste not to be a critic or to show off our mental thesaurus, but to express our thoughts and strengthen our ability to discuss the smells and tastes hitting our senses.

That said, there are some commonly used words that can help give context to the smells and tastes you're assessing. Some relate to balance (for example, "this Daiquiri is very acidic" or "this Negroni is bitter"), some are more ephemeral ("this Martini tastes like heaven"). Starting here, you can dial in to what each of those mean using some of the terms listed here—or your own.

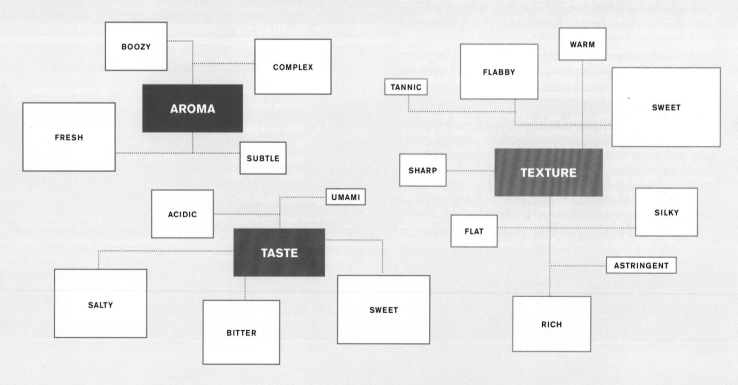

HOW TO TASTE

1. Smell first, taste second. Aroma is fundamental to flavor, so spend a couple extra seconds smelling the spirit or cocktail before you dive in.

2. Take three sips and drink water in between them. The first clears away anything in your mouth, the second introduces the flavor, and the third allows you to contemplate. Go slow. Instead of swallowing each sip, we encourage spitting out each taste into a spit cup to keep your brain sharp.

3. Reflect. Take a moment and write down what you're smelling and tasting. Does the smell or flavor remind you of anything? Do you really think this spirit smells like apple, or did you just have an apple for lunch?

4. Discuss. Vocalizing your thoughts has a way of testing them out. What are other people smelling or tasting? Do you get that, too? It's okay if you don't!

We approach any tasting in three segments: (1) what we smell, (2) what we taste, and (3) the combination of the two, flavor. The first two allow us to isolate our nose and tongue, whereas the final (flavor) brings them together as a cohesive whole—an overall reflection and impression.

A note on smelling spirits: Because of spirits' high proof, if we were to simply sniff as we would a glass of wine, the alcohol would destroy our ability to smell for a couple of minutes. Don't inhale deeply through your nose. Draw the glass toward your nose, then open your mouth slightly and breathe in through your mouth. This will allow the spirit's aroma to enter your nose and bypass most of the aggressiveness of the alcohol. You can throttle this up and down depending on what aroma you're getting: close your mouth slightly to increase the power of the aroma, or open it a bit to decrease.

AROMA

- Smell all three ingredients, one at a time.

- Smell two ingredients next to each other, oscillating each in front of your nose. Make sure to compare each ingredient to the others.

- Write down answers to the following questions:

  ○ Are there similarities between the pear, cider, and pear brandy? (Wild guess: yes.) If so, what are those similarities (and don't just write "pear")? Some examples that may come to mind: yeasty, melon, floral, green.

  ○ Do you see the connection from one to the other? Is it represented in aroma?

  ○ Aside from pear, are there other aromas you smell in either of the two beverages?

  ○ Does this aroma remind you of anything? Don't be afraid of making off-the-wall references; the more personal the connection, the more powerful. Think caramel, radish, or tomato leaf.

TASTE

- Taste all three ingredients individually, moving from the raw pear to the cider, and finally, to the brandy. A reminder: take three sips, keep them small, and drink water in between.

  ○ Do you notice anything different between the aroma and the taste in each ingredient? Jot down your notes. Talk about them.

- Taste the ingredients next to each other.

  ○ How do they compare? Are there differences in how pear is expressed in its raw, fermented, and distilled forms? Perhaps the juiciness of the raw pear aligns with the refreshing funkiness of the cider, or the gritty texture of the raw pear may come through in the distilled pear but is less present in the cider.

  ○ Do you notice the impact alcohol has on the taste of the pear cider and brandy?

  ○ Does the taste remind you of anything?

FLAVOR

- Now that you've critically smelled and tasted, it's time to combine those into a general impression. Look back at your notes and reflect on your discussions.

- How does the single ingredient change in these three states: raw, fermented, and distilled? How different is the aroma and taste of each? How are they similar?

- Is one more "pear-y" than the others—that is, is one more like you expected pear to taste?

- After smelling and tasting each, do you think of the base flavor (pear) in a different way?

In focusing on such a specific flavor, we hope this exercise showed you that there's a surprising amount of variety, even with something we think we know so well. We also revealed that the same flavor, when handled differently—raw, fermented, and distilled—expresses a wide variety of aromas and tastes. Return to this lesson when tasting, allowing some of what you discovered to guide you: do you smell and taste the freshness of the raw ingredient, the luscious fullness of the fermented, or the sharp fieriness of the distilled?

PALATE LESSON #2: FINDING BALANCE

In case you haven't noticed yet: we love the classic Daiquiri. The holy trinity of rum, lime juice, and sugar is the perfect place to start any discussion about balance. In the exercises that follow, we're going to use "Goldilocks" experiments to explore the spectrums of sweet and sour, strong and weak, as well as saltiness, bitterness, temperature, and dilution.

These experiments are best done with at least one other person, and ideally a group of four. Because you'll be making a *lot* of drinks to see each lesson through, feel free to break up the individual experiments into several sessions.

You'll need:

- Cocktail shaker sets: 4

- Jigger(s) (able to measure 2, 1, ¾, and ½ ounces accurately): 1 or more

- Teaspoon: 1

- Hawthorne strainers: 4

- Cone strainers: 4

- Cocktail coupes: 4

- Fresh lime juice: 16 ounces

- Simple syrup (page 287): 14 ounces

- White rum: One 750 ml bottle

- Campari: 3 ounces

SWEET & SOUR

Fresh citrus is powerful stuff, and the best way to balance its sourness is with some sort of sweetener—neutral-flavored simple syrup, in this case. However, simply using them in equal proportions may not yield a well-balanced drink. At Death & Co, we like to add just a touch more lime juice to make it a bigger part of the overall flavor; however, your taste may be different. To see for yourself, make the following three drinks:

Tart Daiquiri

2 ounces white rum

1 ounce fresh lime juice

¼ ounce simple syrup

Balanced Daiquiri

2 ounces white rum

1 ounce fresh lime juice

¾ ounce simple syrup

Sweet Daiquiri

2 ounces white rum

¼ ounce fresh lime juice

1 ounce simple syrup

Just as in the pear-tasting exercise, smell the cocktails first, then taste each three times. Remember, it's okay to spit (especially if you're doing all the lessons in this section in one session). Before moving on to our analysis, discuss with your tasting partner(s):

- What are the differences between the cocktails?

- Do individual ingredients come through more in one version over another?

- Is the perception of alcohol different? This can be felt as a tingling on the tongue, or in a sip that leaves you a little breathless.

- In the process, try as much as possible to ignore your personal preferences and talk more objectively about what you're smelling and tasting. You'll have a preference (we do!), but the exercise is more powerful when you dive in to the flavor and sensory reactions you get from each.

For us, these three Daiquiris represent a critical lesson about the importance of accuracy in measuring cocktails: The difference between too acidic, too sweet, and just right is a tiny margin. Too tart, and the Daiquiri is boozy and bracingly acidic to the point that it hurts your tongue. Too sweet, and the Daiquiri is also too boozy but in an entirely different way, cloying and saccharine.

Some may even find our "balanced" version too tart for them. That's fine—it simply means you have a different preference of sweet to tart—but we suspect your preference is very near to this (back off on the lime to ¾ ounce . . . better?). However, in that example, the components of rum, lime, and sugar have found harmony—they are all present but have combined into something greater than their individual parts. This is the critical goal of cocktails involving citrus. Look for it not only in the recipes you make (or create!), but also in those you drink at bars.

Beyond this, we find it fascinating how aroma changes with the balance of the liquid: the Tart Daiquiri is more astringent on the nose, like the smell of lime zest; the Sweet Daiquiri draws out the lusciousness of the rum with big, fruity aromas; and the Balanced Daiquiri has the sweet smell of a freshly cut lime wheel. These are fantastic sense memories to store away for future use in analyzing other cocktails.

STRONG VERSUS WEAK

Next, you'll make three Daiquiris to experience how alcohol strength can have an impact on flavor. While these three examples throttle up and down on the amount of rum in the recipe, the same could be true of the proof of the rum: using a high-octane bottling, like Wray & Nephew (126 proof), would have the same overall effect as adding more rum.

We advise spitting out your mouthfuls in this lesson. Also, we don't recommend reusing the Balanced Daiquiri from the previous experiment; make a fresh one to properly compare the examples here.

Strong Daiquiri

3 ounces white rum

1 ounce fresh lime juice

¾ ounce simple syrup

Balanced Daiquiri

2 ounces white rum

1 ounce fresh lime juice

¾ ounce simple syrup

Weak Daiquiri

1 ounce white rum

1 ounce fresh lime juice

¾ ounce simple syrup

Tasted side by side, you will likely notice that the Strong Daiquiri wallops both your nose and tongue, almost taking your breath away. On the other end of the spectrum, the Weak Daiquiri is wimpy, lacking body and resulting in a lime-aid-like flavor. It's only with the Balanced Daiquiri that we see how the rum can still be front and center, though checked by a refreshing substructure of lime and sugar in a highly tuned proportion: very near two parts strong (alcohol) to one part sour (lime juice) to one part sweet (simple syrup).

From this, we can learn some important lessons. In high proportions, alcohol can take our breath away and be abrasive, but it can also allow for an extremely focused flavor (think of the pear brandy in the earlier experiment). But alcohol always brings body, or a fullness of flavor, to a cocktail. It's the foundation on which flavor is built, and without it, a cocktail loses complexity.

MANIPULATING FLAVOR: SALT

The use of salt in cocktails is becoming more and more common. Over the years we've found that adding a drop or two of salt solution can have a noticeable impact on many styles of drinks—just as salt helps elevate the flavors of the foods we eat. Note that this doesn't necessarily make a drink *salty;* rather, it amplifies certain flavors while curbing others.

Before starting this experiment, make sure you've made some salt solution (page 299). As you'll see, this may come in handy for general cocktail use (add a drop to your next Negroni; you won't be disappointed). We like to keep a tiny dropper bottle handy at all times.

Balanced Daiquiri

2 ounces white rum

1 ounce fresh lime juice

¾ ounce simple syrup

Bright Daiquiri

2 ounces white rum

1 ounce fresh lime juice

¾ ounce simple syrup

2 drops salt solution

Daiquiri at Sea

1 ounce white rum

1 ounce fresh lime juice

¾ ounce simple syrup

1 teaspoon salt solution

Do you notice anything different between the Balanced and Bright Daiquiris? Just two tiny drops of salt solution have worked some magic—the lime tastes brighter and more present, but the cocktail isn't more acidic. As more salt is added, the effect quickly changes. What was before a surprisingly pleasant Bright Daiquiri turns to a savory mess in the Daiquiri at Sea. This level of salt in the cocktail makes the composition disjointed and impossible to drink.

Identifying "minerally" characteristics when tasting can help isolate a unique flavor profile that—unlike sweet, sour, or strong—is not always obvious. Certain fortified wines (such as manzanilla sherry) have relatively high levels of saltiness. Other ingredients are more subtle—like celery stalks, which have a subtle salinity. Be on the lookout for naturally salty ingredients, as these flavors can be powerful tools in cocktail creation.

FINDING COMPLEXITY: BITTER

At this stage, you should be very familiar with the Balanced Daiquiri. Here, we'll incrementally add a bitter flavor to see how it impacts the drink. To do this, we use Campari, a bittersweet Italian liqueur. To further illustrate the impact of the bitter ingredient, we've pulled back on the lime juice a bit in our base Daiquiri recipe, from 1 ounce to ¾ ounce (lime juice and Campari don't always get along). Note: We don't think any of these examples are particularly delicious; rather, they're instructive, even when they're balanced. You'll notice that the amount of rum decreases as the amount of Campari increases, because Campari adds proof to the drink in addition to bitterness, and we want to keep the alcoholic strength relatively close in the finished cocktail (see the Strong Versus Weak exercise).

Just a Touch Daiquiri

2 ounces white rum

¾ ounce fresh lime juice

¾ ounce simple syrup

1 teaspoon Campari

Tongue-Tingling Daiquiri

1¾ ounces white rum

¾ ounce fresh lime juice

¾ ounce simple syrup

½ ounce Campari

Might as Well Be Grapefruit Juice Daiquiri

1 ounce white rum

¾ ounce fresh lime juice

¾ ounce simple syrup

1 ounce Campari

Tongue-Stripper Daiquiri

¼ ounce white rum

¾ ounce fresh lime juice

¾ ounce simple syrup

1¾ ounces Campari

As you taste through these four versions, you may notice a sensation creeping in. In the Just a Touch Daiquiri, you can notice a subtle increase in complexity. As more Campari is introduced, that complexity starts imparting a sharp edge to the cocktail and a tingling of the tongue. For those unfamiliar with Campari, at this stage you'll likely start reacting to not only Campari's bitterness, but also its medicinal flavor. Don't be disheartened if you're not having a whole lot of fun—push through and keep tasting. At a full ounce of Campari, the cocktail maintains a level of balance but is overshadowed by the red liqueur's pungency. And with 1½ ounces of Campari, the final iteration is a challenge for all but the most bitterly inclined drinkers.

This entire spectrum of drinks can be found throughout the cocktail universe. Drinks with an almost-imperceptible amount of bitterness benefit from greater complexity, such as the Bulldog Front (page 179). Then there are cocktails like the Negroni (page 65) that find an equilibrium between bitter, strong, and sweet. And at the far end are cocktails so bitter that they are, for some, difficult to drink (Pugilist, page 240).

Acclimating yourself to bitter ingredients will take time, but when you find a way to enjoy them, you'll be opened up to a whole new world of flavor. If you've ever enjoyed a radicchio salad, it's the bitterness in the leaf that gives the dish a great level of complexity. Or if you're a fan of grapefruit juice, it's the bitterness of the juice balanced by acidity and sweetness that delivers such a refreshing drink. But bitterness is very individual, and so being able to identify it in various forms (from subtle to heavy-handed) will allow you to choose your own bitter adventure.

TEMPERATURE

When we first started making cocktails, the goal was to make cocktails as cold as possible. We experimented with different sizes of ice, frozen vessels for stirred cocktails, and shaking our Daiquiris really *really* hard (we're still a little sore). It's true, a room-temperature cocktail is often disappointing. But today we have a more nuanced view of temperature. There are times when a bracingly cold cocktail is in order, and other times where a warmer drink allows certain flavors to blossom.

To explore temperature's influence on flavor, we'll make three identical Balanced Daiquiris and present them as frozen, room-temperature, and chilled drinks.

Balanced Daiquiri

2 ounces white rum

1 ounce fresh lime juice

¾ ounce simple syrup

Frozen Daiquiri

At least three hours prior to tasting, assemble one Balanced Daiquiri, shake it as usual, and strain it into a double old-fashioned glass. To keep out any other aromas, cover the drink with plastic wrap and place in your freezer. Just prior to moving on to the experiment, remove the now-frozen glass. Your Daiquiri should be partially frozen. Use a fork to scrape the top, digging in and fluffing the cocktail into a slushy consistency, working quickly so as not to melt the liquid. Return to the freezer until the tasting. When both of the other drinks are completed, remove the Frozen Daiquiri and use spoons to taste it.

Room-Temperature Daiquiri

Assemble a Balanced Daiquiri in a cocktail shaker and add 1 ounce of room-temperature water. Do not add ice to the shaker. Shake for 20 seconds and pour into a coupe.

Chilled Daiquiri

At the same time as you make the Room-Temperature Daiquiri, assemble a Balanced Daiquiri: build, shake with ice, and strain into a coupe.

We particularly like this lesson because it exaggerates versions of cocktails that exist in the wild. As you taste the spoonfuls of Frozen Daiquiri next to the Chilled Daiquiri, you may notice that the brightness of the lime is muted, as cold numbs the palate. The Frozen Daiquiri loses some of its focus and complexity. (Frozen and blended drinks often employ big, bold flavors to push through this numbing effect.)

On the opposite end, a Room-Temperature Daiquiri is a disjointed mess of a cocktail, the lime juice coming through as astringent and the sugar and rum as saccharine. While no one should ever be served one—*ever*—it's not uncommon that a drink will be carefully made, then left to sit and warm up for minutes until delivered to a guest. With this treatment, the overall flavor of an otherwise delicious cocktail is compromised.

While you're tasting these three cocktails, also pay attention to how the Chilled Daiquiri changes as it slowly warms. It'll taste bright and fresh just after it's been strained, while other flavors are brought to life as it warms up—the average life of a cocktail being between 10 and 15 minutes (although given how much we love Daiquiris, for us it's often just one to two minutes). The lime flavor inches its way in, becoming more and more astringent. The rum, too, becomes more pronounced and increasingly fruity, and if it's a rum with a little funk to it, that will start getting louder and louder.

DILUTION

Water is fundamental to almost all cocktails. While there are a few obscure drinks that call for no dilution at all (a style dubbed "scaffa"; we're not crazy about them), all cocktails have an intentional amount of water added. Most often this is done through stirring or shaking, but we also will add precise amounts to prebatched frozen cocktails (page 163), as well as carbonated and draft cocktails (page 169).

This lesson will show you how important dilution is. While this speaks to technique, for the purposes of this lesson, we will learn to recognize when a cocktail has missed the mark, either with too little dilution or too much.

Underdiluted Daiquiri

2 ounces white rum

1 ounce fresh lime juice

¾ ounce simple syrup

Build the drink in a small glass bottle. Chill the bottle in a bath of ice, water, and a few pinches of salt—as though you're chilling a bottle of champagne. Let chill for about 30 minutes. When ready to taste alongside the other drinks, remove from the ice bath, shake the bottle hard, and pour the drink directly into a coupe.

Balanced Daiquiri

2 ounces white rum

1 ounce fresh lime juice

¾ ounce simple syrup

Shake all the ingredients with ice, then double strain into a coupe.

Overdiluted Daiquiri

2 ounces white rum

1 ounce fresh lime juice

¾ ounce simple syrup

1 ounce filtered water

Shake all the ingredients with ice, then double strain into a coupe.

What strikes us most about these three drinks is that, while they're the same cocktail on paper, a small amount of water can make them taste entirely different. You may notice that in the Underdiluted Daiquiri, the flavors are tight and wound up, with each individual ingredient noticeable but lacking harmony as a whole. Conversely, in the Overdiluted Daiquiri, the flavor doesn't have much focus—it tastes, well, watery.

Often, temperature and dilution go hand in hand, but in isolating them in two lessons, we hope you've seen how each independently can change flavors. This will come in handy when considering how a cocktail is going to be served: if its best version is with very little dilution, you'll want to avoid using ice that will add more water content, such as small chipped ice or ice that has been sitting at room temperature for an extended period of time. Alternatively, should your ingredients be full of vibrant flavor, perhaps more dilution while sipping will allow flavors to express themselves in different ways, either by diluting longer or by serving the cocktail with ice that will dilute over time, such as pellet ice in a julep.

We should recognize that there are certain cocktails where dilution is just another subjective decision, most noticeably in the Martini: some love nothing more than a bottle of gin pulled from the freezer, a mist of vermouth in the glass, and no water at all. To each their own!

SPIRITS

In our other books, we've presented the traditional way to learn about a spirit: gather many varieties of one spirit and familiarize yourself with some basic facts (place of origin, raw materials, distillation method, aging), then taste them side by side using proper technique.

While this is helpful as a baseline, it teaches us about booze in an isolated way. While we're fanatical about great-quality spirits, at the end of the day our main focus is understanding how they will work in cocktails. To that end, we've developed a series of experiments that will help you understand each spirit's contribution to a cocktail. Refer to the boxes on pages 48 and 49 for an explanation of how to taste and smell spirits, and the words commonly used to describe them.

In Our Rail

SUBTLE

Ketel One

Grey Goose

Suntory Haku

Absolut Elyx

St. George All-Purpose

St. George Citrus

Craft Method Citrus Reticulata var. Sunshine

Craft Method Citrus Hystrix

Craft Method Citrus Medica var. Sarcodactylis

St. George Green Chile

INTENSE

VODKA

RAW MATERIALS

Most commonly grains, such as wheat, rye, corn, or barley. Less commonly grass (sugarcane), vegetables (sugar beets, potatoes), fruits (apples, grapes), or other sources of sugar (maple syrup, for example).

GEOGRAPHY

Originally from Russia and Poland; today, made all over the world. Some of our favorite brands are made in France and the United States.

CATEGORIES

Unflavored vodka: Neutral tasting, neutral smelling, and crystal clear, unflavored vodka is distilled to a very high proof and cut with water, usually down to 40% ABV. High-quality vodka will offer subtle aromas of grain, citrus, and floral notes, with spice, more grain, and more citrus on the palate.

Flavored vodka: Neutral spirit with additional flavor added by means of one or more of the following: artificial extracts, natural extracts, maceration, infusion, or percolation. While many flavored vodkas are of poor quality, there are producers taking an enlightened approach, for example Hangar One and St. George.

In Cocktails

Though vodka's nuanced flavors are often masked by other ingredients—even in a Martini, the category of cocktails it's most associated with—we often use the spirit to add proof and stretch out other base spirits, to add body, or to soften the texture of a drink.

VODKA

We enjoy vodka for its supreme clarity and subtle flavor, an elegance that requires a particularly well-tuned palate to understand and enjoy. While the cocktail community (which includes us) has historically looked down on vodka as a neutral platform for cocktails, we don't discount this misunderstood, underappreciated spirit, but rather celebrate the fact that very minute differences in base ingredients—wheat, corn, rye, and so on—can shift a cocktail's flavor. To us, those *tiny* differences are the pocket where cocktail mastery lives.

The problem with vodka-based cocktails is that, with the exception of the vodka Martini, they're almost always jam-packed with powerful flavors that make assessing the nuance from one vodka to another nearly impossible. So we need to strip back the components to let the subtly of the vodka come through.

For these two experiments, you'll need three different styles of vodka: one made from potatoes (such as Chopin, Luksusowa, Woody Creek, Boyd & Blair, or the fantastically funky Karlsson's Gold), one from wheat (such as Absolut, Absolut Elyx, Grey Goose, or Ketel One), and one from corn (such as Tito's, Deep Eddy, Prairie, or Crystal Head). Importantly, do not prechill the vodka. The lower temperature will deaden the aroma and flavor of the spirit.

Tasting I: Vodka Soda

Although it sounds boring, simply mixing a spirit with some carbonated water brings two important benefits: first, neutral dilution stretches out the compact flavor of a high-proof spirit, allowing you to dig more deeply into the flavors—and do so in multiple tastes without getting too buzzy. Second, the effervescence of the soda water increases the aroma of the vodka, amping up those little differences in each style.

For this experiment, we're going to build a slightly different vodka soda than you might get from a bar, pulling back on the soda water and dialing in the optimal balance that exposes as much of the differences in the vodka as possible. And we'll leave the traditional lemon or lime garnish out

of the experiment for now (we'll explore the vodka-citrus relationship in the next experiment).

This is a great way to explore any spirit, but with vodka, it's one of the most effective ways we know to draw out flavors and aromas that are otherwise far too subtle for most people to smell or taste. With each, we hope you smelled and tasted differences, albeit small ones, from vodka to vodka. The lesson here is less about making the best vodka soda than about exposing you to something that baffles most novice spirit tasters: if you dig deep enough, there are actually noticeable aromas and flavors drawn from the vodka's base material—and knowing that each has its own characteristics, you can use them for creating more layered and complex cocktails.

Tasting II: Vodka Sour

Now that we have a solid foundation for distinguishing the qualities of different vodkas, we can see how those aromas and flavors interact with vodka's most common companion: citrus (for this experiment, specifically, fresh lemon juice).

As noted earlier, vodka's subtlety makes it very challenging to find differences when mixed with powerful ingredients like citrus and sugar, but here we hope you noticed something. To us, the differences in these three vodka sours is less in aroma and flavor than in texture. A potato-based vodka has an earthy, vegetal undertone. A wheat-based vodka in the sour has a cooling effect; it's almost thin, but refreshingly focused. The corn-based vodka sour is more luscious, and the sweetness of the lemon is more pronounced. If using a rye-based vodka, the sour draws out just a touch more acidity from the lemon juice, making for a slightly more structured cocktail.

When choosing which bottle to use for any given cocktail, think back on this experiment to determine not just what flavors will marry with the other components of the cocktail, but also your preference for the final flavor. Vodka may present tiny shades of difference, but it's those differences that can tip a cocktail from merely good to delicious.

Tasting I

VODKA SOUR

2 ounces vodka

3 ounces chilled seltzer

Supplies

- Three different types of vodka, three collins glasses, chilled seltzer, barspoon, ice.

Instructions

- Add each of your three vodkas to a different glass (no ice yet).

- Smell each vodka, noting the differences in each.

- Pour 3 ounces of chilled seltzer into each glass. Using a barspoon, mix briefly.

- Smell the three glasses again. Have the aromas you identified increased? Likely, they've become more intense.

- Taste each. Do the aromas you called out now come to life as flavors? You may need to taste a couple of times to draw out more differences.

- Add ice to each glass and stir briefly.

- Taste again. Do you notice how those subtle flavors are now pulled back a bit? This is what chilling liquids (or foods) does: dumbs down flavor and aroma.

Tasting II

VODKA SOUR

2 ounces vodka

¾ ounce fresh lemon juice

¾ ounce simple syrup
(page 287)

Supplies

- Three different types of vodka, three cocktail shaker sets, jigger, Hawthorne strainer, three cocktail glasses, ice.

Instructions

- Add each of the three vodkas to a different shaker and smell, noting the differences in aroma.

- Add the remaining vodka sour ingredients to the shakers.

- Add ice, seal, and shake each cocktail for 10 seconds, one at a time (do not strain yet).

- Shake each cocktail for an additional 5 seconds, then quickly strain into a cocktail glass.

- Smell each iteration. Do you notice any difference in the aroma? Then taste each and assess similarly.

In Our Rail

TRADITIONAL

Plymouth

Beefeater

Tanqueray

Fords

Bimini

Tanqueray 10

Monkey 47

St. George Dry Rye

St. George Terroir

Four Pillars Navy Strength

UNCONVENTIONAL

GIN

RAW MATERIALS
Neutral grain spirit, distilled water, and botanicals (endless options, but often among them: juniper, juniper oil, coriander, orange peel, lemon peel, anise, cassia, bitter almonds, caraway, cocoa, angelica root, and orris root). There are two ways of imparting botanical flavors to gin.

Compound gin. Natural or artificial flavorings are added after distillation. Used for making cheaper gins.

Distilled gin. Flavors are adding during the distillation process by one (or both) of the following means: botanicals are steeped in neutral grain spirit before being redistilled (maceration), or raw and/or neutral grain spirit is distilled such that the vapors pass through a botanical basket before being condensed.

GEOGRAPHY
Originally from Holland, gin is now made all over the world. Most major gin brands are distilled in the United Kingdom, with a growing roster of independent brands in the United States.

CATEGORIES
Plymouth: A gentle, citrus-forward style of gin similar to the traditional London dry gins, with an ABV of 41.2%. Distilled in a single distillery in Plymouth, England.

London dry: A big, crisp, high-proof, and aggressive style of gin with prominent flavors of juniper and citrus. Widely considered the benchmark for all other gin styles. Within the London dry category there are "mild" versions (similar to Plymouth), generally around 80 proof and light in flavor profile, and more assertive versions (such as Tanqueray and Beefeater), clocking in at higher ABVs and packing in more botanical flavor.

Contemporary gins: The "Wild West" of gin, a category encapsulating any style of botanical distillate that does not fall directly under one of the preceding categories. Most producers take flavor and/or style cues from classic gin styles and manipulate them by adding previously untried botanicals, removing botanicals, or experimenting with different raw materials for the base spirit.

Old Tom: London dry's predecessor, with a similar juniper-forward flavor but richer body and a sweeter flavor profile. Most old cocktail recipes that call for "gin" are actually referring to the Old Tom style.

Genever: The grandfather of all gin, created by the Dutch as a delivery system for juniper, which was thought to offer protection from the plague (nope, sorry). Distilled from a base of malted-barley wine, then redistilled with botanicals. The flavor profile is sweeter and richer than any other style of gin.

In Cocktails

Because the flavor profiles of gin can vary widely, we take careful consideration in which style—and even specific brand—to use when making a cocktail. If you find yourself needing to make a substitution, choose another gin from the same category with a similar proof and flavor profile. As a (very) general rule, higher-proof gins will be more aggressive and "spicy," while lower-proof gins tend to be more citrusy and floral.

GIN

Generically, when we say "gin," we mean something close to London dry gin—that is, of the Tanqueray and Beefeater heritage. Juniper is ever present, of course, but it's the other botanicals that add up to a sum greater than their parts. Some gins are mild; we'll refer to these in the following experiments as Mild London Dry (such as Plymouth or Fords). Others are higher in proof or have a more intense flavor profile; we'll refer to them as Strong London Dry (such as Beefeater, Tanqueray, or Gordon's).

There are more and more gins coming to market that break the mold. We call these Contemporary Gins (such as Aviation or St. George's multiple expressions: Botanivore, dry rye, and Terroir). Because there's so much diversity in the category, it's impossible to simply group all these new gins into one—but the point here is that they not only taste different from London dry, but their flavor profiles interact with other ingredients uniquely.

To execute these experiments, select a bottle from each of the categories—ideally, Fords, Tanqueray, and St. George Terroir—though the general notes should apply to similar bottles.

Tasting I: Tom Collins

Citrus and gin are classic companions, and there may be no better an example than the famous Tom Collins, a simple mix of gin, lemon juice, sugar, and seltzer. Here, the gin and lemon juice's collaboration is in full focus: with each variation, you'll see how the botanicals and proof will change the flavor and presence of lemon juice, and the effervescence from the seltzer should expose you to how aroma is unique to each.

What we love about this experiment is that all three versions are tasty, no doubt, but they are all noticeably different—and delicious in their own way. The version with Light London Dry (Fords) is refreshing, tart, and easily drinkable in a couple of sips. The Strong London Dry (Tanqueray) is noticeably punchier, with the gin's personality asserting itself, encouraging (slightly) slower sipping. And the Contemporary (St. George Terroir) is still refreshing, but dips far into savory territory.

Tasting II: Negroni

With just three ingredients—gin, Campari, sweet vermouth—in equal proportions, you'd think it'd be hard to mess up a Negroni. Aside from accurate measurements, the selection of each ingredient has a lot to do with how the whole comes together. Above all other considerations, we think the choice of gin for a Negroni is critical.

Whereas the Tom Collins experiment taught us that different styles of gin result in different expressions of the cocktail, the Negroni experiment is an education in how gin's components can, at times, clash. The lesson here is one of composition.

In tasting these three Negronis, we find ourselves gravitating to the more classic style, London dry. You get the spicy juniper punch right in the middle of the palate. We love that, and we find that the slightly more assertive personality of the Strong London Dry pushes through the Campari and sweet vermouth just enough to make the cocktail a touch more complex, whereas the Mild London Dry is deadened. They're both tasty, but our money is on the Strong London Dry Negroni.

The Contemporary Gin Negroni is perplexing but out of whack—it's too boozy and disjointed. This has a lot to do with the powerful flavors in the other ingredients. Both the Campari and the vermouth are sweet and bitter, and both are packed with flavor. Our ideal Negroni celebrates these characteristics but doesn't create chaos; using a gin with a strong personality puts too many cooks in the kitchen.

Perhaps our assessment of the Negroni doesn't match with yours. No problem! If you favored the Contemporary Gin Negroni, that likely means you're drawn to those big, bold flavors. Or you might find the milder flavor of Plymouth (or a similar gin) to be ideal. You just learned something about your palate.

Tasting I

TOM COLLINS

2 ounces gin

1 ounce fresh lemon juice

¾ ounce simple syrup
(page 287)

2 ounces cold seltzer

Supplies

- Three different gins, jigger, three cocktail shaker sets, ice, three collins glasses, Hawthorne strainer.

Instructions

- Add each of the three gins to a different shaker and smell, noting the differences in aroma.

- Add the remaining Tom Collins ingredients to the shakers.

- Add ice and seal the shakers.

- Add 2 ounces seltzer to each collins glass.

- Shake the cocktails, then strain each over the seltzer. Fill the glass with ice and stir briefly.

Tasting II

NEGRONI

1 ounce gin

1 ounce sweet vermouth,
preferably Cocchi vermouth
di Torino

1 ounce Campari

Supplies

- Three different gins, jigger, three cocktail shaker sets, ice, three old-fashioned glasses, three large ice cubes.

Instructions

- Add each of the three gins to a different shaker and smell, noting the differences in aroma.

- Add the remaining Negroni ingredients to the shakers.

- Fill the shakers to the brim with ice and stir each for 20 seconds.

- Strain each cocktail into an old-fashioned glass over 1 large ice cube. For this experiment, you don't need a garnish.

This lesson will aid you as you select gins for your cocktails and when and where to use certain styles. As a general rule, we opt for a milder London dry, like Plymouth, when the other ingredients aren't aggressive. Conversely, when making a cocktail with more assertive ingredients—like Campari or amari—using a stronger London dry will generally make a more complex cocktail. Finally, if the gin is going to be the star of the show—in, say, a Martini—a contemporary gin can be the perfect opportunity to let the gin shine without interruption.

In Our Rail

VEGETAL

Siembra Valles Blanco

Fortaleza Blanco

Cascahuin 48 Plata

Olmeca Altos Blanco

Cimarron Blanco

Tequila Ocho Blanco

El Tesoro Blanco

Tapatio Blanco

Siembra Azul Blanco

Siete Leguas Blanco

FRUITY

TEQUILA

RAW MATERIALS

Agave (a succulent of the lily family—not a cactus!) is cooked and shredded and the juice extracted in preparation for fermentation; cooking happens by either steaming the plant's hearts in a stainless steel pressure cooker or baking them in a neutral clay oven. Generally, steaming is considered a more industrialized process, resulting in a less flavorful tequila, while baking in clay results in a more flavorful and dynamic distillate.

GEOGRAPHY

Tequila is produced exclusively in the Mexican states of Jalisco, Nayarit, Michoacán, Guanajuato, and Tamaulipas, in governmentally designated zones covering more than 26 million acres. The majority (98 percent of total production) comes from the Jaliscan highlands and valley, where the elevation ranges between 800 and 2,300 meters above sea level.

CATEGORIES

100 percent agave: Made entirely from blue agave (*Agave tequilana* Weber var. *azul*), with the allowance of 2 percent added sugars, and distilled twice. We use only this style.

Mixto: Made from at least 51 percent blue agave sugars, with up to 49 percent "other," often nonagave sugars. Mixto is considered the lower quality of the two tequilas.

AGING

Blanco/plata/platinum/white: No aging, though sometimes "rested" in neutral holding tanks for up to 60 days.

Reposado: Matured in oak barrels from 60 days up to 11 months, 30 days.

Añejo: Matured in oak wood barrels with a capacity no larger than 600 liters from 1 year to 2 years, 364 days.

Extra añejo: Matured in small oak barrels for 3 years or longer.

In Cocktails

When choosing tequila for cocktail we usually look to age first. Blanco tequilas are the lightest style and a good fit for refreshing, citrusy drink Reposado tequilas are versatile, working in both citrusy and spirituo cocktails. Añejo tequilas have a pronounced oak-aged flavor and work well in Manhattan variations.

TEQUILA

Good tequila is (rightfully) expensive, and the longer-aged versions tend to be more expensive than the younger. Don't get us wrong; we'd love to incorporate the complexity of aged tequilas in our drinks (and we do in Talisman, page 206), but the expense is hard to justify. Here, we're focusing on two blanco tequilas and one reposado. We hope the first two bottles will expose you to the variety within blancos made in the same general region—one from a higher altitude than the other—showing how the development of slow-growing agave asserts itself in the final spirit. Each contributes to cocktails in different ways. That said, these two geographical anchors do not represent the full spectrum of tequila. Even within Jalisco, the lines get blurry very quickly, as many distilleries source their agave from all over the region; here, we use "highlands" and "valley" as more representative of a flavor profile: highlands tequilas tend to be brighter in aroma and more peppery on the palate, whereas valley tequilas are fruitier and often have a vanilla-like quality.

When choosing a highland blanco tequila, we suggest one of the products from the highly regarded La Alteña distillery: Tequila Ocho, El Tesoro, Siete Leguas, or Tequila Tapatío. Other widely available highland tequilas include Siembra Azul, Cascahuin, and Calle 23. For valley tequila, look for brands like Siembra Valles and Fortaleza.

For the reposado selection, we recommend purchasing an aged version of whichever blanco you chose, either highlands or valley. This will give you a good foundation for how aging impacts the cocktail from the same base style of tequila. We're huge fans of El Tesoro or Siete Leguas reposado from the highlands, and also Fortaleza reposado from the lowlands.

Tasting I: Margarita

Let's all agree: The margarita is a tasty cocktail, regardless of your tequila choice. Not only is it one of the most popular cocktails in the world, but when made properly, it's also a fantastic platform to explore tequila's intrinsic character.

However, there are some noticeable and instructive differences among the three iterations that will either speak to your personal preferences or be a jumping-off point when considering margarita variations of various complexity. For us, the highlands margarita is thirst-quenching, the perfect cocktail for a hot afternoon, with the tequila's sharp character heightening the acidity of the lime juice. The valley margarita is juicy and full, drawing out the sweet orange flavors of the Cointreau. Finally, the reposado makes for an earthier, grittier, and more contemplative margarita. Though we wouldn't reject any version, the clarity of the blanco-based margaritas is a more cohesive harmony—the essence of what a margarita should be.

Tasting II: La Rosita

Though they may seem a world apart in flavor, gin and tequila share some traits that can be useful in cocktails: the botanicals in gin work in a similar fashion to the sharp herbal and vegetal flavors of tequila. Have a favorite gin cocktail? Swap in tequila and give it a shot; it may not be perfect, but it probably works better than you thought it would. Though tequila is most often consumed in refreshing cocktails like the margarita, it can be a versatile player in spirituous cocktails, too. A riff on the Negroni, the La Rosita is an earthy, richly bitter cocktail. Here, we want you to learn how an unexpected spirit substitution (tequila in place of gin) can expose how tequila works alongside big, bitter flavors.

While we love the focus of blanco tequila—a beautiful, pure expression of the agave's innate character—in the presence of a strong flavor such as Campari, the unique personality of the tequila begins to fade. For us, the sharper tones of the highlands blanco is more successful here, but both of the blanco tequilas aren't the best representation of the cocktail. The reposado, though—with its woody spice character—is a fantastic complement to Campari, able to stand up against its bitter flavors to make a more integrated drink. When considering tequila's use in spirit-forward, complex cocktails, a reposado is often a good fit.

Tasting I

MARGARITA

2 ounces tequila

¾ ounce Cointreau

¾ ounce fresh lime juice

¼ ounce simple syrup
(page 287)

Supplies

- Three different tequilas, jigger, three cocktail shaker sets, ice, Hawthorne strainer, three old-fashioned glasses

Instructions

- Add each of the three tequilas to a different shaker and smell, noting the differences in aroma.

- Add the remaining margarita ingredients to the shakers.

- Add ice, seal, and shake each cocktail for 10 seconds, then strain into the glasses. Fill the glasses with ice.

Tasting II

LA ROSITA

1½ ounces tequila

½ ounce Campari

½ ounce sweet vermouth,
preferably Cocchi Vermouth
di Torino

½ ounce dry vermouth,
preferably Dolin dry vermouth

1 dash Angostura bitters

Garnish: 1 lemon twist and
1 orange twist

Supplies

- Three different tequilas, jigger, three cocktail shaker sets, barspoons, three old-fashioned glasses, three large ice cubes.

Instructions

- Add each of the three tequilas to a different shaker and smell, noting the differences in aroma.

- Add the remaining ingredients to each shaker.

- Fill the shakers to the brim with ice.

- Prepare citrus twists and set aside.

- Insert barspoons; working from left to right, stir each cocktail for 5 seconds. Repeat circuit twice.

- Strain each drink into a glass.

- Don't garnish yet; smell and taste each cocktail first, noting the differences among the three versions.

- Express one lemon twist over each cocktail and drop it in. Smell and taste each drink. Repeat with the orange twist.

In Our Rail

MEZCAL

RAW MATERIALS
While tequila can be made from only one variety of agave, mezcal can be made with any wild or cultivated variety of the plant. Espadín is the agave variety most commonly used for making mezcal. The agave must be cooked and shredded before the juice can be extracted in preparation for fermentation; for mezcal, this cooking process happens in pits filled with hot rocks, where the agave is cooked for several days and up to several weeks at a time.

GEOGRAPHY
Traditionally made in five south-central Mexican states: Oaxaca, Durango, San Luis Potosí, Guerrero, and Zacatecas.

CATEGORIES
The type of mezcal has to do with the type of agave used for its production. Notable types include (but are certainly not limited to): Espadín, Tobalá, Barril, and Cupreata.

AGING
Blanco: No aging, though sometimes rested in neutral tanks for up to 60 days.

Reposado/madurado: Matured in oak barrels between 2 months and 11 months, 30 days.

Añejo/añejado: Matured in oak barrels with a capacity no larger than 200 liters for a minimum of 1 year.

In Cocktails

The mezcals we love and frequently use in cocktails are artisanal products, each with its own unique flavor profile. But generally, mezcal adds smoky, briny, and vegetal notes to cocktails, often working in concert with other base spirits to avoid overpowering the drink. While there are aged mezcals, we almost always use unaged versions (blanco or joven) in cocktails. This is in part a cost consideration, but more than that, we gravitate toward the pure expression of the agave's agricultural personality most evident in unaged mezcals.

MEZCAL

Mezcal is a terroir-driven spirit resistant to simple categorization. Its flavor is drawn from the soil in which the agave is grown, the altitude of its region, the impact of years of weather as the agave matures, and the flora of the surrounding ecosystem. The types of agave used in mezcal also vary, from tiny wild species to massive cultivated forms. From there, the nuance of fermentation style and length, yeast strains, distillation technique, and the indescribable influence of the artisan distiller's touch produce a vast spectrum of flavors.

With such variation, it's hard to group mezcal into convenient categories. To make it easier, we're going to focus on the most commonly used agave in mezcal production, Espadín, to demonstrate how a shared base ingredient can display itself in vastly different ways in the final liquid. Though we specify precise bottles, the goal here is contrast; whichever three mezcals you use for the experiments, ensure they're from different producers, regions, and altitudes. If they're available in your area, we recommend acquiring the following: Del Maguey Santo Domingo Albarradas, Mal Bien Espadín, Mezcal Vago Espadín (Aquilino Garcia Lopez).

Tasting I: Paloma

While the margarita is the first cocktail most think of when talking agave spirits, the Paloma is more commonly consumed throughout Mexico. A simple highball of grapefruit soda and (traditionally) tequila is a perfect match for mezcal.

With the first sip, you should be able to notice some stark differences in how the mezcals interact with the grapefruit soda. The Paloma made with the Santo Domingo Albarradas heightens the fruitiness of the grapefruit, pulling its refreshing bitterness to the front of the palate, while the tropical notes in the mezcal are amplified.

The Paloma made with Mal Bien tends to bring a bit more of the pith and bitterness of the grapefruit to the front, finishing with a roasted, savory sweetness. The final drink, made with Mezcal Vago Espadín, is probably the most distinct of the three. This mezcal, clocking in at more than 50% ABV, cuts through the sweetness of the soda and pops with floral aromas. Perfumed with lavender and rose, this cocktail shows how high proof can carry aroma in cocktails.

Tasting II: Martini

Although Martini orthodoxy calls for gin (or vodka), the format is versatile, especially with other clear spirits. Floral, fruity, and minerally; these are all descriptors that can be attributed to both gin and agave-based spirits, so it's no surprise that vermouth and agave have a strong affinity.

For this experiment we're modifying the standard dry Martini to better align with the characteristics of mezcal. The power of mezcal can sometimes overshadow the delicacy of dry vermouth. Blanc vermouth is a better match: the added sweetness helps lift the mezcal's ripe agave characteristics. Additionally, to give the vermouth more room to express itself, we prefer this experiment with a fifty-fifty proportion of mezcal to blanc vermouth, which tamps the mezcal's proof down a touch to let us focus more on how the spirit collaborates with the modifier.

In the drink made with the bottle from Del Maguey Santo Domingo Albarradas, pineapple jumps out of the glass with just a hint of smoke, boosted by the sweet foundation of the blanc vermouth. The mezcal from Mal Bien echoes its savory notes from the Paloma, with flavors of corn and leather. And the Mezcal Vago Espadín–based Martini is bursting with a prominent smoky flavor, thanks to the mezcal's higher alcohol proof, which creates an intense aroma.

Additionally, the Martini format is a great vehicle for exploring how garnishes amplify or modify flavors within the cocktail: citrus twists, olives, pickled onions, and so on. In the first cocktail (Del Maguey), we may opt for a classic lemon twist. The Mal Bien's savory character is perfect territory for a savory garnish, such as a pickled onion. And the floral vibrancy of the Mezcal Vago Espadín invites drawing that flavor out even more, perhaps with a grapefruit twist.

Tasting I

PALOMA

1½ ounces mezcal

6 ounces grapefruit soda

Supplies

- Three different mezcals, jigger, three collins glasses, ice, barspoon.

Instructions

- Add each of the three mezcals to a different glass and smell, noting the differences in aroma.

- Add grapefruit soda to each glass.

- Fill the glasses with ice, and stir briefly.

- Smell and taste each drink.

Tasting II

MARTINI

1½ ounces mezcal

1½ ounces Dolin blanc vermouth

Garnish: 1 lemon twist, 1 grapefruit twist, and/or 1 pickled onion (optional)

Supplies

- Three different mezcals, jigger, three mixing glasses, ice, barspoon, julep strainer, three cocktail glasses.

Instructions

- Add each of the three mezcals to a different mixing glass and smell, noting the differences in aroma.

- Add the remaining Martini ingredients to the mixing glasses. Fill the glasses to the brim with ice and stir until cold and properly diluted.

- Strain each drink into the glasses. Garnish.

CACHAÇA

Brazil has its own sugarcane spirit tradition, cachaça. Distilled from fresh sugarcane juice only once—with some producers favoring column stills for industrial efficiency, or stylistically for a clear flavor, while others use alembics for depth—cachaça's personality is unique. Because of the single distillation (as opposed to the multiple distillations more typical in rum production), the character of the sugarcane juice is wild and funky, similar to rhum agricole in its grassiness, but generally not as aggressive. For cocktail use, we tend to favor unaged bottlings (prata), such as Avuá Prata, Novo Fogo Silver Cachaça, or Yaguara Ouro.

Cachaça also has a long history of aging in barrels made from unique indigenous woods, each of which provides a distinct character different from the flavor contributed by oak. For example, Avuá Amburana (aged in barrels made from the amburana tree) has a spicy, cinnamon-like flavor. Avuá also produces a cachaça in French oak, as well as limited bottlings of other exotic woods: Bálsamo, Jequitibá Rosa, Tapinhoa. Novo Fogo likewise has a range of aged cachaças worth exploring: one and two years in American oak, as well as blends from various barrels, such as American oak plus indigenous zebrawood, Brazil nut wood, or Brazilian teak. Each of these aged products from both producers (and others) is singular in flavor beyond the fruity baseline of the raw cachaça. Because of that, we tend to find use for them as accent pieces, contributing as much proof as they do seasoning to a cocktail—a delicious companion to blanco tequila (see Tandem Jump, page 190), to boost a strawberry-infused gin (Moon River, page 186), to accent aged brandy (see Escadrille, page 195), or to season a funky rhum agricole (see Diamond Heist, page 214).

In Our Rail

LIGHT

El Dorado 3-year

Probitas White

Santa Teresa 1796

Ron del Barilltio 3-Star

Cruzan Black Strap

Avua Prata cachaça

Rhum JM Blanc

Appleton Estate Signature Blend

Wray & Nephew

Hampden Estate Pure Single

FUNKY

RUM

RAW MATERIALS
Sugarcane in various forms, ranging from fresh-pressed sugarcane juice to molasses, the by-product of making refined sugar.

GEOGRAPHY
Rums hail predominately from the Caribbean, though very good rums are made all over the world, including Australia, the United Kingdom, Asia, and the continental United States.

CATEGORIES
Spanish: A lighter style, typically distilled from molasses and filtered to remove the fiery personality of the molasses-based distillate. Many of the rums made in Puerto Rico, Cuba, the Dominican Republic, Venezuela, Guatemala, Nicaragua, Panama, Colombia, Costa Rica, and Ecuador are made in this style.

English: A richer style, often distilled from Demerara sugar. Predominant in the former Caribbean colonies and present-day territories of the United Kingdom.

Jamaican: Also known as "navy" rum, Jamaican rum is always made in pot stills, which gives it both richness and its telltale funky complexity.

French: Also known as rhum agricole, French-style rums are distilled from freshly pressed sugarcane juice (rather than the by-product of the sugar refining process, molasses), which yields a distinctly grassy and earthy flavor profile. Rhum agricole is produced mostly in the French Caribbean, especially Martinique. Haiti has its own particular styles of rhum, from lighter versions to the funky, indigenous Clairin style.

AGING
Although most rum consumed is in a clear form (some unaged, others aged and then stripped of their color through heavy filtration), the world of aged rum is a vast and diverse one, with producers employing aging techniques of various styles (used French or American oak, solera aging) and often blending multiple approaches to create complex bottlings. As with other spirits, the addition of wood aging concentrates the flavor of the rum and changes its color.

In Cocktails

In choosing rum for cocktails, we typically start with a specific style of rum (Spanish, English, Jamaican, or French), asking ourselves which flavor profile will be appropriate with the cocktail's other ingredients. Unless for a cocktail that clearly calls for an aged rum (such as a Manhattan or an Old-Fashioned riff) we typically start with unaged, and layer in aged rum only if the added complexity will benefit the recipe.

RUM

A bottle of rum is a reflection of a style. It might be aged or unaged, light or funky, grassy or buttery. Given the vast variety of rums, when we see recipes that simply call for "rum," our heads explode. Not good enough.

In these experiments, we want to both open your eyes to rum's diversity and show you how different styles are appropriate for different uses. We could use any number of rum types with every gradation of aging, but for this exercise we'll focus on the common Spanish style, and then explore different age categories: first, white rum (such as Flor de Caña 4-year blanco, Plantation 3 Stars, or Bacardi white); then aged rum (such as Flor de Caña 7-year, Diplomático Reserva, Santa Teresa 1796, or Ron Zacapa 23). The goal here is contrast: a white rum (whether unaged or aged, then stripped of color) against one with enough time in oak to develop a richer profile. To these we add a third style: rhum agricole made from fresh sugarcane juice. Its pungent, grassy profile is as loud as spirits come and can make for a deeply delicious addition when used in moderation. If you want to throw a fourth rum into the mix, try a Jamaican style.

Tasting I: Mojito

We've never met a mojito we didn't like; this experiment is no different. The mojito made with white Spanish-style rum is the mojito of our summertime dreams, a crusher that will be consumed within minutes. The focus of the cocktail is really the lime and mint, with the rum acting as more of a foundation. Though its mild grassiness is noticeable, the Spanish-style rum brings richness, allowing the fresh ingredients to shine through.

The woody character of the aged rum doesn't wreck the mojito, but it does change the cocktail's focus from the freshness of the lime and mint to the density of the rum. The cocktail is still refreshing, but it has taken on a more complex flavor. In this way, the aging has seasoned the cocktail.

The rhum agricole mojito turns it up to 11. This cocktail is drinkable, but it feels unbalanced. While the grassiness and

funk of the rhum agricole aligns well enough with the lime and the mint, it definitely overshadows them.

From this lesson, we hope you tasted how the degree of age and complexity in a rum will have a big impact on how it interacts with other flavors. When a cocktail's focus is on fresh, herbal flavors (like a mojito), we lean toward the lighter styles of rums. When our cocktail gets a bit more dense or includes powerful ingredients—for example, amari or rich, darker syrups—we'll probably grab an aged rum.

Tasting II: Mai Tai

If you found yourself returning to the agricole-based mojito—because you liked it or it just made you curious—you're not alone. Agricole rhums are beguiling; on their own, they are fiery and (to the uninitiated) can be more than a little overwhelming. But in cocktails, the rhum's vibrancy shines through as complex, grassy, funky aromas and flavors.

One way to showcase an assertive rum is to mix it with other milder rums to create a new flavor profile. This mixing of multiple rum styles is common in tropical drinks. Here, we explore how the classic mai tai can be expressed differently by splitting the rums in various ways.

We hope each version of the mai tai shows you how different styles of rum in different proportions can influence a cocktail's flavor. For example, the first version maintains the fresh, focused character of the classic mai tai, but with a little extra richness and impression of funky complexity—the aged rum and agricole boosting these flavors, rather than taking over. The second mai tai is rich and gritty, with the agricole's flavor drawing out the aged characteristics of the rum, while the white Spanish-style rum mercifully stretches those flavors out a bit to let the almond and orange flavors of the orgeat shine. The final version is successful in its own unique way: with a big punch of grassy agricole flavor, the aged rum acts like bitters, enhancing the cocktail, while the white rum lengthens the agricole to make an extra-complex drink.

Tasting I

MOJITO

2 ounces rum

Mint leaves and sprigs

¾ ounce simple syrup
(page 287)

1 ounce fresh lime juice

Supplies

- Three different rums, jigger, three cocktail shaker sets, muddler, crushed ice, three double old-fashioned glasses, barspoon, straws.

Instructions

- Add each of three (or four!) rums to a different shaker and smell, noting the differences in aroma.

- Divide the mint leaves evenly among the shakers. Add the simple syrup. Using a muddler, gently press the leaves in each shaker. Do not crush or grind.

- Add the lime juice.

- To each shaker, add about 5 pieces of crushed ice. Seal and shake until you don't hear the sound of the crushed ice.

- Open the shakers and dump the cocktails into glasses. Using a barspoon, scrape any leaves stuck to the inside of the shaker into the glass.

- Fill the glasses to the brim with crushed ice. Garnish each drink with two mint sprigs and insert straws.

Tasting II

MAI TAI 1

1¼ ounces white Spanish-style rum

½ ounce aged Spanish-style rum

¼ ounce white rhum agricole

MAI TAI 2

½ ounce white Spanish-style rum

1¼ ounces aged Spanish-style rum

¼ ounce white rhum agricole

MAI TAI 3

½ ounce white Spanish-style rum

¼ ounce aged Spanish-style rum

1¼ ounces white rhum agricole

Supplies

- Three different rums (as described to the left), jigger, mint leaves and sprigs, and per cocktail 2 ounces simple syrup, 1 ounce fresh lime juice, ¾ ounce orgeat syrup, 3 dashes Angostura bitters, muddler, three cocktail shaker sets, crushed ice, three double old-fashioned glasses.

Instructions

- Add the rums according to the recipes to each of three different shakers and smell, noting the differences in aroma.

- Divide the mint leaves evenly among the shakers.

- Add the orgeat and simple syrup. Using a muddler, gently press the leaves in each shaker. Do not crush or grind. Add the lime juice and bitters.

- To each shaker, add about 5 pieces of crushed ice. Seal and shake until you don't hear the sound of the crushed ice.

- Open the shakers and dump the cocktails into the glasses. Using a barspoon, scrape any leaves stuck to the inside of the shaker into the glass.

- Fill the glasses to the brim with crushed ice. Garnish each drink with two mint sprigs and insert straws.

JIM BRIGGS

Jim Briggs is the CFO for Hunt Companies Finance Trust in New York City.

My interest in making drinks at home with some frequency started when I purchased the original *Death & Co* book, which was my first cocktail book. As a budding cocktail geek, I was immediately engrossed in the techniques for how to build a drink, and the book became my shopping guide for building the beginnings of a home bar.

Even though I owned, and was beginning to bury myself in, the book, I'd never actually been to the bar, something I felt an overwhelming urge to rectify. I picked a day early in the week and made a point of arriving just as the bar was opening, as I wanted to make sure I got in. I was welcomed at the door and seated at the bar near the service station. Jarred Weigand was bartending, and he immediately made me feel welcome with his sincere hospitality and his enthusiastic indulgence of my cocktail curiosity. I still remember my drinks that first night. My last drink of the evening was Some Weird Sin, which absolutely mesmerized me (and was somehow a crystal ball that showed me which spirits and modifiers I was going to fall in love with).

A few months passed before I returned, but when I did, Jarred was behind the bar again and remembered my name—it was like I'd never left. That really epitomized the bar's hospitality. My cocktail journey, with the D&C team as stewards, gained momentum. I'd leave and immediately look forward to my next visit. My freezer is now half full of mixing glasses, Nick & Noras, coupes, old-fashioned glasses, and good ice. My fridge door is full of vermouths, sherry, and several homemade syrups.

As much as you hear that Death & Co drinks contain a lot of ingredients, rare has been a night at the bar where there hasn't been a drink I've found that I can pull off at home. One of these drinks that stands out in my memory is the Warrior Poet (page 270). The cocktail had been off the menu for a while, but I asked for "something brown, stirred, up," was handed that drink, and was wowed. By then the bartenders had a sense of my style, but they also knew how to stretch it just a bit, in a way that they felt would nail it for me. I wouldn't be surprised if "Hey, Jim can make this at home" went into their thinking as well. The Warrior Poet is a pretty simple drink to make; it doesn't contain any obscure ingredients or infusions. I went out and bought Aquavit and Kalani the next day, and they have been staples in my home bar ever since.

To me, Death & Co became, and remains, a place where this cocktail geek can have phenomenal evenings, continuing this very enjoyable journey, surrounded by a D&C team second to none, and people who are just as excited about being there as I am.

SOME WEIRD SIN

Al Sotack, 2017

¾ ounce Old Grand-Dad 114 bourbon

½ ounce Smith & Cross Jamaica rum

½ ounce Zacapa 23-year rum

¼ ounce Amaro Ramazzotti

¼ ounce Lustau Pedro Ximénez sherry

1 teaspoon Cinnamon Syrup (page 283)

1 dash Bitter End Moroccan bitters

Garnish: 1 orange twist

Stir all the ingredients over ice, then strain into a double old-fashioned glass over 1 large ice cube. Express the orange twist over the drink, then place it in the drink.

In Our Rail

SOFT

Buffalo Trace bourbon

Elijah Craig bourbon

Old Forester Signature bourbon

Old Overholt rye

Russell's Reserve 10-year bourbon

Old Grand-Dad 114 bourbon

Wild Turkey rye

Rittenhouse rye

George Dickel rye

Pikesville rye

SPICY

AMERICAN WHISKEY

RAW MATERIALS
Grains including corn, rye, and wheat. Occasionally malted barley is used as well.

GEOGRAPHY
While most American whiskey is made in the southern United States, it can be made anywhere in the country.

CATEGORIES
Bourbon: Made from at least 51 percent corn, typically with a sweet flavor profile and rich mouthfeel.

Rye: Made from at least 51 percent rye, typically with a crisper, spicier profile and lighter mouthfeel than bourbon.

Tennessee sour mash: Made from between 51 and 79 percent corn and filtered through maple charcoal chunks before aging, a step known as the "Lincoln County process."

Canadian whisky: Usually made from mostly corn and lesser quantities of wheat and rye.

AGING
Bourbon, rye, and Tennessee whiskey: Aged in new charred American white oak.

Canadian: Aged a minimum of 3 years in oak barrels.

In Cocktails

When selecting a whiskey for cocktails, we typically first choose between two styles: bourbon or rye. We rarely use Tennessee sour mash whiskey in cocktails, not because we dislike it, but because it's hard to distinguish it in a drink (though we do use whiskey made in Tennessee, Dickel Rye, in the Lord Baltimore on page 236). We also don't typically use Canadian whisky; while there are some brands we love (such as Forty Creek), Canadian whisky is less assertive in a cocktail than bourbon, which we favor for its flavor, availability, and cost. So we ask ourselves: Do we want the sweet flavor and rich texture of a bourbon or a sharper, spicier rye? Next we look at proof and decide whether we need a lower-proof whiskey, the full weight of a bonded one, or something in between.

AMERICAN WHISKEY

Bourbon and rye are the dominant American whiskey styles, but we're seeing new distilleries popping up in every corner of the country that explore new stylistic frontiers. Some of these are closer to a classic bourbon or rye, while others channel a Scottish heritage (such as Clear Creek's McCarthy's single malt) or forge an entirely new path by forgoing any tradition and simply making good whiskey (such as Uncle Nearest)— they shed the strict requirements of any one category to make whiskies that defy neat groupings. Some bourbon and rye producers have added extra enhancement by finishing their whiskies in unique barrels (such as Rabbit Hole's PX cask-finished bourbon) or mashing up traditional bourbon with other styles (as is the case for High West Distillery's "Campfire" whiskey). Which is to say, American whiskey is a vast and ever-changing category.

For these experiments, we're going to start with traditional American whiskies: a high-wheat bourbon, a high-rye bourbon, and a straight-rye whiskey. For a high-wheat bourbon, look for W.L. Weller, Maker's Mark, Old Fitzgerald, and Rebel Yell. For a high-rye bourbon, seek out Old Grand-Dad, Four Roses, Buffalo Trace, and Old Forester. And for the straight rye whiskey, track down a bottle of Rittenhouse rye, Russell's Reserve rye, and Old Overholt rye. All are widely available, affordable, and high quality.

Tasting I: Old-Fashioned

Whiskey, bitters, and a bit of sugar: there's nothing to hide behind in an Old-Fashioned. The whiskey's characteristics are going to be front and center. To get the most out of this experiment, attention to detail is key. The tiny quantities of the other ingredients require that you measure precisely. While our preferred Old-Fashioned calls for a dash of Bitter Truth aromatic bitters for complexity, here we revert to the classic spec with Angostura bitters alone, to keep the conversation squarely focused on the whiskey.

bourbon turns up the complexity. And the straight rye whiskey version is all earthy grit and spice. In this way, what you may have smelled in the spirit alone is amplified in each Old-Fashioned.

We're also fascinated by the incremental addition of citrus twists in each one. With the first twist (lemon peel), the woody character of the whiskey's many years in oak barrels is pulled out, while the addition of the second (orange peel) draws out the grains' personality—the sweetness of the corn in the first two iterations, and the rye's peppery flavor in the third.

Tasting II: Whiskey Sour

The point of this experiment is to highlight American whiskey's affinity for lemon juice, and how lemon juice draws out the unique characteristics of each style. To do this, we're veering away from tradition and using a simplified version of the whiskey sour, sans the traditional egg white.

For us, the combination of bourbon and lemon juice has always elicited sense memories of Tootsie Rolls. This effect is most pronounced in the wheated whiskey sour, less so in the high-rye whiskey sour, then disappears almost entirely in the straight rye sour. While the actual flavor of Tootsie Rolls is our subjective interpretation, there's no denying that style expresses itself differently in the presence of citrus: in the milder forms (wheated bourbon and high-rye bourbon), the Whiskey Sour is a cohesive whole, with no single element dominating the others. The straight rye punches through the cocktail, making a slightly disjointed composition.

Our conclusion? If your citrusy whiskey cocktail is straight-forward, with few ingredients, lean toward bourbon. As the recipe becomes more complicated—say, with the addition of bitter juices like grapefruit, or intense modifiers like amari— consider straight rye, which is powerful enough to prevent the whiskey from getting bulldozed.

Tasting I

OLD-FASHIONED

2 ounces American whiskey

1 teaspoon Demerara Syrup
(page 283)

2 dashes Angostura bitters

Garnish: 1 lemon twist and
1 orange twist

Supplies

- Three different American whiskies, jigger, three mixing glasses, ice, barspoons, julep strainer, three double old-fashioned glasses, three large ice cubes.

Instructions

- Add each of the three whiskies to a different mixing glass and smell, noting the differences in aroma.

- Add the syrup and bitters to each mixing glass. Fill the glasses to the brim with ice.

- Insert barspoons and, working from left to right, stir each cocktail for 5 seconds. Repeat this circuit two more times.

- Strain each Old-Fashioned into a double old-fashioned glass over one large ice cube.

- Don't garnish yet; smell and taste each cocktail first, noting the differences between the three versions.

- Express one lemon twist over each cocktail and drop it in. Smell and taste each drink. Repeat with the orange twist.

Tasting II

WHISKEY SOUR

2 ounces American whiskey

¾ ounces fresh lemon juice

¾ ounces simple syrup
(page 287)

Supplies

- Three different American whiskies, jigger, three cocktail shaker sets, ice, Hawthorne strainer, three double old-fashioned glasses.

Instructions

- Add each of the three whiskies to a different shaker and smell, noting the differences in aroma.

- Add the lemon juice and simple syrup to each shaker.

- Add ice and seal the shakers. Working from left to right, shake each cocktail hard for 5 seconds. Repeat the circuit once more.

- Quickly strain each cocktail into an old-fashioned glass.

- Smell and taste each.

In Our Rail

SCOTCH WHISKY & IRISH WHISKEY

RAW MATERIALS
Malted barley and occasionally grains such as corn or wheat.

GEOGRAPHY
Scotland and Ireland, respectively.

CATEGORIES

Scotch whisky

Single malt: 100 percent malted barley made in a pot still and produced by a single distillery.

Single grain: 100 percent corn or wheat, made in a column still. Used mostly for blending.

Blended malt: 100 percent malted barley whiskies from two or more distilleries.

Blended: A combination of single-malt and grain whiskies.

Irish whiskey

Single malt: 100 percent malted barley made in a pot still and produced by a single distillery.

Grain: Made using no more than 30 percent barley in combination with other unmalted grains, including barley, wheat, or corn, in a column still.

Blended: A combination of single-malt and grain whiskies.

Single pot still whiskey: Made from 100 percent barley, both malted and unmalted, in a pot still.

AGING
Because bourbon producers are required to use brand-new barrels for aging, used bourbon casks are abundant and, post-Prohibition, have been the most common aging vessel for both Scotch and Irish whiskies. More recently, however, distilleries in both countries are experimenting with sherry, port, Madeira, and other types of wine barrels. Both types of whisk(e)y must be aged for at least 3 years.

In Cocktails

We reserve most of the finer scotches for sipping neat, but often reach for blended scotch (or a combination of blended cut with a lesser amount of single malt) for making cocktails. Peaty scotches, most notably those from Islay, are great tools for adding in small amounts to season a drink with their characteristic smoky flavor. With Irish whiskey, we use some of the lighter blends as we would bourbon, and pure pot still whiskeys when we want to showcase the flavor profile of the whiskey as the star of a cocktail.

SCOTCH WHISKY & IRISH WHISKEY

For these experiments, we suggest finding three styles of Scotch whisky that represent three articulations of the category: blended scotch, a mild single malt, and a smoky single malt. Blended scotch isn't necessarily less complex than the others, but generally they are more affordable than single malts, with a milder flavor. Look for bottles such as Famous Grouse or Compass Box Great King Street, or, if you can find it, Street Pumas' blended scotch. Single malts are not categorized as "mild," but we tend to think of certain brands as being more austere than others; look for bottles such as Highland Park 12-year, The Glenlivet 12-year, Auchentoshan Three Wood, or The Balvenie 12-year DoubleWood. Finally, on the far end of the intensity spectrum is smoky single malt scotch made with peated barley. The most intense versions come from Islay; keep an eye out for Caol Ila 12-year, Ardbeg Uigeadail, Laphroaig Quarter Cask, or Bowmore 12-year.

Tasting I: Morning Glory Fizz

This restorative cocktail might look scary to those uninitiated with absinthe but it's delicious and refreshing, and it shows the versatility of Scotch whisky in cocktails. In this experiment we want you to see how the increasing complexity of each scotch presents very different results when a powerful flavor like absinthe is introduced.

We're amazed how these three cocktails drift from refreshing and herbaceous with the blended scotch, to a touch of smoke and cereal grittiness with the mild single malt, to a brutal assault on the senses with the smoky scotch.

Unsurprisingly, we favor the milder versions of Scotch whisky in this style of cocktail. With citrus present, your palate wants more refreshment, and the base spirit should complement that desire. Granted, there's noticeably more complexity in the mild single malt versus the blended, but with the powerful, more-expensive whisky, it's a judgment call whether the complexity is worth the cost. The aggressiveness of the smoky scotch both overpowers the cocktail and conflicts with the absinthe. To us, it's over the top, disjointed, and unsuccessful.

Tasting II: Rob Roy

This experiment explores the collaboration of scotch and vermouth. Here we suggest an Italian vermouth that's neither too bitter nor too light. If you find yourself with a more assertive sweet vermouth (Carpano Antica, for example), you may prefer the bolder whiskies; if you have a milder vermouth (such as Dolin rouge), you may prefer the blended.

Here, the rich and bitter foundation of the sweet vermouth draws out the more subtle flavors from each scotch. The bitter tones of the vermouth slightly overshadow the whisky's personality in the blended scotch version. The mild single-malt version is highly aromatic, with the floral character of the whisky building on the vermouth's botanicals. In the peated version, the smoky scotch is put in check, softened and expanded thanks to the vermouth.

This lesson teaches us a vital consideration when mixing scotch in cocktails: If the base scotch is mild, a strongly flavored ingredient like vermouth can easily overwhelm it. This can be remedied by pulling back on the vermouth in proportion to the whisky; or, as we often do, reserving these milder scotches for citrusy cocktails (see Voodoo Dreams, page 226; Radio Flyer, page 222; Planet Caravan, page 222).

In spirituous cocktails, milder scotches can be matched up with complementary flavors, as in the I Against I (page 234) or the Unforgiven (page 244). A similar trajectory allows the lighter single malts to collaborate with other base spirits, acting in some cases as a split base (see Her Name Is Joy, page 234), a support for another spirit (Phantom Mood, page 239), or the star of the show (Stunt Double, page 204).

With smoky scotch, we rarely put it front and center. As evidenced by the Rob Roy in this experiment, in high proportions these whiskies are disturbingly close to smoking a cigarette (unless that's your thing, man). Rather, we tend to use these powerful whiskies to season in small quantities, as in the Bushido (page 211), Hagakure (page 234), Highwayman (page 234), and Busy Earning (page 230).

Tasting I

MORNING GLORY FIZZ

2 ounces Scotch whisky

¾ ounce fresh lemon juice

¾ ounce simple syrup (page 287)

3 dashes absinthe

1 egg white

2 ounces cold seltzer

Supplies

- Three different Scotch or Irish whiskies, jigger, three cocktail shaker sets, ice, Hawthorn strainer, three fizz glasses, fine strainer.

Instructions

- Add each of the three whiskies to a different shaker and smell, noting the differences in aroma.
- Add the lemon juice, simple syrup, and absinthe to each shaker. Add the egg white.
- Seal the shakers without ice and shake each for 5 seconds.
- Open the shakers, add ice, and seal again.
- Add 1 ounce seltzer to each fizz glass.
- Working from left to right, shake each cocktail hard for 10 seconds. Repeat the circuit one more time.
- Quickly double strain each cocktail into a fizz glass. Top with the remaining 1 ounce of seltzer. Smell and taste each drink.

Tasting II

ROB ROY

2 ounces Scotch whisky

1 ounce sweet vermouth, preferably Cocchi vermouth di Torino

2 dashes Angostura bitters

Supplies

- Three different Scotch or Irish whiskies, jigger, three mixing glasses, ice, barspoons, julep strainer, three cocktail glasses.

Instructions

- Add each of the three whiskies to a different mixing glass and smell, noting the differences in aroma.
- Add the remaining ingredients and fill the glasses to the brim with ice.
- Insert barspoons; working from left to right, stir each cocktail for 5 seconds. Repeat the circuit two more times.
- Strain each Rob Roy into a cocktail glass. Smell and taste each drink.

Irish Whiskey Experiments: These two experiments center around Scotch, but they can both be re-created with Irish whiskey. Though the results will be markedly different, Irish whiskey's diversity presents a similar spread of flavors as does scotch: grab a light and fruity bottle (Tyconnel Irish), another with some pot-still density (Redbreast 12-year), and last, a peated Irish whiskey (Connerara Peated).

JAPANESE WHISKY

The tradition of single-malt Scotch whisky has inspired producers around the globe. There are venerable whiskies made in the Scottish style (St. George Baller and Westward, for example) in the United States, as well as in Taiwan (Kavalan's many iterations), and India (Amrut and Rampur).

In recent years, Japanese whisky has seen a meteoric rise in popularity and, because of a feverish interest by bartenders and aficionados, scarcity in supply and a skyrocketing increase in pricing. We were early adopters, with drinks showing up in our first book, *Death & Co: Modern Classic Cocktails*, using now-revered and rarely found bottles, such as Yamazaki 12-year. Hell, there was a time when Dave would ask for a Rob Roy made with Yamazaki 18-year and no one thought the better of it. Oh, to be young again.

These days, we're more realistic about the use of these pricy products in our drinks. Generally, we tend to use Japanese whisky in collaboration with a more-affordable spirit, not just to spread the cost among multiple ingredients, but because these whiskies work fantastically with other categories of spirits.

Stylistically, in the past many would describe Japanese whisky as being very similar to scotch. While that is true of some bottlings that we use—such as the Hibiki 12-year in the Whiskey Agreement (page 245), Suntory Toki in Bad Sneakers (page 273), or Hibiki Harmony in the Shoganai (page 188)—there are other Japanese whiskies that depart from the scotch tradition. Nikka Coffey Grain Japanese whisky is closer in style to American whiskey in ingredients and distillation techniques, but it still has the elegance that Japanese distillates (or everything Japan-made?) are known for; you'll find it in the Dahlia, Yojimbo, and Sasaki Garden (page 240).

In Our Rail

SAVORY

Reisetbauer carrot eau-de-vie

Rhine Hall mango brandy

Clear Creek Blue Plum brandy

Clear Creek Douglas Fir eau-de-vie

St. George Aqua Perfecta basil
eau-de-vie

Cobrafire eau-de-vie de raisin

Cyril Zangs 00 apple cider
eau-de-vie

Clear Creek pear brandy

Capurro Acholado pisco

St. George framboise eau-de-vie

AROMATIC

_# Spirit Profile

UNAGED BRANDY

RAW MATERIALS
Brandy is most often distilled from fermented fruit (and occasionally vegetables), typically full-flavored, hearty fruits. Some adventurous distillers have experimented with distilling nonfruit ingredients from basil to foie gras to (seriously!) crabs.

GEOGRAPHY
Anywhere in the world, with the best-known eaux-de-vie coming largely from France, Eastern Europe, the Pacific Northwest, and New England.

CATEGORIES
Pisco: Distilled from wine (grape varietals include Torontel, Moscatel, Quebranta, Italia, Albillo, Uvina, and Negra Corriente in Peru; and Muscat, Pedro Ximénez, and Torontel in Chile). Peruvian pisco tends to be made in pot stills, while Chilean piscos are distilled in column stills.

Grappa: Italian spirit made in pot stills from grape skins, seeds, and stems—traditionally those left over from winemaking. While grappa originated in Italy, there are some beautiful grappas made in North America as well.

Marc: Very similar to grappa, the French "eau-de-vie de marc" is also pot-distilled from grape skins, seeds, and stems.

Blanche Armagnac: A crisp, aromatic unaged Armagnac, distinct in both flavor and cocktail use from its aged, far more famous cousin (see Aged Brandy, page 101).

Fruit brandies or eaux-de-vie: Pear (aka poire or poire Williams), cherry (kirschwasser), apple (pomme), raspberry (framboise), and plum (slivovitz).

Singani: In Bolivia, similar grapes are distilled (in both pot and column stills) and called signani.

AGING
No aging, though some eau-de-vie are rested in neutral holding tanks. Some of these styles see sparing use of aging, such as in fine grappas or, occasionally, in pisco. Generally, the brandies presented here (especially for cocktail use) are unaged.

In Cocktails

Unaged fruit brandy is called eau-de-vie ("water of life"), a historical reference to the origins of distillation, wherein the concentration of the liquid through distillation was an exercise in homing in on its quintessence. The hallmark of eau-de-vie, as opposed to other styles of brandy, is a supremely pure expression of the ingredient from which it is distilled. Eaux-de-vie can be very helpful in adding a boost of flavor to fresh ingredients—a quarter ounce of cherry eau-de-vie (kirschwasser) can add deep complexity to a drink (see Verona Cobbler, page 244). As the flavors in eaux-de-vie are extremely concentrated, it's usually best to exercise restraint in the amount used in cocktails—too much can easily overwhelm other ingredients.

UNAGED BRANDY

In the following tasting experiments, we'll show the versatility of these products in two different styles of cocktails—a Spritz and a Martini variation—through three distinct styles of unaged brandy: pear brandy, pisco/singani, and grappa.

We're pear brandy's biggest fanboys. This is our benchmark for unaged brandies. Look for pear brandies that follow the highly fragrant Alsatian tradition: Clear Creek Williams pear brandy, St. George pear brandy, or Massenez Poire Williams. Make sure it's not a liqueur or artificially flavored spirit.

Unlike the base brandy that goes into making cognac, the grape-based brandies of South America are fragrant and highly flavorful. In Chile and Peru, these brandies are called *pisco*; in Bolivia, it's *singani*. Most are produced using highly aromatic grapes and distillation techniques that focus the aroma and flavor pointedly. For piscos, look for brands such as Barsol Acholado, Capurro Acholado, or Macchu. For singani, look for Singani 63.

Made with the leftovers of wine production, grappa is blustery to the uninitiated, but with practice and time, you'll find those overpowering flavors begin to reveal an incredible amount of complexity. We recommend looking for some of the more affordable options, such as Jacopo Poli or Nonino from Italy, or Clear Creek's varietal iterations from Oregon. While we don't use grappa frequently, it does show up occasionally (and sparingly) in our cocktails, such as in the Idyllwild (page 257), Repeater (page 188), and Daisy Bell (page 212).

Tasting I: Basic Spritz

Unaged brandies are focused expressions of their base fruit—there are no added botanicals or flavorings, nor the influence of wood barrels. These spirits are big in personality, and because of that they can be both wonderful in cocktails and occasionally a bully. A little goes a very, very long way.

While we love the individual character of these spirits, in these spritzes the brandy is there to boost the vermouth's characteristics. Beyond showing how much flavor is packed

into unaged brandies, this experiment also exposes the texture of each, a grittiness that creates an added layer of complexity. In the pear brandy spritz, this is reminiscent of biting into a pear, whereas in the pisco (or singani) version, there's almost the impression of grape skin tannins.

Tasting II: Martini

Similar to the mezcal experiment on page 74, building an equal-parts Martini is a great way to explore how a brandy will work in a simple, spirituous cocktail. By doing so, we can experience the characteristics of the spirit as it mingles with the largely cooperative flavors of blanc vermouth—another departure from the traditional dry vermouth, which would be overwhelmed by any of these brandies.

In each of the three "Martini" recipes that follow, we build a slightly different version with a proportion of each brandy, pushing and pulling the composition to show how unaged brandies can play together and how, in collaboration, they express themselves uniquely (or don't, in some cases).

There are any number of variations on this theme that you could explore, but we find these three builds to be instructive in how powerful flavors can be combined to create a new flavor profile. In other words, we're creating a new core flavor in each Martini. The Egalitarian Martini illustrates how, when in (more or less) equal proportion, each brandy competes for attention. In near-equal proportions, the grappa is far too forward even at ½ ounce, overshadowing the other flavors.

The next two iterations shift the focus to either the pear brandy or the pisco/singani and pull back the grappa to a teaspoon. With that, the cocktail suddenly comes more into focus. The Pear-Forward Martini is lifted by the floral undertones of the pisco or singani, while the grappa adds complexity. The Pisco-Forward Martini is more floral, with the pisco's aromatics noticeably lifted, and the pear brandy's aroma doubling down but not making the cocktail overly pear flavored. Each is tasty in its own right.

Tasting I

BASIC SPRITZ

½ ounce unaged brandy

1½ ounces blanc vermouth,
preferably Dolin blanc

¼ ounce fresh lemon juice

2 ounces cold seltzer

Supplies

- Three different unaged brandies, jigger, three wine glasses, ice, barspoon.

Instructions

- Add each of the three brandies to a different wine glass and smell, noting the differences in aroma.

- Add the vermouth and lemon juice to each wine glass. Fill the glasses three-quarters full with ice.

- Stir until the outside of the glass is chilled, about 10 seconds for each drink.

- Add seltzer to each glass and stir briefly to integrate.

- Smell and taste each drink.

Tasting II

EGALITARIAN

¾ ounce pear brandy

¾ ounce pisco or singani

½ ounce grappa

1 ounce Dolin blanc vermouth

PEAR-FORWARD

1½ ounces pear brandy

Supplies

- One bottle each pear brandy, singani, and grappa, jigger, three mixing glasses, ice, barspoon, julep strainer, three cocktail glasses.

Instructions

- Combine the brandies according to the recipes in three separate mixing glasses (or other tasting glasses) and smell.

- Build the cocktail in each mixing glass. Fill the glass to the brim with ice and stir until cold and properly diluted.

- Strain each drink into a cocktail glass. Smell and taste each drink.

In Our Rail

SUBTLE

Bertoux brandy

Clear Creek 2-year apple brandy

Guillon-Painuraud VSOP cognac

Lemorton Selection calvados
domfrontais

Germain-Robin Alambic
American brandy

Louis Roque La Vielle prune eau-de-vie

Domaine du Manoir de Montreuil
Reserve calvados

Hine H VSOP cognac

PM Spirits Bas Armagnac

Lustau Solera Reserva brandy

Pierre Ferrand 1840 cognac

Gourry de Chadville cognac

Lairds bonded apple brandy

INTENSE

The great aged brandies of the world come mainly from France, Italy, and the Americas.

CATEGORIES

Cognac: Double distilled in pot stills from Ugni Blanc, Folle Blanche, and Colombard grapes, and aged in Limousin oak barrels. To be called *cognac*, the spirit must be made in the Cognac region of France.

Armagnac: Distilled from mostly Ugni Blanc grapes using a combination of column and pot stills, aged in oak, and made in the Armagnac region of France.

Brandy de Jerez: Made in the same region as sherry wine in southern Spain and the city of Jerez in Andalusia, and distilled from the neutral Airén grape, Spanish brandy employs the same solera aging process used for the region's famous sherry.

Calvados: French apple brandy with production and aging regulations similar to those for cognac and Armagnac. Crisp apple flavor with loads of barnyard funk. While most calvados is made from only cider apples, some have a minority percentage of pears, specifically from the Domfrontais region in Normandy, France, where 30 percent of the distillate comes from pears.

Straight apple brandy: American apple brandy. Laird's bonded apple brandy follows the same set of standards as bonded whiskies, yielding a rich, spicy, deeply aged spirit. The other major United States apple brandy producer, Clear Creek, makes a 2-year and an 8-year apple brandy, both of which have bright apple flavors more similar to those found in calvados, without the aggressively earthy, funky notes.

Other aged apple brandies: There are many producers (both domestic and international) that make brandy from apples. Depending on the producer, their style is similar to either calvados or American straight apple brandy—or somewhere in between.

simple approaches. However, with aged grape brandies we often reach for VS or VSOP cognac in citrusy Sidecar and Sazerac variations, or in concert with other base spirits; and Armagnac when we want to showcase a specific bottle we love. When selecting apple brandy for cocktails, we ask ourselves if we want the rich, spicy flavors of a straight apple brandy (such as Laird's straight bonded), or the crisp apple flavor and funk of a calvados. If a calvados, the complexity of a VSOP aged is perfectly suited for most cocktails. If the latter, we usually reach for brandy that's been aged around three years, which will bring toasty oak and vanilla flavors to the party and works well alongside other aged spirits.

AGED BRANDY

We adore the purity of unaged brandies for their focused personality. But these experiments are about exploring how *aging* brandy can shape the fruit's inherent flavor into something that isn't found in nature. We focus on three aged brandies here: cognac, calvados, and American straight apple brandy.

For cognac, we tend to use bottlings that have enough age to become complex, but not overly expensive. Targeting a VSOP age range, look for Pierre Ferrand ambré, Pierre Ferrand 1840, Park VSOP cognac, or H by Hine VSOP.

Much like grape-based cognac, apple-based calvados can get expensive real quick, and the brands that are affordable enough to mix in cocktails tend to be too youthful and not complex enough. Here, spring for a bottle in the VSOP range, too: Look for Busnel VSOP, Boulard VSOP, Père Magloire VSOP, or Roger Groult Reserve 3 Ans.

While the French-inspired apple brandies just listed show an incredible amount of finesse due to long aging in reused French oak, an American tradition of using charred new oak spawned a style of apple brandy unique to the United States: straight apple brandy. These spicy, complex brandies are much like a mashup of American whiskey and calvados. Look for the gold standard (and oldest American-made spirit), Laird's bonded apple brandy, bottled in bond, as well as other notable newcomers Black Dirt Distillery apple jack (confusingly, not an applejack by the technical definition, but a straight apple brandy), or Copper & Kings American apple brandy.

Tasting I: Sidecar

Refreshing, tart, and complex, the Sidecar is a great way to ease into exploring aged brandies. The fresh, orange-y complexity of Cointreau draws out the fruity characteristics of each of the three brandies—cognac, calvados, and American straight apple brandy—while the acidity of lemon juice matched with the sweetness of the liqueur allows for easy drinking.

Though all three cocktails are refreshing, they veer in very different directions. The cognac-based Sidecar is the classic. Calvados transforms an already elegant cocktail into a softer, more delicate cocktail. Though there's no cinnamon or cloves in the drink, your brain might be triggered into believing there is—this Sidecar riff is deeply soothing in a holiday-spice sort of way. Pivoting in a spicy direction, the applejack-based Sidecar is grittier and woodsy, with the base spirit pushing through.

Choosing one direction over another is a stylistic choice: do you want soft, gentle flavors, or big, bold ones?

Tasting II: American Trilogy

This experiment showcases the various ways in which brandy can express itself alongside other ingredients—in this case, American whiskey.

For an Old-Fashioned lover, the American Trilogy is a knockout variation, and none of these versions disappoint—but they are so different. The cognac-based version is rich and soothing, with a spiced raisin flavor from the cognac matched with the spicy bite of the rye. Swapping in calvados steers the drink toward an almost buttery softness, the rye inching forward relative to the brandy, but making the cocktail lighter than the American apple brandy version. And in the final, original form of the American Trilogy, the pungency of the Laird's apple brandy (or your other choice) matches assertively with the rye whiskey, a spicy combination that packs a punch.

We find this lesson valuable in teaching us when to use each style for specific end results. If we were aiming for a cocktail with bold, round flavors, cognac would be our choice. Should we be seeking levity and nuance, calvados would surely do the trick. And if spiciness were needed, the Laird's bottled in bond (or a similar style of American apple brandy) would be the right tool for the job.

Tasting I

SIDECAR

1½ ounces aged brandy

¾ ounce fresh lemon juice

1 teaspoon simple syrup
(page 287)

¾ ounce Cointreau

Garnish: 1 orange twist

Supplies

- Three different aged brandies, jigger, three cocktail shaker sets, Hawthorne strainer, ice, three cocktail coupes.

Instructions

- Add each of the three brandies to a different shaker and smell, noting the differences in aroma.

- Add the lemon juice, simple syrup, and Cointreau to the shakers.

- Add ice and seal the shakers.

- Working from left to right, shake each cocktail hard for 10 seconds. Repeat the circuit one more time.

- Quickly strain each cocktail into a coupe. Garnish with the orange twist.

- Smell and taste each drink.

Tasting II

AMERICAN TRILOGY

1 ounce aged brandy

1 ounce rye whiskey

1 teaspoon Demerara Syrup
(page 283)

1 dash Angostura bitters

1 dash Angostura orange bitters

Supplies

- Three different aged brandies, jigger, three mixing glasses, ice, barspoon, julep strainer, three old-fashioned glasses, three large ice cubes.

Instructions

- Add each of the brandies and the rye whiskey to a different mixing glass and smell, noting the differences in aroma.

- Add the Demerara Syrup and both bitters to each mixing glass.

- Fill the mixing glasses to the brim with ice and stir until chilled and properly diluted.

- Strain each drink into single old-fashioned glasses over 1 large ice cube.

MODIFIERS

Our longstanding definition of a "modifier" is any alcoholic ingredient that plays a supporting role to a cocktail's base spirit(s). And as you learned in the preceding section, spirits can also play the supporting role of a modifier—and many ingredients that typically serve as modifiers can moonlight as a base ingredient.

As such, modifiers constitute a *very* broad range of ingredients, and we've profiled dozens of our favorite brands in previous books. But for the purpose of exploring modifiers for your own bar and cocktail-making endeavors, we've divided the category into three groups: liqueurs, fortified wines, and amari. We then break these subcategories down even further by grouping bottles with similar styles, flavor profiles, and proofs, which gets you closer to being able to make selections—and substitutions—based on your needs.

LIQUEURS

Generally speaking, liqueurs are moderately alcoholic (typically 20 to 40 percent) ingredients that add a specific flavor—orange (Cointreau), mint (menthe-pastille), or grapefruit (pamplemousse)—or complex presentation of flavors—such as Chartreuse or Bénédictine. Opposite we plot out the proof and relative sweetness of our most frequently used liqueurs at Death & Co.

AMARI

Amari is a tricky modifier to group into categories. We think of this universally bitter (to varying degrees), mostly sweet, mostly Italian class of alcohol as falling somewhere between a liqueur and a fortified wine. Like liqueurs, most amari are built upon a spirituous base ingredient, typically grape brandy or a grain neutral spirit (though rarely from a fortified wine base), and are sweetened to various degrees. But they're also flavored with varying botanicals common to fortified wines, especially sweet vermouth (which also originated in Italy), often with bitter flavorings like barks, herbs, and citrus peel. Proof-wise, amari can be all over the place, but many land in the 20% to 30% ABV range, while others start inching toward spirit-level proof.

In cocktails, we use amari in various amounts and roles, from a generous pour as base ingredient (such as Don't Forget the Struggle, Don't Forget the Streets, page 250) all the way down to a small amount used as a seasoning in place of bitters (Thieves in the Night, page 242). Because each amari is unique, it can be tricky to swap one out for another in a cocktail without affecting the proof, sweetness, and flavor profile of a drink. Here we group amari into a few general categories, ranging from the lightest (aperitivi) to the densest.

APERITIVI

Aperol, Campari, Suze

LIGHT AMARI

Amaro Meletti, Amaro Montenegro, Amaro Nonino Quintessentia, Lo-Fi gentian amaro

MEDIUM AMARI

Amaro Averna, Amaro CioCiaro, Bigallet China-China Amer, Cynar, Ramazzotti, Cappelletti Pasubio vino amaro, Amaro di Angostura, Braulio amaro, Amaro Nardini

DENSE AMARI

Fernet-Branca, Luxardo Amaro Abano, Capalleti Amaro Sfumato, Forthave Spirits Marseille amaro, Fernet-Vallet

Death & Co's Favorite Modifiers

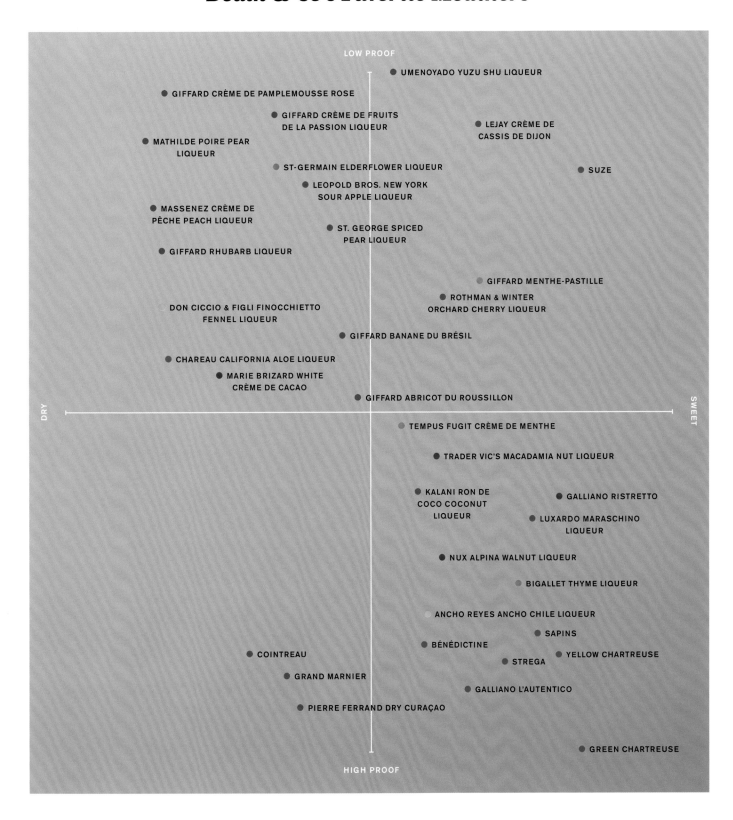

LOW PROOF

UMENOYADO YUZU SHU LIQUEUR

GIFFARD CRÈME DE PAMPLEMOUSSE ROSE

GIFFARD CRÈME DE FRUITS
DE LA PASSION LIQUEUR

LEJAY CRÈME DE
CASSIS DE DIJON

MATHILDE POIRE PEAR
LIQUEUR

ST-GERMAIN ELDERFLOWER LIQUEUR

SUZE

LEOPOLD BROS. NEW YORK
SOUR APPLE LIQUEUR

MASSENEZ CRÈME DE
PÊCHE PEACH LIQUEUR

ST. GEORGE SPICED
PEAR LIQUEUR

GIFFARD RHUBARB LIQUEUR

GIFFARD MENTHE-PASTILLE

ROTHMAN & WINTER
ORCHARD CHERRY LIQUEUR

DON CICCIO & FIGLI FINOCCHIETTO
FENNEL LIQUEUR

GIFFARD BANANE DU BRÉSIL

CHAREAU CALIFORNIA ALOE LIQUEUR

MARIE BRIZARD WHITE
CRÈME DE CACAO

DRY

GIFFARD ABRICOT DU ROUSSILLON

SWEET

TEMPUS FUGIT CRÈME DE MENTHE

TRADER VIC'S MACADAMIA NUT LIQUEUR

KALANI RON DE
COCO COCONUT
LIQUEUR

GALLIANO RISTRETTO

LUXARDO MARASCHINO
LIQUEUR

NUX ALPINA WALNUT LIQUEUR

BIGALLET THYME LIQUEUR

ANCHO REYES ANCHO CHILE LIQUEUR

SAPINS

BÉNÉDICTINE

YELLOW CHARTREUSE

COINTREAU

STREGA

GRAND MARNIER

GALLIANO L'AUTENTICO

PIERRE FERRAND DRY CURAÇAO

GREEN CHARTREUSE

HIGH PROOF

● HERBAL LIQUEUR   ● FLOWER- & HERB-BASED LIQUEUR   ● FRUIT LIQUEUR   ● RICH LIQUEUR   ● VEGETAL LIQUEUR

Death & Co's Favorite Fortified Wines

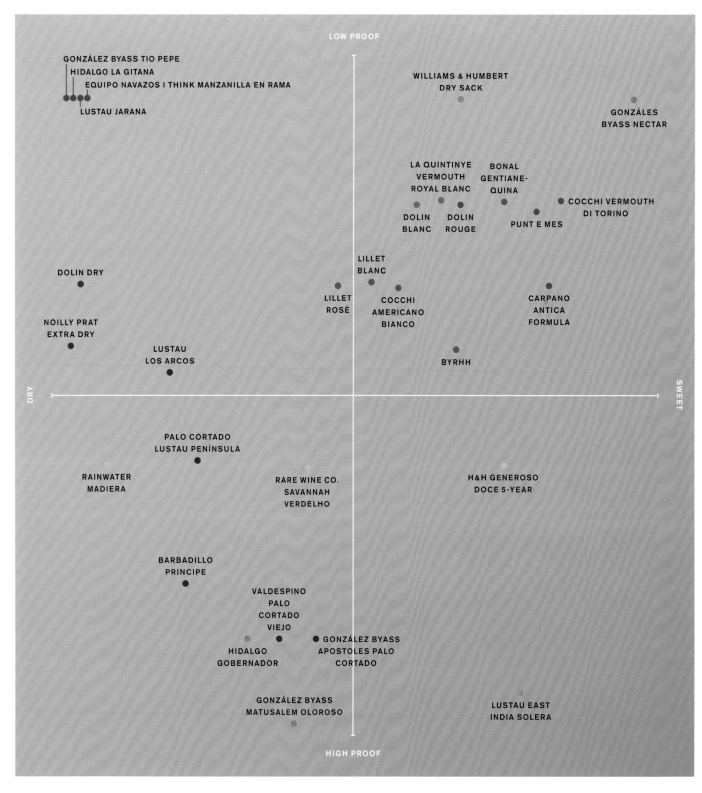

LOW PROOF

GONZÁLEZ BYASS TIO PEPE

HIDALGO LA GITANA

EQUIPO NAVAZOS I THINK MANZANILLA EN RAMA

LUSTAU JARANA

WILLIAMS & HUMBERT
DRY SACK

GONZÁLES
BYASS NECTAR

LA QUINTINYE
VERMOUTH
ROYAL BLANC

BONAL
GENTIANE-
QUINA

COCCHI VERMOUTH
DI TORINO

DOLIN
BLANC

DOLIN
ROUGE

PUNT E MES

DOLIN DRY

LILLET
BLANC

LILLET
ROSÉ

COCCHI
AMERICANO
BIANCO

CARPANO
ANTICA
FORMULA

NOILLY PRAT
EXTRA DRY

LUSTAU
LOS ARCOS

BYRHH

DRY

SWEET

PALO CORTADO
LUSTAU PENÍNSULA

RAINWATER
MADIERA

RARE WINE CO.
SAVANNAH
VERDELHO

H&H GENEROSO
DOCE 5-YEAR

BARBADILLO
PRINCIPE

VALDESPINO
PALO
CORTADO
VIEJO

HIDALGO
GOBERNADOR

GONZÁLEZ BYASS
APOSTOLES PALO
CORTADO

GONZÁLEZ BYASS
MATUSALEM OLOROSO

LUSTAU EAST
INDIA SOLERA

HIGH PROOF

● SWEET VERMOUTH   ● DRY VERMOUTH   ● BLANC VERMOUTH   ● MADEIRA

● FINO SHERRY   ● MANZANILLA SHERRY   ● AMONTILLADO SHERRY   ● CREAM SHERRY   ● OLOROSO SHERRY   ● APERITIF WINES

FORTIFIED WINES

This category includes the most frequently used modifier, vermouth, as well as sherry, madeira, and aperitif wines. Within each category, proof is somewhat consistent (typically between 15 to 18% ABV) and sweetness won't vary as wildly as it does with liqueurs. When looking to make a substitution, you'll first want to work within a stylistic group (such as sweet vermouth or fino sherry), then consider the unique flavor profile of the modifier you're working with and try to find something similar—or make an intentional shift in flavor.

BITTERS

Bitters are added to drinks in minuscule amounts, yet these intensely flavored seasoning agents can have a profound effect on a drink's overall flavor profile. Depending on the makeup of the rest of the cocktail, bitters can serve a couple of different functions. First, they can amplify, or lift, other flavors already present in the drink; for example, a dash of orange bitters can heighten and brighten the citrus flavors in a gin-based Martini. Bitters can also simply add flavors not already present in the cocktail, such as clove and cinnamon notes from Angostura. Last, when dashed over the top of a drink after it's been poured into a serving glass, bitters can work as an aromatic garnish, the first thing you encounter when you bring the glass to your mouth for that first sip.

Because they're high in both proof and concentration of flavor, bitters can be difficult to profile by just tasting a drop on its own. We recommend adding a few dashes to a glass of cold seltzer, which will stretch out the bitters' flavors, making them easier to ascertain, while the bubbles will bring the aromas up to the surface and into your nose. If you're in a hurry (or out of seltzer), you can dash a couple of drops onto the palm of your hand, rub your hands together, and take a big whiff.

Say you want to make a cocktail in this book but don't have the bitters specified in the recipe. Don't throw your shaker down in disgust (or rush to the liquor store) just yet! While most bitters are singular products with a unique flavor profile, you can make an educated substitution. For example, both lemon and grapefruit bitters sit near orange bitters on our graph, so a side-by-side experiment using a Martini (swapping out the recipe's orange bitters for lemon or grapefruit) will show you how these potent ingredients can

shift the flavor profile in a different direction. Other light bitters are worth exploring here as well, such as the Bitter Truth celery or peach bitters. In the chart on page 108, we group our most frequently used bitters according to some general classifications: aromatic, citrus, savory, and spicy (that is, bitters that will add some heat to a drink). We've also attempted to plot them according to their complexity: all bitters are layered with flavor, but some have a dozen or more botanicals, while others have just a few.

We also consider swapping bitters an easy opportunity to riff on a drink without bringing in a whole shelf full of new ingredients, and perhaps a way to improve on the drink, or at least tweak it to your own personal preference. Pro tip: If a drink calls for the granddaddy of all bitters, Angostura, it's a great one to experiment with. In a Manhattan, swap out the Angostura for similar bitters such as the Bitter Truth aromatic bitters, Bitter Truth Jerry Thomas' Own Decanter bitters, or Fee Brothers whiskey barrel–aged bitters. You can extend further into bitters that have a similar complexity, such as Bitter End Jamaican Jerk Bitters or Moroccan bitters.

Another option is to add a second style of bitters to a cocktail that contains bitters. The simplest example is the Old-Fashioned, where the usual Angostura bitters can be accented with complementary, flavoring bitters. Examples to explore include Bittermens Xocolatl mole bitters, Miracle Mile pecan bitters, or Scrappy's cardamom bitters.

NATURAL FLAVOR EXTRACTS

The beauty and honesty of natural ingredients is unmatched, be it freshly pressed juice or herbs plucked straight from the garden. Thanks to human ingenuity, the chemical components of these natural flavors can be isolated and reproduced, but to us there's no fine-tuning of various acids and added flavorings that can match, say, the experience of freshly pressed lime juice in a Daiquiri. Call us romantic.

But there are flavors and ingredients—for example, birch bark or eucalyptus—that are particularly difficult to isolate and access, because of either their rarity or the difficulty of extraction. Enter natural flavor extracts: extremely concentrated, naturally derived flavors in a water-soluble, food-grade, ethyl-alcohol base. These are not infusions as

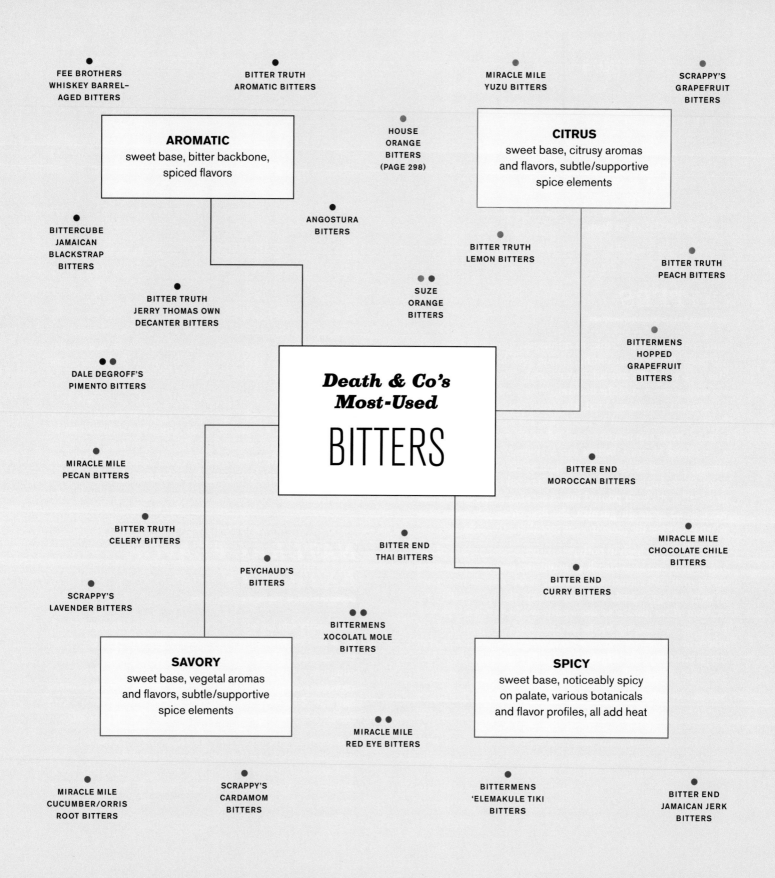

FEE BROTHERS
WHISKEY BARREL–
AGED BITTERS

BITTER TRUTH
AROMATIC BITTERS

MIRACLE MILE
YUZU BITTERS

SCRAPPY'S
GRAPEFRUIT
BITTERS

AROMATIC
sweet base, bitter backbone,
spiced flavors

HOUSE
ORANGE
BITTERS
(PAGE 298)

CITRUS
sweet base, citrusy aromas
and flavors, subtle/supportive
spice elements

BITTERCUBE
JAMAICAN
BLACKSTRAP
BITTERS

ANGOSTURA
BITTERS

BITTER TRUTH
LEMON BITTERS

BITTER TRUTH
PEACH BITTERS

BITTER TRUTH
JERRY THOMAS OWN
DECANTER BITTERS

SUZE
ORANGE
BITTERS

DALE DEGROFF'S
PIMENTO BITTERS

BITTERMENS
HOPPED
GRAPEFRUIT
BITTERS

*Death & Co's
Most-Used*

BITTERS

MIRACLE MILE
PECAN BITTERS

BITTER END
MOROCCAN BITTERS

BITTER TRUTH
CELERY BITTERS

BITTER END
THAI BITTERS

MIRACLE MILE
CHOCOLATE CHILE
BITTERS

PEYCHAUD'S
BITTERS

BITTER END
CURRY BITTERS

SCRAPPY'S
LAVENDER BITTERS

BITTERMENS
XOCOLATL MOLE
BITTERS

SAVORY
sweet base, vegetal aromas
and flavors, subtle/supportive
spice elements

SPICY
sweet base, noticeably spicy
on palate, various botanicals
and flavor profiles, all add heat

MIRACLE MILE
RED EYE BITTERS

MIRACLE MILE
CUCUMBER/ORRIS
ROOT BITTERS

SCRAPPY'S
CARDAMOM
BITTERS

BITTERMENS
'ELEMAKULE TIKI
BITTERS

BITTER END
JAMAICAN JERK
BITTERS

we typically know them; through advanced extraction methods, they are highly potent and focused flavors. A couple of drops will go a very, very long way. Flavor extracts are also distinguished from essential oils, which we steer clear of for cocktails (unless they're floated on top of the drink as an aromatic garnish), as they won't dissolve evenly into the liquid.

Widely used in food production in both natural and artificial forms, flavor extracts are ubiquitous in our everyday lives—the vast majority of processed foods you purchase contain them. While their use in cocktails has little (if any) historical precedent, you can think of them much as other industries do: to add dimension to aroma and taste, to use a flavor in a form not afforded by its natural state, and to safely use some flavors that are difficult (or dangerous) to render without very specialized equipment.

Our first introduction to the world of extracts was in attempting to reproduce a eucalyptus bitters we tasted during a trip to Copenhagen. The memory haunted us, so we sought out a replacement. We ordered a bottle of eucalyptus extract from Terra Spice and were blown away by its power and potency; simply opening the bottle perfumed a room. With trial and error, we found a way to use a tiny amount in a cocktail to reproduce the experience we'd had in Copenhagen, and thus began a longstanding love affair with flavor extracts.

We now use extracts to flavor cocktails, add dimension to syrups, or flavor entire bottles for an instant infusion. We encourage you to explore our cocktail recipes that use extracts; but to understand how they work in a cocktail, we suggest two simple experiments. We encourage exploring extracts for both home and professional use, but in both cases, be extremely careful with their use: a tiny bit goes a (very) long way. Invest in a microgram scale (aka drug scale!) for experimenting.

EXPERIMENT 1: TECHNICOLOR LEMON

In this experiment, we'll explore how incremental additions of extracts can boost flavor. You'll need lemon extract and the ingredients for a classic Tom Collins (page 65). We encourage you to purchase a high-quality natural lemon flavor extract (not lemon oil!), and we recommend those available from Terra Spice Company (see Resources, page 303).

First, open the bottle of extract and carefully bring it toward you. Be careful not to get too close; the power of the extract can easily overwhelm your senses. Make a Tom Collins; smell and taste, paying attention to the lemon juice's presence in the cocktail.

Next, carefully add *one drop* of lemon extract to the cocktail and stir briefly. Smell and taste again; do you notice anything different? The balance of the cocktail remains, but the lemon juice is slightly more present. Add another drop. Suddenly the lemon juice is leaping out of the glass, a more dynamic version of itself. Continue adding drops one at a time and tasting, stopping at five drops. At this point you've likely crossed the threshold from the added flavor being a welcome contribution to the drink's becoming a lemon bomb.

There are plenty of other experiments similar to this that can show how small additions of flavoring can boost the focus on one ingredient. For example, a margarita with a drop of orange extract will amplify the presence of Cointreau, or a drop of lime juice can add a bright vibrancy to a Daiquiri.

EXPERIMENT 2: ADDING DIMENSION

Clearly we love Martinis, especially when a Martini variation maintains the subtlety and nuance of the classic, but modifies it slightly. Flavor extracts have found their way into a number of these drinks (for example, eucalyptus extract in the Telegraph on page 267 or the Marionette on page 201).

Much like the first experiment, this lesson takes a classic cocktail and incrementally adds flavor extract to demonstrate the gradation from subtle accent to over the top. You'll need the ingredients and tools for a classic Martini (page 75), as well as a eucalyptus extract (again, we favor Terra Spice's). Make the Martini, but do not garnish with a lemon twist. Taste it first, then carefully add one drop of eucalyptus extract. Suddenly the vermouth's herbal flavors are more present. Add another drop, and the Martini is all eucalyptus, an important lesson in the power of flavor extracts.

DEVELOPMENT

When you sit down at a bar and pick up a menu, you're holding the product of hundreds of hours of work by bartenders, managers, and designers. This single object, the menu, should be the essence of the bar distilled into a few, clearly presented pages.

Yes, there are opportunities to engage with guests long before they pick up a menu (in our case, through our website, social media, and books). But handing a guest a menu is the first moment we can go deeper, draw people into our world, and engage them in a dialogue. We see the menu as more than just a list of offerings; a menu is an act of hospitality, a piece of intrigue, and an opportunity to communicate what matters to us. To give voice to our values, in a subtle way. The menu, then, is the physical culmination of all our intent in every aspect of our bars.

This chapter is a start-to-finish journey through the life cycle of a menu, starting with defining the menu's scope and structure, outlining our process for collaboration between bartenders to create our cocktails, fine-tuning the details, and then finally bringing it to life.

INTELLECTUAL DEVELOPMENT

Before we even consider creating a cocktail, we need to have a clear and agreed-upon vision for the menu. While guests may interact with the individual drinks that speak to them, our aim is beyond that: a cocktail menu is a composition, one we believe should be cohesive, with drinks complementing and contrasting with each other in an engaging way.

That's why we begin any development process by thinking about our intention. We start by fleshing out a wireframe, sketching broad ideas, hitting the books (or internet) to research how to execute the vision, and finally assembling and fine-tuning the cocktails. We then put the menu back together and make sure it fulfills the original intent, while asking ourselves critical questions: Can we reasonably execute this menu (during both prep and service)? Does this collection of drinks appeal to a broad audience? Are the cocktails *all* delicious?

When launching a new menu, we gather our team for a long brainstorming session to work out the overall ambition and intent. Out of that session emerges the structural makeup of the menu—the total number of cocktails and how they're organized, and the physical size, shape, and material of the menu itself—as well as the philosophical makeup—the menu's overarching narrative, the tone of the copy, the creative direction for the layout and design, and the message we ultimately want the menu to tell our guests. Only when we feel great about every aspect do we begin development.

GIVING THE MENU STRUCTURE

Each Death & Co location has a slightly different narrative perspective, a reflection of the unique communities they call home, the physical design of their space, and the teams that create and execute the cocktails. Our bars aim to be of a place, a refuge from the outside world, but one that's also reflective of it.

That said, each Death & Co location's menu shares a similar structure. Building on the core cocktails explored in *Cocktail Codex*, our menus are generally separated into six categories: Fresh & Lively (highball and spritz variations); Light & Playful (simple sours, like the Daiquiri); Bright & Confident (more complex sours with liqueurs, such as riffs on Sidecars and margaritas); Boozy & Honest

(a place for the Old-Fashioned and its many variations); Elegant & Timeless (a favorite category filled with Martini, Manhattan, and Negroni riffs); and Rich & Comforting (decadent and rich cocktails riffing on the Flip and piña colada). This is also how we've organized all the cocktail recipes found in chapter 5.

This structure is our starting place, and we modify it depending on the needs of each bar. For Death & Co Denver's fall 2019 menu, for example, we decided to not feature a Rich & Comforting section but replace it with a section of group-format cocktails, Grand & Celebratory. Death & Co Denver is a bustling destination for groups of friends and family, and we've learned that the convivial environment is perfectly suited for punch bowls and other group-style drinks. This shift—modifying our base structure to better meet the needs of our guests—is an act of hospitality.

Ultimately, our menu structure must reflect our guests' preferences and needs. In the past, we organized our cocktail menus by spirit type and style, either shaken or stirred (such as "whiskey shaken" or "gin stirred"). This aligned with our guests' expectations at the time: they were likely to select a cocktail based on its base spirit and whether it was refreshing (shaken) or boozy (stirred). As our guests have become better versed in cocktails and more aware of their drinking preferences beyond these narrow boxes, we've also evolved. Today we tend to use multiple base spirits in our cocktails, so we've shifted our focus away from single ingredients and toward the six foundational styles.

Another way we have adapted our menu structure to be as hospitable to our guests as possible is to ensure that each section includes both a nonalcoholic and low-alcohol cocktail. This is a nod to guests who often want to sample multiple cocktails in one session, or who prefer drinks with less (or no) alcohol content. Furthermore, the drinks in each section of the menu are organized from lowest to highest proof. This is a powerful wayfinding tool for both the guest and our team: with a few quick questions, we can direct them to a general area of the menu and cocktails that meet their preferences. Love a Daiquiri? Head over to Light & Playful and check out the Atlantic Pacific (page 193). Negroni fanatic? The Pixee Pecala (page 262) in Elegant & Timeless is right up your alley.

OLD VERSUS NEW: OUR EVOLUTION

In the early days of Death & Co, we would develop menus in isolation: during shifts, bartenders would play around with ideas percolating in their brains, share early versions of drinks with each other (and the occasional trusted industry friend), and eventually gather for a team tasting to workshop their creations. While this method resulted in a canon of delicious cocktails (and tipsy afternoons), over the years we realized we'd created an echo chamber. After working next to each other night after night, our palates and creative processes started to align. During many of our tastings, we noticed that each of us brought forth drinks that looked similar.

Today our process is a bit different. Rather than trying to pluck new cocktails from thin air, we set some parameters for ourselves at the outset by sketching a menu outline: how many drinks we want to offer, and in what styles. Only once that is established do we start developing individual drinks. We've found that giving ourselves lines to color within—but leaving the door open to sketch beyond their boundaries—results in better menus and cocktails.

We separate our menu creation into three parts: *intellectual development,* all the work we do in our head, the sketching of ideas on paper, and research into new techniques and products; *physical development,* testing our ideas using real ingredients, experimenting with syrups and infusions, tasting with our peers, and fine-tuning recipes; and *finalization,* assembling all the pieces of a menu, prepping new ingredients, ordering product, and mapping out how the menu will come to life.

THE MENU WIREFRAME

Of all the tools we've explored to make menu development easier, by far the most helpful is what we call a *wireframe,* or a simple sketch of the menu's structure—sans specific cocktails—that helps us keep it organized and balanced.

We start the wireframe by deciding on the number of sections, number of cocktails, and type of cocktails within each section. Next we list each section in a spreadsheet with a row for each cocktail under that heading. Then we add columns for Style, Flavor Profile, Garnish, Glassware, Bartender (the drink's creator), and finally, Ice.

Gathering the team, we start the brainstorming process. First, are there any cocktails on the current menu we want to keep around? While we don't do this frequently, there are times when we aren't ready to part with a favorite or best-selling drink. If one survives, we write it in.

Next we fill in the wireframe's style column to ensure that we have an even mix of different types of drinks. The team will then begin sketching out ideas. This can happen in a single session, or bartenders will pick certain boxes to develop.

Over the course of several weeks, working in isolation or collaboratively, our bartenders fill up the wireframe with ideas—fully sketched out directions for each cocktail and a rough, untested recipe for the drink. Through experience and clear vision for the intended style, a bartender can generally get close to a final recipe before putting any liquid into a shaker or mixing glass. Research into ingredients and new techniques is completed, and new products are tasted, and a potential recipe comes into view.

Before we move on to the physical stage of menu development, we take a step back from all these bright ideas and look at the big picture. Here is when we get reasonable. Too many times we've fallen in love with menus that required too much prep time or far too expensive equipment, or were otherwise impractical. While having six cocktails made with clarified juice is cool, we just don't have that many centrifuges (boo hoo). We make sure we have enough variety: an appropriate mix of base spirits (not a whole menu of mezcal, *nerds*), glassware (a menu full of coupes = impending dishwashing and freezer storage nightmares), and styles (not everything should be a Negroni variation).

After a final review of the overall menu, the team members are released to work on their drinks. When we circle back together to share our progress (and feedback), the process is more focused because everyone knows their intention. And we're a bit less tipsy at the end of our menu tastings.

ADEEL KHAN & KEJI AMOS

Adeel Khan is the founder and principal of a charter high school in Denver. Keji Amos is a software engineer.

Adeel: My friend Keji and I are into cocktails and were familiar with Death & Co, but we didn't know all the lore around it when it opened in Denver. Our first night there, we sat at the bar next to a lovely couple who knew all about Death & Co, and they had us trying a bunch of different gins.

Keji: Then we went back a couple weeks later during brunch, and that was epic. We were there for five or six hours. I think we drank through at least half of the menu.

Adeel: We asked our server to take us on a little cocktail journey, and they sure did. I was super curious about the training and how seriously they were taking things. Everything is so very intentional. I'm very detail oriented in my work, so I appreciated that. That's when we really fell in love with the bar.

Keji: One of the most memorable cocktails I've had there is As Islay Dying. It smelled like a cigar; I was like *What did you just give me?* They loved that they were pushing our palates into unknown territory.

Adeel: It tastes like a pack of cigarettes, but it's so freaking delicious.

Keji: It feels nice to meet bartenders who actually want to get to know you, more than just "What do you want to drink?" The entire staff is just the warmest group of people. When we see them we're greeted with big smiles and hugs. They're happy to see me, and I'm equally happy to see them.

Adeel: One of the things they're super good about is they never turn us away if the bar is crowded. We squeeze into this little corner of the bar where there aren't any chairs, or sneak upstairs to Suite 6A to have a shot of pear brandy with the team. It's like we don't have to organize a night out with our friends, knowing they'll be there.

Keji: I love talking to different bartenders, having these conversations you don't normally have at a bar. The staff gets excited that we're just a couple of guys who like to geek out about cocktails.

Adeel: Even when they're super busy, they'll entertain our questions: "Why do you use that glass? Why do you crack the ice for that drink?" There's always an answer behind everything they do, and I learn something new every time I go there.

AS ISLAY DYING

Matt Hunt, 2018

¾ ounce Laphroaig 10-year single-malt scotch

¾ ounce The Botanist gin

¾ ounce Dolin blanc vermouth

¾ ounce Dolin dry vermouth

1 teaspoon Dolin Génépy des Alpes liqueur

2 dashes absinthe

Garnish: 1 lemon twist

Stir all the ingredients over ice, then strain into a chilled Nick & Nora glass. Express the lemon twist over the drink and then place it in the drink.

NEW STRATEGIES FOR CREATING DRINKS

In our first book, *Death & Co: Modern Classic Cocktails,* we shared a few strategies we use when developing new cocktails. These included "Mr. Potato Head," wherein we swap one (or more) elements out of a simple classic cocktail to make something entirely new; the regrettably named "Dressing Up Naked Drinks," in which we add layers of complexity to simple specs via an infusion or intensely flavored modifier; "Splitting Hairs," which calls for combining multiple base spirits; and "Concept Drinks," a catchall for drinks that begin with an idea and little else.

Over the years, we've employed these strategies in hundreds of cocktails, so much so that we're barely even aware of them anymore—they've just become part of the natural cocktail development process. But we've also identified a few frequently used approaches to creating new drinks, which we've named as follows.

THE BATCHELOR [SIC]

Many of our cocktails contain small amounts of multiple ingredients, which we blend together in a cheater bottle to create a "batch" to help speed up execution during service. Some of these batches are so good (or are mistakenly made in so large a quantity) that bartenders repurpose them in new drinks. Likewise, certain combinations of ingredients are so revelatory that they get renewed in future drinks.

Examples: Inspector Norse (page 198), Powder House Fizz (page 203), Echo Spring (page 277) Badlands (page 209), Jungleland (page 219), Altimeter Julep (page 229), Get Free (page 232), Outlaw Country (page 239), Dead Language (page 250), Space Cowboy (page 278), Juke Box Hero (page 199), Sundance Kid (page 278), Ginger Man (page 196)

NEW TOY!

It's increasingly rare to come across a new spirit or modifier that isn't already on the radar of other bars—and, thanks to the internet, of many of our guests. However, once in a while we come across a product so novel or so sublime that we fight over who gets to use it first.

Examples: Goldilocks (page 232), Ice Run Julep (page 235), Stoned Love (page 241), Victory Lap (page 244), 20/20 (page 247), Sundance Kid (page 278), Alta Negroni (page 247), This Island Earth (page 206), Doctor Mindbender (page 179), Cloud Nine (page 179)

LIQUID LUNCH

Our bartenders are often inspired by the culinary world when concepting new cocktails. But some drinks are born out of a specific—and often surprising—dish, be it a street taco or Thai soup.

Examples: Banquo's Ghost (page 177), Ida Means Business (page 198), Buko Gimlet (page 193), Concrete Jungle (page 194), Nautilus (page 202), Strange Encounters (page 204), Witchdoctor (page 207), Dragonfly (page 214), Planet Caravan (page 222), Recortador (page 240), Capuchin (page 249), Oculus (page 260), Return of the Mac (page 263), Southern Nights (page 278), Artful Dodger (page 229), Sound and Fury (page 189)

SUPER MR. POTATO HEAD

We've gotten a lot of mileage out of old Mr. Potato Head over the years. So much so that it's nearly impossible to use him to reimagine classic cocktails. Enter Super Mr. Potato Head, a self-referential nod where instead of starting with classics, we start with past Death & Co drinks and swap out multiple components from there.

Examples: Slightly Stormy (page 189), Curtis Park Swizzle (page 194), King Palm (page 199), Full Sail (page 217), Waco Kid (page 226), True Romance (page 268), Harlequin (page 181), Bushido (page 211), Whole Lotta Love (page 207), Andromeda (page 248), Telegraph (page 267), Marionette (page 201), Hurricane Kick (page 218), Good Enough Gatsby (page 196), Rockabilly (page 223)

FANCY FLEX

We're lucky enough to have some singular, expensive, and rare bottles of booze on our back bar. The trouble is, they're too expensive to justify using in a cocktail (at least as a base spirit). A couple of years back we decided to do something about this. Our genius solution: charge double (or more) for the drink! All of our menus now have a "luxury" cocktail section, which showcases drinks crafted around one amazing ingredient. These cocktails are manipulated as little as possible to allow our guests to fully appreciate their investment in that luxury ingredient.

Examples: Cloud Nine (page 179), Hidden World (page 198), King Ghidora (page 199), Marionette (page 201), The Weaver (page 207), Calypso King (page 230), Cipher (page 230), I Against I (page 234), Shadow Box (page 241), Jewel Thief (page 258), Lightning Rod (page 259), Science of Being (page 264), Strange Religion (page 267), Coat of Arms (page 249), Juke Box Hero (page 199)

I'LL JUST HAVE A BEER

Because we spend most of our waking hours thinking about and making cocktails, the first thing we usually want to drink when we're off duty is an icy cold beer. Sometimes our love for brews seeps into our creative process, and we develop drinks to taste specifically like a style of beer, hard cider, or other low-ABV refreshment. It seems like professional beer brewers have a similar (though converse) yearning, as we've collaborated with local breweries to create beers that mimic specific Death & Co cocktails. With Hudson Valley brewery in Beacon, New York, we took our love for the mai tai and let them run free using roasted almonds, lime, and orange to create a double IPA that blurred the line between beer and cocktail. Our friends at Four Noses in Broomfield, Colorado, took license with our Monkey's Fist (page 202) and zeroed in on the drink's passion fruit, carrot, and coconut flavors to create an ale that's loved by cocktail and beer nerds alike.

Examples: Ghost Colors (page 181), Camargo (page 179), Moon Magic (page 185), Scarlet Tanager (page 188), Lone Star (page 236), Bulldog Front (page 179)

PREP SCHOOL STANDOUT

Because we've evolved our cocktail development process so that much of the creative work happens before we mix an actual drink, we're able to experiment more in our kitchen lab, whether by developing new types of infusions or flavored syrups or by finding an excuse to pull out the centrifuge or some other piece of specialized equipment. The result is a sort of backward development process, in which a bartender has an idea for a prep ingredient (syrup, infusion, and the like), then figures out how to build a cocktail around it.

Examples: Wabi-Sabi (page 206), El Topo (page 180), Halo Effect (page 181), Vaquero (page 244), Charlemagne (page 179), Lamplighter Inn (page 277), Scarlet Tanager (page 188), Paper Thin Hotel (page 239)

UNCHARTED TERRITORY

Some drinks start with a question: "Wouldn't it be cool if. . . ." Or "What would it taste like if. . . ." Even though it often seems like it's all been done before, our bartenders are constantly finding challenges to pose to themselves, whether it's to make an odd combination of ingredients work in harmony or to contort a cocktail from its usual form to another (often turning shaken drinks into stirred ones, or vice versa).

Examples: Tandem Jump (page 190), Ginger Man (page 196), Calypso (page 211), Golden Fang (page 218), Birds of Prey (page 230), Double Dragon (page 231), Event Horizon (page 232), Match Grip Julep (page 236), Strip Solitaire (page 241), The Whiskey Agreement (page 245), Tripwire (page 242), Uncanny Valley (page 242), Fuligin (page 253), New Beat (page 259), No Paddle (page 259), One Armed Scissor (page 260), Satisfied Hare (page 264), Sister Midnight (page 265), Trust Fall (page 269)

FLAVOR SYLLOGISMS

We often thumb through *The Flavor Bible* or another similar culinary reference book when brainstorming potential flavor combinations for our drinks. But you can only do so much with celery + apples, grapefruit + cinnamon, or vanilla + pineapple until it all seems overdone and boring. If you find yourself in a similar rut, try one of our favorite new tricks, which we call "flavor syllogisms." This exercise works like this: pick a flavor (Flavor A) and match it with a common affinity (Flavor B). Then take Flavor B and match it with one of its affinities (Flavor C). Then use a little deductive reasoning to see whether the result is delicious: If Flavor A loves Flavor B, and Flavor B loves Flavor C, does Flavor C love Flavor A? The answer isn't always "yes," of course, but it might help you unlock some surprising new affinities. From there, you can sketch out some rough ideas, using a root cocktail or classic as a jumping-off point. Here are some examples:

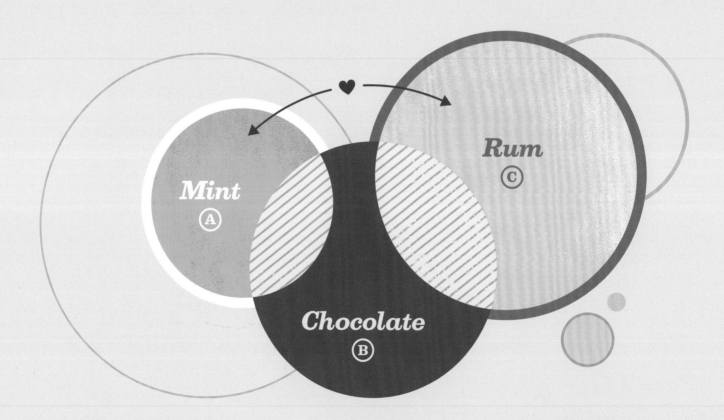

A	B	C	COCKTAIL BRAINSTORM
Apple	Walnut	Honey	Collins variation: Calvados, amontillado sherry, lemon, honey, nocino, seltzer
Pear	Almond	Butter	Mai Tai variation: brown butter–washed rum, pear eau-de-vie, orgeat, lemon juice, Angostura bitters
Pineapple	Banana	Armagnac	Old-Fashioned variation: Plantation pineapple rum, blanche Armagnac, Giffard banane du Brésil, Angostura bitters
Ginger	Cumin	Curry Leaf	Buck variation: gin, ginger-cumin syrup, lemon juice, seltzer, curry leaf
Mint	Chocolate	Rum	Manhattan variation: aged rum, bourbon, sweet vermouth, Giffard menthe-pastille, Bittermens Xocolatl mole bitters
Nuts	Cinnamon	Red wine	Kalimotxo variation: red wine, Avuá amburana cachaça (tastes like cinnamon), cola, Miracle Mile pecan bitters
Vanilla	Lavender	Peach	Martini variation: vodka, blanc vermouth, Galliano l'Autentico (heavy vanilla flavor), Massenez crème de pêche, Scrappy's lavender bitters
Cinnamon	Ginger	Grapefruit	Sidecar variation: cognac, Giffard crème de pamplemousse, Giffard ginger of the Indies liqueur, cinnamon syrup, lemon juice
Chocolate	Cherry	Orange	Sazerac variation: rye whiskey, cognac, curaçao, kirsch rinse
Smoke	Tea	Lemon	Toddy variation: mezcal, oolong tea, lemon peel, cinnamon syrup
Lime	Cilantro	Chiles	Mojito variation: serrano pepper–infused gin, lime juice, muddled sawtooth coriander leaf ("Thai" cilantro) and cucumber, crushed ice, cilantro leaf garnish
Lemon	Pistachio	Apricot	Japanese cocktail variation: cognac, pistachio orgeat, apricot liqueur, lemon juice
Orange	Basil	Watermelon	Coffee Park Swizzle variation: white rum, amontillado sherry, watermelon syrup, Massenez Garden Party basil liqueur, lime juice, crushed ice, basil garnish
Celery	White pepper	Apple	Bamboo variation: celery-infused manzanilla sherry, blanc vermouth, unaged apple brandy, white pepper tincture spray as garnish

DEVELOPING NO-ABV COCKTAILS

Be it for health, mental clarity, or any other reason, more and more of our guests are requesting low- and no-alcohol cocktails—and we find ourselves drawn to both as great opportunities to enjoy more drinks with a clear head.

In the past, bartenders created nonalcoholic cocktails in a pretty simplistic (and lazy) way: make some variation on a sour-style cocktail, toss in some fresh fruit (whatever's currently in the garnish *mise-en-place*, like strawberries, raspberries, or cucumber) or herbs (mint, basil, and so on), and call it a day. This was always an on-the-fly composition made for a special request.

But in recent years we've pivoted our approach and intention: there's no reason a nonalcoholic cocktail can't be composed with the same attention to detail as any based on alcoholic ingredients. Doing so requires attention to a critical element that alcohol brings to a cocktail, one that is lost when you remove it: body. "Body" is the fullness of the drink, the texture that high-proof alcohol brings to cocktails, and the drink's backbone.

There's a lesson to be learned from those original "mock-tails" (a term we avoid, as it implies that alcohol is needed to make a "real" cocktail). When you simply remove the gin in, say, a Tom Collins, you're left with a mix of lemon juice and simple syrup. Topping this with seltzer would leave you with a very thin beverage: watered-down lemonade. To compensate, you must double the amount of both lemon juice and simple syrup, thereby increasing the complexity of flavor and density. At our bars, we have identified four strategies that make up for the body lost without a spirit and yield complex, nonalcoholic cocktails that are more than just doctored-up lemonade.

STRATEGY 1: PURÉES AS BASE

Fruit purées are packed with flavor and texture, an ideal way to bring the robust body needed to a nonalcoholic cocktail. A tropical egg-cream variation, Dave Anderson's Pipe Dream (page 203) is complex, fruity, and deeply refreshing. The success of the cocktail is centered around kiwi purée, which provides a burst of concentrated flavor that's boosted by fresh lime juice and rich coconut cream, seasoned with vanilla, and given levity via seltzer.

STRATEGY 2: MIGHTY VERJUS

Verjus has been a favorite ingredient in our boozy cocktails. This acidic grape juice is the perfect substitute for fresh citrus in a stirred sour (see the Thin White Duke, page 268), but we've also discovered it can act as both the base and the balancer in a nonalcoholic cocktail. Jon Feuersanger's La Luz (page 199) builds a complex cocktail around a base of verjus, then layers in flavoring (Pineapple Pulp Cordial, page 286), a small amount of passion fruit purée for added flavor (and body), fresh lime juice for balance, and a dash of orange flower water for seasoning.

STRATEGY 3: NONALCOHOLIC "SPIRITS"

The increasing availability of artfully made nonalcoholic spirit replacements—such as Seedlip's nonalcoholic spirits or Giffard Aperitif Syrup—provided an exciting opportunity to express nonalcoholic cocktails in styles never before possible, such as in Martini and Old-Fashioned variations. Jon Mateer's Business Casual (page 249) is a great example of how nonalcoholic cocktails are being pushed into new creative territory; his complex Negroni-like variation is made without any booze. It starts with Giffard Aperitif Syrup, then adds more complexity with black tea (a substitute for gin's botanicals) and balance with a red verjus. While the verjus brings acidity, it also brings a great depth.

STRATEGY 4: NO-ABV MILK PUNCH

Milk punch has a long history in cocktails. It's made by combining spirit, milk, sugar, and acid, then allowing the mix to rest and the milk to solidify (thanks to the acidity of the citrus). After straining, the result is a near-clear liquid that retains the milk's richness. The same process can be applied to a nonalcoholic cocktail, such as Matthew Garcia's Liar's Gambit. Centered around a spiced-tea mix (tea, cinnamon, nutmeg, and allspice), Seedlip's Spice 94 nonalcoholic spirit, milk, and small amounts of pineapple syrup and fresh lemon juice, the cocktail is batched in large quantities, clarified, and bottled. Poured per order in a double old-fashioned glass, the Liar's Gambit has the complexity and body of an Old-Fashioned-style cocktail.

DEVELOPING LOW-ABV COCKTAILS

What exactly constitutes a "low-ABV" cocktail is largely subjective. The intent, though, is to create a cocktail that packs less of an alcoholic punch than a full-proof cocktail—roughly half the proof of a standard cocktail—utilizing lower-proof ingredients as the cocktail's core ingredient rather than a spirit. While there is no definitive target ABV for these drinks, our general practice is to construct cocktails with fortified wines as the base ingredients, using spirits as modifiers in smaller quantities. The strategies that follow succeed when the balancing and flavoring elements are adjusted to maintain the cocktail's body.

STRATEGY 1: SPLIT BASE

One of the easiest places to start in creating low-ABV cocktails is to simply split a base spirit with a lower-proof ingredient. In Brian Wyner's Fulton St. Fizz (page 196), a classic Silver Gin Fizz is augmented by pulling back on the gin and introducing dry vermouth and cherry brandy. Because the dry vermouth doesn't have as much body as the gin, the recipe finds an ideal balance with an ounce of sweetener (orgeat), a common strategy for split-base low-ABV cocktails. Similarly, the Common's Park Swizzle (page 212) splits the cocktail's core among cognac, sauternes, and madeira, then layers in complexity with banana liqueur and orgeat.

STRATEGY 2: FLIP THE SCRIPT

Austin Knight's Original Sin (page 260) utilizes another favorite strategy for making low-ABV drinks: taking a Manhattan or Martini template and inversing the proportions of the base spirit and vermouth. Here, the core becomes a split between a Spanish sweet vermouth and an oloroso sherry, accented by an aged rum, and seasoned with nocino (walnut liqueur). Just as in the preceding split-base strategy, lowering proof requires adding more body via the other ingredients.

STRATEGY 3: LOOK TO THE CLASSICS

Cocktail history has plenty of examples of wine-based drinks, and one of the most well-known is the sherry cobbler. These are simple constructions: a small amount of sugar, a few pieces of muddled fruit, crushed ice, and a whole lot of extravagant garnish (which we fondly refer to as "cobbler shit"). In Dave Anderson's Empty Nester (page 231), this idea is expanded by splitting the traditional sherry with an aromatized wine (Bonal Gentiane-Quina) and seasoning the drink with amaro (Amaro Nonino), apple eau-de-vie, and cinnamon syrup.

While it wasn't present on Death & Co Denver's fall 2019 menu, we also love riffing on the classic Bamboo, traditionally a mix of sherry, vermouth, and bitters, served like a Manhattan. While the Bamboo is light on the alcohol, it's big in flavor, and thanks to ever-expanding fortified and aromatized wine, vermouth, amari, and bitters options, variations have become staples in our low-ABV creations (see Noble One, page 239; Sky Ladder, page 265; and Tsukemono, page 269).

KAMA'S ARROW, PAGE 199

LOREZ MEINHOLD

Lorez Meinhold is the executive director of Caring for Denver.

I run a nonprofit called Caring for Denver, which funds alternative responses to incarceration. I basically started that foundation at Death & Co. I live across the street, so my days often begin and end at the bar. During the daytime, it's my office. I'll hold meetings there, or just work on my laptop. Breakfast is usually banana bread with chai butter. When it comes time for cocktails, I'll have a Negroni or some kind of stirred whiskey drink; my go-to now is the Creole Sazerac. I probably spend as much on food and coffee as I do on cocktails there.

The memory of my first visit—which was right after the bar opened—is *comfort*. I sat in a tan leather chair at a table next to the window (this has since become "my table"). I ordered a Bark at the Moon, and the brown butter–washed rum gave me a warmth I'll never forget. I remember being enveloped in this chair, holding a cold drink, and chatting with friends. I was sold.

I meet with plenty of folks who don't drink alcohol, so I love that Death & Co offers plenty of nonalcoholic drinks. I also love their commitment to accessibility: the bar actually has a section that comes down to fit a wheelchair. There aren't enough restaurants and bars here that make those accommodations. It's great that they've created an environment that supports everybody, whether it's people who don't drink, people with disabilities or other lived experiences, or just the community at large.

BARK AT THE MOON

Teddy Lemontagne, 2018

1 ounce Brown Butter–Infused Panama Pacific Rum (page 290)

½ ounce Rittenhouse rye

¼ ounce Amaro Averna

¼ ounce Gonzalez Byass Pedro Ximénez sherry

1 teaspoon Cinnamon Syrup (page 283)

2 dashes Bitter Truth aromatic bitters

Garnish: 1 orange twist

Stir all the ingredients over ice, then strain into a single old-fashioned glass over 1 large ice cube. Express the orange twist over the drink, then place it in the drink.

PHYSICAL DEVELOPMENT

Once our bar staff has a clear plan and a completed wireframe, they dive into testing and fine-tuning their drinks through a series of tastings.

RECIPE TESTING

Much like setting up a bar with proper *mise en place,* the first step in recipe testing is gathering ingredients. Our cocktails can become quite complex, and central to many ideas are special flavors that come from a unique syrup or infusion. These must first be explored and prepared, often requiring more research, stocking our pantry with new ingredients, and occasionally purchasing new equipment. This is exactly how we got our first centrifuge.

When all of the ingredients are ready, we follow a few rules for recipe development. Because each cocktail sits in a specific place on the menu wireframe, we already have a general idea about its root structure and proportion of ingredients before any liquid is poured into a mixing glass or shaking tin. For example, Jon Feuersanger had a vision for a riff on one of our favorite morning revivers, espresso and tonic. From that starting place, Jon knew that he would be riffing off the highball root, using that structure as a starting place for the Long Division (page 185). But having that foresight doesn't mean the cocktail is anywhere near complete. In moving from theory to reality, our ideas almost always need tweaking—more of this, less of that, and fine-tuning.

One parameter we adamantly stick to is the "five tries and you're out rule": after unsuccessfully trying four iterations of a cocktail, if the fifth doesn't land, we move on to something else. This allows us to reset and regroup or, in some cases, to kill the idea entirely. Being forced to step away from an idea we love is a challenge, but it helps us avoid spiraling down endless iterations that can never find their focus.

TASTINGS

Seven weeks before menu launch, we gather the bar team and present our drinks. Even in the early years of Death & Co NYC—and through some very chaotic development sessions—the feedback from our peers has always been paramount to the success of every cocktail. Our intention at these tastings is not to give cocktails-in-progress a simple thumbs-up or thumbs-down (though occasionally one is so delicious it doesn't need tweaks, or is so atrocious that it gets voted off the island). Instead, the tastings are a collaborative environment where we can inject new perspectives into the cocktails.

Sometimes cocktails are completely transformed during the tasting, or a flavor profile that isn't working in one drink finds its place in another. Generally, the first tasting sends the team away with homework. Sometimes there's more work to be done on presented drinks. More frequently, with some recipes finalized and others either paused or unsuccessful, the wireframe is again consulted to identify holes in the overall menu's composition. Bartenders volunteer to fill in the gaps, and the recipe development process resumes.

One to two weeks later, we reconvene for a second (and hopefully final) tasting, and the menu really comes into focus. There are almost always a couple of gaps to fill, and this is where the head bartender will step up and work through some ideas to finalize the menu.

FINALIZATION

Once the menu is locked and loaded, it's tempting to think that the process is over and the menu is ready to launch. Not so fast. Now comes the hours and hours spent trying to figure out the perfect name for the drink and writing descriptive copy to ensure each cocktail is presented clearly to our guests.

NAMING DRINKS

Once a new cocktail has been approved and its recipe finalized, its creator is tasked with giving it a name. In some cases (and for some bartenders), this is the easiest part of the creative process. But for most of us, this is one of the more exasperating steps. In Death & Co's first decade of existence, we took a more "anything goes" approach to drink denomination. Our cocktail names were often inspired by our favorite books, movies, or music; others were nods to classic drinks, industry peers, or inside jokes among the staff. Oh, and plenty of puns. In many cases, our head bartenders were tasked with naming untitled drinks days before a new menu launch, which resulted in some pretty groan-inducing outcomes.

These days, we take a more *intentional* (there's that word again!) approach to naming drinks. Whenever possible, we want a drink's name to evoke its personality, whether by referencing its classic progenitor (Alta Negroni, page 247), hinting at its flavor profile (Bourbon and Birch, page 178), or expressing the feeling a drink might elicit (Hawaii Five-O, page 198). We also try to keep drink names concise, usually two or three words, so there's a consistent cadence across our menus.

The task of keeping our drink names in check falls to one gatekeeper: beverage director Tyson Buhler. Tyson is *not* a fan of puns, so you'll spot few of those on our more recent menus. Even with our more buttoned-up approach to naming cocktails, we can still spot some consistent threads and strategies:

Get Outta Dodge. Naming whiskey drinks after Western movies is a tradition started by Tyson, and one carried out ad nauseum.

Examples: Silverheels, Waco Kid, Highwayman, Unforgiven, Yojimbo, The Lonesome Crowded West, El Topo, Fistful of Dollars, The Magnificent Seven, High Noon

That's So Hardcore. Some of our bartenders and alumni (especially Matthew Belanger and Al Sotack) are fans of punk and hardcore, evident in their own cocktail creations.

Examples: Bulldog Front, Repeater, Full Disclosure, The Argument, Ink & Dagger, Sister Ruby, Comadre, Bikini Kill, Anchor End, Dead Language, Hidden World, I Against I, Jumping the Shark, One Armed Scissor, Palm Dreams

Is the Doctor In? We have a longstanding tradition of naming tiki-style drinks after fictional doctors.

Examples: Doctor Mindbender, Doctor Zhivago, Doctor Strangelove, Serizawa

BRUUUCE! Jersey boy Jarred Weigand always named crushed-ice drinks after his home-state hero.

Examples: Tramps Like Us, Glory Days, Jungleland

Don't Tell Tyson: It's become something of a sport to try to slip a nonconformist name past the censor. Occasionally our bartenders win.

Examples: Trampoline, Shotgun Willie, Sleepy Gary Fizz

WRITING MENU COPY

Menu copy is as much stylistic as it is communicating specific information, and we recognize that your style is likely very different from ours. But we've found some best practices to make our guests' experience more enjoyable, and to help them match their mood to the right cocktail.

For each drink, we could simply list all of its ingredients. But exactly how we list the ingredients will help guests understand whether the cocktail is what they're looking for. Take the Dilly Dally, a low-ABV Martini variation made with a heavy pour of dry vermouth, along with Brennivin aquavit, absinthe, dill, and cucumber. Presenting the cocktail's ingredients three ways suggests three very different cocktails:

DILLY DALLY

Brennivin, dry vermouth, absinthe, dill, cucumber

DILLY DALLY

Cucumber, dill, Brennivin, dry vermouth, absinthe

DILLY DALLY

Dry vermouth, Brennivin, absinthe, dill, cucumber

The first strategy follows what guests often look for first in assessing a cocktail's ingredients—the main spirit—but this implies that the cocktail has a larger proportion of Brennivin than it actually does. The second brings fresh ingredients to the front, but runs the risk of implying that the cocktail is light and vegetal, with an inaccurate emphasis on cucumber as the star of the show. Finally, the last approach lists the ingredients in order of quantity, from largest to smallest, and in the process gives a much more accurate view of what to expect: dry vermouth accented by the Brennivin, with seasoning from absinthe, dill, and cucumber. We almost always employ this strategy, though sometimes we veer away from it in order to send a specific message to our guests.

Overcommunicating, undercommunicating, and finding the sweet spot in between means balancing what's actually in the cocktail with what might distract (or excite!) the guest. At other bars that have a different focus on offerings and aesthetic, we may lean toward minimalism, listing only the flavor profiles or anchor flavors, omitting syrups so as not to trigger guests' bias against sugar (news flash: there's sugar in almost every cocktail). Others get extremely specific and descriptive. We land somewhere in the middle: We list specific ingredients for their individual contribution, and we feel it's valuable to highlight that choice by listing brands in order to communicate the exact composition. For example, we could list a classic Old-Fashioned in three different ways:

THE OVERLY DESCRIPTIVE OLD-FASHIONED

Elijah Craig bourbon from Kentucky, sous vide Demerara syrup, Angostura Trinidadian aromatic bitters, Bitter Truth German aromatic bitters, twists of lemon and orange peel

THE MINIMALIST OLD-FASHIONED

Bourbon and bitters

THE DEATH & CO OLD-FASHIONED

Elijah Craig bourbon, Demerara syrup, Angostura bitters, Bitter Truth aromatic bitters

No one of these is objectively better than the other; these are simply stylistic choices.

Descriptions can also help set up our guests' expectations. For example, the Free Tail (page 180) is a tequila-based collins variation with Lillet rosé, fino sherry, Donn's Mix, lime, and seltzer. Donn's is a tiki-born mix of cinnamon syrup and grapefruit juice (which would be more descriptive to simply list), but by labeling it Donn's Mix, we're nodding to a tropical style and a connection to cocktail history.

PREP: GETTING OUR SHIT TOGETHER

We've learned hard lessons about the dangers of underpreparedness. We now dedicate large blocks of time to preparing every element of the supporting materials needed to make a smooth menu launch, so that the team can focus on getting comfortable with the specs and creating exceptional experiences for their guests.

Our first step is to format all the recipes, both cocktail and any specialized ingredients (including syrups and infusions), in a consistent shorthand style:

Original Sin

- 1.25 ounces Lustau Vermut Rojo
- 0.75 ounce Ron Zacapa 23
- 0.75 ounce Lustau Don Nuño oloroso
- 0.25 ounce Don Ciccio Figli Nocino
- 1 teaspoon Demerara syrup

Method: Stir/strain

Glass: Nick & Nora

Garnish: Orange twist

Origin: Austin Knight, Death & Co Denver 2019

Readers may note that this differs from how we format the recipes in this book, where decimals are converted to fractions, and specific instructions are written out. But we find this format is easiest to recall in the heat of service: bullet points draw the eye to the ingredients, ordered from largest quantity to smallest; Method, Glass, Garnish, and Origin are always in the same order; and we diligently ensure that the product names are precise and consistent throughout the database.

Once a recipe has been finalized, it's moved into a new Evernote folder, "D&C Current Menu," and the previous menu cocktails are moved into the "D&C Master Compendium," an ever-growing collection of original cocktails from all of our bars.

BUDGET VIABILITY

Head bartenders have roughly calculated the cost of each cocktail during the development process, but at this stage the cocktails are all precisely costed to ensure that each is within allowable margins; if not, alternatives are explored. For example, the True Romance (page 268) was finalized with a single-varietal mezcal—a product that, while exceptional, pushed the boundaries of the costs. Working together, the drink's creator, Carey Jenkins, head bartender Alex Jump, and bar manager Jon Feuersanger tried alternatives, settling on Del Maguey Vida mezcal. Tweaking the recipe slightly with the new mezcal, the cocktail was finalized and deemed viable.

BATCHES AND STATION MAP

With all cocktails precisely finalized, we do something simple but vital: we make a long spreadsheet of ingredients that includes every single ingredient used in every cocktail on the new menu. We also list any additional ingredients needed on hand to make general cocktails and Death & Co classics.

We pause and review the recipes to identify which ingredients can be prebatched together to speed up service and maximize quality. An added bonus of batching is that it can fortify otherwise fragile ingredients: for example, the combination of a delicate Lustau manzanilla sherry and Bonal Gentiane-Quina in the Empty Nester (page 231) can be fortified by combining the recipe's Amaro Nonino (which adds sugar and proof) and the Cyril Zangs 00 apple cider eau-de-vie (more proof).

We then reconfigure our primary list to add batches and remove individual ingredients, if appropriate. We also add a number of columns to the right on the spreadsheet for the number of times the ingredient is used on the menu and where the ingredient will live. At the bottom of the spreadsheet, we list glassware and count the number of uses per menu.

From this list we build a number of documents. Using standardized templates, we build prep lists to consolidate every ingredient that needs to be made and what we estimate the daily and weekly prep needs will be. This allows the prep team to plan their schedule and priorities for juicing, syrup making, infusing, batching, and garnish prep.

The list also allows us to make a "station map," a visual outline of where every ingredient lives at each bar station. This includes the speed rail (also called a speed rack, a stainless

steel compartment for bottles attached to the bartender's ice bin); the "cheater box," a custom bar-top fixture that holds small bottles filled with syrups, batches, and other ingredients used in small quantities; the bitters rack, a special rack for bitters bottles and atomizers; the garnish box, a chilled container for holding fresh garnishes; the freezer, which houses specialized ice, glassware, and freezer-bar batches; and the refrigerator, where low-use juices and sparkling wines are stored.

Finding a home for every ingredient can be a maddening game of Tetris, and preparing a detailed and thorough prep plan is grueling in its own way, but once both are complete, we have a clear and focused plan for every element of the menu. From here, we're ready to order new product, prepare ingredients, build batches, and, on the day of the launch, know exactly where everything goes.

MENU LAUNCH

We operate our bars seven days a week, so launching a new menu has become a bit of a grueling art form. Having shut the bar late the previous evening, we arrive the next morning, fire up strong coffee, and reset the whole setup. While there are some bottles that remain in the same location every menu, most of our setups are revamped. Here's what the launch schedule looks like:

3:00 a.m.: At the end of the shift and nightly cleaning, pull all bottles from wells and cart to the liquor room. Double check that new menu ingredients and product are all prepared for next day.

3:30 a.m.: Shot of calvados and a Lyft home.

10:00 a.m.: Arrive at the bar; coffee (very strong).

10:15 a.m.: Strip wells of existing labels, deep clean stations; pull all product from refrigerators; remove glassware from freezers.

10:30 a.m.: Breakfast burritos; continue cleaning.

12:00 p.m.: Pull all new menu items, organize stations: labels, prebatches, new liquor.

1:00 p.m.: Set up first station using well map. Run through the menu one cocktail at a time, touching every ingredient—are they within an easy pivot and in a logical place? Adjust. Also, you definitely forgot something.

2:00 p.m.: Set up remaining stations; stock refrigerators.

2:30 p.m.: Daily fresh juice preparations, garnish prep.

3:00 p.m.: Run to a liquor store for that one bottle that's in three new cocktails but you completely forgot to order from the distributor.

3:15 p.m.: Shot of amontillado sherry (for courage).

4:00 p.m.: Bartenders negotiate who works the service bar (highly coveted during a menu launch) and who works point, where they get to explain the new drinks to guests.

4:50 p.m.: Inhale family meal, suit up, preshift meeting.

4:55 p.m.: Sneaky shot of pear brandy (for focus).

5:00 p.m.: Open for business!

5:05 p.m.: First cocktail served; bartender feels like it's their first shift behind a bar, has existential crisis.

6:00 p.m.: Comfort begins settling in with repeat orders.

7:00 p.m.: Smart-ass table of industry peers orders one of each cocktail on menu; smug service bartender drowns.

7:30 p.m.: Manager keeps eye on ticket times; tells host to slow pace of seating.

9:00 p.m.: Rounds upon rounds served; feeling more comfortable with the new menu.

12:00 a.m.: Daiquiris for everyone! (aka Gangster Daiquiri Time, or GDT.)

1:45 a.m.: Last call. Gratitude.

2:00 a.m.: Final guest out, door locked.

2:05 a.m.: Debrief while cleaning; successes, challenges, opportunities identified; the most delicious and deserved beer ever consumed.

2:30 a.m.: Discussion of how the hell we fit everything in the fridges.

3:00 a.m.: Cleaning and reorganizing complete.

COCKTAILS AT HOME

Guests frequently ask us how to re-create Death & Co cocktails at home. And while we've written three books (and counting?) that can help tremendously with this, the truth is, our intention at the bars is to offer you an experience you *can't* easily replicate at home. This isn't because we're afraid of anyone stealing our secrets—we've published more than a thousand of our recipes, after all. But if it were easy to replicate the Death & Co experience at your home bar, we'd never see you again at ours. And we'd miss you.

Our bars have a few advantages you don't at home: an endless range of products, highly specialized and expensive equipment, and a full-time staff of smart, dedicated professionals whose job is to make you happy and always have something new and exciting to offer. That doesn't make our drinks *better* than ones you make at home; it just makes for a different experience (and one that doesn't require any work on your part!).

In the pages that follow, our goal is to help you craft your own unique cocktail and hospitality experience for your home, rather than re-creating ours. We'll arm you with a carefully curated selection of bottles for your home bar, guidance on how to select the right version of each spirit to suit your needs and tastes, tips on making the most out of each bottle, and ideas for using up any oddball ingredients you bought to make that weird cocktail from our first book, *Death & Co: Modern Classic Cocktails*. Sorry about that.

After you're set up and ready to make drinks, we'll explore some approaches for making drinks at home based on your intention and the occasion, whether it's a solo drink before dinner or a party with a full cocktail menu. We'll also share some fun home-bartending tricks and hacks, which can steer your cocktail making toward convenience—or complexity, if you choose.

BUILDING YOUR HOME BAR

Putting together your first home bar (or expanding your current one) can be daunting, especially if you pick up a cocktail book that calls for a bunch of special ingredients. Even for those of us who enjoy buying and experimenting with new ingredients, it can become a problem: You might start with just a few bottles, but before you know it you've caught the collector's bug, and your "hobby" has snowballed into a storage crisis and a collection of booze worth a small fortune.

The good news? By stocking your bar with a handful of versatile, affordable bottles, you can make loads of famous cocktails, and you have a great liquid pantry for developing endless new creations. And believe us, because we practice what we preach: although we stock our bars with hundreds of brands of liquor, at home we keep things modest and streamlined. Here, we've compiled a dozen spirits and modifiers and a list of fifty cocktails you can make with them (with the addition of citrus, basic sweeteners and bitters, and/or everyday kitchen staples). We based our selections not only on quality but also on value and accessibility— each is widely available and affordable. Though you don't need to stock every single bottle (or specific brand) listed here, the range covered by these twelve bottles will give you a broad foundation of flavors to play with.

12 Bottles = 50 Cocktails

- ◆ **GIN** Beefeater
- ◆ **WHITE RUM** Flor de Caña 4-year
- ◆ **BLANCO TEQUILA** El Tesoro Blanco
- ◆ **BLENDED SCOTCH** Famous Grouse
- ◆ **BOURBON** Elijah Craig 12-year
- ◆ **APPLE BRANDY** Busnel VSOP calvados
- ◆ **GRAPE BRANDY** Paul Beau VS cognac
- ◆ **APERTIVE** Campari
- ◆ **AMARI** Amaro Averna
- ◆ **CURAÇAO** Cointreau
- ◆ **SWEET VERMOUTH** Cocchi Vermouth di Torino
- ◆ **DRY VERMOUTH** Dolin dry vermouth

Extra Ingredients

BASIC BITTERS Angostura, Peychaud's, orange

BASIC SYRUPS simple syrup, Demerara syrup, honey, and so on

BUBBLES seltzer, dry sparkling wine

FRESH CITRUS

KITCHEN STAPLES eggs, dairy, spices

Always Start with a Daiquiri!

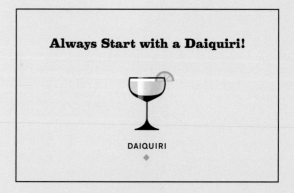

DAIQUIRI
◆

AFFINITY ◆◆

AIRMAIL ◆

AMERICANO ◆◆

BEE'S KNEES ◆

BICICLETTA ◆

BLINKER ◆

BOULEVARDIER ◆◆◆

BREAKFAST
MARTINI ◆◆

BROWN DERBY ◆

CLOVER CLUB ◆◆

CORPSE
REVIVER #1 ◆◆◆

DEAUVILLE ◆◆◆

DELMONICO ◆◆◆◆

FITZGERALD ◆

FRENCH 75 ◆◆

GIMLET ◆

GOLD RUSH ◆

HARVARD ◆◆

JACK ROSE ◆

JAPANESE ◆

LUCIEN GAUDIN ◆◆◆◆

MAMIE TAYLOR ◆

MANHATTAN ◆◆

MARGARITA ◆◆

MARTINI ◆◆

MEXICAN FIRING
SQUAD ◆

MINT JULEP ◆

MOJITO ◆

MORNING GLORY
FIZZ ◆

NEGRONI ◆◆◆

NEGRONI
SBAGLIATO ◆◆

OBITUARY ◆◆

OLD-FASHIONED ◆

OLD PAL ◆◆◆

PAINKILLER ◆

PIÑA COLADA

PINK LADY ◆◆

PRESCRIPTION
JULEP ◆◆

QUEEN'S PARK
SWIZZLE ◆

ROB ROY ◆◆

SIDECAR ◆◆◆

SIESTA ◆◆

SLEEPYHEAD

SOUTHSIDE ◆

TALENT SCOUT ◆

TOM COLLINS

WHISKEY
HIGHBALL ◆

WHISKEY SOUR

WHITE LADY ◆◆

ALINA MARTELL

Alina Martell is a pastry chef who lives in Denver.

Before my husband and I moved to Denver, I lived in the East Village for a few years, within walking distance of the original Death & Co. We made a thousand memories at the New York location and spent so much time there in the years after I first met my husband. It was our Cheers: I'd walk in after work, after a late night in the kitchen, and always run into a friend or two. The bartenders knew what I wanted. My usual was a rye Old-Fashioned that I'd sip until my husband joined me at the bar. Then we'd often switch to Daiquiris. Some nights, one Daiquiri would turn into two, and we'd end up lingering way past last call while we caught up with the staff and tried cocktails they were working on.

We moved to Colorado about a year before the Denver Death & Co opened, and we ended up living in the same neighborhood as the Ramble Hotel and new bar. The Denver bar is physically very different—soaring ceilings, big open tables, roomy booths— but somehow they managed to keep the same super-friendly, super-professional vibe. It feels just as it's supposed to. We go there to have a really good drink from people we know—the pastry chef in me loves the combination of crème de cacao and corn-infused mezcal—and trust and love to catch up with. But now we can sit in a corner booth and watch the city through the windows, and we also go there on weekends just to get coffee in the morning—two things we couldn't do at the New York bar.

Despite their differences, both places feel very much like a home to us. Not just a family, but also the same community.

VAQUERO
Tyson Buhler, 2017

1½ ounces Corn Husk–Infused Del Maguey Chichicapa Mezcal (page 291)

½ ounce Calle 23 reposado tequila

1 teaspoon Demerara Syrup (page 283)

½ teaspoon Marie Brizard white crème de cacao

Garnish: 1 orange twist

Stir all the ingredients over ice, then strain into a double old-fashioned glass over 1 large ice cube. Express the orange twist over the drink, then place it in the drink.

DUSTY BOTTLES

Despite our best efforts at maintaining a minimalist home bar, we often find ourselves with idiosyncratic spirits and modifiers that seldom get used. And if you've mixed your way through our other books, we suspect you have a nice little collection of underused ingredients as well. At home, we see these "dusty bottles" as an opportunity to explore unfamiliar ingredients. We challenge ourselves to use them in larger amounts—and even create drinks around them as a base spirit—in order to use them up. When we're trying to find a new application for a dusty bottle, we think in terms of the following five cocktail concepts, at right.

◆ **GATEWAY COCKTAIL:** The most well-known example of how the ingredient is used. For example, the "gateway cocktail" for Campari is the Negroni.

◆ **SAME SAME, BUT DIFFERENT:** Stepping beyond the Gateway Cocktail. These are recipes that explore a similar theme but in a new format. From the Negroni, you may explore the Old Pal.

◆ **STAR OF THE SHOW:** Using the dusty bottle, which might not typically be used as a "base spirit," as the centerpiece of a cocktail. For example, a Bicicletta is great way to explore Campari as the centerpiece for a cocktail.

◆ **SUPPORTING CHARACTER:** Here, the dusty bottle might not be the base ingredient, but it incontrovertibly changes the cocktail. Continuing our theme of Campari, the La Siesta makes the cocktail more complex and refreshing.

◆ **UNEXPECTED USE:** Recipes that break from tradition or offer an otherwise surprising use of the ingredient.

★ **CLASSIC OR MODERN CLASSIC COCKTAIL:** Widely known cocktail recipes, be they vintage or modern classics.

ABSINTHE

PROOF: 40% to 75% ABV.

HISTORY: Originated in Switzerland in the 1800s and rose to fame among Parisian artists in the later parts of the century.

FLAVOR PROFILE: Herbaceous, with a distinct anise flavor.

GENERAL USE: Heavily diluted with chilled water (and sometimes sugar) to be consumed on its own, or used as a seasoning in cocktails, much like bitters.

- ◆ Sazerac (page 241) ★
- ◆ Moving Target (page 237)
- ◇ Green Beast ★
- ◆ Doctor Zhivago (page 195)
- ◆ Rose Parade (page 240)

APEROL

PROOF: 11% ABV.

HISTORY: Created in 1919 by the Barbieri company but didn't catch on until after WWII.

FLAVOR PROFILE: Bitter orange, rhubarb, grapefruit.

GENERAL USE: Spritzes and other Italian café staples.

- ◆ Paper Plane ★
- ◆ Catamaran (page 274)
- ◇ Aperol Spritz ★
- ◆ Windup Bird (page 191)
- ◆ Subliminal Messages (page 267)

AQUAVIT

PROOF: Typically 40% ABV.

HISTORY: A Scandinavian spirit made with varying botanicals throughout the region. Can be aged or not, depending on its country of origin.

FLAVOR PROFILE: Grain spirit base; botanicals, including caraway, anise, and dill.

GENERAL USE: Traditionally served chilled. We use it in small amounts to add spicy complexity to cocktails.

- ◆ Trident ★
- ◆ Fault Line (page 252)
- ◇ Mr. Wednesday (page 220)
- ◆ Spyglass (page 265)
- ◆ Last Man Standing (page 235)

BLACKSTRAP RUM

PROOF: 40% ABV.

HISTORY: Aged rum with the addition of blackstrap molasses for color and sweetness.

FLAVOR PROFILE: Bitter chocolate, coffee, and sugarcane.

GENERAL USE: Float in mai tais and other tropical cocktails of the tiki era.

- ◆ Dark and Stormy ★
- ◆ Slightly Stormy (page 189)
- ◇ Corn and Oil ★
- ◆ Busy Earning (page 230)
- ◆ Night Train (page 202)

CACHAÇA

PROOF: Around 40% ABV.

HISTORY: Sugarcane distillate produced in Brazil. Usually unaged.

FLAVOR PROFILE: Fresh and grassy, similar to white rhum agricole.

GENERAL USE: Caipirinha.

- ◆ Caipirinha ★
- ◆ Gordons Cup ★
- ◇ Tandem Jump (page 190)
- ◆ Diamond Heist (page 214)
- ◆ Scarlet Tanager (page 188)

CHARTREUSE

PROOF: Yellow, 40% ABV; Green, 55% ABV.

HISTORY: Chartreuse was originally conceived as a medicinal elixir. Carthusian monks have long guarded the recipe for this liqueur named after the mountain on which the original order was founded.

FLAVOR PROFILE: Intensely herbaceous and complex.

GENERAL USE: Sipped neat or on the rocks, or used as an herbaceous modifier in cocktails.

- ◆ Last Word ★
- ◆ Iguanero (page 218)
- ◇ Chartreuse Swizzle ★
- ◆ New Beat (page 259)
- ◆ Bounce House (page 210)

CRÈME DE CACAO

PROOF: 25% ABV.

HISTORY: Chocolate liqueurs have been used worldwide for centuries.

FLAVOR PROFILE: Milk chocolate and vanilla.

GENERAL USE: Dessert drinks—we use it to add richness and chocolate notes to a variety of stirred and shaken drinks.

- ◆ Grasshopper ★
- ◆ Brandy Alexander ★
- ◇ 20th Century ★
- ◆ Chartreuse Alexander (page 274)
- ◆ Queen Snake (page 240)

ISLAY SCOTCH

PROOF: 40% ABV.

HISTORY: Produced on the island of Islay off the western coast of Scotland. Its telltale attribute is the penetrating aroma and flavor of peat.

FLAVOR PROFILE: Smoky with an underlying salinity due to the proximity to the ocean.

GENERAL USE: Served neat or on the rocks, or in cocktails as a rinse or modifying spirit.

- ◆ Penicillin ★
- ◆ Ginger Man (page 196)
- ◇ The Weaver (page 207)
- ◆ Wall of Sound (page 245)
- ◆ Smoking Jacket (page 241)

KALANI RON DE COCO COCONUT LIQUEUR

PROOF: 30% ABV.

HISTORY: Produced in the Yucatan region of Mexico and made by fermenting fresh coconut milk and macerating the liquid with pure cane sugar.

FLAVOR PROFILE: Coconut milk and vanilla.

GENERAL USE: We use Kalani (a lot!) as a modifier to add a tropical flavor to a wide variety of cocktails.

- ◆ Bad Sneakers (page 273)
- ◆ Sky Ladder (page 265)
- ◇ Sea Legs (page 241)
- ◆ Buko Gimlet (page 193)
- ◆ Warrior Poet (page 270)

LUXARDO MARASCHINO LIQUEUR

PROOF: 32% ABV.

HISTORY: Created as a digestif in 1885 by pharmacist Emile Giffard.

FLAVOR PROFILE: Nutty, fruity, and a little funky, with notes of marzipan.

GENERAL USE: As a modifier in cocktails or as an after-dinner *digestivo*.

- ◆ Hemingway Daiquiri ★
- ◆ Siamese Gimlet (page 223)
- ◇ Fancy Free ★
- ◆ Tuxedo #2 ★
- ◆ Get Free (page 232)

MENTHE-PASTILLE

PROOF: 24% ABV.

HISTORY: Created as a digestif by in 1885 by pharmacist Emile Giffard.

FLAVOR PROFILE: Peppermint dominates.

GENERAL USE: Unlike crème de menthe, which is cloudy, menthe-pastille is crystal-clear, allowing it to be used in both stirred and shaken drinks.

- ◆ Stinger ★
- ◆ Space Cowboy (page 278)
- ◇ Arethusa (page 273)
- ◆ Foxtrot (page 253)
- ◆ Junior Marvin (page 184)

PEAR EAU-DE-VIE

PROOF: 40% ABV.

HISTORY: Also known as Poire Williams, pear eau-de-vie is an unaged fruit brandy popular in Europe's Alpine regions.

FLAVOR PROFILE: Bright and aromatic, with a pure, amplified pear flavor.

GENERAL USE: Delicious served chilled as a small nip, or used as an intensely fruity modifier in cocktails.

- ◆ Beyond the Sea (page 178)
- ◆ 41 Jane Does ★
- ◇ Chilled shot with a side of apple cider
- ◆ Telegraph (page 267)
- ◆ Orville Gibson (page 262)

PISCO

PROOF: 40% ABV.

HISTORY: South American brandy produced in both Peru and Chile. The unaged, Peruvian style is the more typical style used in our bars.

FLAVOR PROFILE: Extremely aromatic and floral, with a clean, wine-like texture.

GENERAL USE: Typically used in citrus-driven cocktails.

◆ Pisco Sour ★

◆ City Club (page 194)

◇ Prototype (page 263)

◆ Spritz Roselle (page 189)

◆ Pablo Honey (page 220)

SUZE

PROOF: 15% ABV.

HISTORY: Created in Switzerland in 1885, this bitter aperitif is primarily flavored by gentian root.

FLAVOR PROFILE: Lightly sweet, earthy, and very bitter.

GENERAL USE: Served on the rocks or with seltzer and a slice of citrus. In cocktails, we use it in a similar fashion as Campari.

◆ White Negroni ★

◆ A Clockwork Orange (page 247)

◇ High Atlas (page 218)

◆ La Trinité (page 219)

◆ Ipswitch (page 257)

PLANNING AHEAD: WHAT'S YOUR INTENTION?

In an ideal world, cocktail hour—whether it's out at the bar or at home—is an opportunity to unwind. When you're hosting friends, making cocktails is a catalyst for relaxation, a way to help guests loosen up and enjoy the company of others. Even if you're just mixing a drink to enjoy by yourself, the ritual of fine-tuning a beloved recipe or exploring something new can be meditative. In either case, preparing yourself for the task at hand is vital in removing stress and allowing you to enjoy both the process and the end result.

You've probably heard the phrase *mise en place,* a French kitchen term that means "everything in its place." The gist is this: prepare everything you need ahead of time so that, at the moment of making a dish (or cocktail), all that's left to do is quickly assemble a few components. It's a maxim that the entire hospitality industry holds dear; at any bar or restaurant, there are hours spent each day prepping, cooking, infusing, and putting everything in exactly the right place before guests arrive.

And just as "always be knolling" is more than an organizational method—it's a frame of mind—*mise en place* is a necessary starting point for any bartending, be it in the home or at a bar. *Mise en place* also speaks to intention: before you can start prepping, you need to answer a few questions. First, what do you want out of your drink-making activity? If you're making a couple of casual cocktails for yourself, your *mise en place* can be as simple as grabbing ingredients, ice, glassware, and tools, then making the cocktail. But if you're making drinks for a group, your enjoyment of the process will vastly improve when you commit to mapping out what you're making and prepare beforehand.

As you become more comfortable with this kind of forethought, you'll find a deeper solace in the task and, with that feeling, you'll be able to improve your technique and increase the quality of your drinks. Take, for example, a casual weeknight cocktail: you gather the necessary tools and ingredients, then make the recipe. Over time, you may notice that this requires a lot of running around, and you might reorganize where you keep your tools and ingredients for easier access (and maybe buy a fancy bar cart in the process) to streamline your prep. Or, by storing glassware in a freezer—a couple of mixing glasses, some stemmed coupes, and Nick & Noras—you've thought ahead about how a frozen glass can make a better cocktail (see page 17).

The same evolution will apply to making drinks for a group: with practice, preparing multiple and more ambitious drinks will become easier and increasingly efficient, allowing you more time to focus on the quality of the drinks being made and, importantly, giving you exactly what you want out of the experience, whether it's doing most of the work ahead of time so you can join the party, donning a fake mustache and arm garters to cosplay an old-timey barkeep, or somewhere in between. While every other section of this book can be applied to making one-off drinks at home, the heart of this chapter is meant to give you the skills for entertaining—which isn't just making *more* drinks, but doing so while also enjoying yourself and your company.

Making drinks for a group is as much about execution as it is managing expectations—yours first and then your guests'. Do you want to be the bartender, stationed behind the counter whipping up drinks all night? Do you want to be the untethered host, never anchored to a specific place and task? Or do you want nothing to do with mixing the drinks, but to enjoy everything alongside your guests? Your guests are going to have a good time regardless, so it comes down to your vision for the experience.

Perhaps you're hosting a cocktail party where the cocktails themselves are the focus. In that case, showmanship and the actual making of the drinks are the life of the event. Prepare a concise and focused thematic menu (say, exploring Spritzes, page 96). Set up a bar station in a central location with all the necessary ingredients, tools, and spirits at the ready.

If the gathering is less about the cocktail making and more about the socializing, you may want to consider partially or fully batching (see page 152) the drinks, doing most of the prep hours or days ahead, then quickly executing drinks come party time.

Finally, if you want nothing to do with the making of the drinks and prefer your guests have the option to pour their own, try a fully batched approach (see page 160) or the Freezer Bar (see page 163).

Having formed your intention, you can start deciding what you want to serve.

WRITING THE MENU

Just as in our bars, when preparing an at-home cocktail menu, we begin with *intellectual development* (that is, deciding what the offerings will be) and creating a *wireframe*, or a simple outline used to sketch out the scope and structure of a menu, allowing you to establish your vision and roadmap for getting everything in place.

Grab a piece of paper—or start a spreadsheet, if you're a nerd like us (yes, we plan Thanksgiving dinner this way). On the left side, list the number of drinks you plan to serve. Be practical: a menu of four cocktails is generally manageable. Generally speaking, we prefer a menu with various styles and alcohol contents—say, a spritz, a sour, a collins, and an Old-Fashioned.

Before deciding on any specific cocktails, organize your approach. List the styles of drinks you've decided on, from lightest to strongest. Take a step back and ask yourself: Will these styles of drinks appeal to everyone at the party, or are they too similar? Make this decision now, before you start falling in love with individual recipes and end up with a menu of too-similar drinks.

As an example, let's start with the following cocktail styles:

1. Spritz
2. Margarita
3. Collins
4. Old-Fashioned

If you have a favorite drink you want to feature, add it and build out the other drinks so that they complement or contrast. For example, let's say you're set on serving a Sazerac variation, Matthew Belanger's I Against I (page 234):

1. Spritz
2. Margarita
3. Collins
4. Old-Fashioned: *I Against I*

Next, take a peek at your liquor shelf. Are there any "dusty bottles" (see page 142) that inspire you? Open the refrigerator: Are there any fresh ingredients (fruits, vegetables, herbs) that you want to feature in one or more drinks? Or flip through a cocktail book and pick cocktails that match your style categories and look appealing.

1. Spritz: *Bicycle Wheel, page 178 (seltzer, dry sparkling wine, St. George Bruto Americano, Don Ciccio & Figli Finocchietto fennel liqueur, Giffard crème de pamplemousse rosé)*

2. Margarita: *Talisman, page 206 (Siembra Azul añejo tequila, Siembra Valles Ancestral tequila, Reisetbauer carrot eau-de-vie, Kalani Ron de Coco coconut liqueur, fresh lemon juice, cane sugar syrup, Bitter End Moroccan bitters)*

3. Collins: *The Weaver, page 207 (seltzer, Nikka Taketsuru whisky, Clear Creek Douglas Fir eau-de-vie, Kilchoman Machir Bay single-malt scotch, fresh lemon juice, House Orgeat, yuzu juice)*

4. Old-Fashioned: *I Against I, page 234 (Jamaican rum, blended scotch, Honey Syrup, Peychaud's bitters, Bitter End Jamaican Jerk Bitters, Strega)*

At this point, step back and look at what you're getting yourself into. This is the start of your shopping and prep list. Do you want to commit to pressing fresh juices, making multiple syrups, and sourcing esoteric bottles? Or are you short on time and need to use pantry staples? Most important: Are you *excited* about making these drinks?

If the answer to any of those questions is *no*, it's time to try another approach. One of our favorites is to choose one or two special ingredients to prepare (say, jalapeño-infused tequila and ginger syrup) and use them in multiple drinks in different styles:

1. Shandy: *Ludicrous Speed, page 185 (pilsner, La Favorite rhum agricole blanc, blanc vermouth, jalapeño-infused tequila, fresh lime juice, Pineapple Gomme Syrup)*

2. Swizzle: *Curtis Park Swizzle, page 194 (Singani 63 eau-de-vie, amontillado sherry, Ginger Syrup, fresh lime juice, absinthe, Angostura bitters, mint)*

3. Sour: *Ginger Man, page 196 (Laphroaig 10-year single-malt scotch, fresh cantaloupe and lemon juices, Ginger Syrup, Angostura bitters)*

4. Martini: *Subliminal Messages, page 267 (Del Maguey Santo Domingo Albarradas mezcal, jalapeño-infused blanco tequila, blanc vermouth, Giffard crème de pamplemousse, Aperol)*

You're now at a critical moment. Most people would stop here, gather their ingredients, and consider themselves

ready to make drinks. We implore you to go one step further: write out each recipe and the number of people you think will be joining. As a basic rule of thumb, guests tend to drink one and half drinks per hour, so if you're having ten guests over for an estimated three hours, you may end up serving almost forty-five cocktails! Granted, your friends may not be as thirsty as ours, but you can see how the amount of product, glassware, and ice can quickly add up. If it looks like your wings are going to melt, or if you don't have enough supplies to execute your menu, now's your chance to dial it back a bit.

Use your spreadsheet to do some quick math to figure out precise ingredient quantities. Consider:

1. Do you have enough glassware on hand, or the ability/ desire to wash between rounds?

2. Do you have enough ice? Likely not, so you'll need to purchase or prepare extra in the days leading up to the gathering.

3. If you have more than five guests attending, we highly recommend making one or more batched drinks (see page 160), which will buy you time during the gathering.

4. Consider prepping extra amounts of your specialty ingredients; these are always the star of the show, and the leftovers make for great parting gifts.

5. Dedicate at least one hour the day of the party to prepare fresh ingredients (juices, garnishes, and so on). Keep these chilled for maximum freshness.

COCKTAILS & FOOD

Most food and beverage pairings begin with the food, after which you find a drink to complement it. This approach works perfectly with wine, beer, and sake, but cocktails are a different story. From the powerful acidity of a margarita to the alcoholic punch of an Old-Fashioned or a Manhattan, the intensity of cocktails makes them a challenge to pair with food. This is why we tend to flip the script, starting with the cocktail and finding an appropriate food to match.

Though there are many elements to consider, an easy place to start is to focus on a food's saltiness or richness. Our love of salt is well-documented, but it becomes especially critical when considering how cocktails and food match up. A citrusy cocktail loves a salty fried snack, like french fries; the drink's bright acidity cuts through the heft of the oil and starch. Bitter drinks, like the Negroni, have a natural affinity for salty crunchy snacks, like pretzels (one of our favorite combos); the salt lessens the impression of Campari's bitterness. And there are few things more restorative than a bracingly cold Martini matched with briny oysters (especially with a tangy mignonette); yes, you've just made a deconstructed dirty Martini, straight from the sea.

Cheese pairs nicely with cocktails, too. Try a luscious Brie or other soft cheese with a citrusy cocktail, like a Daiquiri; the citrus cuts through the richness. Or try a hard salty cheese, like pecorino or Parmesan, with a bittered cocktail such as an Aperol Spritz or an Americano. Your taste buds will find relief from the deep flavors of cured meats with a sip of a refreshing cocktail, especially one with bubbles, such as a Tom Collins or highball. Or complement that depth of flavor with a spirituous, dense cocktail, like a Manhattan.

The richness of most desserts is perfect territory for cocktail pairing. If you've ever dashed a bit of Angostura bitters on top of vanilla ice cream, you've experienced an ethereal marriage of spice and creaminess that parallels a root beer float. That same affinity can be explored through cocktails highly influenced by bitters, like an Old-Fashioned (or its many variations). And a bite of really good dark chocolate chased by a sip of a Manhattan is one of life's wonderful pleasures; the bitterness of the sweet vermouth complements the chocolate, with a hint of cacao butter rounding off the whiskey's edges.

You've likely noticed that these examples are mostly small plates, single bites, and sweets—not fully composed meals.

There's a casualness and impermanence that comes with a cocktail—it lasts only a few precious minutes (at least for us). Pairing cocktails throughout a composed meal would be fatiguing to the palate, and you'd risk overconsumption of aggressive flavors that compete with the dishes. That's why we drink cocktails before and after dinner and open bottles of wine, sake, cider, or beer during.

But there are exceptions to this general rule. First, low-ABV cocktails can be a fantastic pairing for composed plates, serving the palate-refreshing role that wine or beer usually fills. But take care to keep the drink's flavors subtle enough so as to not overpower the food. Any variation on the Bamboo, for example, walks the line perfectly: built around a base of food-friendly sherry, it will sip like a more spirituous cocktail, but allow you to still taste the food.

If you really want to pair cocktails throughout a meal, don't let us hold you back. Just be mindful that one doesn't dominate the other. If you're keen on a project, compose a progression of small, concentrated bites with specific cocktails for each. Call it a tasting menu, if you like. We've experimented extensively with this, both at Death & Co with our "Six Bites" menus—where each tiny dish is inspired by a cocktail family—and with coursed tasting menus at the Walker Inn, our dearly departed avant-garde bar in Los Angeles. It's an extravagant endeavor, to be sure, but it can make for a one-of-a-kind dinner party.

NAM HO

Nam Ho is a senior medical director at Health Science Communications and teaching faculty at Columbia University, New York City.

I started going to Death & Co around 2013 when I was a graduate student at Columbia. I didn't have much money to spend on going out in those days, but that didn't stop my love of craft cocktails. I did some research to find the best place to spend my stipend—which led me to Death & Co.

Entering the bar was just a complete shutout of the world, like walking through a curtained portal into a different dimension. I loved sitting at the end of the bar where I could view the entire room and watch the bartenders do their thing. The cash register is right there as well, which meant the bartenders would have a moment for quick chats when they were ringing up checks. In these moments, I'd get to ask about what's in the cheater bottles on the front bar or about the bottles of booze on the back bar. At home, my friends and I would pool our alcohol at get-togethers to make drinks, which allowed me to pick up bottles that I saw at Death & Co and start experimenting in cocktail making.

Once I graduated and got a job, I started going more frequently. I typically show up right at opening time, when there are fewer people and there is more time to chat with the staff. With every new menu release, I make it my mission to work through all of the stirred drinks, usually starting in the back of the menu and working forward. Once that is complete, I start on the shaken drinks. I don't think any shaken cocktail has genuinely surprised me quite like the mai tai that was added in 2019. It was not only the best mai tai I'd ever tasted, but quite possibly the best cocktail I'd ever had. It had the perfect blend of classic mai tai flavors, but was so much more complex and layered.

I don't spend much time by myself at other bars, but here I've become so comfortable with the staff that I never feel alone. It's actually very therapeutic for me; I think I've shared my life story with the staff. Whenever something new happens to me—whether it's about my job, dating, or family—my first impulse is always "I need to get back to Death & Co." Most nights are quiet, uneventful escapes. But when something happens in my life, I need a place to process. I always find myself back at the bar, sipping a drink, waiting for a check to be rung up so I can steal an opinion from the bartenders. I don't do that anywhere else.

MAI TAI (LUXURY)
Matthew Belanger, 2019

1 lime wedge

1½ ounces Habitation Velier WP 2007 Jamaican rum

½ ounce Habitation Velier WP 502 57% Jamaican rum

½ ounce Clément Créole Shrubb

1 ounce fresh lime juice

¾ ounce House Orgeat (page 284)

1 dash Angostura bitters

Garnish: 1 mint sprig, 1 orchid flower, whole nutmeg for grating

Squeeze the lime wedge into a cocktail shaker and drop it in. Add the remaining ingredients and short shake with ice for about 5 seconds, then strain into a double old-fashioned glass. Fill the glass with crushed ice and garnish with the mint sprig and orchid. Grate some nutmeg over the top of the drink and serve with a straw.

DRINKS FOR A CROWD

Let's get something out of the way: In almost every home-entertaining scenario, making every cocktail from scratch each time is a terrible idea. Even if you're motivated to show off your drink-making skills, for any group larger than a couple of people, measuring each ingredient will cause you enormous stress and leave your guests with long, painful gaps between cocktails—a lethal combination of sobriety and awkward small talk, kryptonite for any gathering. We strongly advise you not to treat your home bar as an actual bar, with a limitless menu of options. You don't hand dinner party guests a food menu, do you?

In this section we lay out some efficient (and fun!) approaches to making drinks for a crowd, organized from the least to the most complex.

MINIMALLY BATCHED COCKTAILS: TO EACH HIS/HER/THEIR OWN

If you're not sure about your guests' cocktail preferences, or want to let them craft their own drinks, a choose-your-adventure approach adds an engaging dynamic to hosting. The idea is simple: prepare a base that each guest can combine with their favorite spirit. This base can be anything that helps speed up the process of making a drink, but keeps some element of assembly involved: if a recipe calls for multiple juices and small measurements of modifiers (such as the High Five example on page 154), combining these allows guests to feel engaged in the process while not expecting too much of them. The following are four examples of base mixes that work well here: a boozy Old-Fashioned, a refreshing aperitif, a bubbly brunch staple, and the mighty Bloody Mary. While these examples list specifics, you can take the approach in other directions; we've provided some suggestions to explore.

If you want to leave the drink making to your guests, draw up a little "how-to" guide that coaches them through the process. For example, a Bloody Mary bar should include the following instructions:

1. Choose your booze and add 2 ounces to a glass.

2. Fill the glass all the way with ice (don't skimp!).

3. Top with Bloody Mary mix and stir with a straw for a few seconds.

4. Select your garnishes (follow your heart).

EXAMPLE 1: OLD-FASHIONED YOUR WAY

The Old-Fashioned is a fantastically flexible cocktail formula. While the classic is built on good American whiskey (be it rye or bourbon), *any* spirit can act as the base for a delicious Old-Fashioned, though we generally (but not always) prefer those that have spent time aging in oak barrels. If you and your friends are fans of the Old-Fashioned and its many variations, setting up a DIY Old-Fashioned station allows them to choose their favorite spirit and explore different styles of bitters.

The "base" in this example is two or more aged spirits, be they bourbon, cognac, or aged rum.

To prep, make a batch of Demerara syrup and serve it in a small bottle with a speed pourer (which makes accurate measurement easy); cut and trim citrus twists, then place them in a glass covered with a damp napkin; fill a tall glass with water and add a barspoon and a teaspoon; set out one single old-fashioned glass for each guest; fill an insulated bucket with large blocks of ice (be sure they fit into your glasses) along with tongs; and have a 2-ounce jigger handy. If you like, write out a notecard for your guests with instructions.

Note that here we recommend guests deviate from how we would make the cocktail at a bar. Instead of building the cocktail in a mixing glass, stirring, and pouring over fresh ice, we recommend simply building in the glass to speed up the process.

Old-Fashioned Your Way

Makes 1 drink

DIFFICULTY	ICE
◆ ◇ ◇ ◇	⬙

Prep: Demerara Syrup (page 283)

Ice: One cube or whatever ice you have handy

Ingredients: A selection of at least three aged spirits, such as single-malt scotch, bourbon, rye, cognac, apple brandy, or aged rum; Demerara syrup; Angostura and orange bitters (at least; add others if you want to go crazy).

1 teaspoon Demerara Syrup (page 283)

2 dashes bitters

2 ounces preferred spirit

Garnish: Lemon or orange twist

1. In a single old-fashioned glass, add the Demerara Syrup.

2. Add the bitters.

3. Add the spirit.

4. Using tongs, carefully add an ice block to the glass.

5. Stir until you can perceive a slight chill on the outside of the glass with the back of your hand.

6. Garnish with a citrus twist: lemon, orange, or both.

OTHER COCKTAILS TO TRY WITH THE SAME METHOD

Split-base Old-Fashioneds: Experiment with different base spirits together in different proportions, being mindful not to add more than 2 ounces per cocktail. Tasty combos: scotch with rye, aged rum and bourbon, apple brandy and cognac with everything.

Juleps: Instead of large ice cubes, provide crushed ice; you'll need more than you think. Instead of old-fashioned glasses, provide julep cups. Make sure to offer plenty of mint, which you will sub for the bitters, and a muddler. Any number of spirits can be used.

EXAMPLE 2: HIGH FIVES AND APERITIFS

Light, refreshing, and deeply soothing, the combination of grapefruit juice, lemon juice, and Aperol has proven to be a versatile base for many cocktails, including Alex Day's High Five from *Cocktail Codex*. You can swap out any base spirit in the High Five and be close to a delicious drink, but you can also transform it into a bubbly aperitif with the addition of seltzer or sparkling wine.

To begin, batch your High Five base, scaling up as needed depending on your number of guests.

High Five Your Way

Makes 1 drink

DIFFICULTY	ICE
◆ ◇ ◇ ◇	🧊🧊🧊

1½ ounces preferred spirit

3 ounces High Five Batch (opposite)

Cold seltzer or sparkling wine

Add the spirit and High Five Batch to a wine or collins glass, fill with ice cubes, and stir for 5 seconds. Top with seltzer or sparkling wine. No garnish.

OTHER COCKTAILS TO TRY WITH THE SAME METHOD

Bait and Switch (page 209): Batch the Ancho Reyes, the pineapple juice, lime juice, and Cinnamon Syrup, and swap out the mezcal for your preferred spirit.

High Five Batch

Makes 12 servings

Prep: Select batching; citrus juice and simple syrup prep

Ice: Cubes or whatever ice you have handy

Ingredients: Fresh grapefruit juice, fresh lime juice, Aperol, simple syrup, seltzer or champagne, and a selection of unaged spirits, such as vodka, gin, tequila, mezcal, rum, pisco, Singani, or eau-de-vie (pear brandy . . . just sayin'), or, for a low-ABV option, manzanilla sherry.

12 ounces fresh grapefruit juice

6 ounces fresh lime juice

6 ounces Aperol

6 ounces simple syrup (page 287)

1. Prepare the simple syrup and let cool.

2. Wash and juice the citrus, straining it through a fine-mesh strainer to remove pulp.

3. Combine the grapefruit juice, lime juice, Aperol, and simple syrup in a pitcher. Refrigerate until ready, up to 6 hours ahead of time.

EXAMPLE 3: MIMOSA HOUR

When fruits are at their absolute seasonal best, they can be a perfect match for a nice bottle of crisp sparkling wine—or grower champagne, if you want to be fancy (we do!). This simple-to-assemble riff on the classic peach Bellini or orange-laced Mimosa is a crowd pleaser, the perfect early morning reviver or hot afternoon refresher. You could simply feature one fruit juice option, but providing more than one keeps your guests engaged with minimal effort on your part. The key is the quality of the fruit: if it doesn't taste delicious on its own, it's not going to get better in a cocktail.

Prep:

1. Wash the fruit and juice or purée as appropriate. Pass through a fine-mesh strainer to remove pulp.

2. Refrigerate until ready to serve, up to 2 days.

3. Arrange a self-serve station with flutes, juices and purées in carafes, an ice bucket for the bubbles, and prepared lemon twists in a glass covered with a damp napkin.

Bellini or Mimosa Your Way

Makes 1 drink

DIFFICULTY

◆ ◇ ◇ ◇

Prep: Blending and straining

Ingredients: Fresh seasonal fruit juices (grapefruit, Cara Cara orange, mandarin orange, tangerine), purées (strawberry, peach, nectarine), and/or pressed juice (apple, pear); sparkling wine.

1 ounce fresh fruit juice or purée

Dry sparkling wine, preferably grower champagne

Garnish: 1 lemon twist

1. Add the juice or purée to a champagne flute and carefully top with sparkling wine.

2. Express a lemon twist over the drink and place it in the glass.

OTHER COCKTAILS TO TRY WITH THE SAME METHOD

Sunshine Gun Club (page 279): Batch the fresh orange juice, Vanilla Syrup, acid phosphate, and orange flower water. Add the heavy cream and a preferred unaged spirit (gin, tequila, pisco, and the like).

EXAMPLE 4: BLOODY MARY ADVENTURES

Say you're hosting a brunch and plan to serve Bloody Marys. You could fully batch them ahead of time, but it's more fun to allow your guests to pick their own base spirit: classic variations swap in gin (The Red Snapper) or tequila (Bloody Maria), but why stop there? Amontillado sherry makes a great base for a savory and low-ABV Bloody. Or use mezcal or smoky scotch to make the world's least-subtle Bloody Mary.

Start by preparing a big batch of Bloody Mary mix. Make extra; it'll disappear quickly. (For a group of four, we recommend at least two liters.) This can be done a day ahead and refrigerated until ready.

Basic Bloody Mary Mix

Makes 2 liters (enough for about 4 drinks)

DIFFICULTY ◆ ◇ ◇ ◇   ICE

Prep: Prebatching, juicing

Ice: Cubes

Ingredients: Organic tomato juice, hot sauce, fresh lemon and lime juice, assortment of base spirits, such as vodka, gin, tequila, mezcal, scotch, or amontillado sherry.

Garnishes: An assortment of options, such as lemon and lime wedges, pickled vegetables, celery stalks, cherry tomatoes, salt for rimming the glass, and black pepper for finishing.

1,500 grams organic tomato juice

225 grams Worcestershire sauce

100 grams strained fresh lemon juice

100 grams strained fresh lime juice

40 grams Maggi seasoning

35 grams Tapatío hot sauce

In a large pitcher, combine all of the ingredients and whisk until fully mixed. Refrigerate until ready to use.

Bloody Mary Your Way

Makes 1 drink

Personal interpretation and preferences are highly encouraged in choosing the garnish for a Bloody. Some go extravagant, with a buffet of fresh veggies, pickles, and even bacon strips, while others lean minimalist, with just a citrus wedge—we prefer somewhere in between. A jar full of crunchy pickled vegetables (okra and haricots verts are favorites), plus fresh celery sticks, lemon wedges, and cherry tomatoes make a good start.

Lime wedge (optional)

Kosher salt (optional)

1½ ounces preferred spirit

Basic Bloody Mary Mix (at left)

Garnish: With abandon!

If rimming the glass with salt, rub the outside of a collins glass with the lime wedge and roll it in the salt. Add the spirit and fill the glass with ice cubes. Top with the Basic Bloody Mary Mix and stir until chilled. Garnish with abandon.

HOW WE MEASURE

As a general rule, when making syrups, infusions, and other cocktail building blocks, we use a gram scale for measuring ingredients. Measuring volume by sight, even with measuring cups, tends to be less than accurate, whereas using a scale leads to consistent results.

We use two different gram scales: one that can measure large quantities (up to 4 kilograms), and another that can accurately measure extremely small quantities (down to 0.01 gram).

PARTIALLY BATCHED COCKTAILS

Making drinks is a lot of fun, and sometimes you don't want to give up all the theatrics of stirring and shaking just for efficiency's sake. By selectively combining some of your ingredients hours or even days ahead of time—what we call *partial batching*—you can have your fun while saving yourself a lot of time and headache at party time. The basic idea is this: combine certain ingredients—generally all alcoholic components (such as spirits, wines, and liqueurs)—but hold back on the fresh ingredients (usually citrus juice), thick sweeteners (like Demerara syrup), powerful additives (bitters or absinthe), and effervescent ingredients (seltzer, sparkling wine). Then, when your guests want a drink, combine the partial batch with the remaining ingredients and shake or stir to order. (As a basic rule of thumb, you can shake up to two cocktails per shaker—any more and there's too much liquid for the ice to do its job.)

At our bars, we use this shortcut frequently, especially when a cocktail calls for multiple spirits and modifiers in smaller amounts. By using batches, we save ourselves hours per day.

EXAMPLE 1: CITRUSY COCKTAILS WITH FRAGILE INGREDIENTS (PARTIALLY BATCHED SHAKEN COCKTAIL)

Some cocktail recipes include ingredients that cannot be batched beforehand, mostly notably drinks involving eggs, which will become "cooked" after prolonged exposure to citrus and spirits.

Aquafaba (the liquid used in canned chickpeas), which is often used as a vegan replacement for egg whites in cocktails, is similarly fragile and can't be prebatched. If we were planning to make a Calypso (page 211)—a delicious sake-based cocktail with aquafaba by Death & Co Denver bartender Jonnie Long—or any drink with a fragile ingredient, we'd partially batch the stable, alcoholic ingredients using the following method.

Calypso

Makes 1 drink → 10 drinks

DIFFICULTY ◆ ◆ ◇ ◇

ICE

Advance prep (up to 2 days beforehand):
Batching, syrup preparation

Last-minute prep (up to 8 hours beforehand):
Citrus juicing, aquafaba preparation, final batching

Ice: Large cubes for shaking and serving, or as per recipe

Ingredients: Sake, madeira, banana liqueur, aquafaba, cane sugar syrup

2 ounces junmai sake → 20 ounces (batch)

½ ounce Sercial madeira → 5 ounces (batch)

½ ounce Giffard banane du Brésil → 5 ounces (batch)

¾ ounce fresh lemon juice → 7½ ounces (prep and refrigerate until ready)

½ ounce aquafaba → 5 ounces (prep and refrigerate until ready)

½ ounce Cane Sugar Syrup (page 282) → 5 ounces (prep and refrigerate until ready)

Garnish: Banana leaf, cut into 1 inch-wide strips

1. Make the batch: Combine the sake, madeira, and banana liqueur in a 1-liter bottle. Refrigerate until ready to use.

2. When ready to serve, for every two cocktails add 6 ounces of batch to a cocktail shaker.

3. Add 1½ ounces fresh lemon juice, 1 ounce aquafaba, and 1 ounce cane sugar syrup.

4. Shake with ice, then strain into double old-fashioned glasses with one block of ice in each. Garnish with the banana leaf strips.

OTHER COCKTAILS TO TRY WITH THE SAME METHOD

Slow Hand (page 278): Batch cognac, rum, oloroso sherry, amaretto.

Cloud Nine (page 179): Batch apple eau-de-vie, rhum agricole, absinthe, malic acid solution.

City Club (page 194): Batch pisco, basil eau-de-vie, dry vermouth.

Love Bug (page 201): Batch tequila, mezcal.

EXAMPLE 2: CHAMPAGNE WELCOME (TOPPING WITH BUBBLES)

Welcoming your guests upon arrival with a refreshing champagne-laced aperitif is a graceful host move, but it also calls for careful timing. Prepping most of the drink (without the bubbles!) beforehand allows you to quickly shake the cocktails (this time, up to three per shaker) and top them with bubbly as guests walk through the front door. This straightforward approach can apply to any cocktail that's topped with an effervescent ingredient, be it sparkling wine, seltzer, cider, tonic, ginger beer, or the like.

A great drink to try this on is the Lady Stardust (page 184), a refreshing and complex blend of tequila, amaro, strawberry syrup, and sparkling wine. Your *mise en place* consists of cocktail shakers, flutes, ice, batch, and champagne (open it just before making the drink). Unlike the Calypso, we can fit up to three batches of the Lady Stardust in each shaker, since so much of the drink's volume comes from the champagne. If you use two shakers to double shake, all six drinks come out at exactly the same time.

Lady Stardust

Makes 1 drink → 6 drinks

DIFFICULTY

ICE

Advance prep (up to 2 days beforehand):
Batching, syrup preparation

Last-minute prep (up to 8 hours beforehand):
Citrus juicing, final batching

Ice: Ice cubes for shaking

Ingredients: Blanco tequila, amaro Zucca, Strawberry Syrup, fresh lemon juice, champagne

**1 ounce Siembra Valles Ancestral tequila →
6 ounces**

½ ounce amaro Zucca → 3 ounces

**¾ ounce Strawberry Syrup (page 287) →
4½ ounces (prep and refrigerate until ready)**

**¾ ounce fresh lemon juice → 4½ ounces
(prep and refrigerate until ready)**

2 ounces cold champagne → 12 ounces

1. Make the batch up to 2 days in advance: combine the tequila, amaro, strawberry syrup, and lemon juice in a 1-liter bottle. Seal and shake briefly to mix. Refrigerate until ready to use.

2. When ready to serve, add 9 ounces of batch to each shaker tin.

3. Before shaking, add 2 ounces of champagne to each flute.

4. Shake the batch with ice and double strain, distributing the drink evenly among the six flute glasses.

OTHER COCKTAILS TO TRY WITH THE SAME METHOD

Bastille (page 177): Batch calvados, Pineau des Charentes, Suze; fresh lemon juice, cane sugar syrup, and bitters when finishing.

Black Queen (page 178): Batch gin, amaro, Cocchi Americano, and cherry liqueur; fresh lemon juice, simple syrup, and top with sparkling wine when finishing.

Camargo (page 179): Batch cognac, Campari, Combier crème de rose, and lactic acid solution; cane sugar syrup and dry sparkling wine when finishing.

Crazy Diamond (page 179): Batch cognac, hazelnut eau-de-vie, maraschino liqueur; strawberry syrup, fresh lemon juice, and top with sparkling wine when finishing.

FULLY BATCHED COCKTAILS

You can go a step further by combining all of a cocktail's ingredients beforehand. *Fully batched* drinks allow for extremely quick execution, and they also ensure consistency from glass to glass.

Fully batched drinks present some challenges, though. If a recipe calls for fresh citrus, a fruit purée, or a very volatile ingredient (such as manzanilla sherry, which loses its vibrancy quickly after opening), batching too far ahead of time can affect quality. To keep the cocktail as fresh as possible, we recommend batching no earlier than six hours before its intended use, and after batching, keep chilled until used.

There's also an issue of ingredients separating. The solids in fresh juices or purées will separate and settle as they rest. To remedy this, agitate the batch before serving. Herbs like mint or basil are best used at the moment of drink making; as with tea, steeping herbs for too long will extract unpleasant bitter flavors.

EXAMPLE: PUNCH FOR A CROWD

A proper punch is a crowd-pleasing, deeply crushable mix of citrus, a modest amount of booze, some kind of spice-flavored element, and bubbles. In its simplest form, think of punch as a very large Tom Collins (which, in fact, likely originated as a single-serving punch). Not finding a punch recipe you like in this book? Find any citrus-based cocktail with an effervescent element and scale it up. Voila: punch!

The punch bowl gets a lot of attention, and to us is a fun way of engaging guests. There are tons of punch bowl options available from modern sources, but we love vintage milk-glass punch bowls (Ebay is full of 'em), and don't forget a ladle! That said, a deep salad bowl or large pitcher will suffice—even a stockpot, in a pinch.

Making the punch is a two-step process: prepping and serving. Because punch will sit on ice and generally be topped with something effervescent, it will degrade relatively quickly. To help with this, we mix everything but the bubbles in a pitcher and refrigerate it up to 6 hours in advance, then assemble the punch and add bubbles just as guests begin to arrive. We also tend to serve punch on large blocks of ice versus small chips—keeping the liquid cold but not diluting helps the punch maintain its integrity.

Moonlight Sonata Punch

Makes 4 drinks

DIFFICULTY	ICE
◆ ◆ ◆ ◆	

Advance prep (up to 2 days beforehand):
Syrup preparation

Last-minute prep (up to 6 hours beforehand):
Citrus juicing, final batching

Ice: Cubes, block ice

Ingredients: Irish whiskey, Watermelon Syrup, Cocchi Americano, fresh lemon juice, kirsch, House Orange Bitters, absinthe, Peychaud's bitters, dry sparkling wine

7½ ounces Tyrconnell Irish whiskey

3¾ ounces Watermelon Syrup (page 288)

3¾ ounces Cocchi Americano

3¾ ounces fresh lemon juice

1¼ ounces Massenez Kirsch

5 dashes House Orange Bitters (page 298)

5 dashes absinthe

5 dashes Peychaud's bitters

5 ounces dry sparkling wine

Garnish: Lemon wheels

1. Up to 6 hours in advance, combine all of the ingredients (except the sparkling wine) in a pitcher and refrigerate until ready to use.

2. When ready to serve, add ice cubes to the pitcher and stir to combine.

3. Strain through a large-mesh strainer into the punch bowl with one large block of punch ice.

4. Add the sparkling wine, stirring once to combine. Garnish with lemon wheels.

OTHER COCKTAILS TO TRY WITH THE SAME METHOD

Chinquapin Parish Punch (page 211), **Family Affair Punch** (page 214), **Pirate King Punch** (page 222)

CARBONATED COCKTAILS

If you're a serious home cocktailer, you might already have some way to carbonate liquids at home, be it a soda siphon (aka whip cream charger), SodaStream, or homemade carbonation rig. If not, get on it—your cocktail game will be better for it. In our book *Cocktail Codex* we show how to build your own powerful carbonation rig (and how to carbonate full kegs of cocktails!), but the information is readily available online, and parts can be sourced from a well-stocked local homebrew store.

Once you're geared up, assembling a carbonated cocktail requires a bit more work than throwing together a punch. There are three critical components of carbonation you must consider: temperature, clarity, and dilution. Carbon dioxide bubbles come out of solution more quickly in warmer liquids, so getting all of your ingredients as cold as possible beforehand will help the CO_2 stay put and make for a fizzy drink. In our bars, we store all of the ingredients that are to be carbonated in a refrigerator or freezer.

Carbon dioxide also has a thing for cloudy ingredients: If there are any free-floating particles in the liquid, carbon dioxide will grab on to those little particles, ride them to the surface of the liquid, and quickly disperse into the atmosphere, making for a very sad, very flat cocktail. But carbonated cocktails are most delicious when they have bright, citrusy flavors, which is a problem because fresh citrus, even when finely strained, doesn't react well to forced carbonation. We go to extreme lengths to clarify citrus juices that are destined for carbonated cocktails at our bars, but if you don't have a centrifuge at home (what, you don't?) and you don't want to go through the process of agar clarification (see page 296), there are alternatives that provide the same bright acidity needed to balance a drink. In the recipes that follow, originally formulated for draft or bottled cocktails, we use a number of alternative acids that all help in making a fully carbonated cocktail: citric, lactic, malic, and phosphoric acids, as well as naturally acidic verjus.

Dilution is the final consideration. While each cocktail is a little different, a basic rule of thumb is that every carbonated cocktail should be made up of 50 to 60 percent water. This can be the added water that would come by shaking or stirring, but effervescent ingredients like seltzer, sparkling wine, cider, and beer also count.

In a party setting, a fully carbonated cocktail is a great way to serve something unique, be it out of a large, three-liter bottle or decanted into single-serving bottles to look like a very adult soda.

EXAMPLE: A MAKE-AHEAD CHAMPAGNE COCKTAIL

Blood and Black Lace
Makes 4 drinks

DIFFICULTY

◆ ◆ ◆ ◆

Prep (up to 1 week in advance): Champagne Acid Solution

Ingredients: Amaro Ramazzotti, Old Forester 100 bourbon, Giffard crème de mûre, Vanilla Syrup, Champagne Acid Solution, dry sparkling wine, water

4 ounces Amaro Ramazzotti

2 ounces Old Forester 100 bourbon

1 ounce Giffard crème de mûre

1 ounce Vanilla Syrup (page 288)

1 ounce Champagne Acid Solution (6%) (page 299)

12 ounces dry sparkling wine

2 ounces water

Garnish: Blackberry on a pick

At least 6 hours in advance, chill each ingredient (amaro and bourbon in the freezer, all others in the refrigerator). Combine all the ingredients in a carbonating bottle, charge with CO_2, and gently shake to help dissolve the CO_2 into the liquid. Refrigerate the carbonating bottle for at least 20 minutes, and preferably for 12 hours, before opening. Pour into chilled flutes.

OTHER COCKTAILS TO TRY WITH THE SAME METHOD

Gatekeeper (page 181), **Standing Room Highball** (page 183), **Moon River** (page 186), **Repeater** (page 188), **Ron Coco** (page 188), **Scarlet Tanager** (page 188), **Ursa Major** (page 190), **Banquo's Ghost** (page 177)

THE FREEZER BAR

Thanks to high-proof alcohol's resistance to freezing, we can prebatch a large serving of certain cocktails, dilute it with water, and place it in a freezer to rest and chill until we're ready to drink. When cocktail hour comes around, you simply grab the bottle, pour it into a glass, and garnish. This method works only with spirituous cocktails—that is, drinks that don't involve citrus and that are high enough in proof to resist freezing. If the overall proof of the mixture is 30 percent alcohol or above, it won't freeze in a standard home freezer (most residential units hold temp around 0° Fahrenheit); the freezing point would be -1.75° Fahrenheit. A typical Old-Fashioned or Martini-style cocktail will clock in higher than this, making it perfectly suited for the freezer bar. But if you just freeze the cocktail without adding a bit of water (which is typically added while stirring the drink), the result will be a very stiff, unbalanced drink.

There's an ongoing debate about batching and freezing drinks among those of us who spend far too many hours thinking about cocktails. One camp, the Classicists, will argue that by batching and bottling cocktails, some intangible nuances are lost. The other—let's call them the Rebels—thinks that, with accurate measurement and careful dilution, the only difference between a drink mixed à la minute and one that's been made ahead and stored in the freezer is purely philosophical.

We're not choosing sides here, because each approach has its place, based on your intention for the experience. We place equal weight on what you want out of a cocktail itself and what you want out of the experience of *making* said cocktail. The freezer bar feeds our (frequent) desire to have a quick, perfectly chilled drink, but we can't argue with someone who needs the ritual of mixing a cocktail in the moment to enjoy it.

FREEZER BAR BASICS

The goal with the freezer cocktail is to fully prebatch the cocktail, including water content, store in the freezer, and pour whenever the cocktail is desired. This also allows you to serve exactly how much cocktail you need; instead of mixing a full-size Martini, for example, you can pour a mini Martini.

With any freezer cocktail, we have to account for the water that would be added when stirring. In the case of a stirred drink served up, such as a Manhattan, that amount would fall between 1½ and 2 ounces for a single cocktail. However, adding a full 2 ounces of water to the freezer drink would lower the overall ABV to the point where the cocktail would partially freeze. Instead, we generally start by adding 10 to 15 percent water for cocktails that contain vermouth, like Manhattans and Martinis (depending on the proof of the ingredients), in this case pulling back considerably and adding between ½ and ¼ ounce of water per individual drink.

FREEZER BAR TINY TWEAKS

We almost always have a basic Martini ready to pour from the freezer, though sometimes we want something familiar, but a little extra. Try adding 1 ounce of flavorful liqueur, such as a pear or peach liqueur, to your 750 ml freezer Martini batch. This small addition will add a subtle new layer of complexity. Dave Kaplan is always playing around with his "kitchen sink Martini," which he begins with 5 parts gin to 1 part dry vermouth, to which he adds other modifiers, most often some combination of pear eau-de-vie (or pear liqueur), apple brandy, and blanc vermouth.

Or add ½ ounce of crème de cacao and a small pinch of salt to a Negroni batch. The chocolatey notes hide just under Campari's bitterness, making for a pleasantly rich after-dinner digestif, while the salt helps to tamp down some of the bitterness and accentuates the chocolate flavors.

When exploring, think of flavor affinities not just for the individual ingredients, but how they pair with a finished cocktail. For example, adding a small measure of Cointreau to a batched Manhattan will give it a bright pop. Or, try a splash of aged cachaça, like Avuá amburana, to an Old-Fashioned batch for a little cinnamon spice. And most of all, have fun!

For cocktails served on the rocks—such as a Negroni, an Old-Fashioned, or variations on both—because of the higher proof, you can get away with a bit more water; for Old-Fashioned styles, we recommend around 20 percent added water, or about ½ ounce per individual cocktail, scaling up as you batch multiple cocktails. Also note that the Demerara syrup may separate when stored in the freezer, so give the bottle a few gentle turns before serving. Because the Old-Fashioned (or Negroni) is served on ice, there's no need to dilute the batch with water, though you should let the drink sit on its large block of ice for a few minutes (or speed up the process by stirring it for about 30 seconds) to reach target dilution.

And then there are the bitters to consider. In large batches, bitters magnify in intensity (we don't understand why; it's sorcery). Our basic rule of thumb is to cut the bitters amount in half in any batch over five cocktails, taste, and add more as necessary.

Finally, we need to know the size of the bottle we'll be placing in the freezer. If the bottle were a standard 750 ml (a touch over 25 ounces), we can then map our batch recipe to leave a tiny amount of head room in case the added water expands (which it won't if the batch is boozy enough).

Example: Freezer Bar Manhattan

2 ounces Rittenhouse rye whiskey → 12 ounces

1 ounce Carpano Antica Formula sweet vermouth → 6 ounces

2 dashes Angostura bitters → 6 dashes

3 ounces filtered water

Using a measuring cup, carefully measure all of the ingredients and funnel into the bottle. Seal the bottle, turn it over a few times to mix the ingredients, and taste a small amount. Adjust the bitters as necessary (it may need a couple more dashes; remember that bitters will intensify in a larger batch, so always start with half the recipe's amount). Freeze for at least 3 hours (now's a good time to freeze your Nick & Nora glasses as well). When ready to serve, prepare your garnishes, then divide the batch among the glasses (about 4 ounces each) and garnish.

FREEZER BAR MIXOLOGY: VENTURING BEYOND CONVENIENCE

The Freezer Bar isn't just convenient; it also offers a unique creative strategy: using a fully batched cocktail as a base spirit in other cocktail styles. If you're like us, after a few rounds of a single Freezer Bar cocktail, you may find yourself getting tired of the same drink. Luckily, you have a (mostly full) bottle of delicious and versatile booze that can be used in a number of ways, whether it's to augment other drinks or by infusing the whole batch to make an entirely new cocktail.

Example 1: Freezer Bar Spritz

Turn a freezer bar Negroni, Martini, or other batch made with unaged spirits into a refreshing spritz by adding 1½ ounces of the batch to a wine glass, then ¼ ounce fresh lemon juice. Fill the glass with ice cubes, stir until chilled, then top with cold seltzer and garnish as desired. Also consider adding a small amount (¼ to ½ ounce) of flavorful liqueur—such as Aperol, St-Germain, or crème de pamplemousse—to each drink.

Example 2: Freezer Bar Highball

Any freezer batch can make a delicious base for a simple highball. In a collins glass, combine 2 ounces batch and 4 ounces cold seltzer. Add ice, stir briefly, and garnish with a lemon wedge. Experimenting with different bubbles can be delicious, too: try a Martini or Negroni batch with tonic water, or an Old-Fashioned or Manhattan with ginger ale or ginger beer.

Example 3: Freezer Bar Sour, Fizz, or Collins

With some fresh lemon juice, simple syrup, and a shaker, you can turn pretty much any batch into a refreshing sour, fizz, or collins. The sugar content of your batch needs to be considered in order for your drink to be properly balanced. Start by adding ¼ ounce simple syrup to 2 ounces of batch for each drink. Taste, then add up to ¾ ounce simple syrup until the mix tastes balanced.

2 ounces freezer bar batch

¾ ounce fresh lemon juice

¼ to ¾ ounce simple syrup (page 287)

For a traditional sour: Shake with ice and strain into a coupe.

For a fizz: Dry shake with an egg white, then shake again with ice, strain into a fizz glass, and top with seltzer.

For a collins: Short shake and strain into a collins glass, then add ice cubes and top with seltzer.

FREEZER BAR INFUSIONS

Any freezer bar batch should have enough proof to extract delicious flavors; instead of just infusing one component, why not infuse the entire cocktail? The recipes and suggestions here use a pressure-infusion method (see page 295), but if you don't have an iSi whipper or prefer not to use the technique, in most cases you can combine the infused ingredient with the batch in a sealed container and allow to rest at room temperature for 24 hours or until the flavor is noticeable.

Example 1: Strawberry Negroni

As midsummer approaches, strawberries become their absolute perfect selves. Using a prebatched Negroni, combine 750 ml of batch with 200 grams clean, hulled, and sliced strawberries in a 1-quart iSi. Infuse using the pressure-infusion method on page 295. After infusing, chill and serve. Or use the infused cocktail as a base for a refreshing spritz: combine 1½ ounces Strawberry Negroni, ½ ounce fresh lemon juice, and ½ ounce simple syrup in a wine glass; add ice and stir, then top with 2 ounces chilled dry sparkling wine.

Example 2: Meyer Lemon Martini

Winter citrus reaches its apotheosis when Meyer lemons start showing up at the market. With a highly fragrant peel, the zest can be used to transform a Martini. Using a microplane, prepare 5 grams Meyer lemon zest. Using a prebatched Martini, combine 750 ml of batch with the zest in a 1-quart iSi. Infuse

with the pressure-infusion method on page 295. After infusing, chill and serve. The infused Martini can also be used as a versatile base, perhaps to replace gin in a classic Tom Collins, swapping out the standard lemon juice for the Meyer—peak citrus in technicolor!

Example 3: Chocolate Manhattan or Negroni

Both the Manhattan and the Negroni already have whispers of chocolate flavors, so why not turn them up? Using a prebatched Manhattan or Negroni, combine 750 ml of batch with 30 grams cacao nibs in a 1-quart iSi. Infuse with the pressure-infusion method on page 295. After infusing, chill and serve.

Example 4: Celery Martini

This riff on a dirty Martini avoids brine and instead focuses on savory celery stalks and leaves. Clean and chop 125 grams celery stalk and 10 grams celery leaves. Using a prebatched Martini, combine 750 ml batch with prepared celery and leaves in a 1-quart iSi. Infuse with the pressure-infusion method on page 295. After infusing, chill and serve. For a more refreshing alternative, consider using the infusion as the base for a simple highball: add 2 ounces to a highball glass, add ice and cold seltzer, and garnish with a lime wedge.

FREEZER BAR DIVIDENDS

If you're making a round of stirred cocktails à la minute and you know you'll likely want another round, grab a large mixing glass (a pitcher will work as well) and a small bottle or other freezer-safe vessel. Make four cocktails instead of two, strain the first round, and pour the extra cocktail into the bottle. Seal and freeze until you're ready to drink it. If your cocktail is served on ice, you can certainly grab a fresh large cube, or just top up your glass.

ADAPTING COCKTAILS FOR THE HOME BAR

We'll be the first to admit that many of the cocktail recipes from our bars are complicated, labor-intensive, and built with esoteric (and often expensive) ingredients. We don't say this to intimidate you—on the contrary! At home, we're more like you than you might think: we don't have fully stocked bars, our ice is made in trays, and sometimes (okay, usually) we make compromises when we don't have exactly the right tools or ingredients.

Here we present our **Home Bartender Adaptability Rules**, an outline of components and obstacles that can sometimes stop the home bartender in their tracks, and how to work around them. We've identified areas that are open to compromise and advise you on how to simplify a recipe to suit your available ingredients, tools, time, or personal preference. Over the years we've found that when you have only so many options, you're forced to get creative, and some cool things can come out of that.

ADAPTING MEASUREMENTS

While cocktail recipes have very precise measurements that we implore you to follow, at the heart of these measurements is a ratio of ingredients in proportion. Nowhere is this more important than when scaling up a recipe for a large batch: any error in the proportion of those ingredients when scaling up will only magnify the mistake. Double-check your math.

Can you accurately measure ingredients without a jigger or measuring cup? Of course it's possible, but it takes a lot of practice to accurately measure by eye, so we highly recommend using some kind of measuring device. If you can't find your jigger, look around your kitchen for something that can measure liquid; say, a tablespoon. A tablespoon equals ½ ounce, so you can use this to build a cocktail recipe.

If you make a mistake when measuring ingredients—say you add 1 ounce of simple syrup to finish building a Daiquiri when you meant to add ¾ ounce—you don't need to start over (or drink a slightly too sweet Daiquiri, either). Simply look at the proportion of syrup to citrus and spirit, and add more of the latter two: add ½ ounce rum and ¼ ounce fresh lime juice, then enjoy your Super Daiquiri! (We're also obligated, at this point, to remind you that adding the cheapest ingredients to a shaker or mixing glass first will avoid this issue; you could just throw out the $0.001 worth of simple syrup and start over.)

TWEAKING TEMPERATURE

Of all the characteristics of cocktails, temperature is the one that bartenders obsess over the most. We expend an embarrassing amount of energy and money on making and sourcing the right ice cubes for shaking and stirring cocktails and for keeping those drinks cold in the glass. We religiously deep-freeze our mixing glasses and stemmed glassware; we shake like Muppets to get citrusy cocktails frosty and frothy with aeration.

At home, attaining the same low temperatures as at a professional bar can be the biggest challenge you face. You may find that when making a stirred cocktail, the drink is chilled but not *cold* when it hits its target dilution. Here's how to stay frosty.

USE ENOUGH ICE

Both stirred and shaken cocktails need more ice than you may think. A stirred cocktail should be made with a mixing glass full of ice cubes (see page 35), with a larger proportion of ice to liquid. Simply put: If you see ice bobbing in your mixing glass, add more! For a shaken cocktail (see page 32), after building the drink in the smaller tin, fill it all the way to the brim with whatever ice you have.

This same rule of thumb applies to drinks served on ice: they should be more ice than liquid. Any less and the drink will quickly dilute.

What if you ignore our advice and start stirring a cocktail with just a few pieces of ice? Using your barspoon, give it a taste; does it taste noticeably boozy and barely chilled, or watery and slightly more chilled? If the former, you caught the issue early enough that you can simply add more ice, stir a bit more, and strain. If the latter, add a couple of pieces of ice to the glass and place it in your freezer. Wait 15 minutes, then taste again; hopefully the remaining ice has melted and the cocktail is now balanced and nicely chilled.

A shaken drink is more forgiving, up to a point. If you've just started shaking a drink and realize that you haven't added enough ice, quickly add more ice and resume. But if you've fully shaken a drink, then straw-tasted it and realized you didn't use enough ice (because the drink tastes half chilled and partially diluted), quickly add a few more ice cubes, and shake vigorously for a few seconds (any longer and over-dilution is all but assured), then strain immediately.

ICE FLEX: BREAKING DOWN BIG BLOCKS

These days, most cities are home to at least one commercial ice company that sells their perfectly clear wares to bars and consumers. If you can't find a source for precut ice, you can almost always find a local icemaker that sells big blocks of ice, which you can break down into whatever shapes you like. We usually do this long before guests arrive, then store our hand-shaped cubes in the freezer, but it also makes for a flashy party trick, if you want to take the time to shape your ice to order. Here's a quick primer on how to break it down:

1. Place the block on top of a wire rack set inside a rimmed baking sheet. Let it sit at room temperature for a few minutes to temper (to avoid shattering when you start chipping away).

2. Grab a long, serrated kitchen knife, one that you don't mind beating up (ice will quickly dull the knife's teeth). A new, clean hacksaw will also do the trick.

3. Begin by cutting away slabs of ice that can be broken down into smaller pieces. Let's say you want to make a bunch of 2-inch blocks; use a sawing motion to score one side of your big block about 2 inches from the edge until you have a trench about ⅛ inch deep. Turn the block and continue that score down the next side, and repeat until you have a channel running around all four sides.

4. Next, lay the knife teeth in one of the channels and tap the top, noncutting edge of the blade with a mallet (the serrated teeth will work like tiny ice picks), then repeat with the other sides until the 2-inch slab is released. You now can shape that slab into cubes using the same method.

FREEZE ALL GLASSWARE

This is the hardest thing to convince people to do at home. We get it: your freezer is full of noncocktail foodstuffs, and the thought of cramming your most precious glassware in there among the frozen pizzas, half-eaten pints of ice cream, and mysteriously unlabeled storage containers is, well, scary. However, do it *one time* and taste a Martini or Daiquiri served in a frozen glass next to one served in a room-temperature glass, then decide if you can live with fewer frozen pizzas (or perhaps purchase a supplemental chest freezer). While a chilled glass will keep a drink colder for a longer stretch of time, what's more important to us is the sensory experience of holding a frozen cold glass in our hand when we pick up a drink, and feeling the rim against our lips upon that first sip—it is a certain type of addiction we plan never to kick. Even at our bars, we don't have the space to freeze every style of glassware we use, but we do ensure that every stemmed glass (coupe, Nick & Nora, or Martini) has a home in our freezer. At home, you don't need to stop at stemware; chilled old-fashioned and collins glasses are lovely, if you have the space.

You don't even need a permanent place in your freezer for glasses. So long as you freeze them for about an hour before use, your vessels will be plenty frosty. Or if you can't justify the space (or simply forget to stash them), fill the glassware with ice, top with water, and let it chill for about 5 minutes. Discard the water and ice before using (or drink it; hydrating prior to making and drinking cocktails is never a bad idea).

SERVE THE DRINK IMMEDIATELY

After taking such extensive care to prepare your cocktail, make sure to serve it as quickly as possible. If you let it linger, ice will melt, liquid will start to warm, and for shaken cocktails, texture will die. Drink up!

SKIP THE MIXING GLASS

Our normal protocol is to build all stirred cocktails in a mixing glass with ice and strain over ice. While we believe this makes the highest-quality cocktail in a bar setting, at home the method takes a lot of time; requires rinsing, drying, and letting the glass cool (at least to room temperature!); and requires a lot of precious ice. You can skip it without the quality suffering too much by simply building the cocktail in an old-fashioned glass, adding one large block (highly recommended versus smaller ice cubes), and stirring until you feel a slight chill on the outside of the glass.

SWAP SPIRIT TYPE

Modern cocktail recipes have become increasingly complex, with long lists of ingredients (especially at our bars!), to the point where the type of spirit called for is often so intertwined with the collaborating ingredients that, should you not have that precise spirit, the cocktail won't succeed. Take, for example, the Bad Sneakers (page 273), a mix of Suntory Toki Japanese Whisky, Donn's Mix, coconut, lime, and a tiny bit of smoky scotch. The Toki is such a specific flavor that subbing another Japanese whisky may not be exactly the same, but will probably be tasty enough. But a critical component of the recipe is the smoky, concentrated addition of Laphroaig Islay single-malt scotch. If you don't have another peaty Islay scotch around and try to sub in a blended scotch, like Famous Grouse, the drink will suffer. For this reason, you must be mindful of what substitutions can work—the Toki for another Japanese whisky—and which cannot, like subbing a scotch of an entirely different style for the Laphroaig.

That doesn't mean it's impossible to sub another spirit, you just have to be mindful of what will replace the recipe's called-for spirit type and its affinity for the other ingredients. Take a Daiquiri as an example. Don't have rum? Swap in blanco tequila, gin, or vodka and you'll have a tasty drink—but it won't be a Daiquiri. Or a whiskey sour: if you don't have bourbon or rye, any spirit is going to be tasty, but extra-credit points for subbing in another aged spirit—its complexity will shine alongside the lemon juice.

A basic rule for substituting a completely different style of spirit in a recipe is to stick to spirits that have a similar amount of aging (or none at all). Vodka, gin, white rum, blanco tequila, and mezcal can be swapped interchangeably, in theory, as can whiskies and aged brandies. Will that substitution always make for a perfect cocktail? Maybe not, but it will probably do the trick.

SWAP SPIRIT BRAND

We've gone to excruciating lengths to choose very specific spirit brands for our cocktail recipes; the individual personality of each becomes a central player in the drink's composition, and we get way up on a high horse when selecting the brands based on their provenance and flavor profile. We know that you won't have all of these specific brands, and that's absolutely okay—let's talk about how to sub in what you do have.

We've discussed how you can sub in a different type of spirit if you absolutely need to, but if you're reconfiguring some of the recipes in this book based on your home bar, we highly recommend staying in the same general area: gin for gin, not gin for genever; blanco rum for blanco rum, not blanco rum for heavily aged rum; bourbon for bourbon (or, honestly, rye), not bourbon for Islay scotch. You get the idea. Generally speaking, if you stick to this advice, you can get very close to the original cocktail. (Careful: If you veer outside this advice you might accidentally create a new, delicious cocktail all your own.)

There are some exceptions, though. Thanks to the explosion in craft distilling, the boundaries of spirit types have massively expanded. A few years ago, anyone making a gin would probably be coloring within some expected lines: London dry, or at least London dry, but a little extra. Then the rebels came in and smashed the orthodoxy—people like the fine folks at St. George, who produce a range of gins so deeply individual that they almost always become the central actor in any cocktail. Take, for example, the Apollo cocktail (page 248) calling for St. George dry rye reposado gin, a weirdly delicious hybrid between gin and spicy moonshine. Likely you have only one or two gins in your repertoire, and likely they're the classic London dry style. Subbing one in for the Apollo will be delicious, no doubt, but a very different cocktail.

.... YOU HAVE

As we noted in the preceding temperature section, making
and keeping cocktails cold is fundamental to making them
delicious. Perhaps the most appealing visual in cocktails is
an Old-Fashioned served over a massive hunk of crystal-
clear ice. While this presentation may be familiar in many
bars, not long ago it was a novelty, and even the subject of
scorn by guests who assumed we were shorting them on
booze by adding so much ice to their drinks. While serving
a cocktail with a single cube is beautiful, it also has practical benefits: the large cube has relatively small surface area,
which slows dilution and lengthens the life of the drink.

But if you don't have the room in your freezer for making
big cubes, or you find that you've run out, you can still make
great cocktails. A good middle ground is slightly smaller
cubes (about 1 inch), which pull triple duty in stirring,
shaking, and serving. But you'll probably find yourself in
the unenviable position of only having small, chip ice (what
we affectionately call "shitty ice") to use. Don't fear; just use
a ton of it: pack your shaker full before shaking and fill a
glass all the way to the brim.

Some recipes call for crushed ice to keep a drink viciously
cold, and though you're probably not going to invest in a
special machine to produce small pebbles of ice, you can
approximate the size of crushed ice by cracking cubes using
the back of a heavy spoon (see page 15). The sizing isn't consistent, but with practice you'll be able to quickly assemble
enough ice to use. Make sure to pack the glass tightly and
to top the drink with more ice.

SWAP GLASSWARE

Glassware selection is important, but only to a degree. Even
when we make a case for always serving a Daiquiri in a coupe
or a Martini in a V-shaped glass, your joy will be diminished
only a little bit if you serve the drink in a different glass.

The short of it: You don't need to build a complete arse-
nal of glassware (see page 18). Serve that Daiquiri neat in
an old-fashioned glass, and it will still be delicious. Don't
have a collins glass? Use a highball or your tallest, skinniest
drinking glass. Wine glasses can be used for shaken drinks
served up or on the rocks. And you absolutely don't need
both Martini glasses and Nick & Noras; if you have to pick
one, the latter will be more versatile in the long run.

Just do us one small and deeply important solid: don't ever,
ever serve a cocktail in a warm glass straight out of the
dishwasher—it's the ultimate cocktail blasphemy.

SPECS

Since we published our first Death & Co book, our bars have created almost 1,000(!) new cocktails. While we'd love to share each and every one with you, we simply didn't have enough room in the confines of these pages to fit them all. So we painstakingly (emphasis on the *pain*) whittled the list down to a few hundred of our very favorites, focusing on the drinks we feel are the most accessible at home. We organized the drinks in the same manner we now structure our menus, grouping cocktails in descriptive categories that match one of the core cocktails explored in *Cocktail Codex*: Fresh & Lively (highball and spritz variations); Light & Playful (simple sours); Bright & Confident (complex sours); Boozy & Honest (home of the Old-Fashioned and its many variations); Elegant & Timeless (Martini, Manhattan, and Negroni riffs); and Rich & Comforting (Flips and other decadent and rich cocktails). As always, we encourage you to make our specs your own, whether that's by substituting ingredients, tweaking amounts, or experimenting with other ice or garnishes.

One last reminder on bitters: in the following recipes, bitters are measured in dashes and assume you're using an off-the-shelf retail bitters bottle. If you transfer your bitters to a fancy dasher bottle, double the amount of dashes called for in the recipe.

Fresh & Lively

⊙ LOW ABV   ⊘ NO ABV   ❄ FREEZER BAR   ⧗ PROJECT COCKTAIL   ❀ LOW-PREP COCKTAIL

ACHILLES' HEEL ❄

Matthew Belanger, 2018

- 2 ounces cold seltzer
- 1 ounce Lemorton Selection calvados Domfrontais
- ½ ounce Amrut cask-strength single malt Indian whisky
- ½ ounce Henriques & Henriques rainwater madeira
- ¼ ounce Lejay crème de cassis de Dijon
- ¾ ounce fresh lemon juice
- ½ ounce Demerara Syrup (page 283)
- 2 dashes Miracle Mile Redeye bitters
- Garnish: 1 lemon wheel and 1 coffee bean

Pour the seltzer into a collins glass. Short shake the remaining ingredients with ice for about 5 seconds, then strain into the glass. Fill the glass with ice cubes, garnish with the lemon wheel, and finely grate some of the coffee bean over the top of the drink.

ALPENGLOW ⊘

Tyson Buhler, 2018

For this nonalcoholic highball, I wanted to make a savory-yet-fruity cordial that used tea as a way to balance the sugar and let its tannic, bitter qualities create balance. Fresh bay leaves taste and smell just like Lipton iced tea, so it naturally plays really well with the black tea. —TB

- 2 ounces cold seltzer
- 4 ounces Alpenglow Cordial (page 282)
- ½ ounce fresh lime juice
- Garnish: 1 fresh bay leaf

Pour the seltzer into a collins glass. Short shake the remaining ingredients with ice for about 5 seconds, then strain into the glass. Fill the glass with ice cubes and garnish with the bay leaf.

BANQUO'S GHOST

Matthew Belanger, 2019

I get a lot of inspiration from culinary sources. There's a recipe in the *Alinea* cookbook made with corn, coconut, and cayenne, so I wanted to make a highball around those flavors. Mezcal Vago Elote is a triple-distilled mezcal macerated with corn, so it tastes a bit like cooked corn. —MB

- 1 ounce Compass Box Great King Street Glasgow Blend scotch
- 1 ounce Mezcal Vago Elote
- 1 teaspoon Cane Sugar Syrup (page 282)
- ½ teaspoon lactart
- ½ dash Bitter End Moroccan bitters
- 4 ounces Harmless Harvest coconut water
- Garnish: 1 grapefruit twist

Chill all the ingredients. Combine them in a carbonating bottle, charge with CO_2, and gently shake to help dissolve the CO_2 into the liquid (see page 162 for detailed carbonation instructions). Refrigerate the carbonating bottle for at least 20 minutes, and preferably for 12 hours, before opening. Pour into a fizz glass and fill with ice cubes. Express the grapefruit twist over the drink, then place it in the drink.

BASTILLE ❄

Tyson Buhler, 2017

The goal with this drink was to create something that felt sophisticated and really focused on French ingredients. It's got loads of apple and grape flavors, and the small dash of celery bitters helps ground all of that fruit and complements the bitter Suze. —TB

- 2 ounces dry sparkling wine
- 1½ ounces Domaine du Manoir de Montreuil calvados
- ¾ ounce fresh lemon juice
- ½ ounce Jean-Luc Pasquet Pineau des Charentes
- ½ ounce Suze
- ½ ounce Cane Sugar Syrup (page 282)
- 1 dash Bitter Truth celery bitters

Pour the sparkling wine into a chilled flute. Shake the remaining ingredients with ice, then double strain into the flute. No garnish.

BEYOND THE SEA

Matthew Belanger, 2016

I created this drink when working on my first Death & Co menu. We were down to the wire and needed a sparkling wine drink. Rose water and champagne is a classic flavor combination. Many drinks take a lot of tweaking to get them to the point where they work; this spec was my first pass, and it was approved right off the bat. That was a huge confidence-building moment for me. —MB

2 ounces dry sparkling wine

1 cucumber slice

1¼ ounces Campo de Encanto Acholado pisco

¼ ounce Clear Creek Williams pear brandy

¾ ounce Grapefruit Cordial (page 283)

½ ounce fresh lemon juice

3 drops rose water

Pour the sparkling wine into a chilled flute. In a shaker, gently muddle the cucumber. Add the remaining ingredients and shake with ice, then double strain into the flute. No garnish.

BICYCLE WHEEL ⚜

Matthew Belanger, 2019

This is based on a classic spritz called the Bicicletta. Fennel and citrus is a well-trod culinary combination executed in cocktail form, and the fennel-flavored liqueur from the Don Ciccio guys is a fun flavor to play around with in drinks. —MB

1 ounce cold seltzer

2 ounces dry sparkling wine

1¼ ounces St. George Bruto Americano

½ ounce Don Ciccio & Figli Finocchietto fennel liqueur

1 teaspoon Giffard crème de pamplemousse rose

Garnish: 1 grapefruit half wheel

Pour the seltzer into a chilled wine glass filled with ice cubes. Add the remaining ingredients and stir briefly to combine. Garnish with the grapefruit half wheel.

BLACK POODLE ☉

Amanda Harbour, 2018

When developing cocktails, I usually start with one or two flavors and expand from there. In this case, I was excited about the interaction of three: Pineau des Charentes, whiskey, and amaro. —AH

2 ounces cold seltzer

1 ounce Cucumber Magnesium Syrup (page 283)

1 ounce J. Navarre Vieux Pineau des Charentes

¾ ounce Tyrconnell single-malt Irish whiskey

¼ ounce Amaro Montenegro

½ teaspoon Chareau aloe liqueur

Garnish: 1 cucumber slice

Pour the seltzer into a fizz glass. Stir the remaining ingredients over ice, then strain into the glass. Fill the glass with ice cubes and garnish with the cucumber slice.

BLACK QUEEN ⚜

Al Sotack, 2014

1½ ounces dry sparkling wine

¾ ounce Fords gin

¾ ounce Meletti amaro

½ ounce Cocchi Americano

¾ ounce fresh lemon juice

¼ ounce simple syrup (page 287)

½ teaspoon Rothman & Winter Orchard cherry liqueur

Garnish: 1 lemon twist and 1 brandied cherry

Pour the sparkling wine into a chilled flute. Shake the remaining ingredients with ice, then double strain into the flute. Garnish with the lemon twist and brandied cherry.

BLOOD & BLACK LACE ⌛

Shannon Tebay, 2018

I created this wintry spritz for a winter menu, swapping a darker amaro for Aperol, and augmenting the drink with bourbon. If you don't want to carbonate this drink you can also stir it and strain over the sparkling wine. —ST

1 ounce Amaro Ramazzotti

½ ounce Old Forester 100 bourbon

¼ ounce Giffard crème de mûre

¼ ounce Vanilla Syrup (page 288)

¼ ounce Champagne Acid Solution (page 299)

3 ounces dry sparkling wine

½ ounce water

Chill all the ingredients. Combine them in a carbonating bottle, charge with CO_2, and gently shake to help dissolve the CO_2 into the liquid (see page 162 for detailed carbonation instructions). Refrigerate the carbonating bottle for at least 20 minutes, and preferably for 12 hours, before opening. Pour into a chilled flute.

BOURBON AND BIRCH

Jon Armstrong, 2016

1 ounce cold seltzer

1½ ounces Old Grand-Dad 114 bourbon

½ ounce Amaro Averna

¾ ounce fresh lemon juice

½ ounce House Ginger Syrup (page 284)

¼ ounce Cinnamon Syrup (page 283)

2 drops Terra Spice birch extract

Pour the seltzer into a collins glass. Short shake the remaining ingredients with ice for about 5 seconds, then strain into the glass. Fill the glass with ice cubes. No garnish.

⊙ LOW ABV   ⊘ NO ABV   ❄ FREEZER BAR   ⌛ PROJECT COCKTAIL   ⚜ LOW-PREP COCKTAIL

BULLDOG FRONT ❄

Matthew Belanger, 2017

I pulled this shandy-style drink out of my ass, more or less, and it worked on the first try. It's named after a Fugazi song, but I guess that's not very straight-edge of me to name a drink after their work. —MB

1½ ounces Westbrook Gose beer

1 ounce Beefeater gin

½ ounce Krogstad aquavit

½ ounce Giffard crème de pamplemousse rose

1 teaspoon Campari

¾ ounce fresh lemon juice

½ ounce Cane Sugar Syrup (page 282)

Garnish: 1 lemon wheel

Pour the beer into a pilsner glass. Short shake the remaining ingredients with ice for about 5 seconds, then strain into the glass. Fill the glass with ice cubes and garnish with the lemon wheel.

CAMARGO

Matthew Belanger, 2017

This was inspired by raspberry lambic beer; I wanted to re-create that flavor profile in a spritz. Pasquet Marie-Framboise is Pineau des Charantes flavored with raspberries, and the core of the whole drink. —MB

2½ ounces dry sparkling wine

1 ounce Pasquet Marie-Framboise

½ ounce Paul Beau VS cognac

¼ ounce Campari

¼ ounce Combier crème de rose

¼ ounce Cane Sugar Syrup (page 282)

1 teaspoon Lactic Acid Solution (page 299)

Pour the sparkling wine into a chilled flute. Stir the remaining ingredients with ice, then double strain into the glass. No garnish.

CHARLEMAGNE

Tyson Buhler, 2018

I made this drink for Death & Co Denver's first menu, and after working through a number of boozy, complex drinks, I needed something light and crushable. Even though cucumber is far from a new cocktail ingredient, it pairs perfectly with young spirits and screams "summertime." —TB

1½ ounces Street Pumas Blended scotch

¾ ounce Cucumber Magnesium Syrup (page 283)

4 ounces cold seltzer

Pour the scotch and syrup into a collins glass and fill the glass with ice cubes. Top with the seltzer. No garnish.

CLOUD NINE

Tyson Buhler, 2017

This drink was on one of our first "luxury" menu sections, in which most of the drinks are big, spirituous cocktails that showcase aged spirits. Here, I wanted something that shows off the absurdly delicious Cyril Zangs 00 apple cider eau-de-vie. The rhum agricole lifts up the grassy aromas, and the whole drink tastes like biting into a Granny Smith apple on steroids. —TB

2 ounces cold seltzer

1½ ounces Cyril Zangs 00 apple cider eau-de-vie

½ ounce La Favorite rhum agricole blanc

¾ ounce fresh lime juice

½ ounce Cane Sugar Syrup (page 282)

2 dashes absinthe

1 dash Malic Acid Solution (page 299)

1 egg white

Pour the seltzer into a chilled fizz glass. Dry shake the remaining ingredients, then shake again with ice. Double strain into the glass. No garnish.

CRAZY DIAMOND

Tyson Buhler, 2017

Reisetbauer eau-de-vie, while pricy, are so expressive and unique that getting to play with them is such a treat. It's the most elegant version of Nuts & Berries (a 1980s cocktail made with Frangelico and Chambord) I could think of. —TB

2 ounces dry sparkling wine

1 ounce Paul Beau VS cognac

½ ounce Reisetbauer hazelnut eau-de-vie

¾ ounce Strawberry Syrup (page 287)

½ ounce fresh lemon juice

1 teaspoon Luxardo maraschino liqueur

Pour the sparkling wine into a chilled flute. Shake the remaining ingredients with ice, then double strain into the flute. No garnish.

DOCTOR MINDBENDER

Matthew Belanger, 2019

Copenhagen-based Empirical Spirits makes this really cool vapor-distilled spirit, which has the intensely floral flavor of habanero chiles, but none of the heat. It reminded me of guava, so I took the recipe for a classic Mexican Firing Squad and swapped in the habanero spirit for tequila, and guava syrup for grenadine. There's a tradition in tiki drinks for naming them after doctors; this one is a nod to a G.I. Joe villain. —MB

1 ounce Tapatío 110-proof tequila

½ ounce Tapatío Blanco tequila

½ ounce Empirical Spirits Habanero Spirit

¾ ounce fresh lime juice

¾ ounce Guava Syrup (page 283)

2 dashes Angostura bitters

Garnish: 1 lime wheel

Short shake all the ingredients with ice for about 5 seconds, then strain into a collins glass filled with cracked ice. Garnish with the lime wheel.

DRAMA QUEEN ⚘

Al Sotack, 2015

- 2 ounces dry sparkling wine
- 2 green apple slices
- 1 ounce Tanqueray gin
- ½ ounce Salers Gentien aperitif
- ¾ ounce fresh lemon juice
- ¾ ounce Honey Syrup (page 284)
- 2 dashes Bitter Truth celery bitters
- Pinch of salt

Pour the sparkling wine into a chilled flute. In a shaker, gently muddle the apples. Add the remaining ingredients and shake with ice. Double strain into the flute. No garnish.

DROP STITCH ⊙

Sam Johnson, 2018

When I started working at Death & Co, we had few truly low-ABV cocktails. I created this one around the pairing of pear and celery, which is a fresh take on apples and celery, a flavor combo we riff on frequently at the bar. —SJ

- 1½ ounces cold seltzer
- 1½ ounces Lustau Papirusa Manzanilla Sherry
- ¾ ounce Perry's Tot Navy Strength gin
- ½ ounce Don Ciccio & Figli Finocchietto fennel liqueur
- ¼ ounce Clear Creek pear eau-de-vie
- ¾ ounce fresh lemon juice
- ½ ounce simple syrup (page 287)
- 1 dash absinthe
- Garnish: 1 mint bouquet

Pour the seltzer into a collins glass. Short shake the remaining ingredients with ice for about 5 seconds, then strain into the glass. Fill the glass with ice cubes and garnish with the mint bouquet.

EL TOPO

Matthew Belanger, 2017

The key ingredient in this Bizzy Izzy Highball riff is tepache, a Mexican beverage made from lightly fermented pineapples. We make ours from the skin and pulp left over from juicing pineapple, which is another great way to use up prep waste. —MB

- 1 ounce cold seltzer
- 1½ ounces Lustau Los Arcos amontillado sherry
- 1 ounce Great King St. Glasgow Blend scotch
- 2 ounces Tepache (page 298)
- 1 teaspoon acid phosphate
- ½ teaspoon Citric Acid Solution (page 299)
- 1 dash Angostura bitters
- Garnish: 2 pineapple fronds

Pour the seltzer into a collins glass. Short shake the remaining ingredients with ice for about 5 seconds, then strain into the glass. Fill the glass with ice cubes and garnish with the pineapple fronds.

FLEAS ON TRAPEZE VOL. 1 ⊙

Amanda Harbour, 2019

Everyone at Death & Co loves Clear Creek pear eau-de-vie, but it's extra special to me. The first time I injured myself at work (I sliced my finger on a vegetable peeler), I was nursing my wound in the back, and Alex Day brought me a glass of Clear Creek pear eau-de-vie to cheer me up. That's when I fell in love with the product. I based this low-ABV drink on the combination of pear and fennel; the rest of the ingredients fell into place to make a beautiful highball. —AH

- ¾ ounce Plymouth Navy Strength gin
- ¾ ounce Clear Creak pear eau-de-vie
- ½ ounce Don Ciccio & Figli Finocchietto fennel liqueur

- ½ ounce fresh lime juice
- ½ ounce Cane Sugar Syrup (page 282)
- 2 dashes absinthe
- Garnish: Fennel fronds

Short shake all the ingredients with ice for about 5 seconds, then strain into a collins glass filled with ice cubes. Garnish with the fennel fronds.

FREE TAIL

Adam Griggs, 2019

This play on the classic Bizzy Izzy Highball showcases Siembra Valles tequila, which is a throwback to the style of tequila that was made before the industry was modernized. Its complex flavor profile is more akin to mezcal than the tequilas we drink today, so I added Lillet rosé and fino sherry to add balance and lightness. —AG

- 1 ounce cold seltzer
- 1 ounce Siembra Valles Ancestral tequila
- ½ ounce Lillet rosé
- ½ ounce Tio Pepe fino sherry
- 1 ounce Donn's Mix #1 (page 298)
- ½ ounce fresh lime juice
- 1 teaspoon Cane Sugar Syrup (page 282)
- 1 dash Bittermens Xocolatl mole bitters
- Garnish: 1 grapefruit twist

Pour the seltzer into a collins glass. Short shake the remaining ingredients with ice for about 5 seconds, then strain into the glass. Fill the glass with ice cubes and garnish with the grapefruit twist.

GATEKEEPER ⏳

Shannon Tebay, 2019

For his end-of-shift drink, our doorman Josh would always ask for a "gin spritz," which is not really a thing. He basically wanted a gin and soda, as a way to taste through all of the gins on our back bar. So I wanted to create a cocktail for our "gatekeeper" that was actually a spritz. You don't have to carbonate this drink; instead, stir the drink and strain it over the sparkling wine. —ST

1 ounce Old Raj 110-proof dry gin

½ ounce Cap Corse blanc quinquina

1 teaspoon Cyril Zangs 00 apple cider eau-de-vie

½ ounce Celery Syrup (page 282)

½ teaspoon Malic Acid Solution (page 299)

3 ounces dry sparkling wine

Garnish: 1 apple slice

Chill all the ingredients. Combine them in a carbonating bottle, charge with CO_2, and gently shake to help dissolve the CO_2 into the liquid (see page 162 for detailed carbonation instructions). Refrigerate the carbonating bottle for at least 20 minutes, and preferably for 12 hours, before opening. Pour into a chilled flute and garnish with the apple slice.

GHOST COLORS

Jeremy Oertel, 2017

I developed this drink when super-juicy fruit-bomb IPAs were at the peak of their popularity. Here, I tried to mimic those flavors in something that resembles the vintage tiki cocktail, Cobra's Fang, but with a gin base instead of rum. —JO

1½ ounces Greenhook Ginsmiths Old Tom gin

¾ ounce fresh lime juice

½ ounce fresh grapefruit juice

¼ ounce Massenez crème de pêche peach liqueur

¼ ounce House Ginger Syrup (page 284)

¼ ounce Cinnamon Syrup (page 283)

1 dash Angostura bitters

2 ounces Stillwater Nu-Tropic IPA

Garnish: 1 lime wheel

Shake all the ingredients except the beer with ice, then strain into a collins glass and fill the glass with ice cubes. Top with the beer and garnish with the lime wheel.

GRAMERCY RIFFS

Alex Jump and Jon Feuersanger, 2019

Spritzes usually get locked into a box of bitter, fruity, and bubbly, so Jon and I wanted to show a different side of the Spritz. We also really wanted to get Riesling into a cocktail, so we amplified the subtle dill flavors in Riesling with Svöl aquavit, which is very dill-driven, then we layered on the malic-acid characteristic of the Leopold sour apple. —AJ

1 ounce dry sparkling wine

1 ounce Spring44 vodka

½ ounce Svöl Swedish Style Aquavit

½ ounce Cocchi Americano

½ ounce Leopold Bros. New York sour apple liqueur

½ ounce dry Riesling

½ ounce Cane Sugar Syrup (page 282)

½ ounce fresh lemon juice

Garnish: 1 lemon wheel and 1 apple fan

Pour the sparkling wine into a chilled wine glass. Short shake the remaining ingredients with ice for about 5 seconds, then double strain into the glass. Fill the glass with ice cubes. Garnish with the lemon wheel and apple fan.

HALO EFFECT

Tyson Buhler, 2018

For our first Garden menu at Death & Co Denver, we relied heavily on bottled cocktails. This one was really centered around the apple cordial, which we made from the leftover pulp after juicing apples for other applications. —TB

3 ounces cold seltzer

1 ounce Spring44 vodka

¾ ounce white port

¼ ounce Salers Gentien aperitif

1 ounce Apple Cordial (page 282)

Garnish: 1 mint bouquet

Pour the seltzer into a collins glass. Short shake the remaining ingredients with ice for about 5 seconds, then strain into the glass. Fill the glass with ice cubes. Garnish with the mint bouquet and serve with a straw.

HARLEQUIN

Matthew Belanger, 2018

Forthave is an intensely bitter amaro that tastes like rhubarb and eucalyptus. I based this wintry spritz on a drink that Al Sotack created called the Poison Ivy, so I named it after another female comic book villain. —MB

1½ ounces Fever-Tree tonic

1½ ounces Bonal Gentiane-Quina

1 ounce Domaine du Manoir de Montreuil calvados

½ teaspoon Forthave Spirits Marseille amaro

¼ ounce Honey Syrup (page 284)

1 teaspoon acid phosphate

Garnish: 1 mint bouquet and 1 lemon wheel

Pour the tonic into a wine glass. Shake the remaining ingredients with ice, then strain into the glass. Fill the glass with ice cubes and garnish with the mint bouquet and lemon wheel.

GRAMERCY RIFFS, PAGE 181

HIGHBALL (STANDING ROOM) ⧗

Matthew Belanger, 2019

The addition of shiso and pear-flavored spirits makes this more interesting than the standard Japanese highball. If you don't want to carbonate this in a whipper, you can freeze a batch of everything but the seltzer, then top it with seltzer to serve. —MB

4½ ounces cold seltzer

1½ ounces Suntory Toki Japanese Whisky

½ ounce Glasshouse shiso brandy

¼ ounce Mathilde Poire pear liqueur

1 teaspoon Clear Creek Williams pear brandy

¼ ounce simple syrup (page 287)

½ teaspoon Malic Acid Solution (page 299)

Garnish: 1 shiso leaf

Chill all the ingredients. Combine them in a carbonating bottle, charge with CO_2, and gently shake to help dissolve the CO_2 into the liquid (see page 162 for detailed carbonation instructions). Refrigerate the carbonating bottle for at least 20 minutes, and preferably for 12 hours, before opening. Pour into a collins glass and fill the glass with ice cubes. Garnish with the shiso leaf.

HIGH NOON ❄

Tyson Buhler, 2016

1½ ounces cold seltzer

1½ ounces Great King St. Glasgow Blend scotch

½ ounce Laird's bonded apple brandy

¾ ounce fresh lemon juice

½ ounce Amaro Nonino

½ ounce Demerara Syrup (page 283)

1 dash Miracle Mile Redeye bitters

Garnish: 1 dehydrated lemon wheel

Pour the seltzer into a collins glass. Short shake the remaining ingredients with ice for about 5 seconds, then strain into the glass. Fill the glass with ice cubes and garnish with the dehydrated lemon wheel.

HIGH SPEECH

Matthew Belanger, 2016

I wanted to make a vegetal collins using the main flavors of thyme and bell pepper. —MB

1 lime wedge

Aleppo salt (equal parts Aleppo pepper and kosher salt)

1 ounce cold seltzer

1½ ounces Tanqueray gin

½ ounce Emile Pernot Liqueur de Sapin

1 teaspoon Bigallet thyme liqueur

¾ ounce fresh lemon juice

½ ounce fresh yellow bell pepper juice

½ ounce Cane Sugar Syrup (page 282)

Garnish: 1 dehydrated lemon wheel

Rub the lime wedge along the upper ½ inch of a collins glass, halfway around the circumference, then roll the wet portion in the salt. Pour the seltzer into the glass. Short shake the remaining ingredients with ice for about 5 seconds, then strain into the glass. Fill the glass with ice cubes and garnish with the dehydrated lemon wheel.

HOT GOSSIP ❄

Jon Armstrong, 2017

This is an elevated gin and tonic riff that includes the grapefruit and maraschino duo from a Hemingway Daiquiri, with some Douglas Fir eau-de-vie for pineyness. At the bar we carbonated and bottled each serving of the drink, which was such a pain in the ass to do. The juice wasn't worth the squeeze, as they say, so it makes more sense to build it in a collins glass. —JA

1½ ounces Plymouth Navy Strength gin

2 teaspoons Giffard crème de pamplemousse rose

½ teaspoon Luxardo maraschino liqueur

½ teaspoon Clear Creek Douglas Fir eau-de-vie

5 ounces Fever-Tree tonic

Garnish: 1 lime wedge

Combine all of the ingredients except the tonic in a collins glass, then fill the glass with ice cubes. Top with the tonic and stir once. Garnish with the lime wedge.

HULA HULA HIDEOUT ☉

Tyson Buhler, 2018

Another bottled cocktail from Denver's Garden, this low-ABV piña colada variation utilized the manzanilla sherry we kept on draft throughout the summer, which was always dangerously within arm's reach on hot summer days. —TB

1 ounce cold seltzer

1½ ounces Bodegas Yuste Aurora manzanilla sherry

½ ounce Rhum JM Blanc 100

½ ounce Pineapple Gum Syrup (page 286)

2½ ounces Harmless Harvest coconut water

½ ounce fresh lime juice

Garnish: 1 pineapple frond

Pour the seltzer into a collins glass. Short shake the remaining ingredients with ice for about 5 seconds, then strain into the glass. Fill the glass with ice cubes and garnish with the pineapple frond.

JUNIOR MARVIN ❄

Jon Armstrong, 2015

This is a riff on an Old Cuban. While most Old Cubans are made with dark rum, I tried it with younger and younger rums before settling on a white rum, which led to a comparatively more simple drink, but definitely a crowd-pleaser. I wish more people would treat crème de menthe like absinthe and use it in tiny amounts as an accent. —JA

  2 ounces dry sparkling wine

  1½ ounces El Dorado 3-year rum

  1 teaspoon Kalani Ron de Coco coconut liqueur

  ¾ ounce fresh lime juice

  ½ ounce simple syrup (page 287)

  2 dashes Giffard menthe-pastille

Pour the sparkling wine into a chilled flute. Shake the remaining ingredients with ice, then double strain into the flute. No garnish.

KID DYNAMITE

Matthew Belanger, 2019

There's a classic drink called a Blinker, made with rye, grapefruit juice, and grenadine. It's frequently made like a sour, but the earliest recipes are more like a long drink. You can make this drink with commercial grapefruit soda, or even Squirt. —MB

  1½ ounces Wild Turkey 101 rye

  ½ ounce Empirical Spirits Habanero Spirit

  ¼ ounce House Grenadine (page 284)

  4 ounces grapefruit soda

  Garnish: 1 lime wedge

Combine all of the ingredients except the soda in a double old-fashioned glass and add 1 large ice cube. Top with the soda and stir once. Garnish with the lime wedge.

KID DYNAMITE ⊘

Matthew Belanger, 2019

Whenever we create a nonalcoholic cocktail, we want it to taste as good as the full-proof version of drink (at left). I think this one succeeds. —MB

  2 ounces Seedlip Grove 42 Citrus

  ¼ ounce House Grenadine (page 284)

  4 ounces grapefruit soda

  Garnish: 1 lime wedge

Combine all of the ingredients except the soda in a double old-fashioned glass and add 1 large ice cube. Top with the soda and stir once. Garnish with the lime wedge.

KINGSTON AMERICANO

Tyson Buhler, 2019

  1 ounce Wray & Nephew Jamaican rum

  1 ounce Campari

  4 ounces grapefruit soda

  Garnish: Pinch of salt and 1 grapefruit half wheel

Add the rum and Campari to a collins glass and fill the glass with ice cubes. Top with the soda and stir once. Sprinkle the salt on top of the drink and garnish with the grapefruit half wheel.

KINSALE COOLER ❄❄

Eryn Reece, 2014

  1 ounce cold seltzer

  1 ounce Tanqueray 10 gin

  1 ounce Lustau manzanilla sherry

  ¾ ounce fresh lemon juice

  ½ ounce St-Germain elderflower liqueur

  ½ ounce Suze

  ½ ounce simple syrup (page 287)

  1 dash Scrappy's celery bitters

  Garnish: 1 lemon wheel

Pour the seltzer into a collins glass.

Short shake the remaining ingredients with ice for about 5 seconds, then strain into the glass. Fill the glass with ice cubes and garnish with the lemon wheel.

LADY STARDUST

Tim Miner, 2019

  2 ounces dry sparkling wine

  1 ounce Siembra Valles Ancestral tequila

  ½ ounce Amaro Zucca

  ¾ ounce Strawberry Syrup (page 287)

  ¾ ounce fresh lemon juice

Pour the sparkling wine into a chilled flute. Shake the remaining ingredients with ice, then double strain into the flute. No garnish.

LEFT A WOMAN WAITING

Al Sotack, 2014

  1 strawberry

  1½ ounces Siembra Azul blanco tequila

  ½ ounce Wray & Nephew Jamaican rum

  ¼ ounce Rhum Clément Créole Shrubb

  ¾ ounce fresh lime juice

  ¼ ounce Honey Syrup (page 284)

  ¼ ounce Cinnamon Syrup (page 283)

  2 dashes Peychaud's bitters

  1½ ounces dry apple cider

  Garnish: 1 strawberry and 1 orange wheel

In a shaker, gently muddle the strawberry. Add the remaining ingredients except the cider and shake with ice. Double strain into a collins glass and fill the glass with ice cubes. Top with the cider, garnish with the strawberry and orange wheel, and serve with a straw.

⊙ LOW ABV   ⊘ NO ABV   ❄ FREEZER BAR   ⧖ PROJECT COCKTAIL   ❄❄ LOW-PREP COCKTAIL

LIPSTICK VOGUE ✻

Tyson Buhler, 2016

2 ounces Etienne Dupont Cidre

1½ ounces Lemorton Pommeau de Normandie

¼ ounce Lejay crème de cassis de Dijon

½ ounce Bowmore 12-year scotch

½ ounce fresh lemon juice

¼ ounce simple syrup (page 287)

Garnish: 1 dehydrated apple slice

Pour the cider into a wine glass. Short shake the remaining ingredients with ice for about 5 seconds, then strain into the glass. Fill the glass with ice cubes and garnish with the dehydrated apple slice.

LONG CON

Tyson Buhler, 2015

2 ounces Isastegi Spanish cider

1½ ounces Linie aquavit

½ ounce Laird's bonded apple brandy

¾ ounce fresh lemon juice

½ ounce Demerara Syrup (page 283)

¼ ounce Don's Spices (page 298)

Garnish: 1 apple fan

Pour the cider into a collins glass. Short shake the remaining ingredients with ice for about 5 seconds, then strain into the glass. Fill the glass with ice cubes and garnish with the apple fan.

LONG DIVISION ✻

Jon Feuersanger, 2019

This is a fun variation on an espresso and tonic, which is one of my favorite summertime coffee drinks. The black strap rum and ristretto deepen the coffee flavor and add depth and dynamics. —JF

2 ounces cold tonic water

1 ounce Clear Creek 2-year apple brandy

½ ounce Highland Park 12-year scotch

¼ ounce Cruzan Black Strap rum

¼ ounce Galliano Ristretto

1 ounce cold brew coffee

1 teaspoon Demerara Syrup (page 283)

Pour the tonic into a double old-fashioned glass over 1 large ice cube. Shake the remaining ingredients with ice, then slowly strain over the ice to float the drink over the tonic. No garnish.

LOST CAUSE ☉

Jon Armstrong, 2016

I love super dry, funky, Norman barnyard ciders, so this is my attempt to make a domestic cider taste like that. Combining it with sparkling wine (especially a grower champagne) adds some yeastiness, and the duo of pear liqueur and pear eau-de-vie adds notes of baking spices. At the bar we'd make a batch of this and carbonate it, and we found that its flavors improve with time. —JA

3 ounces Aval cider

2 ounces dry sparkling wine

½ ounce St. George spiced pear liqueur

1 teaspoon Vanilla Syrup (page 288)

1 teaspoon Clear Creek pear eau-de-vie

Chill all the ingredients. Pour the cider and sparkling wine into a chilled flute, then add the remaining ingredients. No garnish.

LUDICROUS SPEED

Tyson Buhler, 2016

A bright, slightly spicy shandy-inspired cocktail that always hits the spot on hot nights. I 100 percent stole this name from concept-cocktail king Brad Farran. —TB

1 lime wedge

Kosher salt

2 ounces Victory Prima Pils

1 ounce La Favorite rhum agricole blanc

½ ounce Jalapeño-Infused Siembra Valles Blanco Tequila (page 291)

¾ ounce fresh lime juice

½ ounce Pineapple Gum Syrup (page 286)

1 fresh makrut lime leaf

Garnish: 1 lime wedge

Rub the lime wedge along the upper ½ inch of a pilsner glass, halfway around the circumference, then roll the wet portion in the salt. Pour the beer into the glass. Shake the remaining ingredients with ice, then strain into the glass and fill the glass with ice cubes. Garnish with the lime wedge.

MOON MAGIC ☉

Alex Jump and Alex Day, 2018

When we opened the Garden Bar, we were bottling a lot of the drinks. This one tastes like a funky root beer. Vanilla and birch play really well with the Pineau, which is a great, versatile base for low-ABV drinks, and gives us an opportunity to talk to guests about an ingredient they haven't tried before. —AJ

3 ounces cava

1½ ounces Park Pineau des Charentes

¼ ounce Rhum JM VSOP

1 ounce Fusion verjus blanc

¼ ounce Vanilla Syrup (page 288)

1 drop Terra Spice birch extract

Garnish: 1 edible flower

Pour the cava into a wine glass. Add the remaining ingredients and fill the glass with ice cubes. Stir once and garnish with the edible flower.

MOON RIVER

Tyson Buhler, 2018

1½ ounces Lillet blanc

1 ounce Strawberry-Infused Plymouth Gin (page 294)

½ ounce Avuá Prata cachaça

½ ounce Marie Brizard white crème de cacao

¼ ounce Lactic Acid Solution (page 299)

1 teaspoon Cane Sugar Syrup (page 282)

1 ounce water

Chill all the ingredients. Combine them in a carbonating bottle, charge with CO_2, and gently shake to help dissolve the CO_2 into the liquid (see page 162 for detailed carbonation instructions). Refrigerate the carbonating bottle for at least 20 minutes, and preferably for 12 hours, before opening. Pour into a chilled flute. No garnish.

MOONRUNNER

Alex Jump and Jon Feuersanger, 2019

This is meant to be a crusher, with the layers of grapefruit flavors on top of the gin base. We make our grapefruit cordial with spent grapefruit, and the Giffard pamplemousse adds a candied citrus note. —AJ

¾ ounce Lillet rosé

1 ounce Beefeater gin

¼ ounce Giffard crème de pamplemousse rose

¾ ounce Grapefruit Cordial (page 283)

¼ ounce fresh lemon juice

1½ ounces sparkling rosé

Garnish: 1 grapefruit half wheel and 1 viola flower

Pour the Lillet rosé into a collins glass. Short shake the remaining ingredients with ice for about 5 seconds, then strain into the glass. Fill the glass with ice cubes and garnish with the grapefruit half wheel and the viola.

OUTRIGGER

Matthew Belanger, 2019

There's a classic tequila drink called Batanga that's said to have been created by the inventor of the Paloma. It's basically a Cuba Libre with tequila instead of rum, but instead of using cola, I brought those flavors to the drink with the Ramazzotti, tamarind syrup, and a drop of cola extract. —MB

4 ounces cold seltzer

1¼ ounces El Tesoro Reposado tequila

½ ounce Amaro Ramazzotti

¼ ounce Hamilton Jamaican Pot Still Black Rum

¾ ounce Tamarind Demerara Syrup (page 288)

1 teaspoon acid phosphate

1 drop Terra Spice cola extract

Garnish: 1 lime wedge

Pour the seltzer into a collins glass. Short shake the remaining ingredients with ice for about 5 seconds, then strain into the glass. Fill the glass with ice cubes and garnish with the lime wedge.

OUTRIGGER ⊘

Matthew Belanger, 2019

Nonalcoholic drinks often need something to give them body, which usually comes from spirits. Here, the pectin from fresh pineapple juice adds a lot of texture. —MB

3 ounces cold seltzer

1½ ounces Seedlip Spice 94

1½ ounces fresh pineapple juice

¾ ounce Tamarind Demerara Syrup (page 288)

1 teaspoon acid phosphate

1 drop Terra Spice cola extract

Garnish: 1 lime wedge

Pour the seltzer into a collins glass. Short shake the remaining ingredients with ice for about 5 seconds, then strain into the glass. Fill the glass with ice cubes and garnish with the lime wedge.

PARALLEL LIVES ⁂

Matthew Belanger, 2019

This riff on one of our staff-favorite classics, the Bizzy Izzy Highball, combines oxidatively aged wine, gin, and pineapple in a highball. St. George's rye-based gin is barrel aged and tastes almost like genever. —MB

1 ounce cold seltzer

1½ ounces Henriques & Henriques rainwater madeira

½ ounce St. George Dry Rye reposado gin

1 ounce fresh pineapple juice

¾ ounce fresh lemon juice

½ ounce simple syrup (page 287)

1 dash Angostura bitters

Garnish: 1 pineapple wedge and Angostura bitters

Pour the seltzer into a collins glass. Short shake the remaining ingredients with ice for about 5 seconds, then strain into the glass. Fill the glass with ice cubes. Garnish with the pineapple wedge and dash some Angostura bitters onto the pineapple.

KINGSTON AMERICANO, PAGE 184

REPEATER ⧗

Matthew Belanger, 2019

I've created a few spritzes that have a similar template (hence the name); this one is very floral, with the grappa pumping up the aromatic quality of the brandy. Instead of carbonating the drink, you can also omit the water, stir, and strain over the sparkling wine. —MB

- 2 ounces dry sparkling wine
- 1¼ ounces Bertoux brandy
- ½ ounce Italicus Rosolio bergamot liqueur
- ¼ ounce Clear Creek Muscat Grappa
- ¼ ounce Bay Leaf Syrup (page 282)
- ½ teaspoon Citric Acid Solution (page 299)
- 1 ounce water
- Garnish: 1 bay leaf

Chill all the ingredients. Combine them in a carbonating bottle, charge with CO_2, and gently shake to help dissolve the CO_2 into the liquid (see page 162 for detailed carbonation instructions). Refrigerate the carbonating bottle for at least 20 minutes, and preferably for 12 hours, before opening. Pour into a chilled flute and garnish with the bay leaf.

RON COCO

George Nunez, 2019

- 1 ounce El Dorado 8-year rum
- 1 ounce oloroso sherry
- 4 ounces Harmless Harvest coconut water
- 1 teaspoon Cane Sugar Syrup (page 282)
- 0.3 g Citric Acid Solution (page 299)
- 2 dashes Angostura bitters
- Garnish: 1 lemon wedge

Chill all the ingredients. Combine them in a carbonating bottle, charge with CO_2, and gently shake to help dissolve the CO_2 into the liquid (see page 162 for detailed

carbonation instructions). Refrigerate the carbonating bottle for at least 20 minutes, and preferably for 12 hours, before opening. Pour into a fizz glass and fill the glass with ice cubes. Garnish with the lemon wedge.

SAVAGE ISLANDS ☉

Tyson Buhler, 2016

This is a low-ABV version of the Bizzy Izzy Highball. I love the fruitiness of the tropical, hazy IPA balanced by the nuttiness of the madeira. —TB

- 2 ounces Stillwater Nu-Tropic IPA
- 2 ounces Henriques & Henriques rainwater madeira
- 1 ounce fresh pineapple juice
- ½ ounce fresh lemon juice
- ½ ounce simple syrup (page 287)
- 1 dash Angostura bitters
- Garnish: 1 dehydrated pineapple slice

Pour the beer into a pilsner glass. Short shake the remaining ingredients with ice for about 5 seconds, then strain into the glass. Fill the glass with ice cubes and garnish with the dehydrated pineapple slice.

SCARLET TANAGER ⧗

Matthew Belanger, 2018

This drink was inspired by an Evil Twin sour beer flavored with niçoise olives and strawberry. —MB

- 1 ounce Cappelletti Vino Aperitivo
- ½ ounce Niçoise Olive–Infused Yaguara Ouro Cachaça (page 293)
- ½ ounce Strawberry Syrup (page 287)
- 1 teaspoon Citric Acid Solution (page 299)
- 1 dash Salt Solution (page 299)
- 1 ounce water
- 3 ounces dry sparkling wine
- Garnish: 1 olive on a skewer

Chill all the ingredients. Combine them in a carbonating bottle, charge with CO_2, and gently shake to help dissolve the CO_2 into the liquid (see page 162 for detailed carbonation instructions). Refrigerate the carbonating bottle for at least 20 minutes, and preferably for 12 hours, before opening. Pour into a chilled flute and garnish with the olive.

SEVEN YEAR ITCH ❀

Eryn Reece, 2014

- 1½ ounces dry sparkling wine
- 1½ ounces Lemorton Selection calvados domfrontais
- ½ ounce yellow Chartreuse
- ¾ ounce fresh lemon juice
- ½ ounce Cane Sugar Syrup (page 282)
- 1 dash Bitter Truth aromatic bitters

Pour the sparkling wine into a chilled coupe. Shake the remaining ingredients with ice, then double strain into the coupe. No garnish.

SHOGANAI

Dave Anderson, 2019

I learned to appreciate the simplicity of highballs when I worked at an izakaya, so I wanted to create a drink in that style. The name actually came to me first: "Shoganai" is Japanese slang that doesn't have an English equivalent, but is a way of saying "it can't be helped" or "I'm throwing in towel." Ironically, the drink took a lot of collaboration to create. Making a highball with champagne instead of soda is complicated, as the wine adds a lot of flavor. The cider was a curveball, too; it was added after Tyson asked "What about Japanese whisky, champagne, and apples?" —DA

- 1 ounce Hibiki Japanese Harmony whisky
- 1 teaspoon Cyril Zangs 00 apple cider eau-de-vie

1 teaspoon Cane Sugar Syrup
(page 282)

2 dashes Champagne Acid Solution
(page 299)

1½ ounces Aval cider

1½ ounces dry sparkling wine

Garnish: 1 apple fan

In a collins glass, combine the whisky, cider eau-de-vie, cane sugar syrup, and champagne acid solution. Fill the glass with ice cubes and top with the cider and sparkling wine. Garnish with the apple fan.

SILVERHEELS ⚜

Jon Feuersanger, 2019

Tyson likes to name cocktails after Westerns, so this cocktail pokes fun at that (Silverheels was the last name of the actor who played Tonto). This is a beer cocktail made with ingredients I love, with the pineapple and crushed ice adding a tiki element. —JF

2 ounces dry apple cider

1 ounce High West Silver oat whiskey

1 ounce Clear Creek 2-year apple brandy

1 ounce fresh pineapple juice

½ ounce Cane Sugar Syrup
(page 282)

½ ounce fresh lemon juice

2 dashes Bittermens 'Elemakule tiki bitters

Garnish: 1 apple slice and 1 mint bouquet

Pour the cider into a pilsner glass. Combine the remaining ingredients in a shaker and whip, shaking with a few pieces of crushed ice, just until incorporated. Dump into the glass and fill the glass with crushed ice. Garnish with the apple slice and mint bouquet and serve with a straw.

SINERGIA ⚜

Brandon Parker, 2018

¾ ounce Rittenhouse rye

½ ounce Laird's bonded apple brandy

¼ ounce Smith & Cross Jamaica rum

¼ ounce St. George spiced pear liqueur

½ ounce fresh lemon juice

½ ounce Cane Sugar Syrup
(page 282)

1½ ounces Lambrusco

Shake all the ingredients except the Lambrusco with ice, then strain into a double old-fashioned glass over 1 large ice cube. Slowly pour the Lambrusco over the back of a spoon to float it on top of the drink. No garnish.

SLIGHTLY STORMY

Alex Jump, Dave Anderson, and Jon Feuersanger, 2019

This is essentially a Dark and Stormy variation, with a nod to Tyson's Starfish and Coffee (page 190), which layers coffee on top of tonic. —AJ

1 ounce tonic water

1½ ounces Jameson Irish whiskey

½ ounce Cruzan Black Strap rum

½ ounce fresh lemon juice

½ ounce House Ginger Syrup
(page 284)

¼ ounce cold brew coffee

Garnish: 1 piece ginger candy on a skewer

Pour the tonic into a collins glass. Short shake the remaining ingredients with ice for about 5 seconds, then strain into the glass. Fill the glass with ice cubes. Garnish with the ginger candy.

SOUND AND FURY

Tyson Buhler, 2015

Raspberry and red bell pepper is an oddball pairing that works remarkably well here, especially alongside the savory and vanilla notes of the Calle 23 blanco tequila. —TB

1 lime wedge

Aleppo salt (equal parts Aleppo pepper and kosher salt)

2 ounces Calle 23 blanco tequila

½ ounce Ancho Reyes ancho chile liqueur

¾ ounce fresh lime juice

½ ounce fresh red bell pepper juice

¾ ounce Raspberry Syrup (page 286)

Garnish: 1 lime wheel

Rub the lime wedge along the upper ½ inch of a collins glass, halfway around the circumference, then roll the wet portion in the salt. Shake the remaining ingredients with ice, then strain into the glass and fill the glass with ice cubes. Garnish with the lime wheel.

SPRITZ ROSELLE

Matthew Belanger, 2019

2 ounces dry sparkling wine

1 ounce Lo-Fi gentian amaro

½ ounce Capurro Acholado pisco

¼ ounce Suze

¼ ounce Giffard passion fruit liqueur

¼ ounce Cane Sugar Syrup
(page 282)

¼ teaspoon Citric Acid Solution
(page 299)

Garnish: 1 edible flower

Pour the sparkling wine into a wine glass. Stir the remaining ingredients over ice, then strain into the glass and fill the glass with ice cubes. Garnish with the edible flower.

STARFISH AND COFFEE

Tyson Buhler, 2016

Right before service, I used to pop around the corner and grab an espresso and tonic from a great little coffee shop in the East Village, which led to the inspiration for this drink. Layering the drink not only looks great, but also creates different flavors throughout the life of the cocktail. I had this drink name, which is a Prince song, on my list for a while, but couldn't match it with the right cocktail until this came along. —TB

- 3 ounces tonic water
- 1 ounce Gosling's Black Seal rum
- 1 ounce Punt e Mes
- 1 ounce cold brew concentrate
- ¼ ounce Vanilla Syrup (page 288)

Pour the tonic into a double old-fashioned glass over 1 large ice cube. Shake the remaining ingredients with ice, then slowly strain over the ice to float the drink over the tonic. No garnish.

TANDEM JUMP

Jarred Weigand, 2018

I'd always wanted to have a tequila sparkling cocktail, but never saw one. I'd also never had a coffee-flavored champagne cocktail, but I knew there was a flavor affinity in there somewhere, as in a Black Velvet. Avuá Amburana is a cinnamon bomb and ties it all together. —JW

- 1½ ounces dry sparkling wine
- 1 ounce Avuá Amburana cachaça
- ½ ounce Tapatío Anejo tequila
- ¼ ounce Galliano Ristretto
- ½ ounce cold brew concentrate
- ½ ounce Pineapple Gum Syrup (page 286)

Pour the sparkling wine into a chilled coupe. Shake the remaining ingredients with ice, then double strain into the glass. No garnish.

TINY FORTUNES

Kenny Martinez, 2019

- 2 ounces cold seltzer
- 1 ounce Woody Creek vodka
- ½ ounce Barsol pisco
- ½ ounce fresh lemon juice
- ¾ ounce Blackberry Syrup (see Raspberry Syrup on page 286 and substitute blackberries for raspberries)
- ¼ ounce Dolin Génépy des Alpes liqueur
- Garnish: 1 lemon wheel and 1 blackberry on a skewer

Pour the seltzer into a collins glass. Short shake the remaining ingredients with ice for about 5 seconds, then strain into the glass. Fill the glass with ice cubes. Garnish with the lemon wheel and blackberry.

URSA MAJOR

Matthew Belanger, 2019

- 4 ounces cold-brewed Rare Tea Company genmaicha
- 2 ounces St. George California rice shochu
- ¼ ounce Marie Brizard white crème de cacao
- ½ ounce Vanilla Syrup (page 288)
- ½ teaspoon lactart
- Garnish: 1 lemon twist

Chill all the ingredients. Combine them in a carbonating bottle, charge with CO_2, and gently shake to help dissolve the CO_2 into the liquid (see page 162 for detailed carbonation instructions). Refrigerate the carbonating bottle for at least 20 minutes, and preferably for 12 hours, before opening. Pour into a fizz glass and fill the glass with ice cubes. Express the lemon twist over the drink, then place it in the drink.

VELVET BUZZSAW

Matt Hunt, 2019

This is the love child of a Campari Spritz and a Clover Club. We kegged this drink and put it on draft. The staff loved it because we sold a ton of these, which bought the bartenders a lot of time. —MH

- 2 ounces cold seltzer
- 1¼ ounces Beefeater gin
- ½ ounce Giffard rhubarb liqueur
- ¼ ounce Campari
- ¼ ounce Dolin blanc vermouth
- ¾ ounce Raspberry Syrup (page 286)
- ½ ounce fresh lemon juice
- Garnish: 1 lemon wheel and 1 viola flower

Pour the seltzer into a wine glass. Stir the remaining ingredients over ice, then strain into the glass. Fill the glass with ice cubes and garnish with the lemon wheel and viola.

WALKIN' AFTER MIDNIGHT ☉

Jarred Weigand, 2018

The pairing of Sauternes and cognac in this collins variation is a smart combination; the fruit notes in both ingredients go well together. The Suze adds a passion fruit flavor and gentian bitterness. —JW

- 2 ounces cold seltzer
- 1 ounce Chateau La Fleur d'Or Sauternes
- 1 ounce Pierre Ferrand ambré cognac
- ½ ounce Suze
- ½ ounce fresh lemon juice
- ½ ounce Passion Fruit Syrup (page 285)
- Garnish: 1 lemon wheel

Pour the seltzer into a collins glass. Short shake the remaining ingredients with ice for about 5 seconds, then strain into the glass. Fill the glass with ice cubes and garnish with the lemon wheel.

WATER-TIGER ✦

Matthew Belanger, 2019

2 ounces Dewazikura Tobiroku sparkling sake

1 ounce Suntory Roku gin

¾ ounce Carpano Bianco vermouth

¼ ounce Chareau aloe liqueur

½ ounce Fusion verjus blanc

1 dash absinthe

Garnish: 1 cucumber slice

Pour the sake into a chilled flute. Stir the remaining ingredients over ice, then double strain into the flute. Garnish with the cucumber slice.

WEIRD FICTION ☉

Al Sotack, 2014

A traditional cobbler wouldn't have a citrusy element, so the acid phosphate creates a cobbler-style drink that drinks like a sour. —AS

1 orange slice

1 ounce Laphroaig 10-year scotch

1 ounce red wine

½ ounce amontillado sherry

¼ ounce yellow Chartreuse

¼ ounce Amaro Nonino

½ ounce Demerara Syrup (page 283)

Scant 1 teaspoon acid phosphate

Garnish: 1 orange slice and at least 2 seasonal berries (raspberry, blackberry, strawberry)

In a shaker, gently muddle the orange slice. Add the remaining ingredients and short shake with ice for about 5 seconds, then strain into a collins glass. Fill the glass with crushed ice and garnish with the orange slice and berries.

WHATEVEREST ☉

Jarred Weigand, 2018

Every menu needs a basic, approachable drink. This one is clean and effervescent, but still interesting. The dill aquavit plays perfectly with the grassy, vegetable notes of tequila. —JW

2 cucumber slices

1 ounce Tapatio Blanco 110 tequila

1 ounce Dolin dry vermouth

½ ounce Gamle Ode dill aquavit

¾ ounce fresh lemon juice

½ ounce simple syrup (page 287)

1 teaspoon House Ginger Syrup (page 284)

1 dash Bitter Truth celery bitters

Garnish: 1 cucumber slice

In a shaker, gently muddle the cucumber slices. Add the remaining ingredients and shake with ice. Double strain into a collins glass and fill the glass with ice cubes. Garnish with the cucumber slice.

WINDUP BIRD

Tyson Buhler, 2014

With its high acidity and salinity, gose is such a fun cocktail ingredient. Here, it helps tame the sweetness and fruitiness of the watermelon syrup and Aperol while still keeping the drink a crowd-pleaser. —TB

1 lemon wedge

Kosher salt

2 ounces Westbrook gose beer

1 ounce Krogstad aquavit

1 ounce Aperol

1 ounce Watermelon Syrup (page 288)

½ ounce fresh lemon juice

½ ounce Chareau aloe liqueur

Rub the lemon wedge along the upper ½ inch of a collins glass, halfway around the circumference, then roll the wet portion in the salt. Pour the beer into the glass. Shake the remaining ingredients with ice, then strain into the glass. Fill the glass with ice cubes. No garnish.

ZOUZOU

Tyson Buhler, 2017

2 ounces cold seltzer

1½ ounces Guillon-Painturaud VSOP cognac

½ ounce Scarlet Ibis Trinidad rum

¾ ounce Cocchi Americano

¾ ounce fresh lemon juice

½ ounce House Ginger Syrup (page 284)

1 teaspoon Rothman & Winter Orchard apricot liqueur

Garnish: 1 orange half wheel

Pour the seltzer into a collins glass. Short shake the remaining ingredients with ice for about 5 seconds, then strain into the glass. Fill the glass with ice cubes and garnish with the orange half wheel.

Light & Playful

⊙ LOW ABV   ⊘ NO ABV   ❄ FREEZER BAR   ⧗ PROJECT COCKTAIL   ❋ LOW-PREP COCKTAIL

ART OF SCRATCHING

Al Sotack, 2015

This crowd-pleaser is a Between the Sheets–style Sidecar meets Daiquiri riff, and uses the same strawberry basil syrup as my Trampoline (page 206). —AS

1 ounce Pierre Ferrand 1840 cognac

1 ounce Wray & Nephew Jamaican rum

1 teaspoon Rhum Clément Créole Shrubb

1 teaspoon Marie Brizard white crème de cacao

¾ ounce Strawberry Basil Syrup (page 287)

½ ounce fresh lemon juice

¼ ounce fresh lime juice

2 dashes Angostura bitters

Garnish: 1 lemon twist

Shake all the ingredients with ice, then double strain into a chilled coupe. Express the lemon twist over the drink and discard.

ATLANTIC PACIFIC

Matthew Belanger, 2017

All rhum agricole has a grassy quality, but La Favorite has a particular briny quality that reminds me of seaweed. I wanted to work that into a Daiquiri that also incorporated the combination of yuzu and nori. If you can't find Diplomático rum, swap in Plantation 3 Stars, Probitas, or Flor de Caña 4. —MB

1½ ounces Diplomático Planas rum

½ ounce Nori-Infused La Favorite Rhum Agricole Blanc (page 293)

½ ounce Umenoyado Yuzu Shu liqueur

¾ ounce fresh lime juice

½ ounce Cane Sugar Syrup (page 282)

Shake all the ingredients with ice, then double strain into a chilled coupe. No garnish.

AWKWARDLY TONGUE TIED

Jarred Weigand, 2015

This was the first cocktail I ever landed on a D&C menu, back when I was promoted from barback to bartender, a move nobody else had made. This was the highest moment of my bartending career. I love the way Fernet pairs with pineapple, and the orgeat and cinnamon syrup amplify those flavors a bit. —JW

2 ounces Fords gin

1 teaspoon Fernet-Branca

½ ounce fresh pineapple juice

½ ounce fresh lime juice

¼ ounce Cinnamon Syrup (page 283)

¼ ounce House Orgeat (page 284)

Garnish: 1 lime wheel

Shake all the ingredients with ice, then double strain into a chilled coupe. Garnish with the lime wheel.

BEACH HOUSE GIMLET ⚜

Shannon Ponche, 2020

1¼ ounces Tanqueray gin

¾ ounce St. George Green Chile vodka

¾ ounce fresh lime juice

½ ounce Cane Sugar Syrup (page 282)

1 teaspoon Giffard crème de banana

1 dash absinthe

Shake all the ingredients with ice, then double strain into a chilled coupe. No garnish.

BUKO GIMLET

Matthew Belanger, 2019

Across the street from Death & Co LA there's an excellent Asian-Californian restaurant called Nightshade, where they serve a delicious take on buko pandan, a Filipino dessert made with pandan gelatin and coconut. I reimagined those ingredients in a cocktail, pulling in a citrusy gin flavored with finger limes as the base. You can usually find frozen pandan leaves in Asian markets, or you can add a drop of pandan extract to cane sugar syrup. —MB

1 ounce Four Pillars Navy Strength gin

¾ ounce Novo Fogo cachaça

¼ ounce Kalani Ron de Coco coconut liqueur

¾ ounce fresh lime juice

½ ounce Pandan Syrup (page 285)

½ ounce Harmless Harvest coconut water

Garnish: Lime zest

Shake all the ingredients with ice, then strain into a double old-fashioned glass over 1 large ice cube. Grate some lime zest over the top of the drink.

CITY CLUB

Matthew Belanger, 2019

This is a Clover Club variation, swapping strawberry and basil in for the classic raspberry. Wray & Nephew rum has a super-high ester count, and adding it to the drink would overwhelm the other delicate flavors, so I opted to spray some of it on top. If you don't have an atomizer, add 1 drop to the top of the cocktail. —MB

1 ounce Capurro Acholado pisco

½ ounce St. George Aqua Perfecta basil eau-de-vie

½ ounce Dolin dry vermouth

¾ ounce fresh lemon juice

¾ ounce Strawberry Syrup (page 287)

1 egg white

Garnish: Wray & Nephew Jamaican rum in an atomizer

Dry shake all the ingredients, then shake again with ice. Double strain into a chilled coupe and spray some rum over the top of the drink.

CONCRETE JUNGLE

Matthew Belanger, 2017

This drink was inspired by the street snack of dried mangos with chile powder and lime, and a variation of a Scott Teague drink called the Firing Pin (page 215), which is also made with Cholula. —MB

1½ ounces Elijah Craig 12-year bourbon

½ ounce Yaguara Ouro cachaça

1 ounce fresh lemon juice

½ ounce House Orgeat (page 284)

¼ ounce Cane Sugar Syrup (page 282)

¼ ounce Perfect Purée mango purée

1 teaspoon Cholula hot sauce

Garnish: 1 orchid flower

Combine all the ingredients in a shaker and whip, shaking with a few pieces of crushed ice, just until incorporated. Dump into a tulip glass and fill the glass with crushed ice. Garnish with the orchid.

CONGRESS PARK SWIZZLE ⊙

Keely Sutherland, 2019

3 to 5 mint leaves

1 ounce Dolin blanc vermouth

½ ounce Appleton Estate Reserve Jamaica rum

½ ounce Rhine Hall mango brandy

¾ ounce fresh lime juice

½ ounce Pineapple Gum Syrup (page 286)

Garnish: 1 mint bouquet and Peychaud's bitters

In a cocktail shaker, gently muddle the mint leaves. Add the remaining ingredients and whip, shaking with a few pieces of crushed ice, just until incorporated. Dump into a collins glass and fill the glass with crushed ice. Garnish with the mint bouquet and dash some Peychaud's bitters over the top of the drink. Serve with a straw.

CRIME DOG

Tyson Buhler, 2018

This is nothing more than a Paloma with the addition of Aperol. At Death & Co Denver, we bottled this drink and it flew off the shelves all summer in the Garden. —TB

3 ounces cold seltzer

1½ ounces Olmeca Altos Blanco tequila

1 ounce Grapefruit Cordial (page 283)

½ ounce Aperol

Garnish: 1 grapefruit twist

Pour the seltzer into a collins glass. Add the remaining ingredients to the glass and fill with ice cubes. Garnish with the grapefruit twist.

CRUEL TO BE KIND ⚜

Al Sotack, 2014

1½ ounces Tanqueray gin

½ ounce Bonal Gentiane-Quina

¾ ounce fresh lime juice

½ ounce fresh grapefruit juice

½ ounce Honey Syrup (page 284)

1 dash Dale DeGroff's pimento bitters

Garnish: 1 lime wheel

Shake all the ingredients with ice, then double strain into a chilled coupe. Garnish with the lime wheel.

CURTIS PARK SWIZZLE

Tyson Buhler, 2018

Beginning with Alex Day's delicious Coffey Park Swizzle, this continues the D&C trend of split-base sherry swizzles. This one uses the floral Singani 63 brandy from Bolivia, and is named after Denver's Curtis Park, which is near our bar. —TB

1 ounce Singani 63 eau-de-vie

1 ounce Lustau Los Arcos amontillado sherry

¾ ounce House Ginger Syrup (page 284)

½ ounce fresh lime juice

2 dashes absinthe

Garnish: 1 mint bouquet and Angostura bitters

Short shake all the ingredients with ice for about 5 seconds, then strain into a collins glass. Fill the glass with crushed ice. Garnish with the mint bouquet and dash some Angostura bitters over the top of the drink. Serve with a straw.

DAISY DE JALISCO

Matthew Belanger, 2019

Drinks in the Standing Room at Death & Co LA are designed to be more sustainable and use waste left over from our prep kitchen. So instead of using fresh lime juice, we make a hopped lime acid—basically a mix of acids that mimics lime juice—and blend citra hops into it, which adds tropical fruit notes. —MB

1½ ounces Cimarron Reposado tequila

½ ounce Blume Marillen apricot eau-de-vie

¾ ounce Pineapple Gum Syrup (page 286)

¾ ounce Hopped Lime Acid (page 299)

Garnish: 1 pineapple wedge

Shake all the ingredients with ice, then strain into a double old-fashioned glass over 1 large ice cube. Garnish with the pineapple wedge.

DHALIA

Tyson Buhler, 2017

Umenoyado umeshu is very different from most found in the United States, and its juicy, rich texture is so good on its own that it doesn't need much enhancement. Here, I added a little whisky, primarily to add proof and dryness to the drink, and spice from the cinnamon syrup and bitters make a very easy-drinking sour. —TB

1½ ounces Umenoyado umeshu

¾ ounce Nikka Coffey Grain Japanese whisky

½ ounce fresh lemon juice

½ ounce Cinnamon Syrup (page 283)

1 dash Bitter Truth aromatic bitters

Garnish: 1 edible flower

Shake all the ingredients with ice, then double strain into a chilled Nick & Nora glass. Garnish with the edible flower.

DIAL 'M' ♣

Al Sotack, 2014

1 ounce Laird's bonded apple brandy

1 ounce Bols genever

1 teaspoon Angostura bitters

1 ounce fresh grapefruit juice

½ ounce maple syrup

Garnish: 1 grapefruit twist

Shake all the ingredients with ice, then strain into a double old-fashioned glass over 1 large ice cube. Express the grapefruit twist over the drink and discard.

DOCTOR ZHIVAGO

Matthew Belanger, 2018

Another one in our ongoing series of tiki drinks named after "doctors." Amrut is a very tasty, very strong whisky from India that has tropical fruit notes. Other than that, it's similar to a Doctor Funk, a 1953 Don the Beachcomber classic. —MB

1 ounce Amrut cask-strength single-malt Indian whisky

½ ounce El Dorado 15-year Demerara rum

½ ounce Batavia arrack

¾ ounce fresh lime juice

¾ ounce House Grenadine (page 284)

6 dashes absinthe

Garnish: 1 orchid flower

Short shake all the ingredients with ice for about 5 seconds, then strain into a collins glass. Fill the glass with crushed ice and garnish with the orchid.

DUNMORE ⊘

Adam Griggs, 2019

This no-ABV, Daiquiri-style cocktail uses Seedlip Spice 94 as its base. I like the Seedlip line of nonalcoholic spirits a lot, but they don't have much texture, so I added a good amount of pineapple juice to beef it up. —AG

1½ ounces Seedlip Spice 94

1½ ounces fresh pineapple juice

1 ounce fresh lime juice

¾ ounce Tonic Syrup (page 288)

¾ teaspoon Perfect Purée mango purée

¾ teaspoon Vanilla Syrup (page 288)

Shake all the ingredients with ice, then double strain into a chilled coupe. No garnish.

ESCADRILLE

Dave Anderson, 2018

This was my first Death & Co spec, and the one I'm most proud of. It's based on the Infante, a classic tequila drink that's basically a tequila Daiquiri with orgeat as the sweetener. In this variation I split the base between brandy and rum to bring an autumnal flavor profile to an otherwise summery cocktail. (You can also use Cobrafire eau-de-vie de raisin in place of the Armagnac.) —DA

1 ounce Domaine d'Espérance blanche Armagnac

¾ ounce Rhum JM Blanc

¼ ounce Avuá Amburana cachaça

1 ounce fresh lime juice

¾ ounce House Orgeat (page 284)

4 dashes St. Elizabeth allspice dram

Garnish: Nutmeg

Shake all the ingredients with ice, then strain into a double old-fashioned glass over 1 large ice cube. Grate some nutmeg over the top of the drink.

FALSE ALARM

Matthew Belanger, 2019

Basically a Mexican Firing Squad with papaya instead of grenadine, similar to Doctor Mindbender. Green chile vodka has tons of cilantro flavor. This drink evokes green papaya salad flavor: chiles, lime, cilantro, a little funk from Clairin. —MB

- 1¼ ounces El Tesoro Blanco tequila
- ½ ounce St. George green chile vodka
- ¼ ounce Clairin Sajous rum
- ¾ ounce fresh lime juice
- ¾ ounce Papaya Syrup (page 285)
- 2 dashes Bittermens Hellfire habanero shrub
- Garnish: 1 lime wheel and 1 piece dried papaya on a skewer

Combine all the ingredients in a shaker and whip, shaking with a few pieces of crushed ice, just until incorporated. Dump into a pilsner glass and fill the glass with crushed ice. Garnish with the lime wheel and dried papaya and serve with a straw.

FALSE ALARM ⊙

Matthew Belanger, 2019

With so many spirits in small amounts, this drink is a pain in the ass to make during service, so we batch the spirits in a cheater bottle. If you're going to make a bunch of these at home, I suggest you do the same. —MB

- 2 ounces Gilles Brisson Pineau des Charentes
- ¼ ounce El Tesoro Blanco tequila
- 1 teaspoon St. George green chile vodka
- ½ teaspoon Clairin Sajous rum
- ¾ ounce Papaya Syrup (page 285)
- ¾ ounce fresh lime juice
- 2 dashes Bittermens Hellfire habanero shrub
- Garnish: 1 lime wheel and 1 piece dried papaya on a skewer

Combine all the ingredients in a shaker and whip, shaking with a few pieces of crushed ice, just until incorporated. Dump into a pilsner glass and fill the glass with crushed ice. Garnish with the lime wheel and dried papaya and serve with a straw.

FINAL CUT

Tyson Buhler, 2016

I'm not sure how the bar team let me get away with using 55% ABV rye and cask-strength bourbon in the fruitiest whiskey sour on the menu, but I figured I'd run with it and float some funky, overproof Jamaican rum over the top for good measure. —TB

- 1½ ounces Pikesville rye
- ½ ounce Booker's bourbon
- 1 teaspoon Campari
- ¾ ounce fresh lemon juice
- ¾ ounce Raspberry Syrup (page 286)
- 1 teaspoon Hamilton Jamaican Pot Still Gold rum

Shake all the ingredients except the rum with ice, then strain into a double old-fashioned glass over 1 large ice cube. Slowly pour the rum over the back of a spoon to float it on top of the drink. No garnish.

FULTON ST. FIZZ

Brian Wyner, 2019

- 1 ounce dry sparkling wine
- ¾ ounce Dolin dry vermouth
- ¾ ounce Beefeater gin
- ½ ounce Rhine Hall cherry brandy
- ¾ ounce fresh lemon juice
- 1 ounce House Orgeat (page 284)
- 1 egg white
- Garnish: Peychaud's bitters

Pour the sparkling wine into a chilled fizz glass. Dry shake the remaining ingredients, then shake again with ice. Double strain into the glass. Dash a stripe of Peychaud's bitters over the top of the drink. No garnish.

GINGER MAN

Tyson Buhler, 2014

I love finding ways to take aggressive or esoteric spirits and make them approachable to all drinkers, and this simple spec does just that. Malt whiskey and melon are a dream pairing, and the spicy ginger is powerful enough to stand up to the Islay scotch and lends a familiar flavor profile. —TB

- 1½ ounces Laphroaig 10-year single malt scotch
- ¾ ounce fresh cantaloupe juice
- ¾ ounce fresh lemon juice
- ½ ounce House Ginger Syrup (page 284)
- 1 dash Angostura bitters

Shake all the ingredients with ice, then double strain into a chilled coupe. No garnish.

GOOD ENOUGH GATSBY

Sean Quinn, 2019

- 1½ ounces Wild Turkey 101 rye
- ½ ounce Clear Creek pear eau-de-vie
- ¾ ounce Cinnamon Syrup (page 283)
- ¾ ounce fresh pineapple juice
- ½ ounce fresh lime juice
- 1 teaspoon Fernet-Branca
- Garnish: 2 pineapple fronds and 1 cinnamon stick

Shake all the ingredients with ice, then strain into a double old-fashioned glass over 1 large ice cube. Garnish with the palm fronds and grate some cinnamon over the top of the drink.

FALSE ALARM, OPPOSITE

GRAMOPHONE

Tyson Buhler, 2018

- 1 ounce Chamomile-Infused Armagnac (page 290)
- 1 ounce Tanqueray London dry gin
- ½ ounce fresh pineapple juice
- ½ ounce fresh lemon juice
- ½ ounce Cinnamon Syrup (page 283)
- ¼ ounce Honey Syrup (page 284)

Shake all the ingredients with ice, then double strain into a chilled coupe. No garnish.

HAWAII FIVE-O

Matthew Belanger, 2017

Gin and rum aren't usually paired in a cocktail, so I challenged myself to build a drink around the combination, using the Saturn, a gin-based tiki classic, as inspiration. —MB

- 1½ ounces Tanqueray gin
- ½ ounce Rhum JM VSOP
- ¾ ounce fresh lime juice
- ½ ounce Orgeat Works Macadamia Nut Syrup
- ¼ ounce Passion Fruit Syrup (page 285)
- 1 teaspoon Trader Vic's macadamia nut liqueur
- 2 dashes Bittermens hopped grapefruit bitters
- Garnish: 1 mint bouquet and nutmeg

Combine all the ingredients in a shaker and whip, shaking with a few pieces of crushed ice, just until incorporated. Dump into a double old-fashioned glass and fill the glass with crushed ice. Garnish with the mint bouquet and grate some nutmeg over the top of the drink. Serve with a straw.

HIDDEN WORLD

Matthew Belanger, 2019

Del Maguey's Santo Domingo Albarradas is a very floral, delicate, and pretty mezcal, and is very different from the smoky, earthy mezcals you typically see in cocktails. Here, I use it in a drink inspired by eating a mango on vacation in Puerto Rico. —MB

- 1 ounce Del Maguey Santo Domingo Albarradas mezcal
- 1 ounce Krogstad aquavit
- ¾ ounce fresh lime juice
- ½ ounce Vanilla Syrup (page 288)
- 2 teaspoons Perfect Purée mango purée
- 1 teaspoon House Ginger Syrup (page 284)
- 1 dash Salt Solution (page 299)
- Garnish: 1 lime wheel

Shake all the ingredients with ice, then strain into a double old-fashioned glass over 1 large ice cube. Garnish with the lime wheel.

HUSTLE & CUSS

Jon Armstrong, 2016

- 2 ounces Buffalo Trace bourbon
- ¼ ounce Marie Brizard white crème de cacao
- ¾ ounce fresh lemon juice
- ½ ounce fresh grapefruit juice
- ¼ ounce Cinnamon Syrup (page 283)
- ¼ ounce maple syrup
- 1 dash Bitter Truth aromatic bitters
- Garnish: 1 grapefruit twist

Shake all the ingredients with ice, then double strain into a chilled coupe. Express the grapefruit twist over the drink, then place it in the drink.

IDA MEANS BUSINESS

Shannon Ponche, 2020

A lot of my cocktails lean savory, and I get a lot of inspiration from food. This cocktail has the flavors of a Thai coconut-based curry, with a base of peppery and earthy flavors from the tequila and Clairin; coconut from the Kalani, and the bitters filling in the blanks with galangal, lemongrass, and makrut lime. Celery is one of my favorite savory elements to use in drinks; it's fresh and light, and can work with both savory and spicy flavors. —SP

- 1¾ ounces Siembra Valles Blanco tequila
- ¼ ounce Clairin Vaval Haitian rum
- ¾ ounce fresh lime juice
- ¾ ounce Celery Syrup (page 282)
- 2 teaspoons Kalani Ron de Coco coconut liqueur
- 1 dash Bitter End Thai bitters

Shake all the ingredients with ice, then double strain into a chilled coupe. No garnish.

INSPECTOR NORSE

Jarred Weigand, 2018

They say some of the best songs are written in five minutes; likewise, this drink basically wrote itself during a subway ride. Our friend Natasha David made a Pimm's and carrot–based drink called the Wildcat at her bar, Nitecap, so I borrowed that combo and added a dill note from the aquavit. This bright-orange drink looks gorgeous, and with its mint garnish, a lot like a carrot. —JW

- 1 ounce Pimm's No. 1
- ¾ ounce Tanqueray gin
- ¼ ounce Gamle Ode dill aquavit
- 1 ounce fresh carrot juice
- ¾ ounce fresh lemon juice
- 2 teaspoons Orgeat Works Macadamia Nut Syrup
- 1 teaspoon Trader Vic's macadamia nut liqueur
- 1 teaspoon House Ginger Syrup (page 284)
- Garnish: 1 mint bouquet

Short shake all the ingredients with ice for about 5 seconds, then strain into a pilsner glass. Fill the glass with crushed ice. Garnish with the mint bouquet and serve with a straw.

JUKE BOX HERO

Tyson Buhler, 2017

This whiskey was the first bottling I had tasted from Barrell Craft Spirits, and I was blown away. They age this whiskey for more than a decade, then finish it in Jamaican barrels, which results in a novel flavor and aroma. While the whiskey is pricy and hard to come by, it gave us a chance to showcase something new to our guests that they likely had never tasted before. —TB

> 1½ ounces Barrell Whiskey Batch 004
>
> ¼ ounce Reisetbauer carrot eau-de-vie
>
> ¾ ounce fresh lemon juice
>
> ¼ ounce Vanilla Syrup (page 288)
>
> 2 teaspoons Orgeat Works Macadamia Nut Syrup
>
> 1 teaspoon Trader Vic's macadamia nut liqueur
>
> 1 dash Angostura bitters

Shake all the ingredients with ice, then double strain into a chilled coupe. No garnish.

KAMA'S ARROW ☉

Tyson Buhler, 2018

You can turn this tropical low-ABV fizz into a truly no-ABV drink by omitting the bitters. —TB

> 2 ounces cold seltzer
>
> 1 ounce Perfect Purée mango purée
>
> ½ ounce fresh lemon juice
>
> 1 ounce Vanilla Syrup (page 288)
>
> ½ ounce Coco López cream of coconut
>
> 1 dash Scrappy's cardamom bitters
>
> Garnish: Crushed pistachio

Pour the seltzer into a chilled fizz glass. Shake the remaining ingredients with ice, then double strain into the glass. Sprinkle some crushed pistachio over the top of the drink.

KINGDOM KEYS ❋

Shannon Tebay, 2018

> 1½ ounces Knappogue Castle 12-year Irish whiskey
>
> ½ ounce Reisetbauer hazelnut eau-de-vie
>
> ¼ ounce Mathilde Poire pear liqueur
>
> ¾ ounce fresh lemon juice
>
> ½ ounce Cane Sugar Syrup (page 282)
>
> ½ dash Scrappy's lavender bitters

Shake all the ingredients with ice, then strain into a double old-fashioned glass over 1 large ice cube. No garnish.

KING GHIDORA

Matthew Belanger, 2016

This luxe tiki drink calls for Yamazaki 12, which is now harder and harder to come by. If you can find some, consider yourself lucky, and celebrate by making this cocktail. If you can't, swap in Hibiki Harmony or Nikka Coffey Grain. —MB

> 1 ounce Yamazaki 12-year whisky
>
> 1 ounce Banks 7 Golden Age rum
>
> ¾ ounce fresh lime juice
>
> ½ ounce Cane Sugar Syrup (page 282)
>
> ½ ounce Perfect Purée papaya purée
>
> 1 teaspoon Marie Brizard white crème de cacao
>
> 1 dash Dale DeGroff's pimento bitters
>
> Garnish: 1 parasol

Combine all the ingredients in a shaker and whip, shaking with a few pieces of crushed ice, just until incorporated. Dump into a double old-fashioned glass and fill the glass with crushed ice. Garnish with the parasol and serve with a straw.

KING PALM ⊘

Tyson Buhler, 2018

This nonalcoholic drink is one we created for D&C Denver. It's a cross between two past D&C drinks, Queen Palm and Piña Colada Deconstruction. Whey provides enough acidity and depth that you may think there was rum hiding in there. —TB

> 1½ ounces kefir whey (made by straining kefir through a cheesecloth-lined sieve)
>
> 1½ ounces Harmless Harvest coconut water
>
> 1 teaspoon Pineapple Gum Syrup (page 286)
>
> 1 teaspoon Cinnamon Syrup (page 283)
>
> Garnish: 1 fresh bay leaf

Stir all the ingredients over ice, then strain into a chilled Nick & Nora glass. Garnish with the bay leaf.

LA LUZ ⊘

Jon Feuersanger, 2019

No-ABV drinks can be challenging. Ingredients interact differently than they do in drinks with alcohol. I looked to Hawaii to inspire this summery drink. The tartness of the pineapple pulp cordial plays with the acidity and sweetness of the passion fruit purée and gives the drink the weight of a Gimlet or Sidecar. It sounds sweet, but it goes down easy. —JF

> 1¾ ounces Fusion verjus blanc
>
> 1 ounce Pineapple Pulp Cordial (page 286)
>
> ½ ounce Perfect Purée passion fruit purée
>
> ¼ ounce fresh lime juice
>
> 1 dash orange flower water
>
> Garnish: 1 lime wedge

Shake all the ingredients with ice, then double strain into a chilled Nick & Nora glass. Garnish with the lime wedge.

LOGAN'S RUN ✻

Eryn Reece, 2015

- 1½ ounces Lustau Los Arcos amontillado sherry
- ½ ounce Nuestra Soledad mezcal
- ¾ ounce fresh lemon juice
- ½ ounce Cane Sugar Syrup (page 282)
- 1 teaspoon Giffard Muroise du Val de Loire

Shake all the ingredients with ice, then double strain into a chilled Nick & Nora glass. No garnish.

LOVE BUG

Sam Penton, 2019

Everyone wants a tequila cocktail these days, so this one came from my wanting to have the most popular drink on the menu. This Daiquiri variation nods to a Clover Club but doesn't contain any modifiers, making it clean, straightforward, and easy to replicate. "Love Bug" is my nickname for my partner, but nobody knew that so it's my secret nod to her. —SP

- 1½ ounces Olmeca Altos Blanco tequila
- ½ ounce Del Maguey Vida mezcal
- ½ ounce fresh lime juice
- ½ ounce fresh pineapple juice
- ½ ounce Raspberry Syrup (page 286)
- 1 egg white
- Garnish: Peychaud's bitters

Shake all the ingredients with ice, then double strain into a chilled coupe. Dash a stripe of Peychaud's bitters over the top of the drink.

LOVE GUN

Scott Teague, 2015

I just wanted to make a cocktail that tastes fucking delicious. One night, David Kaplan and our chef pal Phillip Kirschen-Clark came in, so I brought this drink-in-progress over to them, and they gave me some ideas on how to improve it. What ended up bringing it together was to serve it on a big rock and hit it with some soda, which gave it an effervescent edginess that made it a D&C drink. —ST

- 2 ounces Plantation 3 Stars white rum
- ¾ ounce fresh lemon juice
- ½ ounce Raspberry Syrup (page 286)
- ½ ounce simple syrup (page 287)
- 1 teaspoon St. Elizabeth allspice dram
- 1½ ounces cold seltzer
- Garnish: 1 lemon wheel

Shake all the ingredients except the seltzer with ice, then strain into a double old-fashioned glass over 1 large ice cube. Top with the seltzer and garnish with the lemon wheel.

THE MAGNIFICENT SEVEN

Matthew Belanger, 2015

- 1½ ounces Old Overholt rye
- ¾ ounce Lustau Papirusa manzanilla sherry
- ½ ounce Damoiseau VSOP rhum
- 1 ounce fresh green apple juice
- ¾ ounce fresh lime juice
- ½ ounce House Orgeat (page 284)
- 1 shiso leaf

Shake all the ingredients with ice, then double strain into a chilled coupe. No garnish.

MARIONETTE

Shannon Tebay, 2018

This is a luxe French 75 finished with a beautiful pear cider. —ST

- 2 ounces Eric Bordelet Poire Authentique pear cider
- ¾ ounce Château du Tariquet 15-year Armagnac
- ½ ounce Reisetbauer hazelnut eau-de-vie
- ¼ ounce Clear Creek pear brandy
- ¾ ounce fresh lemon juice
- ½ ounce Vanilla Syrup (page 288)
- 1 drop Terra Spice eucalyptus extract

Pour the cider into a chilled flute. Shake the remaining ingredients with ice, then double strain into the flute. No garnish.

MIRAGE

Shannon Tebay, 2018

Every summer we fight over "Who's going to create 'the watermelon drink?'" because we know it'll be a hit. With this one I made a fizzy liquid salad by adding flavors of tomatoes and watermelon to a mezcal base that's distilled with corn. —ST

- 1½ ounces cold seltzer
- 1 ounce Mezcal Vago Elote
- ½ ounce Siembra Valles Blanco tequila
- ½ ounce Laurent Cazottes 72 Tomatoes
- 1½ ounces Watermelon Syrup (page 288)
- 1 teaspoon acid phosphate
- ½ teaspoon Citric Acid Solution (page 299)
- 1 dash Salt Solution (page 299)

Pour the seltzer into a fizz glass. Short shake the remaining ingredients with 3 ice cubes for about 5 seconds, then strain into the glass and fill the glass with ice cubes. No garnish.

MONKEY'S FIST

Caleb Russell, 2019

1½ ounces Monkey 47 Schwartzwald dry gin

¼ ounce Reisetbauer carrot eau-de-vie

½ ounce Coco López cream of coconut

½ ounce fresh lemon juice

¼ ounce Passion Fruit Syrup (page 285)

1 teaspoon Cane Sugar Syrup (page 282)

Combine all the ingredients in a shaker and whip, shaking with a few pieces of crushed ice, just until incorporated. Dump into a tulip glass and fill the glass with crushed ice. No garnish.

NAUTILUS ❄

Shannon Tebay, 2019

I wanted to re-create, in a colada, the flavors of a delicious Thai soup made with coconut milk and lemongrass. The shochu adds a rice-y flavor, which takes it even further into a Southeast Asian profile. —ST

1½ ounces Kintaro Baisen mugi shochu

½ ounce Rhum JM Blanc 100

1 ounce Coco López cream of coconut

½ ounce fresh lime juice

1 dash Scrappy's celery bitters

½ dash Terra Spice lemongrass extract

Garnish: 1 mint bouquet

Combine all the ingredients in a shaker and whip, shaking with a few pieces of crushed ice, just until incorporated. Dump into a tiki mug and fill the glass with crushed ice. Garnish with the mint bouquet and serve with a straw.

NEON MOON ⊘

Alex Jump, 2018

Tyson named this nonalcoholic drink for me, after a Brooks & Dunn song. At the time he had no idea that Brooks & Dunn was my grandfather's favorite band, and "Neon Moon" was his favorite song. Plus, my grandfather didn't drink! —AJ

1½ ounces cold seltzer

1½ ounces Lime Leaf, Lemongrass & Shiso Syrup (page 284)

1 ounce fresh lime juice

¾ ounce Seedlip Spice 94

1 ounce kefir whey
(made by straining kefir through a cheesecloth-lined sieve)

1 egg white

Garnish: 1 star anise

Pour the seltzer into a chilled fizz glass. Dry shake the remaining ingredients, then shake again with ice. Double strain into the glass. Garnish with the star anise.

NIGHTSHADE

Tyson Buhler, 2016

This is probably the strangest drink I've ever created. It's spicy and savory, and also tropical. I'm not sure I'll revisit this combination anytime soon, but it all came together nicely for this drink. —TB

1½ ounces Brennivin aquavit

1 ounce Orleans Borbon manzanilla sherry

1 ounce fresh tomato juice

½ ounce fresh red bell pepper juice

½ ounce fresh lemon juice

½ ounce House Orgeat (page 284)

1 teaspoon Cholula hot sauce

Garnish: 1 orchid flower and 1 lemon wheel

Combine all the ingredients in a shaker and whip, shaking with a few pieces of crushed ice, just until incorporated. Dump into a pilsner glass and fill the glass with crushed ice. Garnish with the orchid and lemon wheel and serve with a straw.

NIGHT TRAIN ❄

Jeff Hazell, 2014

2 ounces dry sparkling wine

1¼ ounces Appleton Estate V/X rum

½ ounce Zurbaran cream sherry

½ ounce fresh pineapple juice

½ ounce Cane Sugar Syrup (page 282)

½ teaspoon Cruzan Black Strap rum

Pour the sparkling wine into a chilled flute. Shake the remaining ingredients except the rum with ice, then double strain into the flute. Slowly pour the rum over the back of a spoon to float it on top of the drink. No garnish.

OLE BULL

Tyson Buhler, 2018

1½ ounces Linie aquavit

½ ounce Gosling's Black Seal rum

¾ ounce fresh lemon juice

¼ ounce Cinnamon Syrup (page 283)

¼ ounce Marie Brizard white crème de cacao

¼ ounce maple syrup

1 egg white

Dry shake all the ingredients, then shake again with ice. Double strain into a chilled coupe. No garnish.

PALM DREAMS ⚜

Matthew Belanger, 2017

This is pretty much a classic Honeysuckle with an interesting split base and the addition of kalamansi purée. Batavia arrack comes from Indonesia, where kalamansi is a commonly used citrus; the funkiness of the arrack helps push that flavor. —MB

- 1 ounce El Dorado 8-year rum
- ½ ounce Plantation 2000 Jamaican rum
- ½ ounce Batavia arrack
- ¾ ounce fresh lime juice
- ¾ ounce Honey Syrup (page 284)
- 1 teaspoon Boiron kalamansi purée
- 2 dashes Angostura bitters
- Garnish: 1 orange twist

Shake all the ingredients with ice, then double strain into a chilled coupe. Express the orange twist over the drink and discard.

PARACHUTE ⚜

Tyson Buhler, 2017

In this spin on the classic combination of white port and tonic, the addition of savory Salers adds complexity while still keeping the drink in the aperitif category. —TB

- 2 ounces tonic water
- 1 ounce Quinta do Infantado white porto
- 1 ounce Salers Gentien aperitif
- 1 ounce fresh lemon juice
- ¾ ounce simple syrup (page 287)
- 2 dashes Peychaud's bitters
- Garnish: 1 grapefruit half wheel

Pour the tonic into a collins glass. Short shake the remaining ingredients with ice for about 5 seconds, then strain into the glass. Fill the glass with ice cubes and garnish with the grapefruit half wheel.

PIPE DREAM ⊘

Dave Anderson, 2019

I take a lot of pride in making mocktails. We're at over 5,000 feet above sea level in Denver, so I want to be more considerate to people who aren't used to drinking at altitude. This thick, frothy drink gets its name from its likeness to the pipes in the Super Mario Bros. video games. —DA

- 2 ounces cold seltzer
- 1 ounce Perfect Purée kiwi purée
- 1 ounce Vanilla Syrup (page 288)
- ¾ ounce Coco López cream of coconut
- ¾ ounce fresh lime juice
- Garnish: 1 brandied cherry on a skewer

Pour the seltzer into a chilled fizz glass. Short shake the remaining ingredients with ice for about 5 seconds, then double strain into the glass. Garnish with the cherry.

POWDER HOUSE FIZZ

Matthew Belanger, 2019

I wanted to make something frothy like a Ramos Gin Fizz, so I brought back the Gardenia mix to fill the role of heavy cream. All the bartenders hated this mix because it contains butter, which turns your tins slick with fat, so I tweaked the recipe by adding a hydrocolloid, which makes the tins easier to wash. —MB

- 1 ounce cold seltzer
- 1½ ounces Four Pillars Navy Strength gin
- 1 ounce Improved Gardenia Mix (page 298)
- ¾ ounce fresh lime juice
- ¾ ounce Vanilla Syrup (page 288)
- 1 egg white
- Garnish: Lime zest

Pour the seltzer into a chilled fizz glass. Shake the remaining ingredients with ice, then double strain into the glass. Grate some lime zest over the top of the drink.

RANSOM NOTE ⚜

Jeremy Oertel, 2015

- 1 ounce Rittenhouse rye
- 1 ounce Lustau Brandy de Jerez
- ¾ ounce Del Professore vermouth Rosso
- ¼ ounce Ramazzotti
- 1 teaspoon Giffard white crème de cacao
- 1 dash House Orange Bitters (page 298)
- 1 dash Bitter Truth aromatic bitters
- Garnish: 1 lemon twist

Stir all the ingredients over ice, then strain into a chilled Nick & Nora glass. Express the lemon twist over the drink, then place it in the drink.

RAVENMASTER

Tyson Buhler, 2015

I really love the combination of pear and eucalyptus, which I also use in the Telegraph (page 267). Here, it helps to elevate this collins variation. —TB

- 1 ounce cold seltzer
- 1½ ounces Beefeater gin
- ½ ounce Eucalyptus-Infused Yaguara Ouro Cachaça (page 291)
- ¾ ounce fresh lime juice
- ½ ounce Cane Sugar Syrup (page 282)
- ¼ ounce Mathilde Poire
- Garnish: 1 mint bouquet

Pour the seltzer into a collins glass. Short shake the remaining ingredients with ice for about 5 seconds, then strain into the glass. Fill the glass with ice cubes and garnish with the mint bouquet.

RHUM SOUR (STANDING ROOM)

Matthew Belanger, 2019

In Haiti, they call Daiquiris "rhum sours," especially if you make it with Clairin, their indigenous rum that's made in a similar style as rhum agricole. Key lime is the closest thing to what limes taste like in Haiti, and turbinado mimics rapadou, the country's unrefined cane sugar. —MB

- 1 ounce Probitas White blended rum
- ½ ounce Clairin Sajous rum
- ½ ounce key lime cordial
- ½ ounce Turbinado Syrup (page 288)
- ¼ ounce fresh lime juice
- Garnish: 1 lime wedge

Shake all the ingredients with ice, then double strain into a chilled coupe. Garnish with the lime wedge.

RUMOR MILL ❀

Jarred Weigand, 2016

Celery juice gives this Daiquiri variation its awesome texture. When I started developing the drink it tasted muddy, so I added some dry vermouth to bind the flavors and clean it up. It's amazing what a little dry or blanc vermouth can do to a cocktail. —JW

- 1½ ounces dry sparkling wine
- 1 ounce La Favorite rhum agricole blanc
- ½ ounce Dolin dry vermouth
- ½ ounce Cane Sugar Syrup (page 282)
- ½ ounce fresh celery juice
- ½ ounce fresh lime juice
- 1 dash absinthe

Pour the sparkling wine into a chilled flute. Shake the remaining ingredients with ice, then double strain into the flute. No garnish.

SHORT CHANGE HERO

Jon Armstrong, 2015

- 2 ounces Elote-Infused Elijah Craig Bourbon (page 291)
- ¾ ounce fresh lemon juice
- ¾ ounce simple syrup (page 287)
- 1 barspoon pepper jelly
- 1 egg white

Dry shake all the ingredients, then shake again with ice. Double strain into a double old-fashioned glass over 1 large ice cube. No garnish.

SLY FOX ⧗

Tyson Buhler, 2017

We make our Spent Citrus Cordial from garnish trimmings and day-old orange juice. Here, it really shines in this gimlet variation. —TB

- 1½ ounces Perry's Tot Navy Strength gin
- ½ ounce Clear Creek Mirabelle plum
- 1½ ounces Spent Citrus Cordial (page 287)
- 2 dashes Suze orange bitters
- Garnish: 1 dehydrated orange slice

Combine all the ingredients in a shaker and whip, shaking with a few pieces of crushed ice, just until incorporated. Dump into a double old-fashioned glass and fill the glass with crushed ice. Garnish with the dehydrated orange slice and serve with a straw.

STRANGE ENCOUNTERS ⧗

Jarred Weigand, 2016

This drink won a sherry competition in 2018 and got me a trip to Spain. I approached it like a roasted carrot dish. Caramelized carrots have a nuttiness to them, so I added orgeat, along with a big caraway note from the aquavit. —JW

- 1½ ounces Lustau Los Arcos amontillado sherry
- ½ ounce Linie aquavit
- ½ ounce Reisetbauer carrot eau-de-vie
- ¾ ounce fresh lemon juice
- ¼ ounce House Orgeat (page 284)
- ¼ ounce Honey Syrup (page 284)
- ¼ ounce House Ginger Syrup (page 284)
- 1 dash Bitter Truth aromatic bitters

Shake all the ingredients with ice, then double strain into a chilled coupe. No garnish.

STUNT DOUBLE

Javelle Taft, 2019

This Penicillin variation reads like a scotchy Old-Fashioned, but the combination of tart kiwi syrup and Strega really drives the flavor profile on the back end. —JT

- 1 ounce Great King St. Glasgow Blend scotch
- ¾ ounce Kilkerran 12-year single malt scotch
- ¼ ounce Wray & Nephew Overproof Jamaica rum
- 1 teaspoon Strega
- ¾ ounce fresh lemon juice
- ¾ ounce Kiwi Syrup (page 284)
- Garnish: 1 kiwi slice

Shake all the ingredients with ice, then strain into a double old-fashioned glass over 1 large ice cube. Garnish with the kiwi slice.

SLY FOX, PAGE 204

SURF'S UP

Tyson Buhler, 2018

1¾ ounces Plantation 3 Stars white rum

¼ ounce La Favorite rhum agricole blanc

1½ ounces Pineapple Pulp Cordial (page 286)

Garnish: 1 lime wedge

Shake all the ingredients with ice, then double strain into a chilled coupe. Garnish with the lime wedge.

TALISMAN ♣

Shannon Tebay, 2018

We all love the Reisetbauer carrot eau-de-vie and always fight over who gets to use it. Coconut is my favorite flavor, and it makes an unexpectedly delicious pairing with carrot in this smoky margarita variation. –ST

1 ounce Siembra Azul añejo tequila

¾ ounce Siembra Valles Ancestral tequila

¼ ounce Reisetbauer carrot eau-de-vie

1 teaspoon Kalani Ron de Coco coconut liqueur

¾ ounce fresh lemon juice

½ ounce Cane Sugar Syrup (page 282)

2 dashes Bitter End Moroccan bitters

Shake all the ingredients with ice, then strain into a single old-fashioned glass over 1 large ice cube. No garnish.

THIS ISLAND EARTH

Matthew Belanger, 2018

Cognac and rum are often paired up in classic drinks that are made with funky rums. I combine them here in what's basically a papaya Daiquiri. –MB

1½ ounces Paul Beau VS cognac

½ ounce Clairin Sajous rum

1 ounce Papaya Mix (page 298)

¾ ounce fresh lime juice

2 dashes Angostura bitters

Shake all the ingredients with ice, then double strain into a chilled coupe. No garnish.

TRAMPOLINE

Al Sotack, 2014

We served a bazillion of these every night, probably because all of the ingredients are fairly recognizable–and it's delicious. I named it after trampolines because, well, trampolines are fun. –AS

1½ ounces Beefeater gin

¾ ounce Lillet blanc

1 ounce fresh pineapple juice

¾ ounce Strawberry Basil Syrup (page 287)

¾ ounce fresh lime juice

2½ dashes absinthe

2 dashes Peychaud's bitters

Garnish: 1 lime wheel and 1 strawberry

Shake all the ingredients with ice, then strain into a double old-fashioned glass filled with cracked ice cubes. Garnish with the lime wheel and strawberry.

WABI-SABI

Audrey Ludlam, 2019

I lived in Japan for eight months, and during my stay I ate this incredible piece of chocolate layered with wasabi ganache and candied ginger. The memorable bite inspired the white chocolate–wasabi syrup, which makes the drink super creamy, like a piña colada. –AL

1½ ounces High West Silver oat whiskey

½ ounce Suntory Roku gin

1 ounce White Chocolate & Wasabi Syrup (page 288)

¼ ounce Cane Sugar Syrup (page 282)

¾ ounce fresh lemon juice

Garnish: 1 dehydrated lemon wheel and 1 mint bouquet

Combine all the ingredients in a shaker and whip, shaking with a few pieces of crushed ice, just until incorporated. Dump into a tulip glass and fill the glass with crushed ice. Garnish with the dehydrated lemon wheel and mint bouquet. Serve with a straw.

WANING MOON

Tyson Buhler, 2015

1½ ounces Lemorton Selection calvados Domfrontais

½ ounce Clear Creek Douglas Fir eau-de-vie

¾ ounce fresh lemon juice

½ ounce House Orgeat (page 284)

1 teaspoon maple syrup

1 dash Angostura bitters

Shake all the ingredients with ice, then double strain into a chilled coupe. No garnish.

WATER MOCCASIN ♣

Sam Johnson, 2019

Sometimes you can distinguish two ingredients in a drink, and sometimes they become one new and unique flavor. Yuzu and grapefruit create a singular, complex citrus note that goes really well with coconut in this juicy, refreshing gimlet variation. –SJ

1½ ounces Bimini gin

½ ounce Saika Yuzu Shu sake

1 teaspoon Kalani Ron de Coco coconut liqueur

¾ ounce fresh grapefruit juice

½ ounce fresh lemon juice

¼ ounce Cane Sugar Syrup (page 282)

Shake all the ingredients with ice, then double strain into a chilled coupe. No garnish.

THE WEAVER

Sam Johnson, 2018

Yuzu have this intense acidity and an incredible salty-savory flavor, but they are also very aromatic and floral. Sometimes the creative process can be informed by trying to fill gaps, and Death & Co hadn't put out many yuzu drinks. I tried to keep this "luxury" cocktail simple to honor the Nikka whisky, which has a nuttiness that's accented by the orgeat. The name is a reference to Navajo rug making and this idea that the weavers purposefully mess up one little corner of their beautiful, complicated rugs, because a perfect thing is not a living thing. To me, every drink is imperfect, which means we can always revisit and rethink our work. —SJ

1½ ounces cold seltzer

1¼ ounces Nikka Taketsuru whisky

½ ounce Clear Creek Douglas Fir eau-de-vie

¼ ounce Kilchoman Machir Bay single malt scotch

¾ ounce fresh lemon juice

½ ounce House Orgeat (page 284)

1 teaspoon fresh yuzu juice

Pour the seltzer into a collins glass. Short shake the remaining ingredients with ice for about 5 seconds, then strain into the glass. Fill the glass with ice cubes. No garnish.

WHOLE LOTTA LOVE

Matthew Belanger, 2016

Tyson made a punch similar to this spec with Irish whiskey and Cocchi Americano. Nobody ordered it. I turned it into a single-serve cocktail that used every ingredient people wanted at the time, and I named it after the most inoffensively named rock song I could think of. It was the most popular drink on the menu. —MB

1 ounce Wild Turkey 101 rye

1 ounce Lillet rosé

½ ounce Del Maguey Chichicapa mezcal

1 ounce Watermelon Syrup (page 288)

¾ ounce fresh lemon juice

1 dash Peychaud's bitters

Pinch of salt

Shake all the ingredients with ice, then double strain into a chilled coupe. No garnish.

WICKED GAME ☉

Shannon Tebay, 2019

Absentroux is a product I brought to the bar. It's a delicious aromatized wine that incorporates the traditional botanicals used in absinthe, as a way to enjoy that flavor in a more sessionable context, like vermouth. —ST

3 cucumber slices

1 ounce Absentroux

¾ ounce Plymouth gin

¼ ounce Clear Creek Williams pear brandy

¾ ounce fresh lemon juice

¾ ounce simple syrup (page 287)

Garnish: 1 cucumber slice

In a shaker, gently muddle the cucumber slices. Add the remaining ingredients and shake with ice. Double strain into a double old-fashioned glass over 1 large ice cube. Garnish with the cucumber slice.

WING AND A PRAYER

Jeremy Oertel, 2017

1½ ounces Jean-Luc Pasquet Pineau des Charentes

¾ ounce Perry's Tot Navy Strength gin

¾ ounce fresh lemon juice

¾ ounce Donn's Mix #1 (page 298)

1 dash Angostura bitters

1 dash absinthe

Shake all the ingredients with ice, then double strain into a chilled coupe. No garnish.

WITCHDOCTOR

Jillian Vose, 2014

We don't make many blueberry drinks, so I made that my goal, using muffins as my inspiration. It tastes like a blueberry–poppy seed muffin on steroids. —JV

10 blueberries

2 ounces Scarlet Ibis Trinidad rum

¾ ounce Poppy Seed Syrup (page 286)

¾ ounce fresh lemon juice

¼ ounce fresh lime juice

¼ ounce Orgeat Works Macadamia Nut Syrup

1 dash Bitter Truth aromatic bitters

In a shaker, gently muddle the blueberries. Add the remaining ingredients and shake with ice. Double strain into a chilled coupe. No garnish.

Bright & Confident

⊙ LOW ABV   ⊘ NO ABV   ❋ FREEZER BAR   ⧗ PROJECT COCKTAIL   ♣ LOW-PREP COCKTAIL

15 MINUTES OF FAME

Eryn Reece, 2014

- 3 raspberries
- 1 ounce Tapatío Blanco 110 tequila
- 1 ounce Krogstad aquavit
- ½ ounce Plymouth sloe gin
- ¾ ounce fresh lemon juice
- ½ ounce Cane Sugar Syrup (page 282)
- 1 teaspoon House Ginger Syrup (page 284)
- Garnish: 1 raspberry and 1 mint bouquet

In a shaker, gently muddle the raspberries. Add the remaining ingredients and shake with ice. Double strain into a snifter and fill with crushed ice. Garnish with the raspberry and mint bouquet.

AID AND ABET ❄

Eryn Reece, 2015

- 1½ ounces Bigallet China-China Amer
- ½ ounce Tanqueray Malacca gin
- ¾ ounce fresh lemon juice
- ¼ ounce simple syrup (page 287)
- 3 drops orange flower water
- 1 egg white

Dry shake all the ingredients, then shake again with ice. Double strain into a chilled coupe. No garnish.

THE ARGUMENT

Matthew Belanger, 2016

I name a lot of drinks after Fugazi songs, but this was my first. It's a riff on Tyson's Fistful of Dollars, but with blackberries. —MB

- 1½ ounces Lustau Solera Reserva brandy
- ½ ounce Smith & Cross Jamaica rum
- 1 ounce Donn's Mix #1 (page 298)
- ½ ounce fresh lime juice
- ¼ ounce Vanilla Syrup (page 288)
- ¼ ounce Campari
- 3 blackberries

Shake all the ingredients with ice, then double strain into a chilled coupe. No garnish.

BADLANDS

Tyson Buhler, 2018

This is definitely a juice-bar cocktail, but I remember tasting Shannon Ponche's papaya and carrot sangrita at Leyenda in Brooklyn and that combination was just amazing—and the inspiration for this drink. —TB

- 1 ounce Olmeca Altos Blanco tequila
- 1 ounce Ancho Reyes ancho chile liqueur
- ½ ounce fresh lime juice
- ½ ounce Perfect Purée papaya purée
- ½ ounce fresh carrot juice
- ½ ounce fresh orange juice
- ½ ounce Cane Sugar Syrup (page 282)
- Garnish: Summer Royal tea and 1 orchid flower

Combine all the ingredients in a shaker and whip, shaking with a few pieces of crushed ice, just until incorporated. Then strain into a double old-fashioned glass and fill the glass with crushed ice. Sprinkle some tea on top of the drink, garnish with the orchid, and serve with a straw.

BAIT 'N' SWITCH

Jeremy Oertel, 2014

- 1½ ounces Sombra mezcal
- ½ ounce Ancho Reyes ancho chile liqueur
- ½ ounce fresh lime juice
- ½ ounce fresh pineapple juice
- ½ ounce Cinnamon Syrup (page 283)

Shake all the ingredients with ice, then double strain into a chilled coupe. No garnish.

BEACH GOTH ❀

Al Sotack, 2014

1½ ounces Old Forester 100 bourbon

1 ounce Ramazzotti

¾ ounce Giffard banane du Brésil

1 teaspoon Giffard white crème de cacao

¾ ounce fresh lemon juice

½ ounce fresh pineapple juice

Garnish: 1 pineapple wedge dashed with Giffard banane du Brésil

Shake all the ingredients with ice, then strain into a tiki mug filled with crushed ice. Garnish with the pineapple wedge and serve with a straw.

BENICIA PARK SWIZZLE

Eryn Reece, 2014

1 ounce Highland Park 12-year single-malt scotch

1 ounce Lustau Los Arcos amontillado sherry

¾ ounce fresh lemon juice

½ ounce House Ginger Syrup (page 284)

½ ounce Velvet falernum

¼ ounce Giffard Muroise du Val de Loire

Garnish: 1 mint leaf

Combine the scotch, sherry, lemon juice, ginger syrup, and Velvet falernum in a shaker and whip, shaking with a few pieces of crushed ice, just until incorporated. Dump into a pilsner glass and add crushed ice until the glass is about 80 percent full. Swizzle for a few seconds, then pack the glass with crushed ice, mounding it above the rim. Slowly pour the Giffard Muroise over the back of a spoon to float it on top of the drink. Garnish with the mint leaf and serve with a straw.

BLACK AND BLUE

Matthew Belanger, 2017

This is based on a whiskey sour, with a tough-sounding name so whiskey sour drinkers will feel comfortable ordering it. The Port Syrup is very fruity, so I cut it with a savory amaro so the drink didn't become a fruit bomb. —MB

1 ounce Monkey Shoulder Blended Malt scotch

½ ounce Wyoming Whiskey

½ ounce Clear Creek Blue Plum brandy

¾ ounce fresh lemon juice

¾ ounce Port Syrup (page 286)

1 teaspoon Luxardo Amaro Abano

Shake all the ingredients with ice, then strain into a double old-fashioned glass over 1 large ice cube. No garnish.

BLOOD MOON

Tim Miner, 2019

1 ounce Buffalo Trace bourbon

¾ ounce Laird's bonded apple brandy

¼ ounce Massenez framboise eau-de-vie

¾ ounce fresh lemon juice

½ ounce Raspberry Syrup (page 286)

½ ounce Calpico (a concentrated yogurt drink available at Asian markets)

Shake all the ingredients with ice, then double strain into a chilled coupe. No garnish.

BOOM SWAGGER

Al Sotack, 2014

¾ ounce Appleton V/X Jamaican rum

¾ ounce Wild Turkey 101 rye

¼ ounce Lemon Hart 151 rum

¼ ounce Lustau Los Arcos amontillado sherry

¾ ounce fresh lemon juice

½ ounce fresh pineapple juice

¼ ounce Cane Sugar Syrup (page 282)

¼ ounce House Ginger Syrup (page 284)

¼ ounce Cinnamon Syrup (page 283)

Garnish: Angostura and Peychaud's bitters, and 1 pineapple wedge

Combine all the ingredients in a shaker and whip, shaking with a few pieces of crushed ice, just until incorporated. Dump into a pilsner glass and add crushed ice until the glass is about 80 percent full. Swizzle for a few seconds, then pack the glass with ice, mounding it above the rim. Dash some Angostura bitters over the top of the drink, then dash some Peychaud's bitters over the pineapple wedge and garnish with the pineapple wedge. Serve with a straw.

BOUNCE HOUSE

Alex Jump, 2019

When we started working on drinks for the Denver bar, it became glaringly obvious that there weren't many vodka cocktails in the Death & Co canon. But guests always want to have one on the menu, so we make sure we have one. This variation on the Trampoline (page 206) kind of tastes like a Jolly Rancher in the best way. —AJ

1 ounce Spring44 vodka

1 ounce Tio Pepe fino sherry

1 teaspoon Chareau aloe liqueur

1 teaspoon yellow Chartreuse

1 ounce Strawberry Aloe Syrup (page 287)

¾ ounce fresh lemon juice

1 dash Salt Solution (page 299)

Garnish: 1 lemon wheel

Shake all the ingredients with ice, then strain into a double old-fashioned glass over 1 large ice cube. Garnish with the lemon wheel.

BUSHIDO

Matthew Belanger, 2017

- 1½ ounces Nikka Taketsuru whisky
- 2 teaspoons Kalani Ron de Coco coconut liqueur
- 1 teaspoon Laphroaig 10-year single malt scotch
- 1 ounce Donn's Mix #1 (page 298)
- ½ ounce fresh lime juice
- 1 teaspoon Cane Sugar Syrup (page 282)
- 1 dash Scrappy's celery bitters

Shake all the ingredients with ice, then double strain into a chilled coupe. No garnish.

CALAMITY JANE

Shannon Tebay, 2018

I put this drink up to Matt Belanger, and he said "Oh, this has all the Shannon things." One of those "things" is the combination of scotch and Wray & Nephew rum, which I wanted to work into a whiskey sour variation. I also wanted to incorporate strawberries and olive oil, so a touch of soy lecithin keeps the oil in suspension. If you don't have any soy lecithin, add an egg white to the drink and dry shake it first. —ST

- 1½ ounces Buffalo Trace bourbon
- ¼ ounce Bowmore 12-year scotch
- 1 teaspoon Wray & Nephew White Overproof rum
- ½ ounce Dolin blanc vermouth
- ¾ ounce Strawberry Syrup (page 287)
- ½ ounce fresh lemon juice
- 1 teaspoon extra-virgin olive oil
- ½ teaspoon soy lecithin

Shake all the ingredients with ice, then double strain into a chilled coupe. No garnish.

CALYPSO ☉

Jonnie Long, 2019

We have a few employees (and lots of guests) who are vegan, so I wanted to create an egg white–style drink without animal products. Aquafaba is just canned bean liquid, but it works very similarly to eggs whites in a cocktail. —JL

- 2 ounces junmai sake
- ½ ounce Rare Wine Co. Charleston Sercial madeira
- ½ ounce Giffard banane du Brésil
- ¾ ounce fresh lemon juice
- ½ ounce aquafaba
- ½ ounce Cane Sugar Syrup (page 282)
- Garnish: 1 banana leaf

Dry shake all the ingredients, then shake again with ice. Double strain into a double old-fashioned glass over 1 large ice cube. Garnish with the banana leaf.

CAROUSEL

Tim Miner, 2019

- 1 ounce Pierre Ferrand ambré cognac
- ½ ounce St. George absinthe verte
- ½ ounce Tempus Fugit crème de noyaux
- ¾ ounce fresh lime juice
- ½ ounce fresh pineapple juice
- ½ ounce Cane Sugar Syrup (page 282)
- 5 to 6 mint leaves
- Garnish: 1 mint bouquet

Combine all the ingredients in a shaker and whip, shaking with a few pieces of crushed ice, just until incorporated. Dump into a tulip glass and fill the glass with crushed ice. Garnish with the mint bouquet and serve with a straw.

CHINQUAPIN PARISH PUNCH

Eryn Reece, 2014

- 6 ounces Evan Williams single barrel bourbon
- 1½ ounces Dolin blanc vermouth
- 1½ ounces Giffard crème de pêche
- 3 ounces fresh lemon juice
- 1½ ounces fresh orange juice
- ¾ ounce Honey Syrup (page 284)
- ¾ ounce simple syrup (page 287)
- 3 dashes Angostura bitters
- 3 dashes House Orange Bitters (page 298)
- 8 ounces cold seltzer
- Garnish: Lemon wheels and orange half wheels

Combine all of the ingredients except the seltzer in a punch bowl and stir to combine. Add ice cubes and top with the seltzer. Garnish with the lemon wheels and orange half wheels

COMADRE ⚜

Matthew Belanger, 2018

Tamarind liqueur is not something you see in drinks that often. This is basically a Jungle Bird with flavors of cola coming from the tamarind and the amaro. —MB

- 1 ounce Tapatío Reposado tequila
- 1 ounce Von Humboldt's tamarind cordial
- ¾ ounce Amaro Averna
- ¾ ounce fresh pineapple juice
- ½ ounce fresh lime juice
- ¼ ounce Demerara Syrup (page 283)
- 2 dashes Bittermens Xocolatl mole bitters
- Garnish: 1 pineapple wedge and 1 orchid flower

Shake all the ingredients with ice, then strain into a double old-fashioned glass over 1 large ice cube. Garnish with the pineapple wedge and orchid.

COMMON'S PARK SWIZZLE

Caleb Russell, 2019

- 1 ounce Hine H cognac
- ½ ounce Chateau Laribotte Sauternes
- ½ ounce Rare Wine Co. Baltimore rainwater madeira
- ½ ounce Tempus Fugit crème de banane
- ½ ounce fresh lemon juice
- ¼ ounce House Orgeat (page 284)
- 5 to 6 mint leaves
- Garnish: 1 mint bouquet

Combine all the ingredients in a shaker and whip, shaking with a few pieces of crushed ice, just until incorporated. Dump into a collins glass and add crushed ice until the glass is about 80 percent full. Swizzle for a few seconds, then pack the glass with ice, mounding it above the rim. Garnish with the mint bouquet.

CRIMSON AND CLOVER

Matthew Belanger, 2016

- 1 ounce Perry's Tot Navy Strength gin
- ½ ounce Del Maguey Vida mezcal
- ½ ounce Dolin blanc vermouth
- ½ ounce fresh lime juice
- ½ ounce Raspberry Syrup (page 286)
- 1 egg white
- Garnish: 1 grapefruit twist

Dry shake all the ingredients, then shake again with ice. Double strain into a chilled coupe. Express the grapefruit twist over the drink and discard.

CRISS CROSSED

Jeremy Oertel, 2017

- 1½ ounces Rittenhouse rye
- ½ ounce Gamle Ode dill aquavit
- 1 teaspoon Kalani Ron de Coco coconut liqueur
- ¾ ounce fresh lemon juice
- ½ ounce House Ginger Syrup (page 284)
- 1 dash Bitter Truth aromatic bitters

Shake all the ingredients with ice, then double strain into a chilled coupe. No garnish.

DAISY BELL

Matthew Belanger, 2017

Pisco is generally agreeable to the vodka drinker, so we like to keep one on every menu. The drink is named after the song sung by HAL 9000 as he loses his computer mind in *2001: A Space Odyssey*—a premonition of how many times we made this super-popular drink while it was on the menu. —MB

- 1½ ounces Campo de Encanto Acholado pisco
- ½ ounce Ransom Gewürztraminer grappa
- ¼ ounce Marie Brizard white crème de cacao
- ¾ ounce fresh lemon juice
- ½ ounce Raspberry Syrup (page 286)
- 3 drops rose water

Shake all the ingredients with ice, then double strain into a chilled coupe. No garnish.

DARK'S CARNIVAL ❄

Jeremy Oertel, 2015

I named this drink after the setting of Ray Bradbury's *Something Wicked this Way Comes*. Just like the story, it's dark, rich, and a little sinister. —JO

- 1½ ounces El Dorado 3-year rum
- ½ ounce Morenita cream sherry
- ½ ounce Marie Brizard white crème de cacao
- ¼ ounce Hamilton Jamaican Pot Still Gold rum
- ¾ ounce fresh lime juice
- ½ ounce fresh pineapple juice
- 4 drops Bitter End Jamaican Jerk bitters
- Garnish: 1 lime wheel

Shake all the ingredients with ice, then double strain into a chilled coupe. Garnish with the lime wheel.

DAWN PATROL ☉

Shannon Tebay, 2018

This is like a low-ABV reverse Morning Glory Fizz, where the absinthe flavor comes from the wormwood-flavored wine to augment the smoky scotch. Fresh apple has so much pectin that it does this cool thing, making the foam very stiff, almost like a Ramos fizz. —ST

- 1 ounce cold seltzer
- 2 Granny Smith apple slices
- 1½ ounces Absentroux
- ¾ ounce Bowmore 12-year single malt scotch
- ¾ ounce fresh lemon juice
- ½ ounce simple syrup (page 287)
- 1 egg white

Pour the seltzer into a chilled fizz glass. In a shaker, gently muddle the apple slices. Add the remaining ingredients to the shaker and shake with ice. Double strain into the glass. No garnish.

DOCTOR STRANGELOVE, PAGE 214

DIAMOND HEIST

Tyson Buhler, 2014

This drink was really about sliding a bunch of funky, grassy sugarcane distillate into an extremely approachable cocktail. If you put it in a can, you could mistake it for one of the many hazy, tropical IPAs on the market these days. —TB

1½ ounces Rhum JM Blanc

½ ounce Avuá Amburana cachaça

¼ ounce Giffard crème de pêche

1 ounce fresh lime juice

¾ ounce Hopped Pineapple Gum Syrup (page 284)

Garnish: 1 mint bouquet

Short shake all the ingredients with ice for about 5 seconds, then strain into a double old-fashioned glass. Fill the glass with crushed ice. Garnish with the mint bouquet.

DOCTOR STRANGELOVE

Matthew Belanger, 2016

This was the first cocktail that started our trend of naming tiki drinks after fictional doctors. I had a feeling that aloe liqueur and kiwi would go well together, given that they're both weird, green, greasy things. The drink is made using the usual sour proportions, with blanc vermouth stretching the flavors out enough so you can taste the kiwi syrup. —MB

1 ounce El Dorado 3-year rum

¼ ounce Wray & Nephew White Overproof rum

¾ ounce Damoiseau 110-proof rum

¾ ounce Dolin blanc vermouth

¼ ounce Chareau aloe liqueur

¾ ounce fresh lime juice

¾ ounce Kiwi Syrup (page 285)

Garnish: 1 kiwi slice

Short shake all the ingredients with a few ice cubes for about 5 seconds, then strain into a pilsner glass. Fill the glass with crushed ice and garnish with the kiwi slice.

DRAGONFLY

Shannon Tebay, 2018

A women I attended pastry school with made this amazing banana-miso dessert, so I went to Jarred and said "This is going to sound crazy, but I think I can do a drink with miso, banana, and Jamaican rum." I thought he'd push back, but instead he said "Tyson already did that with the Artful Dodger (page 229)." Of course he did. —ST

1 ounce Appleton Estate Reserve Jamaica rum

1 ounce Miso-Infused Pierre Ferrand 1840 Cognac (page 293)

1 ounce fresh lemon juice

½ ounce House Orgeat (page 284)

¼ ounce Giffard banane du Brésil

Garnish: 1 mint bouquet

Shake all the ingredients with ice, then strain into a collins glass. Fill the glass with crushed ice and garnish with the mint bouquet.

EL FUERTE

Tyson Buhler, 2015

2 ounces Old Forester 100 bourbon

¼ ounce Giffard Abricot du Roussillon

2 ounces Tepache (page 299)

½ ounce fresh lemon juice

½ ounce Cane Sugar Syrup (page 282)

1 dash Bittermens Xocolatl mole bitters

1 dash Angostura bitters

Garnish: 1 cinnamon stick

Combine all the ingredients in a shaker and whip, shaking with a few pieces of crushed ice, just until incorporated. Dump into a tiki mug and add crushed ice until the glass is about 80 percent full. Swizzle for a few seconds, then pack the glass with ice, mounding it above the rim. Grate some cinnamon over the top of the drink and serve with a straw.

FADED LOVE

Alex Jump, 2018

This drink sounds all fresh and garden-y, like spa water, but it's weird and vegetal, full of ingredients that nobody knows. But if you're going to give me a sour cocktail, I'd rather it be really herbaceous than floral. —AJ

½ ounce Singani 63 eau-de-vie

½ ounce St. George green chile vodka

½ ounce Suze

½ ounce St-Germain elderflower liqueur

½ ounce fresh lime juice

¼ ounce Parrot Syrup (page 285)

1 dash Salt Solution (page 299)

Garnish: 1 pickled cherry tomato on a skewer

Shake all the ingredients with ice, then strain into a double old-fashioned glass over 1 large ice cube. Garnish with the pickled cherry tomato.

FAMILY AFFAIR PUNCH

Jeremy Oertel, 2014

8 ounces Gamay red wine

3 ounces Greenhook Ginsmiths Old Tom gin

1 ounce Nardini amaro

1 ounce Grand Marnier

3 ounces fresh lemon juice

2 ounces Honey Syrup (page 284)

1 ounce Cinnamon Syrup (page 283)

4 dashes Bitter End Moroccan bitters

8 dashes Dale DeGroff's pimento bitters

8 ounces cold seltzer

Garnish: Lemon wheels

Combine all of the ingredients except the seltzer in a punch bowl and stir to combine. Add ice cubes and top with the seltzer. Garnish with the lemon wheels.

FEVER DREAM

Jeremy Oertel, 2014

This is most popular drink I made at Death & Co. It's a spicy mezcal cocktail with St-Germain, so it obviously checks a lot of boxes. –JO

1 cucumber slice

1½ ounces Arbol-Infused Del Maguey Vida Mezcal (page 290)

½ ounce Suze

½ ounce St-Germain elderflower liqueur

¾ ounce fresh lime juice

½ ounce Cane Sugar Syrup (page 282)

1 dash Bitter Truth celery bitters

In a shaker, gently muddle the cucumber. Add the remaining ingredients and shake with ice. Double strain into a chilled coupe. No garnish.

FIRING PIN

Scott Teague, 2015

This drink is all about precise complexity. I wanted to bring your taste sensors to different places: sweet, smoky, citrusy, spicy, and bitter. It's like a mojito meets a mai tai, then takes on new life when the Campari float sinks into the drink. –ST

2 ounces Sombra mezcal

1 ounce fresh lime juice

½ ounce House Orgeat (page 284)

¼ ounce House Ginger Syrup (page 284)

1 teaspoon Cholula hot sauce

¼ ounce Campari

Garnish: 1 mint bouquet

Combine all the ingredients except the Campari in a shaker and whip, shaking with a few pieces of crushed ice, just until incorporated. Dump into a pilsner glass and fill the glass with crushed ice. Slowly pour the Campari over the back of a spoon to float it on top of the drink. Garnish with the mint bouquet.

FISTFUL OF DOLLARS

Tyson Buhler, 2015

This is one of those drinks that was hated by the end of its time on the menu, as it seemed like there was one on every single ticket coming through the service well. A whiskey sour made with easily understood ingredients will tend to do that. This was the first of many whiskey-based cocktails that we named after Westerns. –TB

1½ ounces Old Grand-Dad bonded bourbon

¼ ounce Cointreau

¼ ounce Campari

1 ounce Donn's Mix #1 (page 298)

¾ ounce fresh lemon juice

1 dash Bitter Truth aromatic bitters

Garnish: 1 orange twist

Shake all the ingredients with ice, then double strain into a chilled coupe. Express the orange twist over the drink, then place it in the drink.

FLYING GUILLOTINE

Matthew Belanger, 2017

1 ounce Dupont Calvados Hors d'Age

½ ounce El Dorado 15-year rum

½ ounce Plantation O.F.T.D. Overproof rum

1 teaspoon Don's Spices (page 298)

¾ ounce fresh lime juice

½ ounce Demerara Syrup (page 283)

½ ounce Perfect Purée guava purée

2 dashes absinthe

1 dash Angostura bitters

Garnish: 1 orchid flower

Shake all the ingredients with ice, then strain into a collins glass. Fill the glass with crushed ice. Garnish with the orchid and serve with a straw.

FORTUNELLA

Tyson Buhler, 2018

1¾ ounces Spring44 vodka

¼ ounce Clear Creek pear eau-de-vie

¾ ounce fresh lime juice

½ ounce House Orgeat (page 284)

½ ounce Rhum Clément Créole Shrubb

1 teaspoon Boiron kalamansi purée

Garnish: 1 lime wheel

Shake all the ingredients with ice, then strain into a double old-fashioned glass over 1 large ice cube. Garnish with the lime wheel.

FULL DISCLOSURE

Matthew Belanger, 2019

1½ ounces Del Maguey Santo Domingo Albarradas mezcal

½ ounce Giffard rhubarb liqueur

1 ounce Donn's Mix #1 (page 298)

¾ ounce fresh lime juice

1 dash Bitter Truth aromatic bitters

Garnish: 1 grapefruit twist

Shake all the ingredients with ice, then double strain into a chilled coupe. Express the grapefruit twist over the drink and discard.

FULL SAIL ☉

Jarred Weigand, 2018

Back in the day, someone had made a drink with Ocho tequila and Granny Smith apple juice, and I loved that bright, refreshing combination, so I pulled it into this low-ABV Daiquiri. —JW

- 1½ ounces Pasquet Pineau des Charentes
- ¾ ounce Ocho 2012 plata tequila
- ½ ounce fresh Granny Smith apple juice
- ½ ounce fresh lime juice
- ¼ ounce Vanilla Syrup (page 288)
- 1 dash absinthe
- 1 dash Angostura bitters
- Garnish: 1 Granny Smith apple slice

Shake all the ingredients with ice, then double strain into a chilled coupe. Garnish with the apple slice.

GALILEO SEVEN

Matthew Belanger, 2018

This combines elements of a Daiquiri #3 (lime and maraschino) and a Mary Pickford (pineapple and maraschino), and is made extra tropical with a base of mango brandy. —MB

- 1 ounce Rhine Hall mango brandy
- ¾ ounce Plantation 3 Stars white rum
- ¼ ounce Neisson rhum agricole blanc
- ¼ ounce Luxardo maraschino liqueur
- ¾ ounce fresh lime juice
- ½ ounce Pineapple Gum Syrup (page 286)
- 2 dashes Peychaud's bitters

Shake all the ingredients with ice, then double strain into a chilled coupe. No garnish.

GARDEN PARK SWIZZLE

Jon Armstrong, 2014

Once you sell one swizzle at the bar, everybody else sees it and soon you're making them all night. One of many "Park" swizzles we made, this one is a riff on the Hyde Park Swizzle, made more interesting with added bitter elements. —JA

- 6 to 8 mint leaves
- 1½ ounces Bombay London dry gin
- ½ ounce Suze
- ¾ ounce fresh lemon juice
- ¾ ounce House Ginger Syrup (page 284)
- ¼ ounce Velvet falernum
- Garnish: Angostura and Peychaud's bitters, and 1 mint bouquet

In a cocktail shaker, gently muddle the mint leaves. Add the remaining ingredients and dry shake, then shake again with ice. Double strain into a pilsner glass and fill the glass with crushed ice. Dash some Angostura and Peychaud's bitters on top of the drink and garnish with the mint bouquet.

GEMINI FLYOVER

Matthew Belanger, 2019

- 1½ ounces Bertoux brandy
- ½ ounce Batavia arrack
- ½ ounce Giffard banane du Brésil
- ¾ ounce fresh lime juice
- ½ ounce Madras Curry Syrup (page 285)
- 1 dash Angostura bitters

Shake all the ingredients with ice, then double strain into a chilled coupe. No garnish.

GEMINI FLYOVER ☉

Matthew Belanger, 2019

- 1 ounce Lustau Los Arcos amontillado sherry
- ½ ounce Bertoux brandy
- 1 teaspoon Batavia arrack
- 1 teaspoon Giffard banane du Brésil
- ¾ ounce fresh lime juice
- ½ ounce Madras Curry Syrup (page 285)
- 1 dash Angostura bitters

Shake all the ingredients with ice, then double strain into a chilled coupe. No garnish.

GLORY DAYS ✳

Jarred Weigand, 2019

A lot of my cocktails are made by plugging and playing elements from previous drinks. I started with the banana-sherry combination from Tyson's King Louie then added the ripe tropical fruit notes of Redbreast whiskey. I'm a Jersey boy, and I always name my crushed-ice drinks after Bruce Springsteen songs. —JW

- 1½ ounces Redbreast 12-year Irish whiskey
- ½ ounce Lustau oloroso sherry
- ½ ounce Tempus Fugit crème de banane
- ¾ ounce fresh lemon juice
- ½ ounce Cane Sugar Syrup (page 282)
- 2 drops Terra Spice birch extract
- 6 to 8 mint leaves
- Garnish: 1 mint bouquet and Tempus Fugit crème de banane, in an atomizer

Combine all the ingredients in a shaker and whip, shaking with a few pieces of crushed ice, just until incorporated. Double strain into a collins glass and fill the glass with crushed ice. Garnish with the mint bouquet and spray the top of the drink with the banana liqueur.

GOLDEN FANG

Jon Armstrong, 2016

Tyson challenged us to put orange juice on the menu, as we always have a surplus of oranges left over from making twists. This one is a riff on the Cobra's Fang, a classic tiki drink. —JA

1½ ounces St. George dry rye reposado gin

½ ounce Perry's Tot Navy Strength gin

¾ ounce fresh lime juice

½ ounce fresh orange juice

½ ounce House Ginger Syrup (page 284)

¼ ounce Passion Fruit Syrup (page 285)

¼ ounce Vanilla Syrup (page 288)

4 drops Scrappy's cardamom bitters

Garnish: 1 orchid flower, 1 mint bouquet, and 1 cinnamon stick

Short shake all the ingredients with ice for about 5 seconds, then strain into a tulip glass. Fill the glass with crushed ice. Garnish with the orchid and mint bouquet. Light the end of the cinnamon stick until smoldering, then insert it into the drink. Serve with a straw.

HAITIAN DIVORCE

Al Sotack, 2014

1½ ounces Barbancourt 8-year rum

½ ounce Wray & Nephew Jamaican rum

1 teaspoon Grand Marnier

1 ounce fresh pineapple juice

1 ounce Hibiscus Shrub (page 298)

¼ ounce fresh lime juice

Garnish: 1 edible flower

Short shake all the ingredients with ice for about 5 seconds, then strain into a pilsner glass. Fill the glass with crushed ice. Garnish with the edible flower and serve with a straw.

HARBORMASTER ⚜

Tim Miner, 2019

¾ ounce La Favorite rhum agricole ambre

¾ ounce Singani 63 eau-de-vie

¾ ounce Galliano l'Autentico

¼ ounce Giffard passion fruit liqueur

¾ ounce fresh lime juice

1 teaspoon simple syrup (page 287)

Shake all the ingredients with ice, then double strain into a chilled coupe. No garnish.

HEART THROB

Scott Teague, 2014

This spec was born out of our "gangster time Daiquiri" sessions . . . goddamn I miss those. For the record, where everyone else called our impromptu "snaquiri" sessions "gangster Daiquiri time," I maintain that it's "gangster time Daiquiri." —ST

2 ounces Flor de Caña 4-year rum

¾ ounce fresh lime juice

½ ounce Giffard crème de pamplemousse rose

½ ounce Cinnamon Syrup (page 283)

Shake all the ingredients with ice, then double strain into a chilled coupe. No garnish.

HIGH ATLAS

Tyson Buhler, 2018

¾ ounce Del Maguey Vida mezcal

¾ ounce Suze

¾ ounce Dolin dry vermouth

1½ ounces Spent Citrus Cordial (page 287)

Garnish: 1 dehydrated orange slice

Combine all the ingredients in a shaker and whip, shaking with a few pieces of crushed ice, just until incorporated.

Dump into a double old-fashioned glass and fill the glass with crushed ice. Garnish with the dehydrated orange slice.

HOTEL CALIFORNIA

Matthew Belanger, 2015

1½ ounces Mount Gay Eclipse rum

1 ounce Pineau des Charentes

½ ounce Wray & Nephew Jamaican rum

¼ ounce Giffard Abricot du Roussillon

¾ ounce fresh lime juice

½ ounce Cinnamon Syrup (page 283)

1 dash Bitter End Moroccan bitters

Shake all the ingredients with ice, then double strain into a chilled coupe. No garnish.

HURRICANE KICK

Jeremy Oertel, 2017

1 ounce Siembra Valles High-Proof tequila

1 ounce Del Maguey Santo Domingo Albarradas mezcal

1 teaspoon Massenez crème de pêche peach liqueur

¾ ounce fresh lime juice

¾ ounce fresh pineapple juice

½ ounce Passion Fruit Syrup (page 285)

1 teaspoon House Ginger Syrup (page 284)

Garnish: 1 mint spring, 1 orchid flower, and 2 pineapple fronds

Combine all the ingredients in a shaker and whip, shaking with a few pieces of crushed ice, just until incorporated. Dump into a collins glass and fill the glass with crushed ice. Garnish with the mint bouquet, orchid, and pineapple fronds. Serve with a straw.

IGUANERO

Matthew Belanger, 2018

I thought the Doctor Strangelove (page 214) was pretty, but I wanted to do something more interesting with the kiwi syrup. This Nuestra Soledad mezcal has a tropical and herbaceous aromatic quality to it, and green Chartreuse creates some room for the grassiness of kiwi to come through in the drink. In the Caribbean, iguanas are so pervasive that they hire guys called "iguaneros" to thin out the pack. —MB

- 1 ounce Nuestra Soledad Lachigui mezcal
- ½ ounce El Dorado 3-year rum
- ½ ounce Avuá Prata cachaça
- ½ ounce green Chartreuse
- 1 ounce Kiwi Syrup (page 285)
- ¾ ounce fresh lime juice
- Garnish: 2 kiwi slices

Short shake all the ingredients with ice for about 5 seconds, then strain into a tulip glass. Fill the glass with crushed ice. Garnish with the kiwi slices and serve with a straw.

JAPHY RYDER

Tyson Buhler, 2014

- 1 ounce St. George Terroir gin
- 1 ounce Clear Creek 8-year apple brandy
- ½ ounce Dolin Génépy des Alpes liqueur
- ¾ ounce fresh lemon juice
- ½ ounce fresh pineapple juice
- ½ ounce House Orgeat (page 284)

Shake all the ingredients with ice, then double strain into a chilled coupe. No garnish.

JUMPING THE SHARK

Matthew Belanger, 2015

- 1 ounce Rhum JM Blanc 100
- ¾ ounce Amaro di Angostura
- ½ ounce Giffard crème de pamplemousse rose
- ¼ ounce Avuá Amburana cachaça
- 1 ounce fresh lime juice
- ½ ounce House Orgeat (page 284)
- 1 dash Angostura bitters
- Garnish: 1 cinnamon stick

Combine all the ingredients in a shaker and whip, shaking with a few pieces of crushed ice, just until incorporated. Dump into a pilsner glass and fill the glass with crushed ice. Garnish with the cinnamon stick and serve with a straw.

JUNGLELAND ⚜

Jarred Weigand, 2017

In this cobbler variation I revisited the combination of Ramazzotti, Giffard banana, and Old Forester in Al Sotack's Beach Goth. I originally wanted to name it "Double Fantasy" after the John Lennon album, but Tyson thought it was too sexual, so I went back to the Springsteen canon. —JW

- 1 orange wheel
- 2 ounces Lustau Palo Cortado Peninsula
- 1 ounce Old Forester Signature bourbon
- ½ ounce Giffard banane du Brésil
- ¼ ounce Ramazzotti
- ¼ ounce Demerara Syrup (page 283)
- Garnish: 1 mint sprig, 1 orange wheel, blackberries, raspberries, and powdered sugar

In a shaker, gently muddle the orange wheel. Add the remaining ingredients and short shake with ice for about 5 seconds, then double strain into a collins glass. Fill the glass with crushed ice. Garnish with the mint sprig, orange wheel, and berries. Dust the top of the drink with powdered sugar and serve with a straw.

LA TRINITÉ

Tyson Buhler, 2019

- 1 ounce Rhum JM VSOP
- ½ ounce Clear Creek 2-year apple brandy
- ½ ounce Suze
- ¾ ounce fresh lemon juice
- ¾ ounce Honey Syrup (page 284)
- ½ dash Scrappy's celery bitters

Shake all the ingredients with ice, then double strain into a chilled coupe. No garnish.

MAROONED

Tyson Buhler, 2017

- 1 ounce Paul Beau VS cognac
- 1 ounce Laird's bonded apple brandy
- ¼ ounce Campari
- ¾ ounce fresh lime juice
- ½ ounce Perfect Purée mango purée
- ½ ounce Vanilla Syrup (page 288)
- Garnish: 1 lime wheel and 1 mint bouquet

Combine all the ingredients in a shaker and whip, shaking with a few pieces of crushed ice, just until incorporated. Dump into a double old-fashioned glass and fill the glass with crushed ice. Garnish with the lime wheel and mint bouquet and serve with a straw.

MONDRIAN

Tyson Buhler, 2018

I'm sure the Denver crew is still cursing my name for this very pretty but pain-in-the-ass cocktail. To make the raspberry powder garnish, simply blitz freeze-dried raspberries in a blender or food processor. —TB

- **2 ounces dry sparkling wine**
- **1 ounce El Tesoro Platinum tequila**
- **¾ ounce Cappelletti Vino Aperitivo**
- **¼ ounce St. George Raspberry Brandy**
- **¾ ounce fresh lime juice**
- **¾ ounce Raspberry Syrup (page 286)**
- **1 egg white**
- **Garnish: Raspberry powder (see above)**

Pour the sparkling wine into a chilled fizz glass. Dry shake the remaining ingredients, then shake again with ice. Double strain into the glass and sprinkle some raspberry powder over the top of the drink.

MOONLIGHT SONATA

Tyson Buhler, 2015

This is the aforementioned punch that Matthew ripped off for his Whole Lotta Love (page 207) that never sold. —TB

- **7½ ounces Tyrconnell single malt Irish whiskey**
- **3¾ ounces Watermelon Syrup (page 288)**
- **3¾ ounces Cocchi Americano**
- **3¾ ounces fresh lemon juice**
- **1¼ ounces Massenez kirsch**
- **5 dashes House Orange Bitters (page 298)**
- **5 dashes absinthe**
- **5 dashes Peychaud's bitters**
- **5 ounces dry sparkling wine**
- **Garnish: Lemon wheels**

Combine all of the ingredients except the sparkling wine in a punch bowl and stir to combine. Add ice cubes and top with the wine. Garnish with the lemon wheels.

MR. WEDNESDAY

Matthew Belanger, 2017

- **1¼ ounces Krogstad aquavit**
- **½ ounce Smith & Cross Jamaica rum**
- **½ ounce Giffard banane du Brésil**
- **¼ ounce Cruzan Black Strap rum**
- **1 ounce fresh lemon juice**
- **¾ ounce House Orgeat (page 284)**
- **Garnish: 1 orchid flower**

Combine all the ingredients in a shaker and whip, shaking with a few pieces of crushed ice, just until incorporated. Dump into a tulip glass and fill the glass with crushed ice. Garnish with the orchid and serve with a straw.

PABLO HONEY ✿

Matthew Belanger, 2019

St. George Terroir gin has fir in its botanical build, but it tastes like rosemary in a drink. I wanted to build a gin sour around that. —MB

- **1 ounce St. George Terroir gin**
- **1 ounce Capurro Acholado pisco**
- **¼ ounce Dolin Génépy des Alpes liqueur**
- **¾ ounce fresh lemon juice**
- **½ ounce fresh grapefruit juice**
- **½ ounce Honey Syrup (page 284)**
- **Garnish: 1 lemon wheel**

Shake all the ingredients with ice, then double strain into a chilled coupe. Garnish with the lemon wheel.

PARADISE LOST

Shannon Tebay, 2018

I started this aggressively funky mai tai riff by swapping pineapple gum syrup for the orgeat. I came to Matt Belanger with the idea for pairing green chile vodka with rhum agricole. "That's fucked up," he said, and walked away. With Matt, this is the ultimate compliment. The drink looks like it'll be tropical and fruity, but it's unexpectedly sulphuric and spicy, like drinking a mai tai in hell. —ST

- **1½ ounces Rhum JM Blanc 100**
- **½ ounce St. George green chile vodka**
- **¼ ounce yellow Chartreuse**
- **1 ounce fresh lime juice**
- **¾ ounce Pineapple Gum Syrup (page 286)**
- **Garnish: 2 pineapple fronds and 1 small dried chile**

Combine all the ingredients in a shaker and whip, shaking with a few pieces of crushed ice, just until incorporated. Dump into a collins glass and fill the glass with crushed ice. Garnish with the pineapple fronds and dried chile and serve with a straw.

PIRATE KING PUNCH

Tyson Buhler, 2015

I named this drink after the TV show *Archer*, which was a staff favorite. It's a pretty classic tiki build that uses up all that fresh orange juice we're always drowning in. —TB

    3 ounces Siembra Valles Blanco tequila

    3 ounces Bacardi Heritage rum

    2 ounces Velvet falernum

    1 ounce Wray & Nephew Overproof Jamaica rum

    ¾ ounce St. Elizabeth allspice dram

    3 ounces fresh lime juice

    2 ounces fresh orange juice

    2 ounces Passion Fruit Syrup (page 285)

    10 dashes Angostura bitters

    Garnish: 1 small cube of bread soaked in 151-proof rum, 1 empty lime shell, and ground cinnamon

Combine all of the ingredients in a punch bowl and stir to combine. Fill the bowl with crushed ice. Place the rum-soaked bread cube in the lime shell and ignite. Place the flaming lime shell on top of the ice and grate some cinnamon over the punch. Serve with straws.

PLANET CARAVAN

Matthew Belanger, 2018

I've always thought that curry and coconut is a fun combination, but I had never used it in a cocktail before. Scotch goes well with flavors in this unusual whiskey sour. —MB

    1½ ounces Great King St. Glasgow Blend scotch

    ½ ounce Batavia arrack

    ½ ounce Kalani Ron de Coco coconut liqueur

    ¾ ounce fresh lime juice

    ½ ounce Cinnamon Syrup (page 283)

    1 dash Angostura bitters

    1 curry leaf

    Garnish: 1 curry leaf

Shake all the ingredients with ice, then strain into a double old-fashioned glass over 1 large ice cube. Garnish with the curry leaf.

RABBLE-ROUSER ⚎

Matthew Belanger, 2018

    3 cucumber slices

    1¼ ounces Capurro Acholado pisco

    1 ounce Martini Riserva Speciale Ambrato vermouth di Torino

    ¼ ounce Bols genever

    1 teaspoon crème de violette

    ¾ ounce fresh lemon juice

    ½ ounce simple syrup (page 287)

    Garnish: 1 cucumber slice

In a shaker, gently muddle the cucumber. Add the remaining ingredients and shake with ice, then double strain into a double old-fashioned glass over 1 large ice cube. Garnish with the cucumber slice.

RADIO FLYER

Matthew Belanger, 2017

Watermelon and jerk bitters are an interesting combo and gives this drink an extra dimension. Jerk bitters pair well with smoky spirits like scotch as well. I wanted to name this in the spirit of stuff you do in the summer as a kid; I originally called it "Wrist Rocket," but nobody knew what that was, and some folks thought it was inappropriate, so I landed on something more classic and wholesome. —MB

    1½ ounces Monkey Shoulder Blended Malt scotch

    ½ ounce Wyoming Whiskey

    ½ ounce Cappelletti Vino Aperitivo

    ¾ ounce fresh lime juice

    ¾ ounce Watermelon Syrup (page 288)

    ½ dash Bitter End Jamaican Jerk bitters

    Garnish: 1 lime wheel

Shake all the ingredients with ice, then strain into a double old-fashioned glass over 1 large ice cube. Garnish with the lime wheel.

RAMBLE ON

Matthew Belanger, 2018

    1 ounce El Tesoro reposado tequila

    ½ ounce Clear Creek 8-year apple brandy

    ½ ounce Zucca Rabarbaro amaro

    ½ ounce Giffard rhubarb liqueur

    ¾ ounce fresh lime juice

    ½ ounce Raspberry Syrup (page 286)

Shake all the ingredients with ice, then double strain into a chilled coupe. No garnish.

RARE HEARTS

Tyson Buhler, 2018

    1 ounce Pierre Ferrand ambré cognac

    1 ounce Weller Special Reserve bourbon

    ½ ounce fresh lemon juice

    ½ ounce green Chartreuse

    ½ ounce Vanilla Syrup (page 288)

    ½ dashes Scrappy's cardamom bitters

Shake all the ingredients with ice, then double strain into a chilled coupe. No garnish.

ROCKABILLY ✲

Adam Griggs, 2019

This is a Mr. Potato Head of the classic Pompadour, a delicious Daiquiri made with a triple base of fancy ingredients. —AG

- 1 ounce Domaine du Manoir de Montreuil calvados
- 1 ounce Navarre Pineau des Charentes Vieux
- ½ ounce Rhum JM VSOP
- ¾ ounce fresh lemon juice
- ½ ounce simple syrup (page 287)

Shake all the ingredients with ice, then double strain into a chilled coupe. No garnish.

SEA EAGLE

Javelle Taft, 2019

We needed a whiskey sour variation for the menu, so I reached back into my childhood and the flavors of a cherry-vanilla Coke. —JT

- 1½ ounces Rittenhouse rye
- ½ ounce Amaro Averna
- ¾ teaspoon Leopold Bros. New York sour apple liqueur
- ¾ teaspoon Luxardo maraschino liqueur
- ¾ ounce fresh lemon juice
- ½ ounce Vanilla Syrup (page 288)

Shake all the ingredients with ice, then strain into a double old-fashioned glass over 1 large ice cube. No garnish.

SIAMESE GIMLET ✲

Jon Armstrong, 2014

- 2 ounces Tanqueray gin
- 1 ounce fresh lime juice
- ½ ounce fresh grapefruit juice
- ½ ounce Cane Sugar Syrup (page 282)
- ¼ ounce Luxardo maraschino liqueur

- 1 dash Bitter Truth Jerry Thomas' Own Decanter bitters
- 1 makrut lime leaf

Shake all the ingredients with ice, then double strain into a chilled coupe. No garnish.

SIDE EYE

Jeremy Oertel, 2017

- 1½ ounces Tapatío Blanco 110 tequila
- ½ ounce Del Maguey Vida mezcal
- ½ ounce Leopold Bros. New York sour apple liqueur
- ¼ ounce Strega
- ¾ ounce fresh lime juice
- ¼ ounce House Ginger Syrup (page 284)
- 1 dash Scrappy's celery bitters
- Garnish: 1 dehydrated green apple slice

Shake all the ingredients with ice, then strain into a double old-fashioned glass over 1 large ice cube. Garnish with the dehydrated apple slice.

SKYLINE

Tyson Buhler, 2018

- 1 ounce Olmeca Altos Blanco tequila
- 1 ounce Krogstad aquavit
- ½ ounce fresh lime juice
- ½ ounce Spent Citrus Cordial (page 287)
- ½ ounce Campari
- ½ ounce Cinnamon Syrup (page 283)

Shake all the ingredients with ice, then double strain into a chilled coupe. No garnish.

SNAKECHARMER

Tyson Buhler, 2019

- 1 ounce Cobrafire eau-de-vie de raisin
- 1 ounce Plantation Barbados 5-year rum
- ¾ ounce fresh lime juice
- ¾ ounce Raspberry Syrup (page 286)
- 1 teaspoon green Chartreuse
- 1 teaspoon Marie Brizard white crème de cacao

Shake all the ingredients with ice, then double strain into a chilled coupe. No garnish.

SNAKECHARMER ☉

Tyson Buhler, 2019

- 1½ ounces Dolin blanc vermouth
- ⅓ ounce Cobrafire eau-de-vie de raisin
- ⅓ ounce Plantation Barbados 5-year rum
- ¾ ounce fresh lime juice
- ¾ ounce Raspberry Syrup (page 286)
- ⅓ teaspoon green Chartreuse
- ⅓ teaspoon Marie Brizard white crème de cacao

Shake all the ingredients with ice, then double strain into a chilled coupe. No garnish.

SOUR SOUL

Matthew Belanger, 2019

- 1 ounce Old Overholt 100-proof rye
- ½ ounce Busnel VSOP calvados
- ½ ounce St. George spiced pear liqueur
- ¾ ounce fresh lemon juice
- ¾ ounce Vanilla Syrup (page 288)
- ½ ounce dry red wine

Shake all the ingredients except the wine with ice, then strain into a double old-fashioned glass over 1 large ice cube. Slowly pour the wine over the back of a spoon to float it on top of the drink.

STAR SAPPHIRE

Matthew Belanger, 2017

I wanted to make an autumnal margarita with sloe gin. I added the baking-spice flavors of pimento bitters to pull it together and ground it in that season. It ended up being a super-purple drink, so I named it after the Green Lantern villain. —MB

- 1 ounce Tapatío 100 blanco tequila
- 1 ounce Reisetbauer sloeberry gin
- ½ ounce Giffard crème de pamplemousse rose
- ¾ ounce fresh lime juice
- ½ ounce Vanilla Syrup (page 288)
- 1 dash Dale DeGroff's pimento bitters
- Garnish: 1 grapefruit half wheel

Shake all the ingredients with ice, then strain into a double old-fashioned glass over 1 large ice cube. Garnish with the grapefruit half wheel.

SUN MEDALLION

Sam Johnson, 2018

A common way for me to come up with a cocktail is to taste a base spirit first, identify a few flavors, then try to bring them out with other ingredients. I taste a lot of apricot in the Singani, so I amplified that with the apricot eau-de-vie, then completed the stone-fruit flavor profile with the oxidative nuttiness of the Sauternes and the macadamia nut syrup. —SJ

- 1 ounce Singani 63 eau-de-vie
- 1 ounce Blume Marillen apricot eau-de-vie
- ½ ounce Chateau La Fleur d'Or Sauternes
- ¾ ounce fresh lemon juice
- ½ ounce Orgeat Works Macadamia Nut Syrup
- 1 egg white
- Garnish: 1 grapefruit twist

Dry shake all the ingredients, then shake again with ice. Double strain into a chilled coupe. Express the grapefruit twist over the drink and discard.

THIEVES IN LAW

Jillian Vose, 2014

This was my first cocktail that used the beloved "Mac Daddy" syrup made by our friend Tiki Adams at Brooklyn-based Orgeat Works. —JV

- 2 ounces Tanqueray Malacca gin
- ½ ounce Dolin Génépy des Alpes liqueur
- ¾ ounce Orgeat Works Macadamia Nut Syrup
- ½ ounce fresh lemon juice
- ½ ounce fresh Granny Smith apple juice

Shake all the ingredients with ice, then double strain into a chilled coupe. No garnish.

TORO BRAVO

Tyson Buhler, 2015

- 3 cucumber slices
- 1½ ounces Lustau Papirusa manzanilla sherry
- ½ ounce Mahon gin
- 1 teaspoon yellow Chartreuse
- ¾ ounce fresh lemon juice
- ½ ounce House Orgeat (page 284)
- Garnish: 1 cucumber ribbon on a skewer

In a shaker, gently muddle the cucumber slices. Add the remaining ingredients and shake with ice. Double strain into a chilled coupe and garnish with the cucumber ribbon.

TRADEWINDS ❅

Tyson Buhler, 2019

- 1 ounce Cimarron Reposado tequila
- ½ ounce Clear Creek 8-year apple brandy
- ½ ounce Glasshouse Trade Winds garam masala brandy
- ¼ ounce Giffard Abricot du Roussillon
- ¾ ounce fresh lemon juice
- ½ ounce Cane Sugar Syrup (page 282)
- 2 dashes Peychaud's bitters
- Garnish: 1 lemon wheel

Shake all the ingredients with ice, then strain into a double old-fashioned glass over 1 large ice cube. Garnish with the lemon wheel.

TRADEWINDS ☉

Tyson Buhler, 2019

1½ ounces Lustau oloroso sherry

¾ ounce fresh lemon juice

½ ounce Cane Sugar Syrup (page 282)

¼ ounce Cimarron Reposado tequila

2 teaspoons Clear Creek 8-year apple brandy

2 teaspoons Glasshouse Trade Winds garam masala brandy

1 teaspoon Giffard Abricot du Roussillon

2 dashes Peychaud's bitters

Garnish: 1 lemon wheel

Shake all the ingredients with ice, then strain into a double old-fashioned glass over 1 large ice cube. Garnish with the lemon wheel.

TRAMPS LIKE US

Tyson Buhler, 2016

While the drink contains more ingredients than I wanted to use, it fell apart whenever I tried to remove anything, and everything gels together in a focused flavor profile we're always striving for. It's obviously named after The Boss, a frequent topic of conversation at the bar for a period of time in 2016. —TB

1 ounce Dorothy Parker gin

½ ounce Krogstad aquavit

½ ounce Massenez framboise eau-de-vie

¼ ounce Campari

¼ ounce Marie Brizard white crème de cacao

¾ ounce fresh lemon juice

½ ounce Raspberry Syrup (page 286)

Garnish: 1 lemon wheel, 1 raspberry, and 1 mint bouquet

Short shake all the ingredients with ice for about 5 seconds, then strain into a double old-fashioned glass. Fill the glass with crushed ice. Garnish with the lemon wheel, raspberry, and mint bouquet and serve with a straw.

VOODOO DREAMS ⚜

Keely Sutherland, 2018

I wanted to make a tasty, warming fall tiki drink with scotch, so I pulled in the banana bread flavors found in the Tempus Fugit banana liqueur. —KS

1 ounce Diplomático Reserva Exclusiva rum

1 ounce Naked Grouse whisky

½ ounce Tempus Fugit crème de banane

½ ounce fresh lemon juice

½ ounce Demerara Syrup (page 283)

2 dashes Bittermens Xocolatl mole bitters

½ dash Salt Solution (page 299)

Garnish: 1 mint bouquet and dried banana slices

Combine all the ingredients in a shaker and whip, shaking with a few pieces of crushed ice, just until incorporated. Dump into a tiki mug and fill the mug with crushed ice. Garnish with the mint bouquet and dried banana slices. Serve with a straw.

WACO KID

Tyson Buhler, 2014

This was my first foray into clarified juices. I took Brad Farran's Blazing Saddles as inspiration and turned it into an acidified Martini of sorts. —TB

2 ounces High West Silver oat whiskey

¾ ounce Dolin blanc vermouth

½ ounce Combier pamplemousse rose liqueur

½ ounce Clarified Lime Juice (page 296)

1 teaspoon Cinnamon Syrup (page 283)

1 dash Bittermens 'Elemakule tiki bitters

Garnish: 1 grapefruit twist

Stir all the ingredients over ice, then strain into a chilled coupe. Express the grapefruit twist over the drink and discard.

WARMORE'S BLUES

Tyson Buhler, 2017

2 ounces Pistachio-Infused Elijah Craig Bourbon (page 294)

¼ ounce Mathilde pêche liqueur

¾ ounce fresh lemon juice

½ ounce Cane Sugar Syrup (page 282)

1 dash Angostura bitters

Shake all the ingredients with ice, then double strain into a chilled coupe. No garnish.

WINDJAMMER

Tyson Buhler, 2018

1 ounce Weller Special Reserve bourbon

½ ounce Appleton Estate Reserve Jamaica rum

½ ounce Hamilton Jamaican Pot Still Gold rum

½ ounce Giffard crème de banane

¾ ounce fresh lemon juice

¼ ounce House Ginger Syrup (page 284)

¼ ounce House Orgeat (page 284)

Garnish: Dried chamomile

Combine all the ingredients in a shaker and whip, shaking with a few pieces of crushed ice, just until incorporated. Dump into a tiki mug and fill the glass with crushed ice. Sprinkle some chamomile over the top of the drink and serve with a straw.

☉ LOW ABV   ◌ NO ABV   ❄ FREEZER BAR   ⧗ PROJECT COCKTAIL   ⚜ LOW-PREP COCKTAIL

Boozy & Honest

ACES AND EIGHTS ❄

Jarred Weigand, 2016

2 ounces El Tesoro Reposado tequila

½ ounce Meletti amaro

1 teaspoon Galliano Ristretto

1 teaspoon Vanilla Syrup (page 288)

1 dash Bittermens Xocolatl mole bitters

Garnish: 1 orange twist

Stir all the ingredients over ice, then strain into a double old-fashioned glass over 1 large ice cube. Express the orange twist over the drink, then place it in the drink.

ALTIMETER JULEP

Jarred Weigand, 2017

I love the way El Tesoro tequila pairs with apple brandy; we've used this combination in numerous drinks. With all of these alpine-y, Christmas-y flavors going on, maple syrup felt like the obvious sweetener for this Old-Fashioned. —JW

1½ ounces El Tesoro Reposado tequila

½ ounce Clear Creek 8-year apple brandy

¼ ounce yellow Chartreuse

¼ ounce Clear Creek Douglas Fir eau-de-vie

¼ ounce maple syrup

Garnish: 1 mint bouquet and 1 dried apple slice

Combine all the ingredients in a julep tin and fill the tin about halfway with crushed ice. Holding the tin by the rim, stir, churning the ice as you go, for about 10 seconds. Add more crushed ice to fill the tin about two-thirds full and stir until the tin is completely frosted. Add more ice to form a cone above the rim. Garnish with the mint bouquet and dried apple slice and serve with a straw.

ARTFUL DODGER ❄

Tyson Buhler, 2015

The combo of miso and banana is so, so good. I wanted to let it shine in a simple, Armagnac and rum–based Old-Fashioned. —TB

1 ounce Miso-Infused Tariquet Classique VS Armagnac (page 293)

1 ounce El Dorado 15-year rum

1 teaspoon Demerara Syrup (page 283)

½ teaspoon Giffard banane du Brésil

Garnish: 1 lemon twist

Stir all the ingredients over ice, then strain into a double old-fashioned glass over 1 large ice cube. Express the lemon twist over the drink and discard.

BACKROADS

Michael Buonocore, 2019

¾ ounce Westward American single malt

¾ ounce Delord 25-year bas Armagnac

½ ounce Dupont Pommeau de Normande

½ teaspoon Amrut peated cask-strength single malt Indian whisky

½ teaspoon Vanilla Syrup (page 288)

1 teaspoon maple syrup

Stir all the ingredients over ice, then strain into a single old-fashioned glass over 1 large ice cube. No garnish.

BADLANDS COBBLER ☉

Matthew Belanger, 2019

1 orange wheel

1½ ounces Carpano Antica Formula vermouth

¾ ounce Fernet-Branca

¾ ounce El Dorado 8-year rum

½ ounce Giffard Banane du Brésil

¼ ounce Demerara Syrup (page 283)

1 drop Terra Spice eucalyptus extract

Garnish: 1 orange wheel, 1 mint bouquet, and powdered sugar

In a shaker, gently muddle the orange wheel. Add the remaining ingredients and shake with ice. Strain into a tulip glass and fill the glass with crushed ice. Garnish with the orange slice and mint bouquet and dust the top of the drink with powdered sugar. Serve with a straw.

BIRDS OF PREY ❋

Matthew Belanger, 2015

It's easy to get tropical flavors into a shaken drink, but much harder to get them into a stirred one. Here, I infused the tequila with mangos and built the rest of the drink around it to showcase that infusion. —MB

1 ounce Dried Mango–Infused Calle 23 Reposado Tequila (page 291)

1 ounce Scarlet Ibis Trinidad rum

½ ounce Ancho Reyes ancho chile liqueur

1 teaspoon Cane Sugar Syrup (page 282)

1 drop Bitter End curry bitters

Garnish: 1 orange twist

Stir all the ingredients over ice, then strain into a double old-fashioned glass over 1 large ice cube. Express the orange twist over the drink, then place it in the drink.

BLACK POWDER ❋

Scott Teague, 2013

I created this drink around the time I fell in love with mixing base spirits. Here, I paired the beautiful grape notes from a super-nice Armagnac with a smoky mezcal. —ST

1 ounce Del Maguey Vida mezcal

1 ounce Tariquet Classique VS Bas-Armagnac

1 teaspoon maple syrup

½ teaspoon St. Elizabeth allspice dram

1 dash House Orange Bitters (page 298)

1 dash Angostura bitters

Garnish: 1 orange twist

Stir all the ingredients over ice, then strain into a double old-fashioned glass over 1 large ice cube. Flame the orange twist over the drink, then place it in the drink.

BUSY EARNING ❋

Tyson Buhler, 2015

Drink writing can be easy when you're working with extremely well-made spirits, such as Redbreast whiskey. I try to give their flavor profile a slight accent, in this case a bit of sarsaparilla and black strap rum, and let the base spirit do the rest of the work. —TB

1½ ounces Redbreast 12-year Irish whiskey

½ ounce Cruzan Black Strap rum

¼ ounce Laphroaig 10-year scotch

1 teaspoon Sarsaparilla Demerara Syrup (page 286)

1 dash Angostura bitters

Garnish: 1 orange twist

Stir all the ingredients over ice, then strain into a double old-fashioned glass over 1 large ice cube. Express the orange twist over the drink, then place it in the drink.

CALYPSO KING ❋

Tyson Buhler, 2016

Here's another drink that really lets the base spirits shine, which is always the goal when working with higher-priced bottles. It doesn't take much when working with old, rich, layered rum. —TB

1 ounce Navazos Palazzi oloroso rum

1 ounce Redbreast 12-year Irish whiskey

1 teaspoon Pineapple Gum Syrup (page 286)

½ teaspoon House Orgeat (page 284)

1 dash Bittermens 'Elemakule tiki bitters

Garnish: 1 grapefruit twist

Stir all the ingredients over ice, then strain into a double old-fashioned glass over 1 large ice cube. Express the grapefruit twist over the drink, then place it in the drink.

CASHMERE THOUGHTS ❋

Jarred Weigand, 2019

When we started playing around with our new centrifuge, Tyson blended some biscotti cookies with kirschwasser and clarified it, and it was delicious. I wanted to create that flavor without so much trouble or technology, and I found this dusty bottle of biscotti liqueur at a liquor store in New Jersey. I thought the drink was rich, elegant, and bad ass, so I named it after a Jay-Z song. —JW

1½ ounces Gourry de Chadeville overproof cognac

¼ ounce Massenez kirschwasser

¼ ounce González Byass Noé Pedro Ximénez

1 teaspoon Faretti biscotti liqueur

1 dash absinthe

Garnish: 1 lemon twist

Stir all the ingredients over ice, then strain into a chilled single old-fashioned glass. Express the lemon twist over the drink and discard.

CIPHER ❋

Sam Johnson, 2019

This is a big-flavored, boozy nightcap, built around an amazing sherry-finished whiskey. After tasting the whiskey, I thought coffee flavors would go well with it, and yellow Chartreuse loves coffee. —SJ

1½ ounces Navazos Palazzi Overseas malt whiskey

½ ounce Avuá Amburana cachaça

¼ ounce Galliano Ristretto

¼ ounce yellow Chartreuse

1 dash Miracle Mile Redeye bitters

1 dash absinthe

Garnish: 1 orange twist

Stir all the ingredients over ice, then strain into a single old-fashioned glass over 1 large ice cube. Express the orange twist over the drink, then place it in the drink.

CITADELLE ❋

Tyson Buhler, 2017

1 ounce Rhine Hall mango brandy

1 ounce Bols genever

1 teaspoon Luxardo maraschino liqueur

½ teaspoon Honey Syrup (page 284)

1 dash House Orange Bitters (page 298)

1 dash absinthe

Garnish: 1 lemon twist

Stir all the ingredients over ice, then strain into a double old-fashioned glass over 1 large ice cube. Express the lemon twist over the drink, then place it in the drink.

CYRANO

Jonnie Long, 2018

Cynar gives this Ti' Punch riff a nice backbone and smooths out the rum. Like a Negroni, the drink starts sweet and finishes dry and spirit-forward, with a long, sugarcane-y finish from the rhum agricole. —JL

1 lime coin (a quarter-size piece of rind with some flesh attached)

1 teaspoon Pineapple Gum Syrup (page 286)

1 ounce Rhum JM VSOP

¾ ounce Cynar

¼ ounce Plantation Pineapple rum

1 dash Angostura bitters

Garnish: 1 mint bouquet

In a single old-fashioned glass, muddle the lime and syrup. Add the remaining ingredients, fill the glass with cracked ice, and stir briefly. Garnish with the mint bouquet.

DIAMOND SQUAD ❋

Matthew Belanger, 2019

1¼ ounces Old Forester 100 bourbon

½ ounce Bertoux brandy

¼ ounce Anchor Hophead vodka

1 teaspoon Pineapple Gum Syrup (page 286)

½ teaspoon Luxardo maraschino liqueur

1 dash Bitter Truth peach bitters

Garnish: 1 lemon twist

Stir all the ingredients over ice, then strain into a single old-fashioned glass over 1 large ice cube. Express the lemon twist over the drink, then place it in the drink.

DIXIELAND JULEP

Tyson Buhler, 2017

1 ounce Pierre Ferrand 1840 cognac

½ ounce Ron Zacapa 23 rum

½ ounce Lemon Hart 151 rum

¼ ounce Fernet-Branca

¼ ounce Bittermens New Orleans coffee liqueur

¼ ounce Pineapple Gum Syrup (page 286)

Garnish: 1 dehydrated pineapple slice, 1 mint bouquet, and 1 coffee bean

Combine all the ingredients in a julep tin and fill the tin about halfway with crushed ice. Holding the tin by the rim, stir, churning the ice as you go, for about 10 seconds. Add more crushed ice to fill the tin about two-thirds full and stir until the tin is completely frosted. Add more ice to form a cone above the rim. Garnish with the pineapple slice and mint bouquet and grate some coffee over the top of the drink. Serve with a straw.

DOUBLE DRAGON ❋

Al Sotack, 2014

1 ounce Yamazaki 12-year (or Nikka Taketsuru) whisky

1 ounce Sombra mezcal

¼ ounce Port Syrup (page 286)

2 dashes Bitter End Moroccan bitters

Garnish: 1 orange twist

Stir all the ingredients over ice, then strain into a double old-fashioned glass over 1 large ice cube. Express the orange twist over the drink, then place it in the drink.

EMPTY NESTER

Dave Anderson, 2019

This is my take on a more bitter and complex sherry cobbler. A tiny amount of Zangs 00 cider eau-de-vie works wonders and makes the drink taste like my mom's apple crisp. The garnish is lavish, but a reminder that cobblers should be exciting and a little over the top. —DA

1 lemon coin (a quarter-size piece of rind with some flesh attached)

1 orange half wheel

1½ ounces Lustau manzanilla sherry

1 ounce Bonal Gentiane-Quina

½ ounce Amaro Nonino

1 teaspoon Cyril Zangs 00 apple cider eau-de-vie

¼ ounce Cinnamon Syrup (page 283)

Garnish: 1 mint bouquet, 1 orange half wheel, 1 apple slice, powdered sugar, and 1 cinnamon stick

In a shaker, gently muddle the lemon coin and orange half wheel. Add the remaining ingredients and whip, shaking with a few pieces of crushed ice, just until the ingredients are incorporated. Strain into a julep tin and fill the tin with crushed ice. Insert the mint bouquet, orange half wheel, and apple slice into the ice; dust the top of the garnishes with powdered sugar and grated cinnamon.

EVENT HORIZON ✳

Sam Johnson, 2018

Here, I'm trying to make a Toronto with Mexican ingredients. Vallet, Mexican fernet, is very dry and astringent, like trying to eat a teaspoon of ground cinnamon. I combine our macadamia nut syrup with macadamia liqueur; this is something I do frequently, as the syrup doesn't have much aroma, so when used in tandem they complete the circle of macadamia nut. —SJ

2 ounces Siete Leguas Añejo tequila

¾ ounce Fernet-Vallet

1 teaspoon Orgeat Works Macadamia Nut Syrup

½ teaspoon Trader Vic's macadamia nut liqueur

Garnish: 1 orange twist

Stir all the ingredients over ice, then strain into a double old-fashioned glass over 1 large ice cube. Express the orange twist over the drink, then place it in the drink.

FALSE SUMMIT ✳

Sam Johnson, 2018

This is the whiskey and aged-rum drinker's pinnacle, full of base tone flavors. Even though there's more whiskey in the build, the drink is really more about the rum, which is so intense you don't need much of it. PX sherry adds extra texture and sweetness, and the rum just sucks that right up. —SJ

1½ ounces Tyrconnell single malt Irish whiskey

½ ounce Navazos Palazzi oloroso rum

2 teaspoons Gonzáles Byass Pedro Ximénez sherry

1 teaspoon Tempus Fugit crème de banane

Garnish: 1 orange twist

Stir all the ingredients over ice, then strain into a single old-fashioned glass over 1 large ice cube. Express the orange twist over the drink and discard.

GET FREE ✳

Matthew Belanger, 2017

I borrowed the combination of maraschino and passion fruit from old-school tiki drinks and put them into a Fancy Free variation. —MB

1 ounce Barrell Whiskey Batch 004

1 ounce El Dorado 15-year Demerara rum

2 teaspoons Luxardo maraschino liqueur

1 teaspoon Giffard passion fruit liqueur

1 dash Bittermens 'Elemakule tiki bitters

Garnish: 1 grapefruit twist

Stir all the ingredients over ice, then strain into a double old-fashioned glass over 1 large ice cube. Express the grapefruit twist over the drink, then place it in the drink.

GOLDEN LANCEHEAD

Matthew Belanger, 2017

I had a hunch that Chareau would work well in a Ti' Punch, as both the aloe liqueur and rhum agricole have a grassy quality. The pear eau-de-vie gives it all a bit of roundness, but you don't detect the pear in the final drink, which is a great example of how pear can improve a drink in the background. —MB

1 lime coin (a quarter-size piece of rind with some flesh attached)

1 teaspoon Cane Sugar Syrup (page 282)

1¼ ounces Rhum JM Agricole Blanc

½ ounce Chareau aloe liqueur

¼ ounce Clear Creek pear eau-de-vie

½ teaspoon green Chartreuse

In a single old-fashioned glass, muddle the lime coin and syrup. Add the remaining ingredients, fill the glass with cracked ice, and stir briefly. No garnish.

GOLDILOCKS ✳

Jillian Vose, 2014

1½ ounces Hamilton Jamaican Pot Still Gold rum

½ ounce Glen Grant 10-year whisky

¼ ounce Amaro CioCiaro

¼ ounce Giffard banane du Brésil

½ teaspoon Cane Sugar Syrup (page 282)

1 dash Bittercube Jamaican Black Strap bitters

Garnish: 1 orange twist

Stir all the ingredients over ice, then strain into a double old-fashioned glass over 1 large ice cube. Express the orange twist over the drink, then place it in the drink.

HAGAKURE ✳

Matthew Belanger, 2018

After Japanese whisky started to get really popular but before they clamped down on allocations, we'd buy every bottle of Yamazaki that we could get our hands on. By the time this drink went on the menu, we were sitting on a massive stockpile of the stuff. This was the most expensive cocktail in the menu, but we sold the shit out of it. If you can't find Yamazaki, use Santori Toki or Nikka Coffey Grain in its place, and it will be almost as good. —MB

1½ ounces Yamazaki 12-year whisky

½ ounce Caol Ila 12-year scotch

¼ ounce Chareau aloe liqueur

1 teaspoon Cane Sugar Syrup (page 282)

½ teaspoon yellow Chartreuse

2 dashes Miracle Mile yuzu bitters

Garnish: 1 lemon twist

Stir all the ingredients over ice, then strain into a single old-fashioned glass over 1 large ice cube. Express the lemon twist over the drink and discard.

CYRANO, PAGE 231

HER NAME IS JOY ❄

Sam Penton, 2019

If I could make one cocktail that would best describe me, this is it. I've always been a lover of rum, and have worked in tiki bars in the past. Highland Park is one of my favorite scotches, so I split the base between that and a funky Jamaican rum, using a Vieux Carré (my favorite classic cocktail) as inspiration. —SP

- 1 ounce Appleton Estate 21-year Jamaica rum
- 1 ounce Highland Park 12-year scotch
- ¼ ounce Lustau oloroso sherry
- 1 teaspoon Bénédictine
- 1 teaspoon Galliano Ristretto
- ½ teaspoon Demerara Syrup (page 283)
- Garnish: 1 orange twist

Stir all the ingredients over ice, then strain into a single old-fashioned glass over 1 large ice cube. Express the orange twist over the drink and discard.

HIGHWAYMAN ❄

Tyson Buhler, 2018

Yet another whiskey-based cocktail named after a Western; the combination of coffee and tropical fruit flavors is really fun to play around with. —TB

- 1¼ ounces Elijah Craig 12-year bourbon
- ½ ounce Bowmore 12-year scotch
- ¼ ounce Smith & Cross Jamaica rum
- 2 teaspoons Galliano Ristretto
- 1 teaspoon Giffard passion fruit liqueur
- Garnish: 1 orange twist

Stir all the ingredients over ice, then strain into a double old-fashioned glass over 1 large ice cube. Express the orange twist over the drink, then place it in the drink.

HONOR AMONGST THIEVES ♣

Tyson Buhler, 2016

We've only served a handful of hot drinks at Death & Co NYC, as they're quite the hassle to make in the small confines of the bar. But this mulled wine riff was fully batched and held in a hot water bath for quick service. —TB

- 3 ounces Saint Cosme Crozes-Hermitage
- ½ ounce Cruzan Black Strap rum
- ½ ounce Amaro sfumato
- ½ ounce Demerara Syrup (page 283)
- 2 dashes Bitter Truth aromatic bitters
- 3 drops Terra Spice birch extract
- Garnish: 1 orange twist and nutmeg

Combine all the ingredients in a small saucepan over medium-low heat and cook, stirring occasionally, until steaming hot but not simmering. Pour into an Irish coffee mug. Express the orange twist over the drink and discard, then grate some nutmeg over the top of the drink.

HOT DREAMS ⧗

Jarred Weigand, 2018

This was my favorite Death & Co spec, and it pretty much wrote itself. Jon Armstrong created the habanero tincture as a way to add spice to drinks without having to use jalapeño-infused tequila. As for the peanut butter–infused rye: a lot of people taste peanuts in Old Overholt, so I amped that up with a fat-wash infusion, then augmented it with a smoky, chocolaty mezcal. Peanut butter loves honey, so honey syrup became the sweetener. We sold so many of this cocktail, because it contains a trifecta of ingredients that makes guests think "I have to have that." —JW

- 1½ ounces Peanut Butter–Infused Old Overholt Bonded Rye (page 293)
- ½ ounce Del Maguey Chichicapa mezcal
- ¼ ounce Gonzáles Byass Nectar Pedro Ximénez dulce sherry
- 1 teaspoon Honey Syrup (page 284)
- 1 dash Bittermens Xocolatl mole bitters
- ½ dash Habanero Tincture (page 299)

Stir all the ingredients over ice, then strain into a single old-fashioned glass over 1 large ice cube. No garnish.

I AGAINST I ♣

Matthew Belanger, 2019

Many Jamaican rum producers buy funky rum from Hampden and blend it into their final product, but Hampden started bottling their rum on its own, and it's more funky than other Jamaican rums by orders of magnitude. Here, it's the star ingredient in a Sazerac variation. —MB

- Strega, to rinse
- 1 ounce Hampden Estate Single Jamaican rum
- 1 ounce Great King St. Glasgow Blend scotch
- ¼ ounce Honey Syrup (page 284)
- 2 dashes Peychaud's bitters
- ½ dash Bitter End Jamaican Jerk bitters
- Garnish: 1 grapefruit twist

Rinse a single old-fashioned glass with Strega and dump. Stir the remaining ingredients over ice, then strain into the glass. Express the grapefruit twist over the drink and discard.

ICE RUN JULEP ❄

Sam Johnson, 2018

The Brooklyn-made Forthave amaro has a cool, mentholated flavor and waxy honey note; it is the keystone of this cool, refreshing julep. —SJ

1 ounce Eagle Rare 10-year bourbon

1 ounce Château de Pellehaut Selection Armagnac

½ ounce Forthave Spirits Marseille amaro

½ teaspoon Grand Marnier

1 teaspoon Honey Syrup (page 284)

Garnish: 1 mint bouquet and 1 orange half wheel

Combine all the ingredients in a julep tin and fill the tin about halfway with crushed ice. Holding the tin by the rim, stir, churning the ice as you go, for about 10 seconds. Add more crushed ice to fill the tin about two-thirds full and stir until the tin is completely frosted. Add more ice to form a cone above the rim. Garnish with the mint bouquet and orange half wheel and serve with a straw.

LASH LARUE ❄

Tim Miner, 2019

1¼ ounces Calle 23 blanco tequila

½ ounce Rhum JM Blanc 100

¼ ounce Reisetbauer carrot eau-de-vie

1 teaspoon Pierre Ferrand dry curaçao

½ teaspoon kümmel liqueur

1 teaspoon Cane Sugar Syrup (page 282)

1 dash House Orange Bitters (page 298)

Stir all the ingredients over ice, then strain into a single old-fashioned glass over 1 large ice cube. No garnish.

LAST MAN STANDING ❄

Alex Jump, 2019

This was my first time working with Reisetbauer carrot eau-de-vie, which quickly became my obsession (as well as everyone else's). It was difficult to work it into this cocktail, which originally started as a Sazerac. —AJ

1½ ounces Russell's Reserve 10-year bourbon

½ ounce Linie aquavit

1 teaspoon Reisetbauer carrot eau-de-vie

1 teaspoon Trader Vic's macadamia nut liqueur

1 teaspoon House Orgeat (page 284)

1 dash Angostura bitters

Garnish: 1 orange twist

Stir all the ingredients over ice, then strain into a single old-fashioned glass over 1 large ice cube. Express the orange twist over the drink, then place it in the drink.

LAST SHADOW ❄

Tyson Buhler, 2014

This cocktail lasted on the menu for only a month or so, as Lemon Hart 151 was discontinued in the US for a time. But the combination of rich rums, cinnamon, and fernet acting as bitters works seamlessly. —TB

1½ ounces El Dorado 15-year rum

½ ounce Lemon Hart 151 rum

½ teaspoon Fernet-Branca

1 teaspoon Cinnamon Syrup (page 283)

1 teaspoon Demerara Syrup (page 283)

Garnish: 1 grapefruit twist

Stir all the ingredients over ice, then strain into a single old-fashioned glass over 1 large ice cube. Express the grapefruit twist over the drink, then place it in the drink.

THE LONESOME CROWDED WEST ❄

Matthew Belanger, 2018

This Old-Fashioned has everything everyone likes, so of course it was the most popular drink on the menu. —MB

1½ ounces Ron del Barrilito 3-Star rum

¾ ounce Amaro Nonino

½ ounce Old Grand-Dad 114 bourbon

½ teaspoon Giffard passion fruit liqueur

1 dash Angostura bitters

Garnish: 1 grapefruit twist

Stir all the ingredients over ice, then strain into a single old-fashioned glass over 1 large ice cube. Express the grapefruit twist over the drink and discard.

LONE STAR ❄

Matthew Belanger, 2018

I wanted to make an Old-Fashioned that had the flavor profile of root beer. The root beer extract obviously has that, but I blew it up with spearmint, allspice, and vanilla flavors, along with a malty genever. —MB

1¾ ounces Tapatío Blanco 110 tequila

¼ ounce Bols genever

¼ ounce Velvet falernum

1 teaspoon Giffard menthe-pastille

1 teaspoon Vanilla Syrup (page 288)

1 dash Dale DeGroff's pimento bitters

1 drop Terra Spice root beer extract

Garnish: 1 orange twist

Stir all the ingredients over ice, then strain into a single old-fashioned glass over 1 large ice cube. Express the orange twist over the drink, then place it in the drink.

LONG STORY SHORT ❄

Jeremy Oertel, 2017

1½ ounces Old Forester Signature bourbon

½ ounce Smith & Cross Jamaica rum

½ teaspoon Cinnamon Syrup (page 283)

½ teaspoon Demerara Syrup (page 283)

½ teaspoon Giffard passion fruit liqueur

1 dash Bitter Truth Jerry Thomas' Own Decanter bitters

Garnish: 1 orange twist

Stir all the ingredients over ice, then strain into a double old-fashioned glass over 1 large ice cube. Express the orange twist over the drink, then place it in the drink.

LORD BALTIMORE ❄

Jon Armstrong, 2016

Old-Fashioneds usually use a citrus twist as an aromatic garnish, but here I use grapefruit liqueur in its place. —JA

1½ ounces George Dickel rye

½ ounce Pikesville 110-proof rye

1 teaspoon Giffard crème de pamplemousse rose

1 teaspoon dark maple syrup

½ teaspoon Amaro di Angostura

Stir all the ingredients over ice, then strain into a double old-fashioned glass over 1 large ice cube. No garnish.

LOST HORIZON ❄

Tyson Buhler, 2018

Laphroaig 10-year scotch, to rinse

1 ounce Appleton Estate Reserve Jamaica rum

1 ounce Hine H VSOP cognac

2 teaspoons Giffard banane du Brésil

1 teaspoon Fernet-Branca

Garnish: 1 orange twist

Rinse a single old-fashioned glass with the Laphroaig and dump. Stir the remaining ingredients over ice, then strain into the glass. Express the orange twist over the drink, then place it in the drink.

THE MANTICORE ❄

Scott Teague, 2014

2 ounces Beefeater gin

¼ ounce Velvet falernum

1 teaspoon Giffard menthe-pastille

1 teaspoon Cinnamon Syrup (page 283)

1½ dashes Peychaud's bitters

Garnish: 1 lemon twist

Stir all the ingredients over ice, then strain into a single old-fashioned glass over 1 large ice cube. Express the lemon twist over the drink and discard.

MATCH GRIP JULEP ❄

Jarred Weigand, 2016

I wanted to create a julep that didn't involve fresh mint, so I reached for Branca Menta, then added cognac and played up its fruit notes with a funky rum, as well as some crème de cacao for body. —JW

1½ ounces Hine H VSOP cognac

½ ounce Appleton Estate Signature rum

1 teaspoon Marie Brizard white crème de cacao

1 teaspoon Fernet-Branca Menta

1 teaspoon Demerara Syrup (page 283)

1 dash Bittermens Xocolatl mole bitters

1 teaspoon Hamilton Jamaican Pot Still Black rum

Garnish: 1 mint bouquet

Combine all the ingredients except the Hamilton rum in a julep tin and fill the tin about halfway with crushed ice. Holding the tin by the rim, stir, churning the ice as you go, for about 10 seconds. Add more crushed ice to fill the tin about two-thirds full and stir until the tin is completely frosted. Add more ice to form a cone above the rim. Drizzle the Hamilton rum over the top of the drink. Garnish with the mint bouquet and serve with a straw.

MIDNIGHT OIL

Tyson Buhler, 2017

1 orange half wheel

1½ ounces Fausse Piste Garde Manger Syrah

1½ ounces Amaro Ramazzotti

½ ounce Laird's bonded apple brandy

¼ ounce yellow Chartreuse

½ ounce Cinnamon Syrup (page 283)

Garnish: 1 blackberry and 1 cinnamon stick

In a cocktail shaker, gently muddle the orange. Add the remaining ingredients and whip, shaking with a few pieces of crushed ice, just until incorporated. Dump into a double old-fashioned glass and fill the glass with crushed ice. Garnish with the blackberry and grate some cinnamon over the top of the drink. Serve with a straw.

MINASENO

Tyson Buhler, 2016

1 ounce Shiitake-Infused Hibiki Harmony Whisky (page 294)

1 ounce Dried Mango–Infused Calle 23 Reposado Tequila (page 291)

1 teaspoon Honey Syrup (page 284)

½ teaspoon Vanilla Syrup (page 288)

1 dash House Orange Bitters (page 298)

Garnish: 1 lemon twist and 1 orange twist

Combine all the ingredients in a shaker and whip, shaking with a few pieces of crushed ice, just until incorporated. Dump into a double old-fashioned glass over 1 large ice cube. Express the lemon and orange twists over the drink, then place in the drink.

MONARCH JULEP ⚜

Tyson Buhler, 2016

1½ ounces J. Rieger Kansas City whiskey

½ ounce Peach Street Peach brandy

½ ounce Hidalgo Gobernador oloroso

¼ ounce Amaro CioCiaro

¼ ounce Massenez crème de pêche peach liqueur

¼ ounce Honey Syrup (page 284)

Garnish: 1 mint bouquet and 1 peach slice

Combine all the ingredients in a julep tin and fill the tin about halfway with crushed ice. Holding the tin by the rim, stir, churning the ice as you go, for about 10 seconds. Add more crushed ice to fill the tin about two-thirds full and stir until the tin is completely frosted. Add more ice to form a cone above the rim. Garnish with the mint bouquet and peach slice and serve with a straw.

MONONOKE ⚜

Shannon Tebay, 2019

1 lemon wheel

2 ounces Choya Kokuto umeshu

1 ounce Lustau Los Arcos amontillado sherry

¼ ounce Dolin Génépy des Alpes liqueur

¼ ounce Cane Sugar Syrup (page 282)

Garnish: 1 lemon wheel, 1 apple slice, and 1 mint bouquet

In a shaker, gently muddle the lemon. Add the remaining ingredients and whip, shaking with a few pieces of crushed ice, just until incorporated. Dump into a collins glass and fill the glass with crushed ice. Garnish with the lemon wheel, apple slice, and mint bouquet. Serve with a straw.

MOUNTAIN OF LIGHT ⚜

Matthew Belanger, 2019

Apple and cardamom are a common combination in food and perfumery. I named the drink after the Cascahuin distillery, which is located on a mountain that is frequently struck by lightning because of its metal content. —MB

1½ ounces Cascahuin 48 Plata tequila

½ ounce Leopold Bros. New York sour apple liqueur

1 teaspoon Rhine Hall apple brandy

1 teaspoon Cane Sugar Syrup (page 282)

1 dash Angostura bitters

3 drops Scrappy's cardamom bitters

Garnish: 1 apple fan

Stir all the ingredients over ice, then strain into a single old-fashioned glass over 1 large ice cube. Garnish with the apple fan.

MOVING TARGET ⚜

Jeremy Oertel, 2016

Absinthe, to rinse

1½ ounces Pierre Ferrand 1840 cognac

½ ounce Rittenhouse rye

½ ounce Jean-Luc Pasquet Marie-Framboise

1 teaspoon Demerara Syrup (page 283)

2 dashes Miracle Mile Redeye bitters

Garnish: 1 lemon twist

Rinse a single old-fashioned glass with absinthe and dump. Stir the remaining ingredients over ice, then strain into the glass. Express the lemon twist over the drink and discard.

NO-LOOK PASS, OPPOSITE

NOBLE ONE ⊙

Javelle Taft, 019

After trying Sam's Sky Ladder (page 265), I wanted to come up with a Bamboo variation that was all about the white port, with a really cool flavor combination of port, apricot, and sherry. I first brought the drink to a tasting as a Bamboo, then we made it into a sour, then it became a collins, then we circled back to the original Bamboo build. —JT

1½ ounces Quinta do Infantado white porto

1½ ounces Alvear Festival pale cream sherry

1 teaspoon Rothman & Winter Orchard apricot liqueur

½ teaspoon Honey Syrup (page 284)

1 dash House Orange bitters (page 298)

Garnish: 1 lemon twist

Stir all the ingredients with ice, then strain into a single old-fashioned glass. Express the lemon twist over the drink and discard.

NO-LOOK PASS ♣

Shannon Ponche, 2020

This drink is totally clear, so it's surprising how much is going on in the glass. I've used the flavor combination of habanero, basil, and peach before, so I'm very comfortable with it, the same way a basketball player is comfortable enough with her body and team to make a no-look pass. —SP

1¼ ounces Agave de Cortes mezcal

¾ ounce Empirical Spirits Habanero Spirit

1 teaspoon Massenez Garden Party basil liqueur

½ teaspoon Giffard crème de pêche

½ teaspoon simple syrup (page 287)

Garnish: 1 basil sprig

Stir all the ingredients with ice, then strain into a single old-fashioned glass over 1 large ice cube. Garnish with the basil sprig.

OUTLAW COUNTRY ❄

Tyson Buhler, 2017

This combination of base spirit, amaro, tropical fruit, and spice is something we've used in many Old-Fashioned variations, but there's always room for more exploration, and it seems to never fail. —TB

1 ounce Old Grand-Dad bonded bourbon

½ ounce Plantation Pineapple rum

¼ ounce Smith & Cross Jamaica rum

¼ ounce Amaro Averna

1 teaspoon Vanilla Syrup (page 288)

1 dash Angostura bitters

Garnish: 1 orange twist

Stir all the ingredients over ice, then strain into a double old-fashioned glass over 1 large ice cube. Express the orange twist over the drink, then place it in the drink.

PAPER THIN HOTEL ❄

Jarred Weigand, 2018

1½ ounces Pistachio-Infused Rittenhouse Rye (page 294)

½ ounce Pierre Ferrand 1840 cognac

1 teaspoon Demerara Syrup (page 283)

½ teaspoon Massenez crème de pêche peach liqueur

2 dashes Angostura bitters

Garnish: 1 orange twist and 1 lemon twist

Stir all the ingredients over ice, then strain into a single old-fashioned glass over 1 large ice cube. Express the orange twist over the drink, then gently rub it around the rim of the glass. Express the lemon twist over the drink, then garnish with both twists.

PAPI CHULEP

Jon Armstrong, 2015

This whole drink is a showcase for the chichicapa, which has flavors of dark chocolate, mint, and bitter orange. I don't build my juleps like most folks; instead of muddling or rubbing the mint inside the tin, I prefer the fresh flavor you get from dry shaking the cocktail with mint. —JA

6 to 8 mint leaves

1½ ounces Cacao Nib–Infused Calle 23 Tequila (page 290)

½ ounce Del Maguey Chichicapa mezcal

¼ ounce Grand Marnier

1 teaspoon Cane Sugar Syrup (page 282)

Garnish: 1 mint bouquet

Dry shake all the ingredients, then shake again with ice. Double strain into a julep tin and fill the tin with crushed ice. Garnish with the mint bouquet and serve with a straw.

PHANTOM MOOD ❄

Jeremy Oertel, 2017

I love an Old-Fashioned with a bit of spiciness that kicks up on the finish, a little extra burn on the end. —JO

1½ ounces Torres 15-year brandy

½ ounce Springbank 10-year scotch

¼ ounce González Byass Nectar Pedro Ximénez dulce sherry

1 teaspoon Caffo Amaretto

1 dash absinthe

1 dash Miracle Mile chocolate chile bitters

Garnish: 1 orange twist

Stir all the ingredients over ice, then strain into a double old-fashioned glass over 1 large ice cube. Express the orange twist over the drink, then place it in the drink.

PRIMROSE ❊

Jarred Weigand, 2018

This is one of those drinks that doesn't involve any infusions, special syrups, or weird juices. I love writing drinks that can be replicated anywhere. —JW

  1½ ounces Domaine d'Espérance blanche Armagnac

  ½ ounce Del Maguey Santo Domingo Albarradas mezcal

  ½ ounce Italicus Rosolio bergamot liqueur

  1 teaspoon simple syrup (page 287)

  1 dash House Orange Bitters (page 298)

  Garnish: 1 lemon twist

Stir all the ingredients over ice, then strain into a single old-fashioned glass over 1 large ice cube. Express the lemon twist over the drink, then place it in the drink.

PUGILIST

Tyson Buhler, 2015

Prizefighter #1, a vermouth and Fernet–based smash from Nick Jarrett, is a one of the best modern cocktails, and this drink plays off of that while morphing into more of a cobbler. —TB

  1 grapefruit half wheel

  1½ ounces Carpano Antica Formula vermouth

  ¾ ounce Fernet-Branca

  ¾ ounce Amaro Averna

  ½ ounce Cruzan single-barrel rum

  ½ ounce Pineapple Gum Syrup (page 286)

  Pinch of salt

  Garnish: 1 mint bouquet, 2 raspberries, 2 blackberries, and powdered sugar

In a shaker, gently muddle the grapefruit. Add the remaining ingredients and whip, shaking with a few pieces of crushed ice, just until incorporated. Dump into a double old-fashioned glass and fill the glass with crushed ice. Garnish with the mint bouquet and berries, and dust the top of the drink with powdered sugar. Serve with a straw.

QUEEN SNAKE ❊❊

Shannon Tebay, 2019

I often find myself coming up with an unexpected flavor combination, asking the other bartenders to "hear me out." Here, it's raisin eau-de-vie, Douglas Fir, and lychee—weird, but it works. —ST

  1 lime coin (a quarter-size piece of rind with some flesh attached)

  1½ ounces Cobrafire eau-de-vie de raisin

  ½ ounce Clear Creek Douglas fir eau-de-vie

  2 teaspoons Giffard Lichi-Li lychee liqueur

  1 teaspoon Marie Brizard white crème de cacao

In a single old-fashioned glass, muddle the lime coin. Add the remaining ingredients, fill the glass with cracked ice, and stir briefly. No garnish.

RECORTADOR ❊

Matthew Belanger, 2017

Can you put the flavors of an al pastor taco into a cocktail and make it taste great? Make this drink and let me know. —MB

  1¼ ounces Tapatío Blanco 110 tequila

  ½ ounce Del Maguey San Luis del Rio mezcal

  ¼ ounce St. George green chile vodka

  ¼ ounce Pineapple Gum Syrup (page 286)

  1 teaspoon green Chartreuse

  1 dash House Orange Bitters (page 298)

  ½ dash Bittermens Hellfire habanero shrub

Stir all the ingredients over ice, then strain into a double old-fashioned glass over 1 large ice cube. No garnish.

ROSE PARADE ❊

Jeremy Oertel, 2014

  Absinthe, to rinse

  Emile Pernot Fraise de Boise liqueur, to rinse

  1½ ounces Campo de Encanto Acholado pisco

  ½ ounce Kappa pisco

  ¾ ounce Cocchi Americano

  1 teaspoon Combier crème de rose

  1 dash House Orange Bitters (page 298)

Rinse a single old-fashioned glass with absinthe and Fraise de Boise and dump. Stir the remaining ingredients over ice, then strain into the glass. No garnish.

SASAKI GARDEN ❊

Sam Johnson, 2019

I used to live in SoHo, and I would walk through the Sasaki Garden on the NYU campus every day on my way to the bar. I'd sit under the cherry blossom trees there as a little reprieve before service. This drink is my ode to that park. It looks like an Old-Fashioned variation, but it's more like a Rusty Nail. —SJ

  1½ ounces Nikka Coffey Grain Japanese whisky

  ½ ounce Avuá Amburana cachaça

  2 teaspoons Caffo Amaretto

  1 teaspoon Rothman & Winter Orchard apricot liqueur

  1 dash House Orange Bitters (page 298)

  Garnish: 1 lemon twist

Stir all the ingredients over ice, then strain into a single old-fashioned glass over 1 large ice cube. Express the lemon twist over the drink, then place it in the drink.

SAZERAC (STANDING ROOM) ❄

Matthew Belanger, 2019

This is a great drink to batch at home. Combine the ingredients in a bottle, add a touch of water (see page 160), and keep it in the freezer. —MB

Absinthe, to rinse

1½ ounces Busnel calvados

½ ounce Old Grand-Dad 114 bourbon

½ ounce Giffard rhubarb liqueur

½ teaspoon Cane Sugar Syrup (page 282)

1 dash Bitter Truth celery bitters

Rinse a single old-fashioned glass with absinthe and dump. Stir the remaining ingredients over ice, then strain into the glass. No garnish.

SEA LEGS ❄

Tyson Buhler, 2015

I add a good amount of Kalani, a delicious-but-overpowering coconut liqueur, in this cocktail, which allowed me to get away with using some pretty aggressive rums and aromatic eau-de-vie. —TB

1 ounce Barbancourt 8-year rum

¾ ounce Scarlet Ibis Trinidad rum

¼ ounce Lost Spirits Navy Style rum

½ ounce Kalani Ron de Coco coconut liqueur

1 teaspoon Reisetbauer hazelnut eau-de-vie

1 dash Fee Brothers whiskey barrel–aged bitters

Garnish: 1 lemon twist

Stir all the ingredients over ice, then strain into a single old-fashioned glass over 1 large ice cube. Express the lemon twist over the drink and discard.

SHADOW BOX ❄

Shannon Tebay, 2019

Del Bac is an American single malt, and every year they release a distiller's cut that's finished in a particular barrel. This one was finished in madeira casks, so all the ancillary ingredients here are meant to pull out the flavors of the fortified wine. —ST

1 ounce Del Bac Distiller's Cut single malt whiskey

1 ounce Pellehaut Armagnac

1 teaspoon Giffard Crème de Framboise liqueur

1 teaspoon Orgeat Works Macadamia Nut Syrup

1 dash Bittermens Xocolatl mole bitters

Garnish: 1 orange twist

Stir all the ingredients over ice, then strain into a single old-fashioned glass. Express the orange twist over the drink, then place it in the drink.

SMOKING JACKET ❄

Jon Armstrong, 2014

Laphroaig scotch, to rinse

1½ ounces Hine H cognac

½ ounce Busnel VSOP calvados

1 teaspoon Demerara Syrup (page 283)

3 dashes Peychaud's bitters

1 dash Angostura bitters

Rinse a single old-fashioned glass with the Laphroaig and dump. Stir the remaining ingredients over ice, then strain into the glass. No garnish.

STONED LOVE ☉

Shannon Tebay, 2017

This was my first Absentroux drink; it's basically a low-ABV absinthe frappé. The drink is vegetal and tastes a little bit like weed. —ST

3 ounces Absentroux

½ ounce simple syrup (page 287)

1 teaspoon Giffard menthe-pastille

1 teaspoon St. George absinthe

1 teaspoon Clear Creek pear eau-de-vie

Garnish: 1 mint bouquet, and absinthe in an atomizer

Short shake all the ingredients with ice for about 5 seconds, then strain into a tulip glass. Fill the glass with crushed ice. Garnish with the mint bouquet and spray some absinthe over the top of the drink. Serve with a straw.

STRIP SOLITAIRE ❄

Alex Jump, Dave Anderson, and Jon Feuersanger 2019

We wanted to create a pineapple Old-Fashioned, and once we nailed it we were like, "this is so simple, but so fucking good." Dave came up with the name; he's one of the best cocktail namers of all time. —AJ

2 ounces Evan Williams bonded bourbon

½ ounce Giffard Caribbean pineapple liqueur

½ teaspoon Cane Sugar Syrup (page 282)

2 dashes Angostura bitters

1 dash Bittermens 'Elemakule tiki bitters

Garnish: 1 dehydrated pineapple wedge

Stir all the ingredients over ice, then strain into a single old-fashioned glass over 1 large ice cube. Garnish with the dehydrated pineapple wedge.

SWEET DYNAMITE

Shannon Tebay, 2019

I use the phrase "mind mouth" a lot to describe things I can taste in my head; it's almost like synesthesia. When you've worked with flavors long enough, you just kind of know what will work together before you actually taste it. Here, I wanted to combine fennel and passion fruit in a julep, and Matt suggested I use the Krogstad aquavit, which has a big fennel note. —ST

1 ounce Krogstad aquavit

¾ ounce Appleton Estate Reserve Jamaica rum

¼ ounce Lemon Hart 151 rum

¼ ounce Giffard passion fruit liqueur

1 teaspoon Cinnamon Syrup (page 283)

Garnish: 1 mint bouquet

Combine all the ingredients in a julep tin and fill the tin about halfway with crushed ice. Holding the tin by the rim, stir, churning the ice as you go, for about 10 seconds. Add more crushed ice to fill the tin about two-thirds full and stir until the tin is completely frosted. Add more ice to form a cone above the rim. Garnish with the mint bouquet and serve with a straw.

THIEVES IN THE NIGHT ⚜

Jarred Weigand, 2018

I love creating juleps; it's really fun to do crushed ice drinks that don't contain any juice. Sombra mezcal tastes like it was made to go with gin, but I needed something else to link them together, and Amaro Braulio—with its uplifting, alpine flavors—is perfect for that. —JW

1 ounce Sombra mezcal

1 ounce St. George Terroir gin

¼ ounce Amaro Braulio

¼ ounce maple syrup

Garnish: 1 mint bouquet and dark chocolate

Combine all the ingredients in a julep tin and fill the tin about halfway with crushed ice. Holding the tin by the rim, stir, churning the ice as you go, for about 10 seconds. Add more crushed ice to fill the tin about two-thirds full and stir until the tin is completely frosted. Add more ice to form a cone above the rim. Garnish with the mint bouquet, shave some chocolate over the top of the drink, and serve with a straw.

TRADITION

Tyson Buhler, 2014

1 ounce Caol Ila 12-year scotch

½ ounce Lemorton Selection calvados Domfrontais

1 teaspoon Galliano Ristretto

1 teaspoon Honey Syrup (page 284)

1 teaspoon Cinnamon Syrup (page 283)

1 dash Angostura bitters

3 ounces boiling water

Garnish: 1 orange twist and 1 cinnamon stick

Combine all the ingredients except the water in an Irish coffee mug. Add the boiling water. Express the orange twist over the drink and discard. Garnish with the cinnamon stick.

TRIPWIRE ❄

Shannon Tebay, 2018

What would a stirred piña colada taste like? This. —ST

1 ounce Kilkerran 12-year single malt scotch

¾ ounce Ron del Barrilito 3-Star rum

¼ ounce Smith & Cross Jamaica rum

½ teaspoon crème de cacao

1 teaspoon Pineapple Gum Syrup (page 286)

2 dashes Bittermens Xocolatl mole bitters

Garnish: 1 lemon twist

Stir all the ingredients over ice, then strain into a single old-fashioned glass over 1 large ice cube. Express the lemon twist over the drink, then place it in the drink.

UNCANNY VALLEY ❄

Dave Anderson, 2019

I always wanted to make a gin-based Sazerac, and I'm a big fan of Phil Ward's Elder Fashion, which combines gin and St-Germain in an Old-Fashioned. I found that gin and tequila work very well together: tequila is grassy, gin is herbaceous, and those flavors are adjacent to one another. I opted for a reposado tequila to give the drink that oaky quality you expect in an Old-Fashioned. —DA

Reisetbauer carrot eau-de-vie, to rinse

1 ounce St. George dry rye reposado gin

¾ ounce Ocho reposado tequila

¼ ounce Coriander-Infused Ransom Old Tom (page 291)

1 teaspoon agave nectar

1 dash Bitter Truth celery bitters

Garnish: 1 lemon twist

Rinse a single old-fashioned glass with the Reisetbauer and dump. Stir the remaining ingredients over ice, then strain into the glass. Express the lemon twist over the drink, then place it in the drink.

UNFORGIVEN ❄

Jon Feuersanger, 2018

This is a *very* complex Sazerac, layering multiple sweet elements beginning with the Drambuie, and with the cherry brandy acting like bitters to lift the drink's floral notes. —JF

Laphroaig 10-year scotch, to rinse

1¼ ounces Monkey Shoulder scotch

½ ounce Pierre Ferrand 1840 cognac

¼ ounce Brugal 1888 rum

¼ ounce Drambuie

1 teaspoon Demerara Syrup (page 283)

½ teaspoon Rhine Hall cherry brandy

2 dashes Peychaud's bitters

2 dashes Angostura bitters

Garnish: 1 orange twist

Rinse a single old-fashioned glass with the Laphroaig and dump. Stir the remaining ingredients over ice, then strain into the glass. Express the orange twist over the drink and discard.

VANTAGE POINT ❄

Javelle Taft, 2019

It's ironic that Old-Fashioned style cocktails are usually our most popular drinks, but often the last ones developed for a menu. Here, I started with a Toki Highball, Japan's most notable cocktail, and started deconstructing it. Toki whisky is a young blend with lots of pear, honey, and rose on the nose; Bertoux adds nuances of juicy stone fruit that intensify those flavors, while the Caol Ila pushes the Toki's subtle smoky notes. Our original intention was to add seltzer and make this into a highball, but we realized that the drink was better without bubbles. —JT

1½ ounces Suntory Toki Japanese whisky

½ ounce Bertoux brandy

¼ ounce Italicus Rosolio bergamot liqueur

¼ ounce Caol Ila 12-year scotch

½ teaspoon simple syrup (page 287)

1 dash House Orange Bitters (page 298)

Garnish: 1 lemon twist

Stir all the ingredients with ice, then strain into a single old-fashioned glass over 1 large ice cube. Express the lemon twist over the drink and place it in the drink.

VAQUERO ❄

Tyson Buhler, 2017

This drink was all about the corn-infused mezcal. By toasting dried corn husks and making a sous-vide infusion, the husks not only accentuate the roasted flavor of the agave but also add an almost mineral spiciness to the mezcal. Chichicapa tastes like chocolate-covered green chilies, so the crème de cacao was an obvious addition to complement the spirit. —TB

1½ ounces Corn Husk–Infused Del Maguey Chichicapa (page 291)

½ ounce Calle 23 reposado tequila

1 teaspoon Demerara Syrup (page 283)

½ teaspoon Marie Brizard white crème de cacao

Garnish: 1 orange twist

Stir all the ingredients over ice, then strain into a double old-fashioned glass over 1 large ice cube. Express the orange twist over the drink, then place it in the drink.

VERONA COBBLER

Sam Johnson, 2019

I recommend using a good champagne in this sparkling wine–based cobbler, so that the other ingredients can amplify its flavor profile. Orgeat does a lot of the lifting here and gives the drink richness, while the rose water is barely perceptible but brightens up the drink and plays well with the floral kirsch. —SJ

3 ounces dry sparkling wine

¾ ounce Domaine d'Espérance blanche Armagnac

¼ ounce Massenez Kirsch Vieux cherry brandy

½ ounce House Orgeat (page 284)

3 drops rose water

Garnish: 1 grapefruit twist

Pour the sparkling wine into a tulip glass. Add the remaining ingredients and fill the glass with crushed ice. Express the grapefruit twist over the drink and insert it into the ice. Serve with a straw.

VICTORY LAP ☉

Matthew Belanger, 2019

I was inspired to make this by the Cazottes, which is somewhere between an aperitif and an eau-de-vie made with heirloom tomatoes. It has a really bizarre fresh tomato flavor and aroma of tomato vines. It's probably the most expensive ingredient we've ever put on a menu. So the rest of the drink is configured to showcase the Cazottes while spending as little money as possible. —MB

2½ ounces Dolin dry vermouth

½ ounce Cazottes 72 Tomates

1 teaspoon Merlet crème de fraise des bois strawberry liqueur

½ teaspoon Vanilla Syrup (page 288)

2 dashes absinthe

Garnish: 1 lemon twist

Stir all the ingredients over ice, then strain into a single old-fashioned glass. Express the lemon twist over the drink and discard.

⊙ LOW ABV   ⊘ NO ABV   ❄ FREEZER BAR   ⧗ PROJECT COCKTAIL   ✿ LOW-PREP COCKTAIL

WALL OF SOUND ❅

Shannon Tebay, 2017

This was the first time I did the "Shannon thing" of combining bourbon, smoky scotch, and a crazy Jamaican rum. The whole thing was built around the Rum Fire rum, which is similar to Wray & Nephew. This Sazerac riff drinks like a Phil Spector song sounds—hence the name. —ST

> Laphroaig 10-year scotch, to rinse
>
> 1½ ounces Elijah Craig 12-year bourbon
>
> ½ ounce Bowmore 12-year scotch
>
> 1 teaspoon Rum Fire rum
>
> 1 teaspoon Cane Sugar Syrup (page 282)
>
> 1 teaspoon Kalani Ron de Coco coconut liqueur
>
> 2 dashes Bittermens 'Elemakule tiki bitters
>
> Garnish: 1 grapefruit twist

Rinse a single old-fashioned glass with the Laphroaig and dump. Stir the remaining ingredients over ice, then strain into the glass. Express the grapefruit twist over the drink and discard.

WARSPITE ❅

Matthew Belanger, 2016

> 1¼ ounces Plymouth gin
>
> ¾ ounce Aperol
>
> ½ ounce Plymouth sloe gin
>
> ¼ ounce Clear Creek Blue Plum brandy
>
> 1 teaspoon St. Elizabeth allspice dram
>
> Garnish: 1 orange twist

Stir all the ingredients over ice, then strain into a double old-fashioned glass over 1 large ice cube. Express the orange twist over the drink, then place it in the drink.

WHEELWRITER NO. 10 ❅

Emily Horn, 2019

This drink (named after the model of Ray Bradbury's first typewriter) is a Sazerac riff, but also kind of like a Manhattan, or even a Negroni. So it's a bit of a Frankenstein, but very tasty. —EH

> Absinthe, to rinse
>
> 1½ ounces Busnel VSOP calvados
>
> ½ ounce Famous Grouse scotch
>
> ½ ounce Coffee Bean–Infused Campari (page 290)
>
> 1 teaspoon Marie Brizard white crème de cacao
>
> ½ teaspoon Demerara Syrup (page 283)

Rinse a chilled Nick & Nora glass with absinthe and dump. Stir the remaining ingredients over ice, then strain into the glass. No garnish.

THE WHISKEY AGREEMENT ❅

Scott Teague, 2014

The drink's name is dead giveaway: it's no easy feat to make American, Irish, Scottish, and Japanese whiskey (and whisky) get along in one glass. I quite possibly tried all of the whiskeys (and whiskies) in the back bar before landing on this quartet. —ST

> ½ ounce Old Grand-Dad 114 bourbon
>
> ½ ounce Tyrconnell single malt Irish whiskey
>
> ½ ounce Highland Park 12-year scotch
>
> ½ ounce Hibiki 12-year blended single malt Japanese whisky
>
> 1 teaspoon Cinnamon Syrup (page 283)
>
> ½ teaspoon St. Elizabeth allspice dram
>
> 1 dash Angostura bitters

> 1 dash Bittermens hopped grapefruit bitters
>
> Garnish: 1 orange twist and 1 lemon twist

Stir all the ingredients over ice, then strain into a double old-fashioned glass over 1 large ice cube. Express the orange twist over the drink, then gently rub it around the rim of the glass. Express the lemon twist over the drink, then garnish with both twists.

YEAR OF THE TREES ❅

Matthew Belanger, 2019

> 1½ ounces Knob Creek 100 bourbon
>
> ½ ounce Mal Bien Espadin mezcal
>
> ½ ounce Amaro Nonino
>
> 1 teaspoon Demerara Syrup (page 283)
>
> 1 dash Angostura bitters
>
> 1 drop Terra Spice sarsaparilla tincture
>
> Garnish: 1 orange twist

Stir all the ingredients over ice, then strain into a double old-fashioned glass over 1 large ice cube. Express the orange twist over the drink, then place it in the drink.

Elegant & Timeless

☉ LOW ABV   ⊘ NO ABV   ❄ FREEZER BAR   ⧗ PROJECT COCKTAIL   ❅ LOW-PREP COCKTAIL

20/20 ♣

Jon Armstrong, 2015

For me, this drink cracked the code of using carrot eau-de-vie in a cocktail, with all the other ingredients stretching out the carrot flavor. The build is like a 50/50 Martini, but one of our regulars named the drink after carrots' effect on your vision. —JA

- 1½ ounces Plymouth gin
- 1½ ounces Alvear Festival pale cream sherry
- 1 teaspoon Reisetbauer carrot eau-de-vie
- ½ teaspoon Grand Marnier
- 1 dash absinthe
- Garnish: 1 lemon twist

Stir all the ingredients over ice, then strain into a chilled Nick & Nora glass. Express the lemon twist over the drink, then place it in the drink.

ACADIA ♣

Keely Sutherland, 2019

I was having a hard time coming up with a luxe Manhattan-style cocktail, so I decided on an ode to my home state of Maine: apples are abundant there, Douglas Fir eau-de-vie tastes like drinking a pine tree, and maple syrup is a big Maine industry. —KS

- 1 ounce Macallan 15-year scotch
- 1 ounce Clear Creek 8-year apple brandy
- ¾ ounce Cocchi vermouth di Torino
- 2 teaspoons Clear Creek Douglas Fir eau-de-vie
- 1 teaspoon maple syrup
- 1 dash House Orange Bitters (page 298)
- 1 dash Angostura bitters

Stir all the ingredients over ice, then strain into a chilled Nick & Nora glass. No garnish.

A CLOCKWORK ORANGE ❊

Matthew Belanger, 2017

- 1 ounce Tanqueray No. Ten gin
- 1 ounce Dolin blanc vermouth
- ½ ounce Clear Creek Mirabelle eau-de-vie
- ½ ounce Mandarine Napoléon liqueur
- 1 teaspoon Suze
- Garnish: 1 lemon twist

Stir all the ingredients over ice, then strain into a double old-fashioned glass over 1 large ice cube. Express the lemon twist over the drink, then place it in the drink.

ACES & TWOS ❊

Adam Griggs, 2019

This is basically a Mr. Potato Head Martinez, which you can batch and freeze as well. —AG

- 1½ ounces Hayman's Old Tom gin
- ¾ ounce Cesar Florido Moscatel Dorado
- ¼ ounce Amaro CioCiaro
- ½ ounce Carpano Antica Formula vermouth
- 1 dash Angostura bitters
- 1 dash House Orange Bitters (page 298)
- Garnish: 1 brandied cherry

Stir all the ingredients over ice, then strain into a chilled Nick & Nora glass. Garnish with the brandied cherry.

ALTA NEGRONI ❊

Matthew Belanger, 2019

- 1 ounce St. George Terroir gin
- 1 ounce Cocchi Americano
- ½ ounce Salers Gentien aperitif
- ½ ounce Pajarote Toronja Arandense & Romero Licor
- Garnish: 1 grapefruit wheel

Stir all the ingredients over ice, then strain into a double old-fashioned glass over 1 large ice cube. Garnish with the grapefruit wheel.

ANCHOR END ❋

Matthew Belanger, 2018

St. George Bruto Americano is super bitter, with a big grapefruit note. I'd had a drink at the Walker Inn (RIP) that was like a grapefruit shandy with apple brandy in it, so I re-created that flavor profile in a Negroni. —MB

1¼ ounces Clear Creek 8-year apple brandy

1 ounce Cocchi Americano

¾ ounce St. George Bruto Americano

¼ ounce Anchor Hophead vodka

1 dash Scrappy's grapefruit bitters

Garnish: 1 grapefruit twist

Stir all the ingredients over ice, then strain into a double old-fashioned glass over 1 large ice cube. Express the grapefruit twist over the drink and discard.

ANDROMEDA ❋

Matthew Belanger, 2019

This Boulevardier-style cocktail riffs on Brian Miller's Cure for Pain, with a split vermouth-port modifier. Granada-Vallet is an aperitivo made in Mexico that tastes similar to Campari, but is more dry. —MB

1½ ounces Barrell Dovetail whiskey

½ ounce Carpano Antica Formula vermouth

½ ounce Dow's ruby port

1 teaspoon Granada-Vallet bitter pomegranate liqueur

1 teaspoon Galliano Ristretto

Garnish: 1 grapefruit twist

Stir all the ingredients over ice, then strain into a chilled martini glass. Express the grapefruit twist over the drink and discard.

APHRODITE ☉

Adam Griggs, 2018

I had Alex Day in the back of my mind when I was developing this, as he loves all things low-ABV. Aigre doux is an underrated cocktail ingredient; it's basically a mix of cider vinegar and apple ice wine that's bright and aromatic, and a great way to add intense apple flavor in small amounts. —AG

1½ ounces Lustau Los Arcos amontillado sherry

1½ ounces Byrrh Gran Quinquina

¼ ounce Blume Marillen apricot eau-de-vie

1 teaspoon Demerara Syrup (page 283)

½ teaspoon Dupont Aigre Doux

Garnish: 1 lemon twist

Stir all the ingredients over ice, then strain into a chilled Nick & Nora glass. Express the lemon twist over the drink, then place it in the drink.

APOLLO ❋

Matthew Belanger, 2019

Buddha's Hand vodka is flavored with the zest of the finger-shaped citrus and adds an intense perfume to this Vesper variation. —MB

1½ ounces St. George Dry Rye reposado gin

¾ ounce Hangar One Buddha's Hand vodka

½ ounce Cocchi Americano

1 teaspoon Luxardo maraschino liqueur

1 dash House Orange Bitters (page 298)

1 dash absinthe

Garnish: 1 lemon twist

Stir all the ingredients over ice, then strain into a chilled Nick & Nora glass. Express the lemon twist over the drink, then place it in the drink.

AS ISLAY DYING ❋

Matt Hunt, 2018

I love the simplicity of equal-parts cocktails, like the Negroni or Naked and Famous. In this one, I was trying to marry an Islay gin and an Islay scotch, with the Génépy and absinthe tying everything on the midpalate. —MH

¾ ounce Laphroaig 10-year scotch

¾ ounce The Botanist gin

¾ ounce Dolin blanc vermouth

¾ ounce Dolin dry vermouth

1 teaspoon Dolin Génépy des Alpes liqueur

2 dashes absinthe

Garnish: 1 lemon twist

Stir all the ingredients over ice, then strain into a chilled Nick & Nora glass. Express the lemon twist over the drink and discard.

BELCARO ❋

Jon Feuersanger, 2018

This Vieux Carré variation shows off the affinity between Irish whiskey and apple brandy. I brought the Bénédictine over from the classic spec, and the banana liqueur adds a lovely banana bread flavor. —JF

1 ounce Jameson Black Barrel Irish whiskey

1 ounce Dupont Fine Reserve calvados

¾ ounce Cocchi vermouth Di Torino

1 teaspoon Bénédictine

1 teaspoon Tempus Fugit crème de banane

2 dashes Bitter Truth aromatic bitters

2 dashes Peychaud's bitters

Garnish: 1 lemon twist

Stir all the ingredients over ice, then strain into a single old-fashioned glass over 1 large ice cube. Express the lemon twist over the drink, then place it in the drink.

BETWEEN THE LINES ❋

Jarred Weigand, 2017

Brandy has the uncanny ability to go with just about anything; it's like the Swiss Army knife of spirits. In this Martini variation, it forms a split base with gin, and is accented by the alpine flavors of Génépy. —JW

1½ ounces Domaine D'Espérance blanche Armagnac

½ ounce St. George Terroir gin

½ ounce Dolin dry vermouth

½ ounce Dolin Génépy des Alpes liqueur

Garnish: 1 lemon twist

Stir all the ingredients over ice, then strain into a chilled Nick & Nora glass. Express the lemon twist over the drink and discard.

BIKINI KILL ❋

Al Sotack, 2014

1¾ ounces Pineapple-Infused Tanqueray Gin (page 294)

½ ounce Dolin dry vermouth

¼ ounce El Dorado 3-year rum

¼ ounce Combier pamplemousse rose liqueur

1 teaspoon St-Germain elderflower liqueur

Garnish: 1 grapefruit twist

Stir all the ingredients over ice, then strain into a chilled Nick & Nora glass. Express the grapefruit twist over the drink and discard.

BLUE MOUNTAIN ❋

Matthew Belanger, 2018

This is basically a classic Hanky-Panky with additional flavors of rum, banana, and eucalyptus layered on top. —MB

1¼ ounces Plymouth gin

1 ounce Carpano Antica Formula vermouth

½ ounce Fernet-Branca

¼ ounce Smith & Cross Jamaica rum

¼ ounce Giffard banane du Brésil

1 drop Terra Spice eucalyptus extract

Garnish: 1 mint bouquet

Stir all the ingredients over ice, then strain into a double old-fashioned glass over 1 large ice cube. Garnish with the mint bouquet.

BUSINESS CASUAL ⊘

Jon Mateer, 2019

1¼ ounces Giffard Aperitif Syrup

¾ ounce chilled brewed black tea

1 ounce Red Verjus Syrup (page 286)

1 teaspoon Cane Sugar Syrup (page 282)

Garnish: 1 orange half wheel

Stir all the ingredients over ice, then strain into a double old-fashioned glass over 1 large ice cube. Garnish with the orange half wheel.

CAPUCHIN ❋

Matthew Belanger, 2018

Apricot and cumin frequently show up together in Middle Eastern and Moroccan food, so I paired those flavors in a Rob Roy variation. Here, the cumin comes from kümmel, a Dutch liqueur that was used a lot in old-school cocktails. —MB

1½ ounces Monkey Shoulder blended scotch

¾ ounce Punt e Mes

½ ounce Linie aquavit

1 teaspoon Giffard Abricot du Roussillon

½ teaspoon kümmel

Garnish: 1 lemon twist

Stir all the ingredients over ice, then strain into a chilled Nick & Nora glass. Express the lemon twist over the drink and discard.

CLOCKMAKER ❋

Tyson Buhler, 2019

¾ ounce Rittenhouse rye

¾ ounce Linie aquavit

½ ounce Cocchi Americano

½ ounce Rare Wine Co. Boston Bual madeira

½ ounce Amaro Nardini

Stir all the ingredients over ice, then strain into a chilled Nick & Nora glass. No garnish.

COAT OF ARMS ❋

Tyson Buhler, 2017

This is a luxe cocktail made with stupid-good ingredients. I take no credit for this tasting so great. —TB

1 ounce Paul Beau Hors d'Age cognac

½ ounce Clear Creek Douglas Fir eau-de-vie

½ ounce yellow Chartreuse V.E.P.

½ ounce Carpano Antica Formula vermouth

Stir all the ingredients over ice, then strain into a chilled martini glass. No garnish.

CODE OF THE WEST ❋

Eryn Reece, 2015

1 ounce Four Roses single barrel bourbon

1 ounce Domaine du Manoir de Montreuil calvados

¾ ounce Zurbaran cream sherry

¼ ounce yellow Chartreuse

1 teaspoon Cinnamon Syrup (page 283)

Garnish: 1 orange twist

Stir all the ingredients over ice, then strain into a double old-fashioned glass over 1 large ice cube. Express the orange twist over the drink, then place it in the drink.

DARK HORSE ❄

Jeremy Oertel, 2017

1½ ounces Appleton Estate 21-year Jamaica rum

½ ounce Bordelet calvados

½ ounce Amaro Nardini

½ ounce Grand Marnier

Garnish: 1 lemon twist

Stir all the ingredients over ice, then strain into a chilled Nick & Nora glass. Express the lemon twist over the drink, then place it in the drink.

DEAD LANGUAGE ❄

Matthew Belanger, 2017

Tyson created a drink called Sound and Fury that combines raspberry and chile liqueur in a shaken drink; I wanted to revisit those flavors in a Manhattan context. The drink also shares some DNA with Thomas Waugh's Red Ant, which was one of the first times we combined a fruit liqueur and a corresponding fruit brandy to deepen the flavor of the fruit without making the drink too sweet. —MB

1½ ounces Rittenhouse rye

¾ ounce Cocchi vermouth di Torino

½ ounce Ancho Reyes ancho chile liqueur

½ teaspoon Giffard crème de framboise

½ teaspoon Massenez framboise eau-de-vie

1 dash Bittermens Xocolatl mole bitters

Garnish: 1 grapefruit twist

Stir all the ingredients over ice, then strain into a chilled Nick & Nora glass. Express the grapefruit twist over the drink and discard.

DEAD RINGER ❄

Eryn Reece, 2014

Sombra mezcal, to rinse

1½ ounces Ron Zacapa 23 rum

1 ounce Principe amontillado sherry

¾ ounce Amaro Nonino

¼ ounce Kronan Swedish Punsch

1 teaspoon Cane Sugar Syrup (page 282)

Rinse a single old-fashioned glass with mezcal and dump. Stir the remaining ingredients over ice, then strain into the glass. No garnish.

DISTRICT B-13 ❄

Jon Armstrong, 2014

Brandy drinks are often the last ones to be developed for a menu. We have nothing against brandy, but we're usually thinking about other spirits first. This is riff on a brandy Manhattan, splitting the aromatized wine between vermouth and sherry. Alex Day likes to say that if you want to make a Manhattan variation more interesting, add a teaspoon of maraschino liqueur, so I took his advice. —JA

2 ounces Hine H cognac

¾ ounce Carpano Antica Formula vermouth

½ ounce Hidalgo oloroso sherry

¼ ounce Cynar

1 teaspoon Luxardo maraschino liqueur

Garnish: 1 lemon twist

Stir all the ingredients over ice, then strain into a chilled Nick & Nora glass. Express the lemon twist over the drink and discard.

DOMINO ♣

Matthew Belanger, 2019

1½ ounces Suntory Roku gin

1½ ounces Lillet rosé

½ ounce Clear Creek pear brandy

1 teaspoon Luxardo maraschino liqueur

1 dash Scrappy's grapefruit bitters

Garnish: 1 grapefruit twist

Stir all the ingredients over ice, then strain into a chilled martini glass. Express the grapefruit twist over the drink and discard.

DON'T FORGET THE STRUGGLE, DON'T FORGET THE STREETS ♣

Al Sotack, 2015

This is one of my simplest cocktails, as well as the one with the longest name. It's my version of an agave-based Negroni. —AS

1 ounce Del Maguey Chichicapa mezcal

1 ounce Amaro Nardini

1 ounce Lustau Los Arcos amontillado sherry

Stir all the ingredients over ice, then strain into a chilled Nick & Nora glass. No garnish.

ALEX JUMP'S MARTINI, PAGE 254

DREAMSCAPE ⊙

Tyson Buhler, 2017

This drink's ingredients lived in a corner of our selection of cheater bottles that was seemingly reserved for my weird, low-ABV stirred drinks that were rarely ordered (see also: Easy Rider, page 252; Modern Lovers, page 259; and Periscope, page 262). –TB

1½ ounces Lemorton Pommeau de Normandie

1½ ounces Escubac Botanical Spirit

½ ounce Leopold Bros. New York sour apple liqueur

1 teaspoon Aggazzotti Nocino Riserva

1 dash Angostura bitters

Garnish: 1 dried apple slice

Stir all the ingredients over ice, then strain into a double old-fashioned glass over 1 large ice cube. Garnish with the dried apple slice.

EASY RIDER ❄

Tyson Buhler, 2017

Absinthe, to rinse

1½ ounces Tresmontaine "Tabacal" Rancio Sec

1½ ounces González Byass La Copa vermouth

1 teaspoon Merlet crème de fraise des bois strawberry liqueur

½ teaspoon Vanilla Syrup (page 288)

1 dash House Orange Bitters (page 298)

Garnish: 1 lemon twist

Rinse a single old-fashioned glass with absinthe and dump. Stir the remaining ingredients over ice, then strain into the glass. Express the lemon twist over the drink and discard.

EMERALD CITY ❄

Shannon Tebay, 2018

I like to take shitty '80s drinks and elevate them, and this is my appletini. The intense apple eau-de-vie is the star of this show; it makes the drink taste way more apple-y than it is. –ST

1½ ounces Reisetbauer Blue gin

¾ ounce Cyril Zangs 00 apple cider eau-de-vie

½ ounce La Quintinye blanc vermouth

½ ounce Absentroux

1 dash Bitter Truth celery bitters

1 dash absinthe

Garnish: 1 apple fan

Stir all the ingredients over ice, then strain into a chilled martini glass. Garnish with the apple fan.

FADED MEMORIES ❄

Tyson Buhler, 2018

This is one of the stranger drinks I've ever put together, but it's crazy complex and surprisingly approachable. Sake and scotch is a really fun combination that is very underexplored. –TB

1 ounce Asahiyama Junmai sake

1 ounce Beniotome shochu

½ ounce Mathilde Poire pear liqueur

½ ounce Trimbach Mirabelle plum eau-de-vie

1 teaspoon Laphroaig 10-year scotch

1 dash House Orange Bitters (page 298)

Stir all the ingredients over ice, then strain into a single old-fashioned glass over 1 large ice cube. No garnish.

FASHION DISTRICT ❄

Chris Norton, 2019

This drink is similar to something my grandfather, who was from Modena, used to drink. I originally wanted to use white balsamic vinegar in this Manhattan variation, but Jonnie Long turned me on to aigre doux (sweet and sour), and I became obsessed with it. It adds this beguiling flavor that nobody can put their finger on. –CN

1½ ounces Tyrconnell single malt Irish whiskey

½ ounce Rittenhouse rye

½ ounce Cappelletti Vino Aperitivo

½ ounce Carpano Antica Formula vermouth

½ teaspoon Dupont Aigre Doux

2 dashes Angostura bitters

Garnish: 1 lemon twist

Stir all the ingredients over ice, then strain into a double old-fashioned glass over 1 large ice cube. Express the lemon twist over the drink and discard.

FAULT LINE ❄

Shannon Tebay, 2017

You could call this a carrot Negroni, with other earthy and vegetal flavors complementing the carrot eau-de-vie: artichoke from the Cynar and caraway from the aquavit. While the name evokes something divisive, the drink was more well received than I expected, and I still make it a lot when people ask for something bizarre but approachable. –ST

1½ ounces Linie aquavit

1 ounce Cocchi vermouth di Torino

¾ ounce Cynar

1 teaspoon Reisetbauer carrot eau-de-vie

Garnish: 1 orange twist

Stir all the ingredients over ice, then strain into a double old-fashioned glass over 1 large ice cube. Express the orange twist over the drink, then place it in the drink.

⊙ LOW ABV   ⊘ NO ABV   ❄ FREEZER BAR   ⧗ PROJECT COCKTAIL   ⚜ LOW-PREP COCKTAIL

FIVE POINTS ❄

Jon Feuersanger, 2018

This cold-season Manhattan carries on the tradition of naming Manhattan riffs after the borough's neighborhoods. —JF

1½ ounces Ocho reposado tequila

½ ounce Del Maguey Vida mezcal

½ ounce Punt e Mes

½ ounce Amaro Nardini

1 teaspoon Don Ciccio & Figli Nocino

2 dashes Bittermens Xocolatl mole bitters

Garnish: 1 orange twist

Stir all the ingredients over ice, then strain into a chilled Nick & Nora glass. Express the orange twist over the drink, then place it in the drink.

FOXTROT ❄

Amanda Harbour, 2019

Menthe-pastille is usually something you stay away from in larger amounts, but its big menthol flavor works well with mezcal and tequila in this Martini variation. It's a playful drink named after a playful dance, and you'll be surprised how palatable it is. You can definitely make a batch of this and keep it in the freezer. —AH

¾ ounce Sombra mezcal

¾ ounce Olmeca Altos Blanco tequila

½ ounce Giffard menthe-pastille

½ ounce Dolin dry vermouth

½ ounce Dolin blanc vermouth

Garnish: 1 lemon twist

Stir all the ingredients over ice, then strain into a double old-fashioned glass over 1 large ice cube. Express the lemon twist over the drink and discard.

FROSTBITE ☉

Matthew Belanger, 2019

This is a low-ABV version of the Stinger, swapping out the traditional cognac for Pineau des Charentes. —MB

1½ ounces Gilles Brisson Pineau des Charentes

1 ounce Rhine Hall apple eau-de-vie

½ ounce Giffard menthe-pastille

2 dashes absinthe

Stir all the ingredients over ice, then strain into a chilled Nick & Nora glass. No garnish.

FULIGIN ❄

Jeremy Oertel, 2014

I wanted to create the darkest drink possible, so I paired two molasses-y rums with the raisinated flavor PX sherry. Fuligin is a blacker-than-black color from Gene Wolfe's book *The Shadow of the Torturer*. —JO

1½ ounces El Dorado 15-year rum

½ ounce Cruzan Black Strap rum

½ ounce Amaro Averna

¼ ounce Lustau Pedro Ximénez sherry

1 teaspoon Smith & Cross Jamaica rum

1 teaspoon Clément Créole Shrubb

1 dash Bitter End Moroccan bitters

Garnish: 1 orange twist

Stir all the ingredients over ice, then strain into a chilled Nick & Nora glass. Express the orange twist over the drink and discard.

GAME LOVES GAME ❅

Al Sotack, 2014

2 cucumber slices

1 ounce Perry's Tot Navy Strength gin

1 ounce dry white wine

½ ounce Dolin dry vermouth

¼ ounce Bonal Gentiane-Quina

¼ ounce green Chartreuse

½ ounce Honey Syrup (page 284)

1 drop rose water

Garnish: 1 cucumber ribbon on a skewer

In a shaker, gently muddle the cucumber slices. Add the remaining ingredients and shake with ice. Double strain into a collins glass and fill the glass with crushed ice. Garnish with the cucumber ribbon.

THE GOLDEN BOUGH ❄

Sam Johnson, 2018

This Vieux Carré variation showcases the flavors of prune brandy, with the walnut liqueur adding a rich butter flavor. —SJ

1½ ounces Louis Roque La Vieille prune eau-de-vie

½ ounce Elijah Craig 12-year bourbon

¾ ounce Cocchi vermouth di Torino

1 teaspoon Nux Alpina walnut liqueur

1 dash absinthe

1 dash Angostura bitters

Garnish: 1 orange twist

Stir all the ingredients over ice, then strain into a double old-fashioned glass over 1 large ice cube. Express the orange twist over the drink, then place it in the drink.

D&C FAMILY MARTINI ALBUM

If you've ever had any doubt that the Martini is the most personalized and individualistic cocktail, take a look at what happens when we asked the Death & Co team to share their very favorite Martini specs. Though these drinks look similar on the page and are all based on a core of gin and vermouth, their differences are noticeable, if subtle, in the glass, revealing something about their creators' personality. Or to paraphrase French gastronome Jean Anthelme Brillat-Savarin: "Tell me how you Martini, and I'll tell you who you are."

ALEX DAY'S MARTINI

Alex Day, partner

2½ ounces Tanqueray No. Ten gin

¾ ounce Dolin dry vermouth

1 dash House Orange Bitters (page 298)

Garnish: 1 lemon twist

Stir all the ingredients over ice, then strain into a chilled Nick & Nora glass. Express the lemon twist over the drink, then place it in the drink.

ALEX JUMP'S MARTINI

Alex Jump, head bartender, Death & Co Denver

1½ ounces Tanqueray No. Ten gin

1½ ounces Noilly Prat extra dry vermouth

1 dash House Orange Bitters (page 298)

Garnish: 1 olive and 1 lemon twist

Stir all the ingredients over ice, then strain into a chilled Nick & Nora glass. Garnish with the olive. Express the lemon twist over the drink, then place it in the drink.

DAVID'S MARTINI

David Kaplan, partner

2½ ounces Tanqueray No. Ten gin

¼ ounce Dolin blanc vermouth

¼ ounce Noilly Prat extra dry vermouth

1 dash Angostura orange bitters

¾ ounce filtered water

Garnish: 1 lemon twist

If making a batch of Martinis for your freezer bar, scale up the recipe to your desired amount, combine in a bottle, and freeze for at least 2 hours. If making one drink, omit the water and stir all the ingredients over ice, then strain into a chilled Nick & Nora glass. Express the lemon twist over the drink and discard.

DEVON'S MARTINI

Devon Tarby, partner

2 ounces Beefeater gin

1 ounce Dolin dry vermouth

1 dash House Orange Bitters (page 298)

Garnish: 1 olive and 1 lemon twist

Stir all the ingredients over ice, then strain into a chilled Nick & Nora glass. Garnish with the olive. Express the lemon twist over the drink and discard.

JON'S MARTINI

Jon Feuersanger, general manager, Death & Co Denver

2 ounces Leopold's Navy Strength American gin

1 ounce Dolin blanc vermouth

½ dash absinthe

Garnish: 1 olive and 1 grapefruit twist

Stir all the ingredients over ice, then strain into a chilled Nick & Nora glass. Garnish with the olive. Express the grapefruit twist over the drink, then place it in the drink.

MATTHEW'S MARTINI

Matthew Belanger, general manager, Death & Co Los Angeles

1½ ounces Four Pillars Navy Strength gin

1½ ounces La Quintinye blanc vermouth

1 dash House Orange Bitters (page 298)

Garnish: 1 lemon twist

Stir all the ingredients over ice, then strain into a chilled Nick & Nora glass. Express the lemon twist over the drink, then place it in the drink.

MIKE'S MARTINI

Mike Shain, director of operations

- 1½ ounces Tanqueray London dry gin
- 1½ ounces Dolin dry vermouth
- 1 dash House Orange Bitters (page 298)
- Garnish: 1 lemon twist

Stir all the ingredients over ice, then strain into a chilled Nick & Nora glass. Express the lemon twist over the drink and discard.

SHANNON'S MARTINI

Shannon Tebay, head bartender, Death & Co New York

- 1½ ounces Beefeater gin
- 1½ ounces Dolin dry vermouth
- 1 dash Bitter Truth celery bitters
- Garnish: 1 olive and 1 lemon twist

Stir all the ingredients over ice, then strain into a chilled Nick & Nora glass. Garnish with the olive. Express the lemon twist over the drink and discard.

TYSON'S MARTINI

Tyson Buhler, beverage director

- 2½ ounces Tanqueray London dry gin
- ¾ ounce Dolin dry vermouth
- Garnish: 1 olive and 1 lemon twist

Stir all the ingredients over ice, then strain into a chilled Nick & Nora glass. Garnish with the olive. Express the lemon twist over the drink and discard.

WES'S MARTINI

Wes Hamilton, culinary director

- 1½ ounces Plymouth gin
- 1½ ounces Dolin dry vermouth
- 1 dash House Orange Bitters (page 298)
- Garnish: 1 lemon twist

Stir all the ingredients over ice, then strain into a double old-fashioned glass over 1 large ice cube. Express the lemon twist over the drink, then place it in the drink.

WILLIE'S MARTINI

Willie Rosenthal, associate director of operations, Death & Co Denver

- 2½ ounces St. George Terroir gin
- ¾ ounce Cocchi Americano

Stir the ingredients over ice, then strain into a chilled Nick & Nora glass. No garnish.

HOME STRETCH ❋

Jeremy Oertel, 2016

1 ounce Tapatío Anejo tequila

1 ounce Domaine du Manoir de Montreuil calvados

¾ ounce Carpano Antica Formula vermouth

¼ ounce Vanilla Syrup (page 288)

1 drop Terra Spice root beer extract

1 dash Miracle Mile pecan bitters

Garnish: 1 orange twist

Stir all the ingredients over ice, then strain into a double old-fashioned glass over 1 large ice cube. Express the orange twist over the drink, then place it in the drink.

HUMMINGBIRD ⚜

Matthew Belanger, 2018

1½ ounces Dorothy Parker gin

1½ ounces Kamoizumi umeshu

½ ounce Trimbach Mirabelle plum eau-de-vie

¼ ounce Dolin Génépy des Alpes liqueur

½ teaspoon Cane Sugar Syrup (page 282)

Garnish: 1 umeboshi plum

Stir all the ingredients over ice, then strain into a chilled martini glass. Garnish with the umeboshi plum.

HUNT & PECK ⚜

Scott Teague, 2015

1½ ounces Rittenhouse rye

½ ounce Sombra mezcal

½ ounce Carpano Antica Formula vermouth

¼ ounce Amaro Averna

1 teaspoon Campari

Garnish: 1 orange twist and 1 brandied cherry

Stir all the ingredients over ice, then strain into a chilled Nick & Nora glass. Express the orange twist over the drink and discard. Garnish with the brandied cherry.

IDYLLWILD ❋

Tyson Buhler, 2016

I had the honor of putting up Death & Co's first vodka cocktail, which of course is made with a vodka that drinks more like a grape-based eau-de-vie than the typical grain-based spirit. It's subtle, grassy, and aromatic; this makes for a great freezer cocktail. —TB

1½ ounces Craft Distillers DSP CA 162 vodka

1 ounce Silver Needle Tea–Infused Dolin Blanc Vermouth (page 294)

½ ounce Ransom Gewürztraminer grappa

1 dash Miracle Mile cucumber/orris root bitters

Garnish: 1 cucumber slice

Stir all the ingredients over ice, then strain into a chilled Nick & Nora glass. Garnish with the cucumber slice.

INK & DAGGER ❋

Al Sotack, 2014

This Vieux Carré variation is inspired by my favorite stirred drink, but I also think about it a lot in the context of a bar like Death & Co, where we've been criticized for using too many ingredients and overcomplicating things. But even the classic Vieux Carré is a seven-bottle pickup, so sometimes more is better. —AS

1 ounce Rittenhouse rye

1 ounce Laird's bonded apple brandy

½ ounce Maurin Quina

¼ ounce Carpano Antica Formula vermouth

¼ ounce Amaro Nardini

1 teaspoon Bénédictine

1 dash Peychaud's bitters

1 dash Bitter Truth aromatic bitters

Garnish: 1 orange twist

Stir all the ingredients over ice, then strain into a single old-fashioned glass over 1 large ice cube. Express the orange twist over the drink, then place it in the drink.

IPSWITCH ❋

Jonnie Long, 2019

Träkal is Patagonia's first distillate, with all of its botanicals sourced within thirty miles of the distillery. It's an unaged spirit made from an apple and pear eau-de-vie base, with a cool, floral flavor profile. You can also batch this Martini variation and keep it in the freezer. —JL

1½ ounces Plymouth gin

½ ounce Träkal

¾ ounce Cocchi Americano

1 teaspoon Suze

½ teaspoon St-Germain elderflower liqueur

Garnish: 1 lemon twist

Stir all the ingredients over ice, then strain into a chilled Nick & Nora glass. Express the lemon twist over the drink and discard.

IRISH WRISTWATCH ⚜

Eryn Reece, 2014

1 ounce Redbreast 12-year Irish whiskey

½ ounce Louis Roque La Vieille prune eau-de-vie

¾ ounce Punt e Mes

½ ounce Amaro Nonino

Stir all the ingredients over ice, then strain into a chilled Nick & Nora glass. No garnish.

IRON PATH ☉

Sam Johnson, 2018

Because there's no water in it, this is an odd recipe that looks like a reverse Manhattan but drinks like sangria. Instead of chilling all the ingredients separately, you can make a big batch of this and keep it in the fridge. —SJ

2 ounces Manos Negras Malbec

1 ounce Amaro Pasubio

¾ ounce El Dorado 8-year rum

½ ounce Cinnamon Syrup (page 283)

1 dash Angostura bitters

Garnish: 1 orange half wheel and 2 raspberries and/or blackberries on a skewer, 1 cinnamon stick

Chill all ingredients beforehand. Combine the ingredients in a single old-fashioned glass over 1 large ice cube. Garnish with the orange half wheel and berries, and grate some cinnamon over the top of the drink.

JEWEL THIEF ❄

Shannon Tebay, 2019

Amrut tastes like scotch that was made in the tropics, I guess because that's exactly what it is—you can somehow taste the heat of Southern India in the flavor profile. Here, I pair it with flavors of coffee, passion fruit, and cardamom, a trio that has an affinity in Middle Eastern and subcontinent cuisines, underlining the idea that what grows together, goes together. —ST

1½ ounces Amrut cask-strength single malt Indian whisky

¾ ounce Henriques & Henriques rainwater madeira

¼ ounce Galliano Ristretto

1 teaspoon Giffard passion fruit liqueur

½ dash Scrappy's cardamom bitters

Garnish: 1 orange twist

Stir all the ingredients over ice, then strain into a single old-fashioned glass over 1 large ice cube. Express the orange twist over the drink and discard.

KISSY SUZUKI ❄

Matthew Belanger, 2016

1½ ounces Mizu lemongrass shochu

¾ ounce St. George All-Purpose vodka

¾ ounce Cocchi Americano

½ teaspoon Luxardo maraschino liqueur

½ teaspoon kirschwasser

1 dash House Orange Bitters (page 298)

1 dash absinthe

Stir all the ingredients over ice, then strain into a chilled martini glass. No garnish.

LA DISPUTE ❄

Matthew Belanger, 2015

1 ounce Damoiseau VSOP rhum

1 ounce Dupont Fine Reserve calvados

½ ounce Pasquet Pineau des Charentes

½ ounce Leopold Bros. New York sour apple liqueur

1 teaspoon Dolin Génépy des Alpes liqueur

Garnish: 1 dehydrated apple slice

Stir all the ingredients over ice, then strain into a double old-fashioned glass over 1 large ice cube. Garnish with the apple slice.

LAMPLIGHTER ❄

Shannon Tebay, 2019

1¾ ounces Bowmore 12-year scotch

¾ ounce Cocchi vermouth di Torino

¼ ounce Reisetbauer carrot eau-de-vie

¼ ounce Pierre Ferrand dry curaçao

1 dash Bitter End Moroccan bitters

Garnish: 1 orange twist

Stir all the ingredients over ice, then strain into a chilled Nick & Nora glass. Express the orange twist over the drink, then place it in the drink.

LIFE ON MARS ❄

Matthew Belanger, 2019

1½ ounces Barrell Dovetail whiskey

1 ounce Taylor Fladgate ruby port

½ ounce Carpano Antica Formula vermouth

1 teaspoon Kronan Swedish Punsch

2 dashes Miracle Mile Redeye bitters

Garnish: 1 brandied cherry

Stir all the ingredients over ice, then strain into a chilled coupe. Garnish with the brandied cherry.

LIGHTNING ROD ✼

Shannon Tebay, 2017

This was my first time using Siembra Valles Ancestral tequila, which I'd first tasted when Jarred poured me a shot of it. I immediately knew I had to use it in a luxe cocktail, so I built a Negroni variation around it, with the supporting ingredients in smaller proportions. —ST

1½ ounces Siembra Valles Ancestral tequila

¾ ounce Cocchi vermouth di Torino

½ ounce Campari

1 teaspoon Marie Brizard white crème de cacao

1 teaspoon Giffard passion fruit liqueur

Garnish: 1 orange twist

Stir all the ingredients over ice, then strain into a double old-fashioned glass over 1 large ice cube. Express the orange twist over the drink, then place it in the drink.

MARIE PARADIS ✼✼

Eryn Reece, 2014

2 ounces Pierre Ferrand 1840 cognac

¾ ounce Dolin blanc vermouth

½ ounce Pasquet Marie-Framboise

½ ounce Neige apple ice wine

1 teaspoon Cane Sugar Syrup (page 282)

Stir all the ingredients over ice, then strain into a chilled Nick & Nora glass. No garnish.

MODERN LOVERS

Tyson Buhler, 2016

1½ ounces Charles Fournier Riesling

1½ ounces Cocchi Americano

½ ounce Dupont Fine Reserve calvados

1 teaspoon Strega

1 dash Angostura bitters

Garnish: 1 lemon twist

Stir all the ingredients over ice, then strain into a chilled Nick & Nora glass. Express the lemon twist over the drink, then place it in the drink.

NEGRONI (STANDING ROOM) ✼

Tyson Buhler, 2019

1 ounce Cimarron Blanco tequila

1 ounce Aperol

1 ounce Dolin blanc vermouth

½ ounce Rhine Hall mango brandy

¼ ounce fresh cucumber juice

Garnish: 1 coriander flower

Stir all the ingredients over ice, then strain into a double old-fashioned glass over 1 large ice cube. Garnish with the coriander flower.

NEW BEAT ✼

Jarred Weigand, 2017

I hadn't seen a stirred-and-up blanco tequila or rhum agricole drink before, so I found bottles of both that shared a vegetal profile. The fennel flavors of the Finocchietto liqueur bridge the two spirits nicely. —JW

1 ounce Siembra Azul Blanco tequila

1 ounce Rhum JM Agricole Blanc

½ ounce Don Ciccio & Figli Finocchietto fennel liqueur

½ ounce Cocchi Americano

1 teaspoon green Chartreuse

1 dash Bitter Truth celery bitters

Garnish: 1 lemon twist

Stir all the ingredients over ice, then strain into a chilled Nick & Nora glass. Express the lemon twist over the drink and discard.

NIGHTWING ✼

Matthew Belanger, 2018

1 ounce Siembra Valles Ancestral tequila

1 ounce East India Solera sherry

½ ounce Plantation Pineapple rum

½ ounce Amaro Ramazzotti

1 dash Bittermens Xocolatl mole bitters

Stir all the ingredients over ice, then strain into a chilled Nick & Nora glass. No garnish.

NITE TRIPPER ✼

Jon Armstrong, 2015

2 ounces Wild Turkey 101 rye

¾ ounce Dolin dry vermouth

½ ounce Cynar

1 teaspoon Combier pamplemousse rose liqueur

½ teaspoon St-Germain elderflower liqueur

Garnish: 1 grapefruit twist

Stir all the ingredients over ice, then strain into a chilled Nick & Nora glass. Express the grapefruit twist over the drink and discard.

NO PADDLE ✼

Teddy Lamontagne, 2019

1¼ ounces Rabbit Hole bourbon

¾ ounce Dolin blanc vermouth

½ ounce Campari

¼ ounce St. George raspberry eau-de-vie

1 teaspoon Giffard crème de pamplemousse rose

Garnish: 1 lemon twist

Stir all the ingredients over ice, then strain into a single old-fashioned glass over 1 large ice cube. Express the lemon twist over the drink, then place it in the drink.

NO SHADE IN THE SHADOWS ❄

Jeremy Oertel, 2015

Unaged Armagnac is fun to play around with; I usually treat it like a grappa or pisco. Here, I pair it with pineapple-infused gin in a Martinez variation. –JO

1¼ ounces Domaine d'Esperance blanche Armagnac

¾ ounce Pineapple-Infused Tanqueray Gin (page 294)

¾ ounce Cocchi vermouth di Torino

1 teaspoon Luxardo maraschino liqueur

1 dash absinthe

Garnish: 1 lemon twist

Stir all the ingredients over ice, then strain into a chilled Nick & Nora glass. Express the lemon twist over the drink, then place it in the drink.

OCULUS ❄

Shannon Tebay, 2018

I ate an apple and fennel salad somewhere that made me want to turn those flavors into a cocktail. In a way, this is an appletini, but a more savory and complex one. –ST

1½ ounces Domaine du Manoir de Montreuil calvados

½ ounce Brennivin aquavit

½ ounce Don Ciccio & Figli Finocchietto fennel liqueur

½ ounce Lillet blanc

1 teaspoon Cyril Zangs 00 apple cider eau-de-vie

1 dash absinthe

Garnish: 1 lemon twist

Stir all the ingredients over ice, then strain into a chilled Nick & Nora glass. Express the lemon twist over the drink and discard.

OLD CASTILLE ♣

Jillian Vose, 2014

1 ounce Domaine du Manoir de Montreuil calvados

1 ounce Clear Creek 2-year apple eau-de-vie

½ ounce Blandy's 5-year Malmsey madeira

½ ounce Fusion verjus blanc

¼ ounce Cinnamon Syrup (page 283)

1 dash Bittermens Xocolatl mole bitters

Garnish: 1 lemon twist and 1 rosemary sprig

Stir all the ingredients over ice, then strain into a chilled Nick & Nora glass. Express the lemon twist over the drink and discard, then garnish with the rosemary sprig.

ONE ARMED SCISSOR ❄

Matthew Belanger, 2018

I wanted to make a Martini with an intense vegetal vibe, and Clairin Vaval has lots of herbs in its mash bill, and tastes like yellow bell peppers to me. I ended up with this weird, avant-garde drink, so I named it after a song by the post-hardcore band At the Drive-In. –MB

1¼ ounces Beefeater gin

½ ounce St. George green chile vodka

¼ ounce Clairin Vaval Haitian rum

¾ ounce Dolin blanc vermouth

1 teaspoon Strega

1 dash absinthe

1 dash House Orange Bitters (page 298)

Garnish: 1 orange twist

Stir all the ingredients over ice, then strain into a chilled Nick & Nora glass. Express the orange twist over the drink, then place it in the drink.

OPPOSITES ATTRACT ☉

Jeremy Oertel, 2017

2 ounces Lustau East India Solera sherry

1 ounce Nuestra Soledad San Luis del Rio mezcal

1 teaspoon Giffard elderflower liqueur

½ teaspoon Elisir Novasalus vino amaro

Stir all the ingredients over ice, then strain into a chilled Nick & Nora glass. No garnish.

ORIGINAL SIN ♣

Austin Knight, 2019

1¼ ounces Lustau Vermut Rojo

¾ ounce Ron Zacapa 23 rum

¾ ounce Lustau Don Nuño oloroso sherry

¼ ounce Don Ciccio & Figli Nocino

1 teaspoon Demerara Syrup (page 283)

Garnish: 1 orange twist

Stir all the ingredients over ice, then strain into a chilled Nick & Nora glass. Express the orange twist over the drink, then place it in the drink.

ORVILLE GIBSON

Matthew Belanger, 2019

At Death & Co LA, we work with as many California-based ingredients as possible. Sea gin is distilled with seaweed, so it has this wild umami note that's amplified by the seaweed-infused pear brandy in this 50/50 Martini. —MB

1½ ounces Oakland Spirits Co. Automatic Sea gin

¾ ounce Dolin blanc vermouth

¾ ounce Dolin dry vermouth

1 teaspoon Dashi Kombu–Infused Pear Brandy (page 291)

Garnish: Dashi Kombu–Infused Pear Brandy in an atomizer

Stir all the ingredients over ice, then strain into a single old-fashioned glass over 1 large ice cube. Spray some of the infused pear brandy over the top of the drink.

PARQUET COURTS ❄

Tyson Buhler, 2016

1 ounce Tariquet 15-year Bas-Armagnac

¾ ounce Avuá Amburana cachaça

¼ ounce Reisetbauer hazelnut eau-de-vie

¾ ounce Carpano Antica sweet vermouth

1 teaspoon Vanilla Syrup (page 288)

1 dash Angostura bitters

Stir all the ingredients over ice, then strain into a chilled Nick & Nora glass. No garnish.

PART TIME LOVER ❄

Jillian Vose, 2014

1½ ounces Dorothy Parker gin

¾ ounce Orleans Borbon manzanilla sherry

¾ ounce Dolin blanc vermouth

¼ ounce green Chartreuse

½ teaspoon Luxardo maraschino liqueur

1 dash absinthe

Garnish: 1 lemon twist

Stir all the ingredients over ice, then strain into a chilled Nick & Nora glass. Express the lemon twist over the drink and discard.

PERISCOPE ⊙

Tyson Buhler, 2017

2 ounces Imbue bittersweet vermouth

¾ ounce Monkey 47 Schwartzwald dry gin

½ ounce Mandarine Napoléon liqueur

1 teaspoon Marie Brizard white crème de cacao

1 dash House Orange Bitters (page 298)

1 dash Angostura bitters

Garnish: 1 orange twist

Stir all the ingredients over ice, then strain into a chilled Nick & Nora glass. Express the orange twist over the drink, then place it in the drink.

PIXEE PECALA ❄

Shannon Tebay, 2019

¾ ounce Del Maguey Chichicapa mezcal

¾ ounce Rhine Hall mango brandy

½ ounce Ancho Reyes ancho chile liqueur

½ ounce Aperol

½ ounce Cocchi vermouth di Torino

Garnish: 1 orange twist

Stir all the ingredients over ice, then strain into a double old-fashioned glass over 1 large ice cube. Express the orange twist over the drink, then place it in the drink.

PLOT TWIST ⊙

Shannon Tebay, 2019

Amaro Abano has pungent black-pepper flavors, so I thought it would be delicious paired with the flavors of cherries in a low-ABV Martinez riff. —ST

1½ ounces González Byass La Copa vermouth

1½ ounces Ransom Old Tom gin

½ ounce Leopold Bros. Michigan tart cherry liqueur

1 teaspoon Luxardo Amaro Abano

Garnish: 1 orange twist

Stir all the ingredients over ice, then strain into a chilled Nick & Nora glass. Express the orange twist over the drink and discard.

⊙ LOW ABV　　⊘ NO ABV　　❄ FREEZER BAR　　⧖ PROJECT COCKTAIL　　✳ LOW-PREP COCKTAIL

PONIENTE ❊

Matthew Belanger, 2017

Though you can make a single serving of this drink, it makes a lot more sense to put together a big batch and store it in the freezer. —MB

- 1½ ounces Noilly Prat extra dry vermouth
- 1 ounce Cadenhead's Old Raj gin
- 1 ounce Tio Pepe fino sherry
- ¼ ounce extra-virgin olive oil
- Garnish: 1 olive

Combine all the ingredients in a storage container, then freeze for 24 hours. Strain the solidified oil, and pour the drink into a chilled martini glass. Garnish with the olive.

POPEYE DOYLE ❊

Tyson Buhler, 2017

- ¾ ounce Navazos Palazzi oloroso rum
- 1 ounce Springbank 10-year scotch
- ¾ ounce Caffo Amaretto
- ¼ ounce Massenez kirsch
- ¼ ounce Cherry Heering
- Garnish: 1 brandied cherry

Stir all the ingredients over ice, then strain into a single old-fashioned glass over 1 large ice cube. Garnish with the brandied cherry.

PROTOTYPE ❊

Tyson Buhler, 2017

- 1½ ounces Barsol Acholado pisco
- ½ ounce Cocchi vermouth di Torino
- ½ ounce Campari
- ½ ounce Giffard rhubarb liqueur
- 1 teaspoon Wray & Nephew Overproof Jamaica rum
- Garnish: 1 grapefruit twist and 1 rhubarb ribbon on a skewer

Stir all the ingredients over ice, then strain into a double old-fashioned glass over 1 large ice cube. Express the grapefruit twist over the drink and discard, then garnish with the rhubarb ribbon.

RASPBERRY DIVA ❊

Jeremy Oertel, 2015

Eryn Reece named this drink after one of our porters, who was legitimately scared of fruit. —JO

- 1½ ounces Dorothy Parker gin
- ½ ounce Dolin dry vermouth
- ½ ounce Dolin blanc vermouth
- 1 teaspoon St-Germain elderflower liqueur
- ½ teaspoon Clear Creek framboise eau-de-vie
- Garnish: 1 lemon twist and 1 raspberry

Stir all the ingredients over ice, then strain into a chilled Nick & Nora glass. Express the lemon twist over the drink and discard. Garnish with the raspberry.

REEF BREAK ❊

Tyson Buhler, 2019

I love Martinis that have a fruit element to them (see Al Sotack's Bikini Kill, page 249), and I wanted to do something in a similar vein. This style of drink can be a challenge with guests, because it looks more approachable on paper than in the glass, but we love them (the fruity Martinis and the guests) all the same. —TB

- 1¾ ounces Suntory Haku vodka
- 1 ounce Lustau Jarana fino sherry
- ¼ ounce El Dorado 3-year rum
- 1 teaspoon Giffard passion fruit liqueur
- 1 teaspoon Cinnamon Syrup (page 283)
- Garnish: 1 grapefruit twist

Stir all the ingredients over ice, then strain into a chilled Nick & Nora glass. Express the grapefruit twist over the drink and discard.

RETURN OF THE MAC ☉

Jeremy Oertel, 2016

Macvin du Jura is a super funky fortified wine that pairs well with the raisin flavors of the amber vermouth. Add some carrot eau-de-vie and the malty notes of Irish whiskey, and you have carrot cake in a glass. —JO

- 1½ ounces Noilly Prat Ambré vermouth
- 1 ounce Macvin du Jura
- ½ teaspoon Reisetbauer carrot eau-de-vie
- ½ ounce Connemara Irish whisky
- 1 teaspoon Orgeat Works Macadamia Nut Syrup
- 1 dash Angostura bitters
- 1 dash Miracle Mile pecan bitters

Stir all the ingredients over ice, then strain into a chilled Nick & Nora glass. No garnish.

RHAPSODY IN BLUE ❊

Matthew Belanger, 2019

Amaro Pasubio is made with wild mountain blueberries, so I wanted to make a Boulevardier with that flavor profile. Celery bitters give it a little lift and help to sharpen the blueberry. —MB

- 1½ ounces Rittenhouse rye
- ¾ ounce Dolin blanc vermouth
- ¾ ounce Cappelletti Pasubio vino amaro
- 1 dash Bitter Truth celery bitters
- Garnish: 1 blueberry

Stir all the ingredients over ice, then strain into a chilled Nick & Nora glass. Garnish with the blueberry.

RIVER CHILD ☉

Matthew Belanger, 2018

Sake is usually meant to be consumed during the same season in which it was made, but the producer of Kamoizumi Red Maple sake accidentally left a bottle in the back of his freezer, as the story goes, and realized it actually improved with age. Bottles of Red Maple are now aged at about 41° Fahrenheit for two years, resulting in a rich, unique flavor profile that is potent enough to work as a base spirit. —MB

> 2 ounces Kamoizumi 2-year Red Maple sake
>
> 1 ounce Dolin blanc vermouth
>
> ¼ ounce Chareau aloe liqueur
>
> ¼ ounce Anchor Genevieve gin
>
> Garnish: 1 cucumber slice

Stir all the ingredients over ice, then strain into a chilled Nick & Nora glass. Garnish with the cucumber slice.

RUBY SOHO ❄

Matthew Belanger, 2016

Using a strawberry-infused spirit in this Negroni variation gives you a much fresher flavor than a strawberry liqueur. At the bar we clarify the infusion with a centrifuge, but you can also simply macerate strawberries in the mezcal and strain them out. —MB

> 1 ounce Paul Beau VS cognac
>
> ½ ounce Strawberry-Infused Sombra Mezcal (page 294)
>
> ¾ ounce Cocchi vermouth di Torino
>
> ¾ ounce Gran Classico Bitter
>
> 1 dash Bittermens Xocolatl mole bitters
>
> Garnish: 1 orange twist

Stir all the ingredients over ice, then strain into a double old-fashioned glass over 1 large ice cube. Express the orange twist over the drink, then place it in the drink.

SAN PATRICIA'S BATTALION ❄

Eryn Reece, 2014

> 1½ ounces Redbreast 12-year Irish whiskey
>
> ¾ ounce Dolin blanc vermouth
>
> ½ ounce Del Maguey Chichicapa mezcal
>
> ¼ ounce St-Germain elderflower liqueur
>
> 1 teaspoon Bittermen's Citron Sauvage
>
> Garnish: 1 grapefruit twist

Stir all the ingredients over ice, then strain into a chilled Nick & Nora glass. Express the grapefruit twist over the drink, then place it in the drink.

SATISFIED HARE ☉

Sam Penton, 2018

I was tasked with creating a low-ABV Martini, which is something I hadn't done before. I started with the banana-infused vermouth, which I'd seen in a Manhattan variation at a cocktail competition. (That vermouth became a favorite staff shot.) I also hadn't worked much with Armagnac, but the two fell together in a clean, 50/50 Martini that more adventurous drinkers will enjoy. —SP

> 1½ ounces Delord Napoléon Armagnac
>
> ¾ ounce Banana-Infused Dolin Blanc Vermouth (page 290)
>
> ¾ ounce Dolin dry vermouth
>
> 1 teaspoon Cinnamon Syrup (page 283)
>
> 1 dash absinthe
>
> Garnish: 1 lemon twist

Stir all the ingredients over ice, then strain into a chilled Nick & Nora glass. Express the lemon twist over the drink and discard.

SCIENCE OF BEING

Jarred Weigand, 2016

This is a small cocktail, about 2½ ounces, but Tobola is this big, beautiful expression of agave, and adding any more would overpower the other ingredients. The result is a tiny Martini with bold, smoky flavors and lovely floral attributes. —JW

> 1½ ounces Del Maguey Tobala mezcal
>
> 1 ounce Lillet rosé
>
> 1 teaspoon Cinnamon Syrup (page 283)
>
> 1 dash Peychaud's bitters

Stir all the ingredients over ice, then strain into a chilled martini glass. No garnish.

SHADOWS AND WHISPERS ❄

Tyson Buhler, 2017

> 1 ounce Mic Drop bourbon
>
> 1 ounce Copper & Kings Floodwall apple brandy
>
> ¾ ounce Henriques & Henriques 5-year vino generoso doce madeira
>
> ½ ounce Grand Marnier Cuvée Centenaire
>
> 1 dash Angostura bitters

Stir all the ingredients over ice, then strain into a chilled Nick & Nora glass. No garnish.

SHOTGUN WILLIE ❄

Tyson Buhler, 2018

I developed this cocktail for the first Denver menu before I arrived in the city, and I named it after Willie Nelson. Little did I know that there's a certain infamous strip club in Denver bearing the same name (oops). The drink itself is dry, savory, and a bit strange, and reminds me of the smell of meat that's been dry-rubbed and thrown on the grill. —TB

1¼ ounces Siete Leguas Reposado tequila

½ ounce St. George green chile vodka

¾ ounce Alvear Festival pale cream sherry

¼ ounce Jalapeño-Infused Siembra Valles Blanco Tequila (page 293)

1 teaspoon Grand Marnier

½ teaspoon kümmel liqueur

Garnish: 1 pickled carrot or 1 pickled radish slice

Stir all the ingredients over ice, then strain into a chilled Nick & Nora glass. Garnish with the pickled carrot or radish slice.

SISTER MIDNIGHT ❄

Jon Armstrong, 2016

My goal was to create a three-ingredient stirred rum drink. I started with Appleton, yellow Chartreuse, and pear liqueur, but someone suggested adding a little funky rum to make it more interesting. In essence, it was a simple cocktail we made more complicated because we could. —JA

1½ ounces Appleton Estate Signature Blend Jamaica rum

½ ounce Smith & Cross Jamaica rum

½ ounce yellow Chartreuse

½ ounce St. George spiced pear liqueur

Stir all the ingredients over ice, then strain into a chilled Nick & Nora glass. No garnish.

SKY LADDER ☉

Sam Johnson, 2018

This low-ABV cocktail drinks like a Bamboo, with a slightly oily coconut flavor from the Kalani. Use the highest quality of bottled yuzu juice that you can find. —SJ

1½ ounces Lustau manzanilla sherry

¾ ounce Dolin dry vermouth

¾ ounce Dolin blanc vermouth

1 teaspoon Kalani Ron de Coco coconut liqueur

1 teaspoon simple syrup (page 287)

½ teaspoon bottled yuzu juice

Garnish: 1 grapefruit twist

Stir all the ingredients over ice, then strain into a single old-fashioned glass. Express the grapefruit twist over the drink and discard.

SPINDRIFT ❄

Sam Johnson, 2018

I love a drink that's perfectly clear and served on a big rock, but it often doesn't work because those drinks die quickly on ice. White Negronis are the exception, but it's difficult to create a new White Negroni variation because there aren't a lot of clear bitter ingredients. Once I found the Luxardo Bitter Bianco, everything else fell into place, with the floral fruitiness of the plum eau-de-vie bridging the gin and the bright grapefruit liqueur. —SJ

1 ounce Bimini gin

½ ounce Clear Creek Mirabelle plum eau-de-vie

¾ ounce Luxardo Bitter Bianco

¾ ounce Dolin dry vermouth

1 teaspoon Giffard crème de pamplemousse rose

Garnish: 1 lemon twist

Stir all the ingredients over ice, then strain into a double old-fashioned glass over 1 large ice cube. Express the lemon twist over the drink, then place it in the drink.

SPYGLASS ❄

Tyson Buhler, 2017

1¾ ounces Plymouth gin

¼ ounce Krogstad aquavit

½ ounce Dolin dry vermouth

½ ounce Don Ciccio & Figli Finocchietto fennel liqueur

1 teaspoon Marie Brizard white crème de cacao

Garnish: 1 lemon twist

Stir all the ingredients over ice, then strain into a chilled Nick & Nora glass. Express the lemon twist over the drink and discard.

ST GEORGE AND THE DRAGON ❄

Al Sotack, 2014

I wanted this Bobby Burns riff to have a specifically peaty accent. The combination of smoky and bitter flavors with absinthe is hard to balance, but once you dial it in, it's so good. —AS

1¾ ounces Redbreast 12-year Irish whiskey

¾ ounce Punt e Mes

¼ ounce Laphroaig 10-year single malt scotch

¼ ounce Bénédictine

2 dashes absinthe

Garnish: 1 lemon twist

Stir all the ingredients over ice, then strain into a chilled Nick & Nora glass. Express the lemon twist over the drink and discard.

STAY MUM ⚜

Tyson Buhler, 2018

I love the classic Chrysanthemum cocktail, and Thai basil has a distinct anise flavor that works great with the heavy dose of absinthe. —TB

3 Thai basil leaves

2½ ounces Dolin dry vermouth

½ ounce Bénédictine

1 teaspoon Cyril Zangs 00 apple cider eau-de-vie

4 dashes absinthe

Garnish: 1 lemon twist

In a shaker, gently muddle the basil. Add the remaining ingredients and shake with ice. Double strain into a chilled Nick & Nora glass. Express the lemon twist over the drink, then place it in the drink.

STRANGE RELIGION ⚜

Jon Feuersanger, 2019

With our luxury cocktails, we get the opportunity to work with ingredients made with the highest intention—we don't use expensive ingredients just for the sake of it. Monkey 47 gin is made in Germany and contains a whopping 47 botanicals; you can drink it neat, and it's an experience in itself. A classic Martini showcases the bartender's understanding of ingredients, and hopefully this drink does as well. Because Monkey 47 has a lighter, more delicate flavor profile, a traditional dry vermouth would bully it, so I used a plum wine instead. A teaspoon of mango brandy works as seasoning to lift the other flavors, like playing harmony under a solo. —JF

1½ ounces Monkey 47 Schwartzwald dry gin

1¼ ounces Tozai Blossom of Peace plum wine

¼ ounce Giffard Lichi-Li lychee liqueur

1 teaspoon Rhine Hall mango brandy

1 dash absinthe

½ teaspoon Cane Sugar Syrup (page 282)

Garnish: 1 umeboshi plum

Stir all the ingredients over ice, then strain into a chilled martini glass. Garnish with the umeboshi plum.

STRANGERS ON A TRAIN ⚜

Matthew Belanger, 2017

1 ounce St. George dry rye reposado gin

1 ounce Domaine du Manoir de Montreuil Réserve calvados

¾ ounce Noilly Prat Ambré vermouth

¼ ounce Clear Creek cranberry liqueur

1 teaspoon Luxardo maraschino liqueur

1 dash House Orange Bitters (page 298)

Garnish: 1 orange twist

Stir all the ingredients over ice, then strain into a chilled Nick & Nora glass. Express the orange twist over the drink, then place it in the drink.

SUBLIMINAL MESSAGES ⚜

Jeremy Oertel, 2015

1 ounce Del Maguey Santo Domingo Albarradas mezcal

1 ounce Jalapeño-Infused Siembra Valles Blanco Tequila (page 293)

1 ounce Dolin blanc vermouth

¼ ounce Giffard crème de pamplemousse rose

½ teaspoon Aperol

Garnish: 1 lemon twist

Stir all the ingredients over ice, then strain into a chilled Nick & Nora glass. Express the lemon twist over the drink, then place it in the drink.

SUGAR MAGNOLIA ⚜

Tyson Buhler, 2017

1½ ounces Tyrconnell single malt Irish whiskey

½ ounce Redbreast 12-year Irish whiskey

½ ounce Lustau manzanilla sherry

½ ounce Dolin blanc vermouth

1 teaspoon Combier rose liqueur

1 teaspoon Campari

1 teaspoon Cane Sugar Syrup (page 282)

1 dash Peychaud's bitters

1 dash absinthe

Garnish: 1 lemon twist

Stir all the ingredients over ice, then strain into a chilled Nick & Nora glass. Express the lemon twist over the drink, then place it in the drink.

TELEGRAPH ⚜

Tyson Buhler, 2018

The first drink I put together for the opening of D&C Denver, this is essentially a Ravenmaster (page 203) turned into a Martini. We serve it straight from the freezer with a very small amount of added water, to keep the rich texture and to let the pear and eucalyptus flavors shine. —TB

1¾ ounces Beefeater London dry gin

¼ ounce Clear Creek pear eau-de-vie

1 teaspoon Mathilde Poire pear liqueur

¾ ounce Cocchi Americano

1 drop Terra Spice eucalyptus extract

Garnish: 1 lemon twist

Stir all the ingredients over ice, then strain into a chilled Nick & Nora glass. Express the lemon twist over the drink and discard.

TERMS OF TREATY ❋

Eryn Reece, 2014

1 ounce Buffalo Trace bourbon

1 ounce Pierre Ferrand 1840 cognac

½ ounce Zurbaran cream sherry

½ ounce Giffard banane du Brésil

1 teaspoon Demerara Syrup (page 283)

1 dash Bitter Truth Jerry Thomas' Own Decanter bitters

Stir all the ingredients over ice, then strain into a chilled Nick & Nora glass. No garnish.

THIN WHITE DUKE ❋

Tyson Buhler, 2016

This is an odd, but very pretty and floral Martini variation. I like to think the name fits the drink. —TB

1 ounce Barbancourt white rum

¾ ounce blanche Armagnac Domaine d'Esperance

¼ ounce Clear Creek Blue Plum brandy

½ ounce La Quintinye blanc vermouth

½ ounce Dolin dry vermouth

1 teaspoon Fusion verjus blanc

½ teaspoon Cane Sugar Syrup (page 282)

Garnish: 1 lemon twist

Stir all the ingredients over ice, then strain into a chilled Nick & Nora glass. Express the lemon twist over the drink and discard.

THUNDER ROAD ☉

Matthew Belanger, 2016

1 ounce Ransom sweet vermouth

1 ounce Lustau oloroso sherry

1 ounce Clear Creek 8-year apple brandy

1 teaspoon Sarsaparilla Demerara Syrup (page 286)

1 dash Angostura bitters

Garnish: 1 lemon twist

Stir all the ingredients over ice, then strain into a double old-fashioned glass over 1 large ice cube. Express the lemon twist over the drink, then place it in the drink.

TIGER TANAKA ⁂

Matthew Belanger, 2018

The key to making this Vesper variation is to let the shiso sit in the mixing glass for a couple of minutes before stirring. At this point, we'd named so many Vesper variations after female James Bond villains that I opted for a vaguely Japanese dude from a Bond novel. —MB

1 ounce Siembra Valles Blanco tequila

1 ounce Monkey 47 Schwartzwald dry gin

1 ounce Noilly Prat dry vermouth

¼ ounce green Chartreuse

1 shiso leaf

Garnish: 1 shiso leaf

Stir all the ingredients over ice, then strain into a chilled Nick & Nora glass. Garnish with the shiso leaf.

TOUCH OF EVIL ❋

Jon Armstrong, 2015

This rum-forward drink is a riff on two things: a Cynar julep that I found in the indie book *Rogue Cocktails* by Maks Pazuniak, and a Hanky-Panky, which also combines maraschino with Fernet. This is a total bartender's cocktail: it's boozy as fuck and bitter as hell, but it's approachable if you like those ingredients. —JA

1½ ounces Cynar

1 ounce El Dorado 8-year rum

½ ounce Appleton Estate Signature Blend Jamaica rum

1 teaspoon Luxardo maraschino liqueur

½ teaspoon Fernet-Branca

½ dash Salt Solution (page 299)

Garnish: 1 orange twist

Stir all the ingredients over ice, then strain into a chilled Nick & Nora glass. Express the orange twist over the drink and discard.

TRUE ROMANCE ❋

Carey Jenkins, 2019

I love Tarantino movies, and I wanted my first D&C cocktail to be named after Tarantino's introduction into film. It's essentially a mezcal Negroni inspired by Scott Teague's Straight Razor. It's meant to be a slow sipper; as it dilutes, the flavors open up, the drink loses some of its bitterness, and it tastes brighter and more summery. —CJ

¾ ounce Del Maguey Vida mezcal

¾ ounce Olmeca Altos reposado tequila

½ ounce Cynar

½ ounce Punt e Mes

½ ounce Ancho Reyes ancho chile liqueur

2 dashes Bitter Truth celery bitters

Garnish: 1 orange half wheel

Stir all the ingredients over ice, then strain into a double old-fashioned glass over 1 large ice cube. Garnish with the orange half wheel.

TRUST FALL ❄

Shannon Tebay, 2017

The name comes from the fact that this was my first Death & Co drink. I'd asked one of our servers what kind of drink she'd like to see on a Death & Co menu, and she said she'd love a good lychee Martini. —ST

1½ ounces Beefeater gin

½ ounce Singani 63 eau-de-vie

½ ounce Dolin blanc vermouth

¼ ounce Giffard Lichi-Li lychee liqueur

1 teaspoon Raspberry Syrup (page 286)

1 dash Peychaud's bitters

1 dash absinthe

Garnish: 1 grapefruit twist

Stir all the ingredients over ice, then strain into a chilled martini glass. Express the grapefruit twist over the drink and discard.

TSUKEMONO ☉

Tyson Buhler, 2016

This Bamboo variation highlights a beautiful sake, livened up with a dash of pickled cucumber brine. —TB

2 ounces Musashino Junmai daiginjo sake

¾ ounce Dolin blanc vermouth

¾ ounce Lustau manzanilla sherry

1 teaspoon Cane Sugar Syrup (page 282)

2 dashes Miracle Mile yuzu bitters

2 dashes Tsukemono Brine (page 299)

Garnish: 1 pickled cucumber slice

Stir all the ingredients over ice, then strain into a chilled martini glass. Garnish with the pickled cucumber slice.

VIGILANTE ❄

Tyson Buhler, 2016

1¼ ounces Wild Turkey rye

1 ounce Noilly Prat Ambré vermouth

½ ounce Cyril Zangs 00 apple cider eau-de-vie

¼ ounce Clear Creek Douglas Fir eau-de-vie

1 teaspoon Demerara Syrup (page 283)

1 dash Angostura bitters

Garnish: 1 apple slice

Stir all the ingredients over ice, then strain into a chilled Nick & Nora glass. Garnish with the apple slice.

VIPERINE ❄

Matthew Belanger, 2018

In the first Death & Co book, there were a ton of variations on the Diamondback, which is basically a Manhattan with yellow Chartreuse instead of vermouth, so they're always preposterously boozy (and always named after snakes). Cobrafire is a high-proof blanche Armagnac; the Pasquet Marie-Framboise lowers the proof and dries out the drink a bit. —MB

1½ ounces Cobrafire eau-de-vie de raisin

½ ounce yellow Chartreuse

½ ounce Pasquet Marie-Framboise

1 teaspoon Massenez framboise eau-de-vie

Garnish: 1 raspberry

Stir all the ingredients over ice, then strain into a chilled martini glass. Garnish with the raspberry.

VOYAGER ❄

Sam Johnson, 2019

This falls somewhere between a Boulevardier and a Negroni, with predominant flavors of caraway, banana, honey, and cream sherry to give the drink a crazy-long finish. —SJ

1½ ounces Linie aquavit

¾ ounce Morenita cream sherry

¼ ounce Forthave Spirits Marseille amaro

¼ ounce Giffard banane du Brésil

Garnish: 1 orange twist

Stir all the ingredients over ice, then strain into a double old-fashioned glass over 1 large ice cube. Express the orange twist over the drink, then place it in the drink.

WAITING GAME ❄

Jeremy Oertel, 2017

1½ ounces Louis Roque La Vielle prune eau-de-vie

½ ounce Amrut cask-strength single malt Indian whisky

½ ounce Cocchi vermouth di Torino

½ ounce Henriques & Henriques 5-year vino generoso doce madeira

¼ ounce Amaro Nardini

Garnish: 1 lemon twist

Stir all the ingredients over ice, then strain into a chilled Nick & Nora glass. Express the lemon twist over the drink, then place it in the drink.

WARRIOR POET ✳

Tyson Buhler, 2014

This simple Manhattan variation utilizes the very cool combination of coconut and celery. The aquavit pairs well with the soft spice of the rye. —TB

- 1 ounce Wild Turkey 101 rye
- 1 ounce Linie aquavit
- ¾ ounce Carpano Antica Formula vermouth
- ¼ ounce Kalani Ron de Coco coconut liqueur
- 1 dash Bitter Truth celery bitters
- Garnish: 1 lemon twist

Stir all the ingredients over ice, then strain into a chilled Nick & Nora glass. Express the lemon twist over the drink and discard.

WILD SHEEP CHASE ✳

Jeremy Oertel, 2015

- 1¾ ounces Campo Encanto Acholado pisco
- ¾ ounce Dolin dry vermouth
- ¼ ounce Aperol
- 1 teaspoon green Chartreuse
- ½ teaspoon Merlet crème de fraise des bois strawberry liqueur
- 1 dash absinthe
- Garnish: 1 lemon twist

Stir all the ingredients over ice, then strain into a chilled Nick & Nora glass. Express the lemon twist over the drink and discard.

WINSLET ✳

Eryn Reece, 2014

- 1 ounce Greenhook Ginsmiths Old Tom gin
- 1 ounce Busnel VSOP calvados
- ½ ounce Orleans Borbon manzanilla sherry
- ½ ounce Dolin blanc vermouth
- ¼ ounce Élixir combier
- 1 teaspoon Cane Sugar Syrup (page 282)
- 1 dash absinthe
- Garnish: 1 lemon twist

Stir all the ingredients over ice, then strain into a double old-fashioned glass over 1 large ice cube. Express the lemon twist over the drink, then place it in the drink.

WIZARD AND GLASS ✳

Matthew Belanger, 2018

Rose and rhubarb is an aromatic pairing common in perfume-making; I wanted to feature that in a Manhattan. Aquavit adds a savory edge that keeps the drink from being too floral and grounds it in Manhattan territory. —MB

- 1 ounce Wild Turkey 101 rye
- 1 ounce Linie aquavit
- ¾ ounce Carpano Antica Formula vermouth
- ¼ ounce Giffard rhubarb liqueur
- 1 teaspoon Combier crème de rose
- 1 dash absinthe
- 1 dash Peychaud's bitters
- Garnish: 1 grapefruit twist

Stir all the ingredients over ice, then strain into a chilled Nick & Nora glass. Express the grapefruit twist over the drink and discard.

YELLOWJACKET ✳

Jon Armstrong, 2016

This is me trying to combine the flavors of an expensive mezcal with a cheaper one. —JA

- 1 ounce Nuestra Soledad San Luis del Rio mezcal
- ¾ ounce Alvear Festival pale cream sherry
- ½ ounce St. George green chile vodka
- ½ ounce Clear Creek Douglas Fir eau-de-vie
- ½ ounce yellow Chartreuse

Stir all the ingredients over ice, then strain into a chilled Nick & Nora glass. No garnish.

Rich & Comforting

ARETHUSA ⊙

Matthew Belanger, 2019

This is a low-ABV Grasshopper variation, with a very minty amaro base and a bit of smoke from the mezcal. —MB

1 ounce Amaro Braulio

½ ounce Agave de Cortes mezcal

½ ounce Marie Brizard white crème de cacao

½ ounce Giffard menthe-pastille

¾ ounce heavy cream

6 to 8 mint leaves

Garnish: 1 mint leaf

Shake all the ingredients with ice, then strain into a double old-fashioned glass over 1 large ice cube. Garnish with the mint leaf.

BAD SNEAKERS

Tyson Buhler, 2018

1½ ounces Suntory Toki Japanese Whisky

1 ounce Donn's Mix #1 (page 298)

½ ounce Coco López

½ ounce fresh lime juice

2 teaspoons Kalani Ron de Coco coconut liqueur

1 teaspoon Laphroaig 10-year scotch

Garnish: Toasted coconut flakes and grapefruit zest

Combine all the ingredients in a shaker and whip, shaking with a few pieces of crushed ice, just until incorporated, then dump into a double old-fashioned glass and fill the glass with crushed ice. Garnish with the toasted coconut flakes, grate some grapefruit zest over the drink, and serve with a straw.

BANZAI WASHOUT

Alex Jump, 2019

I'm two for two on making blue-hued cocktails work on the first try. The coconut flakes used as a garnish are the remnants from our coconut-infused campari, which turns them into pretty pink petals. If you haven't made that infusion, you can use regular coconut flakes instead. —AJ

1½ ounces Spring44 vodka

½ ounce Giffard blue curaçao

¼ ounce Caffo Amaretto

½ ounce Coco López cream of coconut

½ ounce fresh lemon juice

½ ounce fresh pineapple juice

Garnish: Campari-Infused Toasted Coconut (page 300)

Combine all the ingredients in a shaker and whip, shaking with a few pieces of crushed ice, just until incorporated, then dump into a tulip glass and fill the glass with crushed ice. Garnish with the coconut flakes and serve with a straw.

BAT COUNTRY

Jonnie Long, 2019

I love Vietnamese coffee, both hot and cold, so I wanted to translate its flavors into a drink that could also be served at either temperature. —JL

COLD

¾ ounce Pierre Ferrand ambré cognac

½ ounce Batavia arrack

¼ ounce Grand Marnier

¼ ounce Galliano Ristretto

½ ounce Milk Syrup (page 285)

1 ounce cold brew coffee

Garnish: 1 dehydrated lemon wheel

Combine all the ingredients except the cold brew in a collins glass and fill the glass with crushed ice. Slowly pour the cold brew over the back of a spoon to float it on top of the drink. Garnish with the dehydrated lemon wheel and serve with a straw.

HOT

¾ ounce Pierre Ferrand ambré cognac

½ ounce Batavia arrack

¼ ounce Galliano Ristretto

½ ounce Demerara Syrup (page 283)

3 ounces hot coffee

Garnish: Grand Marnier cream (¼ ounce Grand Marnier whisked with 1 ounce heavy cream)

Combine all the ingredients in an Irish coffee mug. Spoon a layer of the Grand Marnier cream on top.

BROSE COLLINS

Tyson Buhler, 2018

I loved root beer floats as a kid, and I wanted to do a cocktail in that style. The grain-based whiskey, rice-based sake, and oat sorbet all blend together really well to create a creamy, tart dessert cocktail. —TB

1 ounce cold seltzer

1½ ounces Redbreast 12-year Irish whiskey

1 ounce Joto junmai nigori sake

¾ ounce simple syrup (page 287)

½ ounce fresh lemon juice

Garnish: 1 scoop oat milk sorbet

Pour the seltzer into a chilled fizz glass. Shake the remaining ingredients with ice, then double strain into the glass. Top with the sorbet.

BUM LEG

Adam Griggs, 2019

This is probably my most conceptually driven cocktail. I went to the British Virgin Islands on vacation with my girlfriend and her family, and I learned that her mother's favorite cocktail is the resort classic Lime in a Coconut. When we got back home, I decided to create a tiki-style drink in her honor. The drink is named after her thirty-pound cat. —AG

1 ounce Plantation Barbados 5-year rum

½ ounce Smith & Cross Jamaica rum

½ ounce Lustau oloroso sherry

1 ounce unsweetened coconut milk

¾ ounce fresh lime juice

½ ounce Coco López cream of coconut

½ ounce Demerara Syrup (page 283)

2 dashes Angostura bitters

Garnish: Lime zest and nutmeg

Combine all the ingredients in a shaker and whip, shaking with a few pieces of crushed ice, just until incorporated.

Dump into a tiki mug and add crushed ice until the glass is about 80 percent full. Swizzle for a few seconds, then pack the glass with ice, mounding it above the rim. Grate some lime zest and nutmeg over the top of the drink and serve with a straw.

CATAMARAN

Shannon Tebay, 2018

1½ ounces Bimini gin

½ ounce Perry's Tot Navy Strength gin

½ ounce Aperol

1 ounce Donn's Mix #1 (page 298)

½ ounce fresh lemon juice

½ ounce Coco López cream of coconut

Garnish: 1 orchid flower and 1 cinnamon stick

Shake all the ingredients with ice, then strain into a tulip glass. Fill the glass with crushed ice and garnish with the orchid and cinnamon stick.

CHARTREUSE ALEXANDER ⚜

Jon Armstrong, 2015

Back when we had a "redemption" menu of maligned classic drinks, I wanted to revisit the Brandy Alexander, adding a good amount of Chartreuse. —JA

¾ ounce green Chartreuse

¾ ounce Pierre Ferrand 1840 cognac

¾ ounce heavy cream

½ ounce Marie Brizard white crème de cacao

1 dash Bittermens Xocolatl mole bitters

Garnish: Nutmeg

Shake all the ingredients with ice, then double strain into a chilled martini glass. Grate some nutmeg over the top of the drink.

CLAY PIGEONS

Tyson Buhler, 2018

3 ounces hot brewed coffee

1 ounce Leopold Bros. Maryland rye

¼ ounce Giffard banane du Brésil

½ ounce Bénédictine

Garnish: Toasted Oat Cream (page 300) and nutmeg

Combine all the ingredients in an Irish coffee mug and stir to combine. Spoon some toasted oat cream on top of the drink and grate some nutmeg over the top of the drink.

ECHO CHAMBER ⚜

Jeremy Oertel, 2016

1½ ounces Calle 23 blanco tequila

½ ounce Clear Creek pear eau-de-vie

1 teaspoon Fernet-Branca

½ ounce fresh lime juice

½ ounce Coco López cream of coconut

¼ ounce Vanilla Syrup (page 288)

1 drop Terra Spice eucalyptus extract

Garnish: 1 mint bouquet

Combine all the ingredients in a shaker and whip, shaking with a few pieces of crushed ice, just until incorporated. Dump into a tiki mug and fill the glass with crushed ice. Garnish with the mint bouquet.

⊙ LOW ABV   ⃠ NO ABV   ❄ FREEZER BAR   ⧖ PROJECT COCKTAIL   ⚜ LOW-PREP COCKTAIL

LITTLE COCONUT, PAGE 277

ECHO SPRING

Sam Johnson, 2019

This fall tiki drink came on the heels of reworking the gardenia mix, which is essentially a spiced honey-butter syrup. On your first sip, the cocktail tastes like apple butter, and it finishes dry and very tart, so it begs you to keep drinking, like a good Daiquiri. —SJ

1¼ ounces Domaine du Manoir de Montreuil Selection calvados

½ ounce Rhum JM VO rhum agricole

¼ ounce Cyril Zangs 00 apple cider eau-de-vie

¾ ounce fresh lemon juice

½ ounce Vanilla Syrup (page 288)

½ ounce Improved Gardenia Mix (page 298)

1 dash Angostura bitters

Garnish: 1 apple fan and 1 cinnamon stick

Short shake all the ingredients with ice for about 5 seconds, then strain into a pilsner glass. Fill the glass with crushed ice. Garnish with the apple fan, insert a cinnamon stick in the drink, and serve with a straw.

LAMPLIGHTER INN ⊘

Alex Jump, 2019

We're always trying to figure out how to repurpose waste at the bar. Death & Co Denver sells a lot of coffee in the morning and afternoon, so we have a ton of spent coffee grounds that we use to make a damn fine syrup. The syrup stars in this nonalcoholic drink, which tastes like an old-school malt soda. —AJ

1½ ounces cold seltzer

1½ ounces heavy cream

1½ ounces Spent Coffee Grounds Syrup (page 287)

½ ounce fresh lemon juice

1 egg white

Garnish: 1 coffee bean

Pour the seltzer into a chilled fizz glass. Dry shake all the ingredients, then shake again with ice. Double strain into the glass. Shave some coffee bean over the top of the drink.

LITTLE COCONUT

George Nunez, 2019

1 ounce Rittenhouse rye

½ ounce Avuá Amburana cachaça

¼ ounce Smith & Cross Jamaica rum

¼ ounce Amaro Averna

¾ ounce Cinnamon Syrup (page 283)

½ ounce coconut milk

½ ounce Coco López cream of coconut

1 whole egg

Garnish: Nutmeg

Dry shake all the ingredients, then shake again with ice. Double strain into an Irish coffee mug and grate some nutmeg over the top of the drink.

SABROSA ✤

Jarred Weigand, 2017

I was really into the cool combination of celery and coconut, so I worked it into this fun piña colada variation. Green Chartreuse is a perfect fit with celery, and tequila rounds it all out. *Sabrosa* is Spanish for "tasty"—and the name of a groovy Beastie Boys instrumental track. —JW

1½ ounces Siembra Valles Blanco tequila

½ ounce green Chartreuse

¼ ounce Velvet falernum

¾ ounce Coco López cream of coconut

½ ounce fresh celery juice

½ ounce fresh lime juice

Garnish: 1 mint bouquet

Combine all the ingredients in a shaker and whip, shaking with a few pieces of crushed ice, just until incorporated. Dump into a tiki mug and fill the glass with crushed ice. Garnish with the mint bouquet and serve with a straw.

SLEEPY GARY FIZZ

Matt Hunt, 2019

I threw so many names at Tyson for this drink, and I couldn't believe he went for this one. I learned a trick from a bartender at the NoMad restaurant, who told me that you can add dairy to a citrus cocktail if you include a green tea infusion, which keeps the dairy from breaking. —MH

2 ounces cold seltzer

1½ ounces Barsol Acholado pisco

¼ ounce Avuá Prata cachaça

1 ounce Tropic of Capricorn Greek Yogurt Syrup (page 288)

¾ ounce fresh lemon juice

¾ ounce Cinnamon Syrup (page 283)

Garnish: Tropic of Capricorn green tea leaves

Pour the seltzer into a fizz glass. Short shake the remaining ingredients with ice for about 5 seconds, then double strain into the glass. Sprinkle some green tea leaves over the drink.

SLOW HAND

Alex Jump, 2019

We had a ton of Paul Beau at the bar; few people come to Death & Co and order a glass of super-expensive cognac. So I used it to create something lush, creamy, and nutty—a good after-dinner drink, but still citrusy and refreshing. —AJ

- 1 ounce Paul Beau Hors d'Age cognac
- 1 ounce Brugal 1888 rum
- 1 ounce Vanilla Syrup (page 288)
- ¼ ounce El Maestro Sierra 15-year oloroso sherry
- ¾ ounce fresh lemon juice
- 1 egg white
- ½ teaspoon Caffo Amaretto

Dry shake all the ingredients, then shake again with ice. Double strain into a chilled coupe. No garnish.

SOUTHERN NIGHTS

Alex Jump, 2018

Developing this drink was such a pain in the ass. Originally, I wanted to make something that tasted like drinking a carrot cake. I love peanuts and sherry together, and I've worked a lot with peanut-infused sherry, so I tried pairing it with carrot eau-de-vie, but I couldn't get it to work. This drink taught me that sometimes you have to let go of what you want a drink to be and just allow it to show you what it wants to be. So I swapped in cognac, but it was boring and flat. Tyson suggested adding a little aquavit, and suddenly—finally—it worked. —AJ

- ¾ ounce Pierre Ferrand ambré cognac
- ¾ ounce Linie aquavit
- ¾ ounce Peanut-Infused Lustau Don Nuño Oloroso Sherry (page 293)
- ½ ounce Cane Sugar Syrup (page 282)
- ¼ ounce fresh lemon juice

- 1 barspoon mascarpone cheese
- Garnish: 1 piece of peanut brittle

Shake all the ingredients with ice, then strain into a double old-fashioned glass and fill the glass with crushed ice. Garnish with the peanut brittle and serve with a straw.

SPACE COWBOY ⚜

Jarred Weigand, 2019

One of the bartenders had used a blend of crème de pêche and menthe-pastille in a cocktail, and someone got overexcited and made 3 quarts of the batch, so we had tons of it left over. I developed this drink so we could use it up. I love the way peach, mint, and dill go together, and the Elijah Craig picks up the dill perfectly. For texture and tang, I added Greek yogurt. The name is a nod to the Steve Miller Band, but I also think this drink is way out there. —JW

- 1½ ounces Elijah Craig 12-year bourbon
- ½ ounce Gamle Ode dill aquavit
- 1 teaspoon Massenez crème de pêche peach liqueur
- ½ teaspoon Giffard menthe-pastille
- ¾ ounce fresh lemon juice
- ½ ounce Cane Sugar Syrup (page 282)
- 1 teaspoon Greek yogurt

Shake all the ingredients with ice, then double strain into a chilled coupe. No garnish.

SUNDANCE KID

Tyson Buhler, 2015

This was the first drink where we used the green chile vodka from St. George, a distillery we absolutely love, and the combination of chiles and coconut works great in a creamy, refreshing cocktail. —TB

- 1 ounce Del Maguey Vida mezcal
- ¾ ounce St. George green chile vodka
- ¼ ounce Jalapeño-Infused Siembra Valles Blanco Tequila (page 293)
- ¾ ounce fresh lime juice
- ½ ounce Coco López cream of coconut
- ½ ounce Vanilla Syrup (page 288)
- Garnish: 1 mint bouquet and toasted coconut

Combine all the ingredients in a shaker and whip, shaking with a few pieces of crushed ice, just until incorporated. Dump into a tiki mug and fill the glass with crushed ice. Garnish with the mint bouquet and toasted coconut and serve with a straw.

SUNSHINE GUN CLUB

Jon Armstrong, 2016

There are only a few classic drinks made with orange juice—including the mimosa, the Monkey Gland, and the screwdriver—so there's not a lot of fertile ground for inspiration. So I found my muse in an Orange Julius, taking the flavors of the frozen treat and "adultifying" them. —JA

3 ounces fresh orange juice

1½ ounces Banks 5-Island white rum

1 ounce Vanilla Syrup (page 288)

1 ounce heavy cream

1 teaspoon acid phosphate

5 drops orange flower water

Garnish: 1 orange wedge

Dry shake all the ingredients, then shake again with ice. Double strain into a collins glass. Garnish with the orange wedge and serve with a straw.

SUNSHINE LADY

Al Sotack, 2014

1¾ ounces Kilbeggan Irish whiskey

¾ ounce Hibiscus Honey Syrup (page 284)

¼ ounce Wray & Nephew Overproof Jamaica rum

¼ ounce Aperol

2 dashes Peychaud's bitters

1 egg yolk

Garnish: Dark chocolate

Dry shake all the ingredients, then shake again with ice. Double strain into a chilled Nick & Nora glass and shave some chocolate over the top of the drink.

VINTAGE EGGNOG

Tyson Buhler, 2015

Makes about 30 cocktails

I'm still haunted by the experience of cracking hundreds of eggs, and blending gallons of dairy and pounds of sugar for these batches. Though it does makes me smile a little bit knowing that the Death & Co New York team is suffering through the same prep every holiday season, our guests would crucify us if we didn't put it on the menu. Due to high demand, it's tough for us to keep up with the long aging process, but if you have the patience, let this nog age for a few months, and the flavor and texture will change drastically over time. —TB

50 ounces white sugar

30 ounces whole milk

33 eggs

One 750 ml bottle Old Grand-Dad 114 bourbon

12½ ounces Smith & Cross Jamaicia rum

12½ ounces Blandy's 5-year Malmsey madeira

12½ ounces Pierre Ferrand ambré cognac

20 ounces heavy cream

Working in batches, blend the sugar and milk until the sugar is dissolved. Transfer to a large container. Working in batches, blend the eggs and milk mixture at low speed until the eggs are well blended. Transfer to another container and add the remaining ingredients. Pour the mixture from one container to another a few times until well blended. Funnel into bottles and age in the refrigerator for at least 2 weeks (and up to 2 years!) before serving.

APPENDICES

BAR PREP RECIPES & TECHNIQUES

SYRUPS & CORDIALS

ALPENGLOW CORDIAL

1,000 grams simple syrup (page 287)

5 grams lactic acid

5 grams fresh bay leaf

5 grams loose black tea

25 grams dried hibiscus flowers

Fill a large basin with water and place an immersion circulator inside. Set the circulator to 135° Fahrenheit.

Put all the ingredients in a bowl and stir to combine. Transfer to a sealable, heatproof plastic bag. Seal the bag almost completely,

then press out as much air as possible by dipping the bag (other than the unsealed portion) in the water. Finish sealing the bag, then remove it from the water.

When the water has reached 135° Fahrenheit, place the bag in the basin and cook for 2 hours.

Place the bag in an ice bath and let cool to room temperature. Pass the syrup through a fine-mesh sieve. If any particles remain in the syrup, strain it through a paper coffee filter or Superbag. Transfer to a storage container and refrigerate until ready to use, up to 2 weeks.

APPLE CORDIAL

450 grams cane sugar

300 grams water

100 grams apple pulp

Malic Acid

Citric Acid

Combine the sugar and water in a blender and process until the sugar has dissolved. Pass the syrup through a fine-mesh sieve. If any particles remain in the syrup, strain it through a paper coffee filter or Superbag.

Calculate 4 percent of the weight (multiply by 0.04) to get X grams. Calculate 1 percent of the weight (multiply by 0.01) to get Y grams. Stir in X grams of malic acid and Y grams of citric acid. Pour into a storage container and refrigerate until ready to use, up to 2 weeks.

BAY LEAF SYRUP

1,000 grams simple syrup (page 287)

10 grams fresh bay leaf

2 grams citric acid

Fill a large basin with water and place an immersion circulator inside. Set the circulator to 135° Fahrenheit.

Put all the ingredients in a bowl and stir to combine. Transfer to a sealable, heatproof plastic bag. Seal the bag almost completely, then press out as much air as possible by dipping the bag (other than the unsealed portion) in the water. Finish sealing the bag, then remove it from the water.

When the water has reached 135° Fahrenheit, place the bag in the basin and cook for 2 hours.

Place the bag in an ice bath and let cool to room temperature. Pass the syrup through a fine-mesh sieve. If any particles remain in the syrup, strain it through a paper coffee filter or Superbag. Transfer to a storage container and refrigerate until ready to use, up to 2 weeks.

CANE SUGAR SYRUP

300 grams unbleached cane sugar

150 grams unfiltered water

Combine the sugar and water in a blender and process until the sugar has dissolved. Pour into a storage container and refrigerate until ready to use, up to 2 weeks.

CELERY SYRUP

1 bunch celery

White sugar

Ascorbic acid

Juice the celery and strain into a container. Weigh the juice. Add the same amount of sugar by weight to a blender. Calculate 0.5 percent of the weight of the juice (multiply by 0.005) to get X grams. Add

X grams of ascorbic acid to the blender, along with the celery juice. Process until the sugar has dissolved. Pour into a storage container and refrigerate until ready to use, up to 2 weeks.

CINNAMON SYRUP

500 grams simple syrup (page 287)

10 grams crushed cinnamon sticks

0.1 gram kosher salt

Fill a large basin with water and place an immersion circulator inside. Set the circulator to 145° Fahrenheit.

Put all the ingredients in a bowl and stir to combine. Transfer to a sealable, heatproof plastic bag. Seal the bag almost completely, then press out as much air as possible by dipping the bag (other than the unsealed portion) in the water. Finish sealing the bag, then remove it from the water.

When the water has reached 145° Fahrenheit, place the bag in the basin and cook for 2 hours.

Place the bag in an ice bath and let cool to room temperature. Pass the syrup through a fine-mesh sieve. If any particles remain in the syrup, strain it through a paper coffee filter or Superbag. Transfer to a storage container and refrigerate until ready to use, up to 2 weeks.

CUCUMBER MAGNESIUM SYRUP

250 grams strained fresh cucumber juice

250 grams white sugar

1 gram ascorbic acid

2.5 grams malic acid powder

1.5 grams magnesium

Combine all of the ingredients in a blender and process until the sugar has dissolved. Transfer to a storage container and refrigerate until ready to use, up to 2 weeks.

DEMERARA SYRUP

300 grams demerara sugar

150 grams filtered water

Fill a large basin with water and place an immersion circulator inside. Set the circulator to 145° Fahrenheit.

Combine the sugar and water in a blender and process until the sugar has dissolved, about 2 minutes.

Pour the mixture into a sealable, heatproof plastic bag. Seal the bag almost completely, then press out as much air as possible by dipping the bag (other than the unsealed portion) in the water. Finish sealing the bag, then remove it from the water.

When the water has reached 145° Fahrenheit, place the bag in the basin and cook for 2 hours.

Place the bag in an ice bath and let cool to room temperature. Transfer to a storage container and refrigerate until ready to use, up to 2 weeks.

GRAPEFRUIT CORDIAL

250 grams strained grapefruit juice

250 grams white sugar

2.5 grams citric acid

10 grams grapefruit zest

1 gram Salt Solution (page 299)

Fill a large basin with water and place an immersion circulator inside. Set the circulator to 135° Fahrenheit.

Put all the ingredients in a bowl and whisk until blended. Transfer to a sealable, heatproof plastic bag. Seal the bag almost completely, then press out as much air as possible by dipping the bag (other than the unsealed portion) in the water. Finish sealing the bag, then remove it from the water.

When the water has reached 135° Fahrenheit, place the bag in the basin and cook for 2 hours.

Place the bag in an ice bath and let cool to room temperature. Pass the syrup through a fine-mesh sieve lined with several layers of cheesecloth. If any particles remain in the syrup, strain it again through a paper coffee filter or Superbag. Transfer to a storage container and refrigerate until ready to use, up to 2 weeks.

GUAVA SYRUP

333 grams white sugar

222 grams Boiron guava purée

111 grams unfiltered water

2.5 grams malic acid

1.6 grams citric acid

Combine all the ingredients in a blender and process until the sugar has dissolved. Pour into a storage container and refrigerate until ready to use, up to 2 weeks.

HIBISCUS HONEY SYRUP

1,000 grams Honey Syrup (page 284)

30 grams dried hibiscus flowers

Fill a large basin with water and place an immersion circulator inside. Set the circulator to 135° Fahrenheit.

Add the honey syrup and hibiscus to a sealable, heatproof plastic bag. Seal the bag almost completely, then press out as much air as possible by dipping the bag (other than the unsealed portion) in the water. Finish sealing the bag, then remove it from the water.

When the water has reached 135° Fahrenheit, place the bag in the basin and cook for 2 hours.

Transfer the bag to an ice bath and let cool to room temperature. Pass the syrup through a fine-mesh sieve. If any particles remain in the syrup, strain it again through a paper coffee filter or Superbag. Transfer to a storage container and refrigerate until ready to use, up to 4 weeks.

HIBISCUS SYRUP

1,000 grams simple syrup (page 287)

30 grams dried hibiscus flowers

Fill a large basin with water and place an immersion circulator inside. Set the circulator to 135° Fahrenheit.

Add the simple syrup and hibiscus to a sealable, heatproof plastic bag. Seal the bag almost completely, then press out as much air as possible by dipping the bag (other than the unsealed portion) in the water. Finish sealing the bag, then remove it from the water.

When the water has reached 135° Fahrenheit, place the bag in the basin and cook for 2 hours.

Transfer the bag to an ice bath and let cool to room temperature. Pass the syrup through a fine-mesh sieve. If any particles remain in the syrup, strain it again through a paper coffee filter or Superbag. Transfer to a storage container and refrigerate until ready to use, up to 4 weeks.

HONEY SYRUP

400 grams wildflower honey

200 grams warm filtered water

Combine the honey and water in a bowl and whisk until thoroughly blended. Transfer to a storage container and refrigerate until ready to use, up to 2 weeks.

HOPPED PINEAPPLE GUM SYRUP

500 grams white sugar

30 grams gum arabic

3 grams citric acid

500 grams strained fresh pineapple juice

7 grams Citra hop pellets

Fill a large basin with water and place an immersion circulator inside. Set the circulator to 140° Fahrenheit.

In a blender, combine the sugar, gum arabic, and citric acid. Turn the blender on and slowly add the pineapple juice; process until well mixed. Transfer to a sealable, heatproof plastic bag and add the hops. Seal the bag almost completely, then press out as much air as possible by dipping the bag (other than the unsealed portion) in the water. Finish sealing the bag, then remove it from the water.

When the water has reached 140° Fahrenheit, place the bag in the basin and cook for 1 hour.

Transfer the bag to an ice bath and let cool to room temperature. Pass the syrup through a fine-mesh sieve. If any particles remain in the syrup, strain it again through a paper coffee filter or Superbag. Transfer to a storage container and refrigerate until ready to use, up to 4 weeks.

HOUSE GINGER SYRUP

250 grams unpeeled fresh ginger, washed and coarsely chopped

About 300 grams unbleached cane sugar

Juice the ginger and pass the juice through a fine-mesh sieve. Weigh the ginger juice, then multiply the weight by 1.5 and weigh out that much sugar.

Combine the ginger juice and sugar in a blender and process until the sugar has dissolved. Pour into a storage container and refrigerate until ready to use, up to 2 weeks.

HOUSE GRENADINE

250 grams POM Wonderful pomegranate juice

250 grams unbleached cane sugar

1.88 grams malic acid powder

1.25 grams citric acid powder

0.15 gram Terra Spice orange extract

Combine all the ingredients in a blender and process until the sugar has dissolved.

Transfer to a storage container and refrigerate until ready to use, up to 3 weeks.

HOUSE ORGEAT

800 grams unsweetened, unflavored almond milk

1,200 grams superfine sugar

14 grams Pierre Ferrand ambré cognac

18 grams Lazzaroni amaretto

3 grams rose water

Combine the almond milk and sugar in a saucepan over medium-low heat and cook, stirring occasionally, until the sugar has dissolved. Remove from the heat and stir in the cognac, amaretto, and rose water. Let cool to room temperature, then transfer to a storage container and refrigerate until ready to use, up to 2 weeks.

KIWI SYRUP

250 grams strained fresh kiwi juice

250 grams superfine sugar

15 grams vodka

Combine the kiwi juice, sugar, and vodka in a blender and process until the sugar has dissolved. Pour into a storage container and refrigerate until ready to use, up to 1 week.

LIME LEAF, LEMONGRASS & SHISO SYRUP

1,000 grams simple syrup (page 287)

100 grams chopped, smashed lemongrass

15 grams fresh makrut lime leaves

5 grams shiso leaves

Fill a large basin with water and place an immersion circulator inside. Set the circulator to 135° Fahrenheit.

Combine all the ingredients in a sealable, heatproof plastic bag. Seal the bag almost completely, then press out as much air as possible by dipping the bag (other than the unsealed portion) in the water. Finish sealing the bag, then remove it from the water.

When the water has reached 135° Fahrenheit, place the bag in the basin and cook for 2 hours.

Transfer the bag to an ice bath and let cool to room temperature. Pass the syrup through a fine-mesh sieve. If any particles remain in the syrup, strain it again through a paper coffee filter or Superbag. Transfer to a storage container and refrigerate until ready to use, up to 2 weeks.

MADRAS CURRY SYRUP

1,000 grams simple syrup (page 287)

5 grams madras curry powder

Fill a large basin with water and place an immersion circulator inside. Set the circulator to 135° Fahrenheit.

Put all the ingredients in a bowl and stir to combine. Transfer to a sealable, heatproof plastic bag. Seal the bag almost completely, then press out as much air as possible by dipping the bag (other than the unsealed portion) in the water. Finish sealing the bag, then remove it from the water.

When the water has reached 135° Fahrenheit, place the bag in the basin and cook for 2 hours.

Place the bag in an ice bath and let cool to room temperature. Pass the syrup through a fine-mesh sieve. If any particles remain in the syrup, strain it through a paper coffee filter or Superbag. Transfer to a storage container and refrigerate until ready to use, up to 2 weeks.

MILK SYRUP

250 grams white sugar

250 grams whole milk

½ ounce 20% Citric Acid Solution (page 299)

Combine the sugar and milk in a jar. Shake vigorously until the sugar has dissolved. Add the citric acid and shake again. Transfer to a storage container and refrigerate until ready to use, up to 1 week.

PANDAN SYRUP

500 grams Cane Sugar Syrup (page 282)

20 grams pandan leaves

Fill a large basin with water and place an immersion circulator inside. Set the circulator to 135° Fahrenheit.

Combine the syrup and pandan leaves in a sealable, heatproof plastic bag. Seal the bag almost completely, then press out as much air as possible by dipping the bag (other than the unsealed portion) in the water. Finish sealing the bag, then remove it from the water.

When the water has reached 135° Fahrenheit, place the bag in the basin and cook for 2 hours.

Transfer the bag to an ice bath and let cool to room temperature. Pass the syrup through a fine-mesh sieve. Transfer to a storage container and refrigerate until ready to use, up to 2 weeks.

PAPAYA SYRUP

333 grams white sugar

222 grams Perfect Purée papaya purée

111 grams filtered water

2 grams citric acid

Combine all the ingredients in a blender and process until the sugar has dissolved. Transfer to a storage container and refrigerate until ready to use, up to 2 weeks.

PARROT SYRUP

1,000 grams simple syrup (page 287)

60 grams fresh parsley leaves

20 grams carrot greens

Fill a large basin with water and place an immersion circulator inside. Set the circulator to 145° Fahrenheit.

Combine all the ingredients in a sealable, heatproof plastic bag. Seal the bag almost completely, then press out as much air as possible by dipping the bag (other than the unsealed portion) in the water. Finish sealing the bag, then remove it from the water.

When the water has reached 145° Fahrenheit, place the bag in the basin and cook for 2 hours.

Transfer the bag to an ice bath and let cool to room temperature. Pass the syrup through a fine-mesh sieve. Transfer to a storage container and refrigerate until ready to use, up to 1 week.

PASSION FRUIT SYRUP

333 grams white sugar

222 grams Perfect Purée passion fruit purée

111 grams filtered water

Combine all the ingredients in a blender and process until the sugar has dissolved. Transfer to a storage container and refrigerate until ready to use, up to 2 weeks.

PINEAPPLE GUM SYRUP

250 grams unbleached cane sugar

15 grams gum arabic

1.5 grams citric acid

250 grams strained fresh pineapple juice

Fill a large basin with water and place an immersion circulator inside. Set the circulator to 145° Fahrenheit.

Combine the sugar, gum arabic, and citric acid in a blender and process for 30 seconds. With the blender running, slowly add the pineapple juice and continue to process until all the dry ingredients have dissolved, about 2 minutes.

Pour the mixture into a sealable, heatproof plastic bag. Seal the bag almost completely, then press out as much air as possible by dipping the bag (other than the unsealed portion) in the water. Finish sealing the bag, then remove it from the water.

When the water has reached 145° Fahrenheit, place the bag in the basin and cook for 2 hours.

Place the bag in an ice bath and let cool to room temperature. Strain through a paper coffee filter or Superbag, transfer to a storage container, and refrigerate until ready to use, up to 1 week.

PINEAPPLE PULP CORDIAL

450 grams unbleached cane sugar

450 grams filtered water

100 grams pineapple pulp (left over from juicing pineapple)

Malic acid

Citric acid

Combine the sugar, water, and pineapple pulp in a blender and process until the sugar has dissolved. Strain the mixture through a paper coffee filter or Superbag. Calculate 2 percent of the weight (multiply by 0.02) to get X grams.

Calculate 3 percent of the weight (multiply by 0.03) to get Y grams. Stir in X grams of malic acid and Y grams of citric acid. Pour into a storage container and refrigerate until ready to use, up to 2 weeks.

POPPY SEED SYRUP

1,000 grams simple syrup (page 287)

10 grams poppy seeds

Fill a large basin with water and place an immersion circulator inside. Set the circulator to 135° Fahrenheit.

Combine the syrup and poppy seeds in a sealable, heatproof plastic bag. Seal the bag almost completely, then press out as much air as possible by dipping the bag (other than the unsealed portion) in the water. Finish sealing the bag, then remove it from the water.

When the water has reached 135° Fahrenheit, place the bag in the basin and cook for 2 hours.

Transfer the bag to an ice bath and let cool to room temperature. Pass the syrup through a fine-mesh sieve. If any particles remain in the syrup, strain it again through a paper coffee filter or Superbag. Transfer to a storage container and refrigerate until ready to use, up to 2 weeks.

PORT SYRUP

2 cups Taylor Fladgate 10-year tawny port

Demerara sugar

In a saucepan, bring the port to a boil over medium-high heat and cook until reduced by one-fourth, about 12 minutes. Let cool slightly, then weigh the liquid. Add twice the weight in sugar to a blender, then add the reduced port. Process until the sugar has dissolved. Let cool to room temperature, then transfer to a storage container and refrigerate until ready to use, up to 6 weeks.

RASPBERRY SYRUP

500 grams simple syrup (page 287)

150 grams fresh raspberries

2.5 grams citric acid

Fill a large basin with water and place an immersion circulator inside. Set the circulator to 135° Fahrenheit.

Put all the ingredients in a bowl and stir to combine. Transfer to a sealable, heatproof plastic bag. Seal the bag almost completely, then press out as much air as possible by dipping the bag (other than the unsealed portion) in the water. Finish sealing the bag, then remove it from the water.

When the water has reached 135° Fahrenheit, place the bag in the basin and cook for 2 hours.

Place the bag in an ice bath and let cool to room temperature. Pass the syrup through a fine-mesh sieve. If any particles remain in the syrup, strain it through a paper coffee filter or Superbag. Transfer to a storage container and refrigerate until ready to use, up to 2 weeks.

RED VERJUS SYRUP

130 grams red verjus

60 grams Vanilla Syrup (page 288)

31.5 grams Cinnamon Syrup (page 283)

In a bowl, whisk together all the ingredients until combined. Transfer to a storage container and refrigerate until ready to use, up to 2 weeks.

SARSAPARILLA DEMERARA SYRUP

710 grams filtered water

12 grams dried sarsaparilla

Demerara sugar

In a saucepan, combine the water and sarsaparilla. Bring to a boil over medium-high heat and cook for 5 minutes. Pass the mixture through a fine-mesh sieve and weigh the liquid. Add twice the weight in sugar to a blender and add the liquid. Process until the sugar has dissolved. Let cool to room temperature, then transfer to a storage container and refrigerate until ready to use, up to 2 weeks.

SIMPLE SYRUP

250 grams white sugar

250 grams filtered water

Combine the sugar and water in a bowl and whisk until the sugar has dissolved. Transfer to a storage container and refrigerate until ready to use, up to 2 weeks.

SPENT CITRUS CORDIAL

Citrus trimmings and juiced hulls

Fresh orange juice

White sugar

Vodka

Citric acid

Weigh the citrus trimmings and hulls. Measure out the same weight (each) of orange juice and sugar. Combine everything in a vacuum sealing bag and use a vacuum sealer to remove all of the air and seal. (Alternatively, combine the ingredients in a sealable plastic bag and squeeze out as much air as possible before sealing.) Let the mixture sit for 12 hours. Cut one of the bag's corners and strain the liquid through a fine-mesh sieve. Weigh the liquid. Calculate 10 percent of the weight of the liquid (multiply by 0.10) and place that much vodka in a storage container. Calculate 2 percent of the weight of the liquid (multiply by 0.02) and add that much citric acid to the storage container. Add the liquid to the storage container and shake well. Refrigerate until ready to use, up to 1 week.

SPENT COFFEE GROUNDS SYRUP

300 grams spent coffee grounds

300 grams unbleached cane sugar

150 grams filtered water

150 grams cold brew concentrate

Fill a large basin with water and place an immersion circulator inside. Set the circulator to 135° Fahrenheit.

Combine all the ingredients in a bowl and stir to combine. Transfer to a sealable, heatproof plastic bag. Seal the bag almost completely, then press out as much air as possible by dipping the bag (other than the unsealed portion) in the water. Finish sealing the bag, then remove it from the water.

When the water has reached 135° Fahrenheit, place the bag in the basin and cook for 2 hours.

Place the bag in an ice bath and let cool to room temperature. Pass the syrup through a paper coffee filter or Superbag. Transfer to a storage container and refrigerate until ready to use, up to 2 weeks.

STRAWBERRY ALOE SYRUP

550 grams hulled strawberries

550 grams aloe juice

550 grams white sugar

Fill a large basin with water and place an immersion circulator inside. Set the circulator to 135° Fahrenheit.

Combine all the ingredients in a bowl and stir to combine. Transfer to a sealable, heatproof plastic bag. Seal the bag almost completely, then press out as much air as possible by dipping the bag (other than the unsealed portion) in the water. Finish sealing the bag, then remove it from the water.

When the water has reached 135° Fahrenheit, place the bag in the basin and cook for 2 hours.

Place the bag in an ice bath and let cool to room temperature. Pass the syrup through a paper coffee filter or Superbag. Transfer to a storage container and refrigerate until ready to use, up to 2 weeks.

STRAWBERRY BASIL SYRUP

1 pound hulled strawberries

3 cups filtered water

Pectinex Ultra SP-L

12 basil leaves

Superfine sugar

Weigh the strawberries and water. Calculate 0.2 percent of the weight (multiply by 0.002) to get X grams. Place the strawberries, water, and X grams of Pectinex in a blender and blend for 5 minutes. Transfer to a saucepan and bring to a boil over medium heat. Boil for 5 minutes, then add the basil. Boil for 5 minutes longer, then turn off the heat. Let cool for 10 minutes, then strain the liquid through a fine-mesh sieve. Weigh the liquid and add an equal amount of sugar. Transfer to a blender and process until the sugar has dissolved. Skim any foam from the surface, then transfer to a storage container and refrigerate until ready to use, up to 2 weeks.

STRAWBERRY SYRUP

250 grams hulled strawberries

250 grams unbleached cane sugar

0.5 gram Pectinex Ultra SP-L

Combine the strawberries and sugar in a blender and process until very smooth. Once the sugar has dissolved, add the Pectinex to a blender and process for 10 seconds. Transfer to a centrifuge container. Weigh the filled container and fill each of the other containers with an equal weight of water. Run the centrifuge at 4,500 rpm for 12 minutes. Remove the containers and carefully strain the syrup through a paper coffee filter or Superbag, being careful not to disturb the solids that have collected on the bottom of the container. Transfer to a storage container and refrigerate until ready to use, up to 1 week.

TAMARIND DEMERARA SYRUP

500 grams filtered water

1,000 grams Demerara sugar

180 grams tamarind paste

Combine the water, sugar, and tamarind paste in a blender and process until the sugar has dissolved, about 2 minutes. Pour into a storage container and refrigerate until ready to use, up to 2 weeks.

TONIC SYRUP

1,000 grams white sugar

690 grams filtered water

150 grams strained fresh orange juice

100 grams strained fresh lemon juice

60 grams strained fresh lime juice

12 grams citric acid

10 grams finely grated orange zest

8 grams dried orange peel

8 grams finely grated zest

7.5 grams Terra Spice quinine extract

6 grams kosher salt

6 grams finely grated zest

3 grams coriander seeds

3 grams juniper berries

2.5 grams cinnamon bark

2 grams dried lemon peel (granules)

1.5 grams star anise

1 gram ground mace

Fill a large basin with water and place an immersion circulator inside. Set the circulator to 140° Fahrenheit.

Put all the ingredients in a bowl and stir to combine. Transfer to a sealable, heatproof plastic bag. Seal the bag almost completely, then press out as much air as possible by dipping the bag (other than the unsealed portion) in the water. Finish sealing the bag, then remove it from the water.

When the water has reached 140° Fahrenheit, place the bag in the basin and cook for 90 minutes.

Place the bag in an ice bath and let cool to room temperature. Pass the infusion through a fine-mesh sieve. If any particles remain in the infusion, strain it again through a paper coffee filter or Superbag. Transfer to a storage container and refrigerate until ready to use, up to 2 weeks.

TROPIC OF CAPRICORN GREEK YOGURT SYRUP

1.5 grams August Uncommon Tea Tropic of Capricorn tea leaves

113 grams hot (200° F) water

125 grams full-fat Greek yogurt

125 grams simple syrup (page 287)

In a heatproof container, combine the tea and hot water and let steep for 5 minutes. Strain the tea through a fine-mesh sieve and transfer to a blender. Add the yogurt and simple syrup and blend for 2 minutes at low speed. Transfer to a storage container and refrigerate until ready to use, up to 2 weeks.

TURBINADO SYRUP

See Demerara Syrup (page 283) and substitute turbinado sugar for the Demerara sugar.

VANILLA SYRUP

500 grams simple syrup (page 287)

2 grams vanilla extract

Combine the simple syrup and vanilla extract in a storage container and shake to combine. Refrigerate until ready to use, up to 2 weeks.

WATERMELON SYRUP

250 grams strained fresh watermelon juice

250 grams superfine sugar

14 grams vodka

Combine the watermelon juice, sugar, and vodka in a blender and process until the sugar has dissolved. Pour into a storage container and refrigerate until ready to use, up to 1 week.

WHITE CHOCOLATE & WASABI SYRUP

375 grams melted white chocolate

375 grams Coco López cream of coconut

375 grams unsweetened coconut milk

375 grams Cane Sugar Syrup (page 282)

15 grams wasabi powder

2 grams matcha tea powder

Combine all the ingredients in a blender and process until smooth. Transfer to a storage container and refrigerate until ready to use, up to 1 week.

PECTINEX ULTRA SP-L

This enzyme aids in clarification by breaking apart bonds in solids within a syrup. We use Pectinex only when we want to clarify ingredients that contain pectin, processing them either in a centrifuge, or by simply mixing in Pectinex and allowing the liquid to sit.

How to Make
CENTRIFUGE SYRUPS

Centrifuge syrups can begin with any type of syrup, which is then spun at an incredibly high speed (up to 4,500 rpm) to separate out any solids. Although this requires advanced equipment, it can produce beautiful results. We use this technique when a translucent syrup will create a more visually appealing drink or when we plan to carbonate the cocktail (see page 162).

We use refurbished laboratory centrifuges from Ozark Biomedical. Our preferred unit—the Jouan CR422, which costs $3,500 to $4,000—can spin 3 quarts of liquid at a time and clarify it in just 10 to 15 minutes. That said, there are now units available for culinary use that are far less expensive.

Don't have a centrifuge? That's okay; you can use much of the following method, then allow the syrup to sit overnight so the enzymes do their work, and then strain the syrup through at least four layers of cheesecloth overnight in the refrigerator. It won't be as crystal clear, but it will be as close as you can get without a machine.

Method

1. Prepare a base syrup using one of the previously described methods.

2. Measure the weight of a centrifuge container using a gram scale, then add the syrup and calculate the difference. (Or, if your scale has a tare function, place the container on it, zero the scale, then add the syrup and determine its weight.)

3. Calculate 0.2 percent of the weight of the syrup (multiply by 0.002) to get X grams.

4. Stir X grams of Pectinex Ultra SP-L into the syrup. Cover and let sit for 15 minutes.

5. Weigh the filled container and fill each of the other containers with an equal weight of water. Each container in a centrifuge must weigh exactly the same in order to keep the machine in balance. (An off-balance centrifuge is dangerous!)

6. Run the centrifuge at 4,500 rpm for 12 minutes.

7. Remove the containers and carefully strain the syrup through a paper coffee filter or Superbag, being careful to not disturb the solids that have collected on the bottom of the container.

8. If any particles remain in the syrup, strain it again.

9. Transfer to a storage container and refrigerate until ready to use.

Tools

Gram scale

Centrifuge containers with lids

Centrifuge

Superbag or paper coffee filter

INFUSIONS

ARBOL-INFUSED DEL MAGUEY VIDA MEZCAL

One 750 ml bottle Del Maguey Vida mezcal (reserve the bottle)

5 chiles de arbol, torn into large pieces

Place the mezcal and chiles in a bowl and stir to combine. Let stand at room temperature for up to 30 minutes, tasting often to monitor the heat level. Strain through a fine-mesh sieve, then funnel back into the mezcal bottle and refrigerate until ready to use, up to 1 month.

Pass the infusion through a fine-mesh sieve. If any particles remain in the infusion, strain it again through a paper coffee filter or Superbag. Funnel back into the mezcal bottle and refrigerate until ready to use, up to 3 months.

SUPERBAGS

A Superbag is a fine-mesh bag strainer that can be purchased online (we get ours from Modernist Pantry). Not only are Superbags reusable, but the material is so strong that you can squeeze the bag with force to speed up some filtrations. Superbags come in various sizes and micron perforations: 100, 250, 400, and 800 microns (800 is the coarsest size). For syrups and infusions, we recommend a medium-size 250 micron bag.

BANANA-INFUSED DOLIN BLANC VERMOUTH

200 grams peeled ripe (but not brown) bananas

One 375 ml bottle Dolin blanc vermouth (reserve the bottle)

Thinly slice the bananas. Combine them with the vermouth in a bowl. Cover and refrigerate for 12 hours. Strain through a paper coffee filter, Superbag, or fine-mesh sieve lined with several layers of cheesecloth, then funnel back into the vermouth bottle and refrigerate until ready to use, up to 3 months.

BROWN BUTTER–INFUSED PANAMA PACIFIC RUM

One 750 ml bottle Panama Pacific rum (reserve the bottle)

150 grams brown butter, melted

Combine the rum and brown butter in a bowl, cover, and let sit at room temperature for 24 hours. Transfer to the freezer and freeze for 24 hours. Carefully poke a hole in the solidified butter and drain the liquid out (reserve the butter for another use). Strain the liquid through a paper coffee filter, Superbag, or fine-mesh sieve lined with several layers of cheesecloth, then funnel back into the rum bottle and refrigerate until ready to use, up to 3 months.

CACAO NIB–INFUSED CALLE 23 REPOSADO TEQUILA

One 750ml bottle Calle 23 Reposado tequila

30 grams cacao nibs

Fill a large basin with water and place an immersion circulator inside. Set the circulator to 130° Fahrenheit.

Combine the tequila and cacao nibs in a bowl and stir to combine. Transfer to a sealable, heatproof plastic bag. Seal the bag almost completely, then press out as much air as possible by dipping the bag (other than the unsealed portion) in the water. Finish sealing the bag, then remove it from the water.

When the water has reached 130° Fahrenheit, place the bag in the basin and cook for 120 minutes.

Place the bag in an ice bath and let cool to room temperature. Pass the infusion through a fine-mesh sieve. If any particles remain in the infusion, strain it through a paper coffee filter or Superbag. Transfer to a storage container and refrigerate until ready to use, up to 3 months.

CHAMOMILE-INFUSED ARMAGNAC

One 750 ml bottle PM Spirits VS Armagnac (reserve the bottle)

5 grams dried chamomile flowers

Combine the Armagnac and chamomile in a bowl and stir to combine. Let stand at room temperature for 30 minutes, stirring occasionally. Pass the infusion through a fine-mesh sieve. If any particles remain in the infusion, strain it again through a paper coffee filter or Superbag. Funnel back into the rum bottle and refrigerate until ready to use, up to 3 months.

COFFEE BEAN–INFUSED CAMPARI

One 1 liter bottle Campari (reserve the bottle)

6 grams whole coffee beans

Combine the Campari and coffee beans in a bowl and stir to combine. Cover and let stand at room temperature for 24 hours, stirring occasionally. Pass the infusion through a fine-mesh sieve. If any particles remain in the infusion, strain it again through a paper coffee filter or Superbag. Funnel back into the Campari bottle and refrigerate until ready to use, up to 3 months.

CORIANDER-INFUSED RANSOM OLD TOM

One 750 ml bottle Ransom Old Tom gin (reserve the bottle)

35 grams lightly toasted coriander seeds

Fill a large basin with water and place an immersion circulator inside. Set the circulator to 135° Fahrenheit.

Combine the gin and coriander seeds in a sealable, heatproof plastic bag. Seal the bag almost completely, then press out as much air as possible by dipping the bag (other than the unsealed portion) in the water. Finish sealing the bag, then remove it from the water.

When the water has reached 135° Fahrenheit, place the bag in the basin and cook for 2 hours.

Transfer the bag to an ice bath and let cool to room temperature. Pass the infusion through a fine-mesh sieve. If any particles remain in the infusion, strain it again through a paper coffee filter or Superbag. Funnel back into the gin bottle and refrigerate until ready to use, up to 3 months.

CORN HUSK–INFUSED DEL MAGUEY CHICHICAPA MEZCAL

14 grams fresh corn husks

One 750 ml bottle Del Maguey Chichicapa mezcal (reserve the bottle)

Preheat the oven to 400° Fahrenheit. Spread the corn husks on a baking sheet and toast until lightly browned and crisp in spots, but not completely dried out.

Fill a large basin with water and place an immersion circulator inside. Set the circulator to 135° Fahrenheit.

Combine the corn husks and mezcal in a sealable, heatproof plastic bag. Seal the bag almost completely, then press out as much air as possible by dipping the bag (other than the unsealed portion) in the water. Finish sealing the bag, then remove it from the water.

When the water has reached 135° Fahrenheit, place the bag in the basin and cook for 2 hours.

Transfer the bag to an ice bath and let cool to room temperature. Pass the infusion through a fine-mesh sieve. If any particles remain, strain it again through a paper coffee filter or Superbag. Funnel the infusion back into the mezcal bottle and refrigerate until ready to use, up to 4 weeks.

DASHI KOMBU–INFUSED PEAR BRANDY

30 grams dashi kombu

One 750 ml bottle Clear Creek pear eau-de-vie (reserve the bottle)

Tear the kombu into 1-inch strips. Place the kombu and brandy in a bowl and stir to combine. Let stand for 45 minutes, stirring occasionally. Pass the infusion through a fine-mesh sieve. If any particles remain in the infusion, strain it again through a paper coffee filter or Superbag. Funnel back into the brandy bottle and refrigerate until ready to use, up to 3 months.

DRIED MANGO–INFUSED CALLE 23 REPOSADO TEQUILA

One 750ml bottle Calle 23 Reposado tequila

75 grams dried mango

Fill a large basin with water and place an immersion circulator inside. Set the circulator to 135° Fahrenheit.

Put all the ingredients in a bowl and stir to combine. Transfer to a sealable, heatproof plastic bag. Seal the bag almost completely, then press out as much air as possible by dipping the bag (other than the unsealed portion) in the water. Finish sealing the bag, then remove it from the water. When the water has reached 135° Fahrenheit, place the bag in the basin and cook for 1 hour.

Place the bag in an ice bath and let cool to room temperature. Pass the infusion through a fine-mesh sieve. If any particles remain in the infusion, strain it through a paper coffee filter or Superbag. Transfer to a storage container and refrigerate until ready to use, up to 3 months.

ELOTE-INFUSED ELIJAH CRAIG BOURBON

1 ear of corn, shucked

One 750 ml bottle Elijah Craig 12-year bourbon (reserve the bottle)

Preheat the oven to 425° Fahrenheit. Roast the corn directly on the oven rack, turning it over every few minutes, until roasted and lightly browned in spots, about 18 minutes.

In a bowl, combine the roasted corn and bourbon. Cover and let sit for 24 hours. Pass the infusion through a fine-mesh sieve. If any particles remain in the infusion, strain it again through a paper coffee filter or Superbag. Funnel back into the bourbon bottle and refrigerate until ready to use, up to 3 months.

EUCALYPTUS-INFUSED YAGUARA OURO CACHAÇA

5 grams Terra Spice eucalyptus extract

One 750 ml bottle Yaguara Ouro cachaça

Add the eucalyptus extract to the bottle of cachaça and shake well. The infusion will last indefinitely.

JALAPEÑO-INFUSED SIEMBRA VALLES BLANCO TEQUILA

4 jalapeños

One 750 ml bottle Siembra Valles Blanco tequila (reserve the bottle)

Halve the jalapeños lengthwise, then scrape the seeds and membranes into

How to Make
SOUS VIDE INFUSIONS

At our bars, we use the sous vide (vacuum sealing) technique not only to extract flavor for syrups but also to flavor alcohol. We've adopted this method for two reasons. First, heat speeds the infusion process. Second, heating the mixture at a precise temperature without allowing any liquid to evaporate yields infusions that are more subtle and nuanced than those made using any other method. Importantly, the temperature remains consistent throughout the process, allowing us to select exactly the right temperature to preserve the flavors we want (typically the flavor of the raw ingredient) without extracting off-flavors.

Most of our sous vide infusions employ temperatures between 135° and 145° Fahrenheit. The lower end of that range is suitable for delicate ingredients such as fruits; the higher end is best for sturdier flavors, like coconut, nuts, or dried spices. As you'll see in the method that follows, at the end of the cooking time we submerge the infusion in an ice bath, which condenses any vapor present in the bag and preserves the alcohol content.

METHOD

1. Fill the basin with water and place the immersion circulator inside.

2. Set the circulator to the desired temperature.

3. Carefully measure the ingredients by weight and combine them in a bowl.

4. Transfer the mixture to a sealable, heatproof plastic bag. Seal the bag almost completely, then press out as much air as possible by dipping the bag (other than the unsealed portion) in the water. The counterpressure from the water will push the rest of the air out. Finish sealing the bag, then remove it from the water.

5. When the circulator has reached the desired temperature, place the sealed bag in the basin.

6. Carefully remove the bag when the specified time is up.

7. Transfer the bag to an ice bath to cool.

8. Strain the infusion through a fine-mesh sieve to remove any solids.

9. Transfer the infusion to a storage container and refrigerate until ready to use.

Tools

Large water basin

Immersion circulator

Gram scale

Bowl

Sealable, heatproof plastic bag, such as a freezer bag

Ice bath

Fine-mesh sieve

Airtight glass or plastic storage container

a container. Add the flesh of 2 of the jalapeños (reserve the flesh of the other 2 for another use). Add the tequila and stir to combine. Let stand at room temperature for up to 20 minutes, tasting often to monitor the heat level. Strain through a fine-mesh sieve lined with several layers of cheesecloth, then funnel back into the tequila bottle and refrigerate until ready to use, up to 1 month.

MISO-INFUSED PIERRE FERRAND 1840 COGNAC

One 750 ml bottle Pierre Ferrand 1840 cognac (reserve the bottle)

1 tablespoon white miso paste

Combine the cognac and miso in a blender and process until well blended. Divide the liquid evenly among your centrifuge containers. Weigh the filled containers and adjust the amount of liquid in each as needed to ensure their weights are exactly the same; this is important for keeping the machine in balance. Run the centrifuge at 4,500 rpm for 12 minutes.

Remove the containers and carefully strain the infusion through a paper coffee filter or Superbag, being careful not to disturb the solids that have collected on the bottom of the containers. If any particles remain in the infusion, strain it again. Funnel back into the cognac bottle and refrigerate until ready to use, up to 2 months.

MISO-INFUSED TARIQUET CLASSIQUE VS ARMAGNAC

One 750 ml bottle Tariquet Classique VS Bas-Armagnac (reserve the bottle)

1 tablespoon white miso paste

Combine the Armagnac and miso in a blender and process until well blended. Divide the liquid evenly among your centrifuge containers. Weigh the filled containers and adjust the amount of liquid in each as needed to ensure their weights are exactly the same; this is important for

keeping the machine in balance. Run the centrifuge at 4,500 rpm for 12 minutes.

Remove the containers and carefully strain the infusion through a paper coffee filter or Superbag, being careful not to disturb the solids that have collected on the bottom of the containers. If any particles remain in the infusion, strain it again. Funnel back into the Armagnac bottle and refrigerate until ready to use, up to 2 months.

NIÇOISE OLIVE–INFUSED YAGUARA OURO CACHAÇA

One 750 ml bottle Yaguara Ouro cachaça (reserve the bottle)

250 grams niçoise olives

Combine the cachaça and olives in a bowl and stir to combine. Cover and let stand at room temperature for 24 hours, stirring occasionally. Pass the infusion through a fine-mesh sieve. Transfer to a container, cover, and freeze for 24 hours. Strain again through a fine-mesh sieve.

Divide the liquid evenly among your centrifuge containers. Weigh the filled containers and adjust the amount of liquid in each as needed to ensure their weights are exactly the same; this is important for keeping the machine in balance. Run the centrifuge at 4,500 rpm for 12 minutes.

Remove the containers and carefully strain the infusion through a paper coffee filter or Superbag, being careful not to disturb the solids that have collected on the bottom of the containers. If any particles remain in the infusion, strain it again. Funnel back into the cachaça bottle and refrigerate until ready to use, up to 3 months.

NORI-INFUSED LA FAVORITE RHUM AGRICOLE BLANC

One 750 ml bottle La Favorite rhum agricole blanc (reserve the bottle)

10 grams aonori (dried seaweed flakes)

Combine the rum and aonori in a bowl and stir to combine. Let stand at room temperature for 15 minutes, stirring occasionally. Pass the infusion through a fine-mesh sieve. If any particles remain in the infusion, strain it again through a paper coffee filter or Superbag. Funnel back into the rum bottle and refrigerate until ready to use, up to 3 months.

PEANUT BUTTER–INFUSED OLD OVERHOLT RYE

One 750 ml bottle Old Overholt rye (reserve the bottle)

40 grams organic creamy peanut butter

Combine the rye and peanut butter in a blender and blend until smooth. Transfer to a bowl, cover, and freeze for 12 hours. Carefully poke a hole in the solidified peanut butter and drain the liquid out. Strain the liquid through a paper coffee filter, Superbag, or fine-mesh sieve lined with several layers of cheesecloth, then funnel back into the rye bottle and refrigerate until ready to use, up to 1 month.

PEANUT-INFUSED LUSTAU DON NUÑO OLOROSO SHERRY

180 grams raw, shelled peanuts

One 750 ml bottle Lustau Don Nuño oloroso sherry (reserve the bottle)

Preheat the oven to 350° Fahrenheit. Spread the peanuts on a rimmed baking sheet and roast until golden brown, 20 to 25 minutes. Transfer the peanuts to a bowl and let cool to room temperature. Add the sherry, cover, and refrigerate for 12 hours. Pass the infusion through a fine-mesh sieve. If any particles remain in the infusion, strain it again through a paper coffee filter or Superbag. Funnel back into the sherry bottle and refrigerate until ready to use, up to 3 months.

PINEAPPLE-INFUSED TANQUERAY GIN

One 750 ml bottle Tanqueray gin (reserve the bottle)

350 grams cubed pineapple (about 1½-inch cubes)

Combine the gin and pineapple in a bowl and stir to combine. Let stand at room temperature for 4 hours, stirring occasionally. Pass the infusion through a fine-mesh sieve. If any particles remain in the infusion, strain it again through a paper coffee filter or Superbag. Funnel back into the gin bottle and refrigerate until ready to use, up to 3 months.

PISTACHIO-INFUSED ELIJAH CRAIG BOURBON

One 1 liter bottle Buffalo Trace bourbon (reserve the bottle)

27 grams Fiddyment Farms pistachio paste

Combine the bourbon and pistachio paste in a blender and process until smooth. Transfer to a storage container, cover, and freeze for 24 hours. Carefully poke a hole in the solidified fat and drain the liquid out. Strain through a paper coffee filter, Superbag, or fine-mesh sieve lined with several layers of cheesecloth, then funnel back into the bourbon bottle and refrigerate until ready to use, up to 3 months.

PISTACHIO-INFUSED RITTENHOUSE RYE

One 750 ml bottle Rittenhouse rye (reserve the bottle)

40 grams Fiddyment Farms pistachio paste

Combine the rye and pistachio paste in a blender and blend until smooth. Transfer to a bowl, cover, and freeze for 12 hours. Carefully poke a hole in the solidified paste and drain the liquid out. Strain through a paper coffee filter, Superbag, or fine-mesh sieve lined with several layers of cheesecloth, then funnel back into the rye bottle and refrigerate until ready to use, up to 1 month.

SHIITAKE-INFUSED HIBIKI HARMONY WHISKY

One 750 ml bottle Hibiki Harmony whisky

7 grams dried shiitake mushrooms

Fill a large basin with water and place an immersion circulator inside. Set the circulator to 135° Fahrenheit.

Combine the whisky and mushrooms in a sealable, heatproof plastic bag. Seal the bag almost completely, then press out as much air as possible by dipping the bag (other than the unsealed portion) in the water. Finish sealing the bag, then remove it from the water.

When the water has reached 135° Fahrenheit, place the bag in the basin and cook for 2 hours.

Place the bag in an ice bath and let cool to room temperature. Pass the infusion through a fine-mesh sieve. If any particles remain in the infusion, strain it again through a paper coffee filter or Superbag. Transfer to a storage container and refrigerate until ready to use, up to 3 months.

SILVER NEEDLE TEA–INFUSED DOLIN BLANC VERMOUTH

One 750 ml bottle Dolin blanc vermouth (reserve the bottle)

10 grams Silver Needle white tea leaves

Combine the vermouth and tea leaves in a bowl and stir to combine. Let stand at room temperature for 30 minutes, stirring occasionally. Pass the infusion through a fine-mesh sieve. If any particles remain in the infusion, strain it again through a paper coffee filter or Superbag. Funnel back into the vermouth bottle and refrigerate until ready to use, up to 3 months.

STRAWBERRY-INFUSED PLYMOUTH GIN

One 750 ml bottle Plymouth gin (reserve the bottle)

500 grams hulled and halved strawberries

Combine the gin and strawberries in a bowl and stir to combine. Cover and refrigerate for 24 hours. Pass the infusion through a fine-mesh sieve. If any particles remain in the infusion, strain it again through a paper coffee filter or Superbag. Funnel back into the gin bottle and refrigerate until ready to use, up to 3 months.

STRAWBERRY-INFUSED SOMBRA MEZCAL

700 grams hulled strawberries

700 grams Sombra mezcal

5 grams ascorbic acid

Pectinex Ultra SP-L

Kieselsol

Chitosan

Wash and hull the strawberries. Combine the strawberries, mezcal, and ascorbic acid in a blender and process until very smooth.

Strain the mixture through a paper coffee filter or Superbag. Calculate 2 percent of the weight (multiply by 0.02) to get X grams. Stir in X grams of pectinex and kieselsol. Cover and let sit for 15 minutes. Stir in X grams of chitosan and let sit 15 minutes more. Stir in X grams of kieselsol.

Transfer to a centrifuge container. Weigh the filled container and fill each of the other containers with an equal weight of water. Run the centrifuge at 4,500 rpm for 12 minutes. Remove the containers and carefully strain the infusion through a paper coffee filter or Superbag, being careful not to disturb the solids that have collected on the bottom of the container. Transfer to a storage container and refrigerate until ready to use, up to 1 week.

PRESSURIZED INFUSIONS

Manipulating pressure is a valuable way to extract flavor from ingredients that are extremely fragile: those that perish too quickly to allow for extended maceration, or those that change dramatically with any amount of heat. We use two different techniques for pressurized infusions: rapid infusions using an iSi whipper (a gadget more typically used to make whipped cream) and nitrous oxide (N_2O); and vacuum infusions using a chamber vacuum machine (instructions for making vacuum infusions can be found in *Cocktail Codex*).

In rapid pressurized infusion, flavors are extracted quickly by using compressed gas to force liquid into a solid ingredient. All of the ingredients are placed in the chamber of an iSi whipper and charged with N_2O, which forces the liquid into the cells of the solid ingredient, somewhat like a sponge sucking up water. When the pressure is released, the liquid is pulled back out of the solid ingredient, now carrying its flavor. Rapid infusions are particularly useful for extracting delicate flavors, such as those of fresh herbs, as well as with ingredients that have a wide range of flavors, such as cacao nibs. Because the infusion process is so quick—usually around 10 minutes—it doesn't run the risk of extracting any of the off-flavors than can come with long maceration times.

METHOD

1. Carefully measure the ingredients by weight.

2. Put the ingredients in an iSi whipper, taking care not to fill it higher than the "Max" line. Seal tightly. Charge with one of the N_2O cartridges, then shake the canister about five times. Change the cartridge, then charge and shake again. We recommend allowing the mixture to sit under pressure for 10 minutes, shaking it every 30 seconds or so.

3. Point the canister's nozzle at a 45-degree angle into a container. Vent the gas as quickly as possible without spraying liquid everywhere; the quicker the venting, the better the infusion. When all of the gas is out, open the canister and take a listen. Once there is no longer audible bubbling, you can proceed. Strain the infusion through a paper coffee filter or Superbag.

4. Funnel the infusion back into the original liquor bottle and refrigerate until ready to use. Because these infusions extract delicate flavors, they are best used within a month—though some delicate flavors (such as the basil in the Silver Needle Tea–Infused Dolin Blanc Vermouth, see opposite) are most vibrant within 1 week.

Tools

Gram scale

iSi whipper, preferably 1-quart capacity

2 N_2O cartridges

Large, deep container

Paper coffee filter or Superbag

Storage container

Clarification is the process of removing cloudy particles from a liquid, thereby making it transparent. While we could clarify juices for our cocktails using a paper filter, we prefer to use either a mechanical centrifuge or agar.

How to Clarify Juice with Agar

METHOD

1. Juice the fruit or other fresh produce, then strain the juice through a fine-mesh sieve.

2. Measure the weight of a container using a gram scale, then add the juice and calculate the difference—or, if your scale has a tare function, place the container on it, zero the scale, then add the juice and determine its weight. Record the weight of the juice.

3. Calculate 25 percent of the weight of the juice (multiply by 0.25). Measure out that amount of water and put it in a separate container.

4. Add the weights of the juice and water, then calculate 0.2 percent of the combined weight (multiply by 0.002) to get X grams; this is the amount of agar you'll use.

5. In a saucepan, combine the water and agar. Cook over medium heat, whisking constantly, until the agar is dissolved.

6. Remove from the heat, add the juice, and whisk until combined.

7. Pour the mixture into one of the containers, then put the container in the ice bath. Allow the mixture to set up, about 10 minutes.

8. Meanwhile, line a fine-mesh sieve with several layers of cheesecloth and set it over a bowl.

9. When the agar has set, use a whisk to break it into curd-like chunks. Transfer the chunks to the cheesecloth-lined sieve.

10. Gently gather the edges of the cheesecloth and form the mass into a ball. Squeeze out the liquid; don't squeeze too hard, or some of the agar may come through.

11. If any particles are still present in the clarified juice, pass the liquid through a paper coffee filter or Superbag.

12. Transfer to a storage container and refrigerate until ready to use.

Tools

Juicer

Fine-mesh sieve

Several bowls or other containers

Gram scale

Saucepan

Cheesecloth

Agar

Paper coffee filter or Superbag

Storage container

Why bother with clarifying? Honestly, sometimes we just like to play with people's expectations: When they see a crystal-clear drink that resembles a Martini, they assume it will be boozy and sharp. But if they take a sip and taste a shockingly bright and acidic Daiquiri, that's a fun surprise. Clarification also serves a practical purpose: when making fully carbonated cocktails (which we explored in the *Cocktail Codex*), removing any particulate matter allows the carbon dioxide to disseminate more uniformly throughout the drink.

One final note: Because clarified juices tend to be more fragile than fresh juices, we recommend using them within 1 day. The exception would be if they're mixed into batched or kegged cocktails with sweeteners and spirits that will help preserve their delicate flavor.

How to Clarify Juice with a Centrifuge

METHOD

1. Juice the fruit or other fresh produce, then strain the juice through a fine-mesh sieve.

2. Measure the weight of a centrifuge container using a gram scale, then add the juice and calculate the difference—or, if your scale has a tare function, place the centrifuge container on it, zero the scale, then add the juice and determine its weight. Record the weight of the juice.

3. Calculate 0.2 percent of the weight of the juice (multiply by 0.002) to get X grams.

4. Stir X grams of Pectinex Ultra SP-L and kieselsol into the juice. Cover and let sit for 15 minutes.

5. Stir X grams of chitosan into the juice. Cover and let sit for 15 minutes.

6. Right before putting the container in the centrifuge, stir in X grams of kieselsol.

7. Weigh the filled container and fill each of the other containers with an equal weight of water. Each container in a centrifuge must weigh exactly the same in order to keep the machine in balance.

8. Run the centrifuge at 4,500 rpm for 12 minutes.

9. Remove the containers and carefully strain the juice through a fine-mesh sieve lined with several layers of cheesecloth (or through a Superbag) being careful to not disturb the solids that have collected on the bottom of the container.

10. Transfer to a storage container and refrigerate until ready to use.

Tools

Juicer

Fine-mesh sieve

Centrifuge

Gram scale

Centrifuge containers with lids

Pectinex Ultra SP-L

Kieselsol (a fining agent for wine and juice)

Chitosan (a fining solution for wine and juice, used in conjunction with Kieselsol)

Cheesecloth

Storage container

HOUSE BITTERS, MIXES, JUICES & SHRUBS

ACID-ADJUSTED ORANGE JUICE

500 grams strained fresh orange juice

16 grams citric acid powder

10 grams malic acid powder

Combine all the ingredients in a bowl and whisk until the powders have dissolved. Transfer to a storage container and refrigerate until ready to use, up to 3 days.

DONN'S MIX #1

400 grams strained fresh grapefruit juice

200 grams Cinnamon Syrup (page 283)

Combine the grapefruit juice and cinnamon syrup in a bowl and whisk until thoroughly blended. Transfer to a storage container and refrigerate until ready to use, up to 2 weeks.

DON'S SPICES

200 grams Vanilla Syrup (page 288)

200 grams St. Elizabeth allspice dram

Combine the vanilla syrup and allspice dram in a bowl and whisk until thoroughly blended. Transfer to a storage container and refrigerate until ready to use, up to 2 weeks.

HIBISCUS SHRUB

500 grams champagne vinegar

22.5 grams dried hibiscus flowers

Superfine sugar

Filtered water

In a bowl, combine the vinegar and hibiscus. Cover and let sit for at least 12 hours or up to 48 hours (longer is better). Pass the liquid through a fine-mesh sieve and pour into a saucepan. Bring the mixture to a boil, then lower the heat and simmer until the liquid is reduced by about one-fourth, about 15 minutes. Let cool slightly, then weigh the liquid. Add the mixture, an equal weight of sugar, and half as much water to a blender. Process until the sugar has dissolved. Transfer to a storage container and refrigerate until ready to use, up to 1 year.

HOUSE ORANGE BITTERS

100 grams Fee Brothers West Indian orange bitters

100 grams Angostura orange bitters

100 grams Regans' orange bitters

Combine all the ingredients in a bowl and stir to combine. Transfer to a storage container and store at room temperature until ready to use, up to 1 year.

IMPROVED GARDENIA MIX

100 grams filtered water

5 grams Ticaloid 210 S (gum stabilizer)

450 grams melted unsalted butter

150 grams Cinnamon Syrup (page 283)

75 grams Vanilla Syrup (page 288)

75 grams St. Elizabeth allspice dram

Place the water and Ticaloid in a blender and let sit for 5 minutes. Add the butter and blend until smooth. Add the remaining ingredients and blend again. Transfer to a storage container and refrigerate until ready to use, up to 1 week.

PAPAYA MIX

600 grams Perfect Purée papaya purée

400 grams Cane Sugar Syrup (page 282)

200 grams Marie Brizard white crème de cacao

30 grams Citric Acid Solution (page 299)

Combine all the ingredients in a bowl and whisk until thoroughly blended. Transfer to a storage container and refrigerate until ready to use, up to 2 weeks.

TEPACHE

15 grams cinnamon bark

5 grams coriander seeds

5 grams whole star anise

5 grams white peppercorns

2 grams cardamom pods

2,000 grams water

500 grams piloncillo (Mexican raw cane sugar)

1 pineapple (with skin), chopped

Lightly crush all the spices, then toast in a dry skillet over medium-low heat until fragrant. Transfer to a heatproof bowl or storage container. In a saucepan, combine the water and piloncillo and heat over medium-low heat, whisking occasionally, until the sugar has dissolved. Pour the solution over the spices and add the pineapple. Cover the container with cheesecloth and secure with a rubber band. Let sit at room temperature in a dark place for 4 days, stirring daily. Pass through a fine-mesh sieve. If any particles remain in the tepache, strain it again through a paper coffee filter or Superbag. Transfer to a storage container and refrigerate until ready to use, up to 2 weeks.

TSUKEMONO BRINE

1 large or 2 or 3 small cucumbers (unpeeled), sliced

Kosher salt

500 grams rice vinegar

500 grams water

250 grams white sugar

125 grams sesame seeds

Place the cucumber slices in a colander and toss with 2 teaspoons salt. Let sit for 1 hour, then rinse well and let dry.

In a bowl, combine the vinegar, water, sugar, and 1 teaspoon salt and whisk until the sugar and salt have dissolved. Add the cucumbers and sesame seeds and toss. Transfer to a storage container and refrigerate for at least 24 hours before using.

SOLUTIONS & TINCTURES

CHAMPAGNE ACID SOLUTION

94 grams unfiltered water

3 grams tartaric acid powder

3 grams lactic acid powder

Combine all the ingredients in a glass bowl and stir until the powders have dissolved. Transfer to a glass dropper bottle or other glass container and refrigerate until ready to use, up to 6 months.

CITRIC ACID SOLUTION

100 grams filtered water

20 grams citric acid powder

Combine the water and citric acid in a glass bowl and stir until the powder has dissolved. Transfer to a glass dropper bottle or other glass container and refrigerate until ready to use, up to 6 months.

HABANERO TINCTURE

150 grams vodka (reserve the bottle)

25 grams habanero peppers, thinly sliced

Combine the vodka and peppers in a bowl, cover, and let sit for 24 hours. Pass through a fine-mesh sieve. If any particles remain in the infusion, strain it again through a paper coffee filter or Superbag. Funnel back into the vodka bottle and refrigerate until ready to use, up to 1 month.

HOPPED LIME ACID

250 grams filtered water

9 grams citric acid powder

6 grams malic acid powder

2 grams Citra hop pellets

1 gram kosher salt

Combine all the ingredients in a blender and process until the powders and salt have dissolved. Strain through a paper coffee filter or Superbag. Transfer to a storage container and refrigerate until ready to use, up to 6 months.

LACTIC ACID SOLUTION

100 grams filtered water

10 grams lactic acid powder

Combine the water and lactic acid in a glass bowl and stir until the powder has dissolved. Transfer to a glass dropper bottle or other glass container and refrigerate until ready to use, up to 6 months.

MALIC ACID SOLUTION

80 grams filtered water

20 grams malic acid powder

Combine the water and malic acid in a glass bowl and stir until the powder has dissolved. Transfer to a glass dropper bottle or other glass container and refrigerate until ready to use, up to 6 months.

SALT SOLUTION

70 grams filtered water

30 grams kosher salt

Combine the water and salt in a glass bowl and whisk until the salt has dissolved. Transfer to a glass dropper bottle or other glass container and refrigerate until ready to use, up to 6 months.

GARNISHES

CAMPARI-INFUSED TOASTED COCONUT

1 Liter bottle Campari
(reserve the bottle)

500 grams toasted coconut

Combine the Campari and toasted coconut in a bowl and stir to combine. Cover and let stand at room temperature for 24 hours, stirring occasionally. Pass the infusion through a fine-mesh sieve and reserve the coconut flakes. If any particles remain in the infusion, strain it again through a paper coffee filter or Superbag. Funnel back into the Campari bottle and refrigerate until ready to use, up to 3 months.

Place the coconut flakes in a dehydrator until dry. Transfer to a storage container and store at room temperature until ready to use, up to 2 weeks.

DEHYDRATED APPLE SLICES

In a bowl, whisk 2 cups water with 1 teaspoon kosher salt until the salt has dissolved. Thinly slice apples (use a mandoline if you have one) and add to the water; this step prevents browning. Let soak for 15 minutes, then drain.

Set a dehydrator to 135° Fahrenheit or preheat the oven to its lowest setting. Arrange the apple slices on the dehydrator rack or a wire rack set inside a rimmed baking sheet, leaving about ½ inch of space between slices. Dehydrate or bake with the door propped open slightly until completely dried and brittle, 6 to 8 hours. Transfer to a storage container lined with paper towels. Store at room temperature until ready to use, up to 1 month.

DEHYDRATED CITRUS WHEELS OR PINEAPPLE WEDGES

Set a dehydrator to 135° Fahrenheit or preheat the oven to its lowest setting. Arrange the fruit on the dehydrator rack or a wire rack set in a rimmed baking sheet, leaving about ½ inch of space between each. Dehydrate or bake with the door propped open slightly until completely dried and brittle, 8 to 12 hours. Transfer to a storage container lined with paper towels. Store at room temperature until ready to use, up to 1 month.

TOASTED OAT CREAM

2 ounces steel-cut oats

16 ounces heavy cream

Preheat the oven to 350° Fahrenheit. Spread the oats on a rimmed baking sheet and toast until lightly browned and fragrant, about 10 minutes. Let cool slightly, then transfer to a bowl and add the heavy cream. Cover and refrigerate for 24 hours. Pass the infusion through a fine-mesh sieve. Transfer to a storage container and refrigerate until ready to use, up to 5 days.

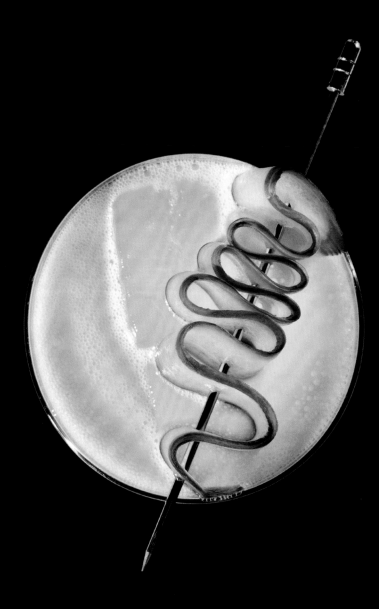

How to Make
CENTRIFUGE INFUSIONS

Generally speaking, making a centrifuge infusion involves first blending solid ingredients with booze to maximize surface contact and speed the infusion process, then using a centrifuge to separate the solids and clarify the liquid. Note that with this process, some of the liquids from the solid ingredient end up in the infusion. This can yield delicious results, but the infusion may be more prone to spoilage and therefore have a shorter life span.

It can take some trial and error to figure out the right proportion of booze to flavoring ingredient. With dry ingredients, such as dried fruits or graham crackers, start with a 1-to-4 ratio by weight of flavoring ingredients to booze. For ingredients that contain water, such as bananas or strawberries, start with a 1-to-2 ratio. With ingredients that have very subtle flavor, such as watermelon, you might use a 1-to-1 ratio.

METHOD

1. Carefully measure the ingredients by weight. Combine the ingredients in a blender and process until the solids are completely puréed.

2. Weigh the container or, if your scale has a tare function, place the container on it, zero the scale, then add the syrup and determine its weight.

3. Strain the mixture into the container through a fine-mesh sieve to remove any large particles.

4. Weigh the filled container, then subtract the weight of the container to determine the weight of the liquid—the baseline weight for the following calculation.

5. Calculate 0.2 percent of the weight of the liquid (multiply by 0.002) to get X grams. Stir X grams of Pectinex Ultra SP-L (see page 288) into the liquid. Cover and let sit for 15 minutes.

6. Stir again to mix any separated liquid, then divide the liquid evenly among the centrifuge containers. Weigh the filled containers and adjust the amount of liquid in each as needed to ensure their weights are exactly the same; this is important for keeping the centrifuge in balance. (An off-balance centrifuge is dangerous!)

7. Run the centrifuge at 4,500 rpm for 12 minutes.

8. Remove the containers and carefully strain the infusion through a paper coffee filter or Superbag, being careful not to disturb the solids that have collected on the bottom of the containers. If any particles remain in the infusion, strain it again.

9. Transfer to a storage container and refrigerate until ready to use.

Tools

Gram scale

Fine gram scale

Blender

Bowl or other vessel

Fine-mesh sieve

Centrifuge

Paper coffee filter or Superbag

Storage container

RESOURCES

ART OF DRINK (artofdrink.com)
For phosphoric acid solution, labeled "Extinct Acid Phosphate Solution."

ASTOR WINES & SPIRITS
(astorwines.com)
For a vast selection of spirits.

AUGUST UNCOMMON TEA
(august.la)
For loose-leaf teas, including Metropolitan and Tropic of Capricorn.

BEVERAGE ALCOHOL RESOURCE
(beveragealcoholresource.com)
For aspiring bartenders and liquor professionals.

CHEF SHOP (chefshop.com)
For honey, Fusion Napa Valley verjus, maraschino cherries, and other pantry staples.

COCKTAIL KINGDOM
(cocktailkingdom.com)
For all matter of barware, as well as bitters, syrups, and cocktail books, including facsimiles of some vintage classics.

CRYSTAL CLASSICS
(crystalclassics.com)
For glassware from Schott Zwiesel and other brands.

DRINK UP NY (drinkupny.com)
For hard-to-find spirits and other boozy ingredients.

DUAL SPECIALTY STORE
(dualspecialtystorenyc.com)
For spices, nuts, and bitters.

IN PURSUIT OF TEA
(inpursuitoftea.com)
For rare and exotic teas.

ISI (www.isi.com/us/culinary/)
For whippers, soda siphons, and chargers.

KEGWORKS (kegworks.com)
For carbonation and draft cocktail tools, as well as acids, glassware, and bar essentials.

LIBBEY (libbey.com)
For durable glassware.

MARKETSPICE (marketspice.com)
For one-of-a-kind tea blends.

MICRO MATIC (micromatic.com)
For keg cocktail equipment.

MODERNIST PANTRY
(modernistpantry.com)
For Superbags, Dave Arnold's Spinzall centrifuge, carbonation tools, and powders used for infusions and clarifications.

MONTEREY BAY SPICE COMPANY (herbco.com)
For bulk herbs, spices, and teas.

MOREBEER (morebeer.com)
For keg cocktail equipment.

MTC KITCHEN (mtckitchen.com)
For Japanese glassware, tools, and kitchen equipment.

ORGEAT WORKS (orgeatworks.com)
For orgeat, macadamia nut syrup, and toasted almond syrup.

OZARK BIOMEDICAL
(ozarkbiomedical.com)
For refurbished medical centrifuges.

PERFECT PURÉE (perfectpuree.com)
For pristine fruit purées.

POLYSCIENCE
(polyscienceculinary.com)
For immersion circulators, the Smoking Gun, and other high-tech tools.

STEELITE (steelite.com)
For coupes and Nick & Nora glasses.

TERRA SPICE COMPANY
(terraspice.com)
For an extensive selection of spices, sugars, dried fruits, and dried chiles.

T SALON (tsalon.com)
For loose-leaf teas and tisanes.

UMAMI MART (umamimart.com)
For Japanese bar tools, glassware, and so much more.

THE DEATH & CO BOOKSHELF

COCKTAILS & MIXOLOGY

Arnold, Dave. *Liquid Intelligence: The Art and Science of the Perfect Cocktail.* New York: Norton, 2014.

Bainbridge, Julia. *Good Drinks: Alcohol-Free Recipes for When You're Not Drinking for Whatever Reason.* Emeryville, CA: Ten Speed Press, 2020.

Baiocchi, Talia. *Sherry: A Modern Guide to the Wine World's Best-Kept Secret, with Cocktails and Recipes.* Emeryville, CA: Ten Speed Press, 2014.

Bartels, Brian. *The United States of Cocktails: Recipes, Tales, and Traditions from All 50 States (and the District of Columbia).* New York: Abrams, 2020.

Broom, Dave. *The Way of Whisky: A Journey Around Japanese Whisky.* London: Mitchell Beazley, 2017.

Brown, Derek, and Robert Yule. *Spirits, Sugar, Water, Bitters: How the Cocktail Conquered the World.* London: Rizzoli, 2019.

Cate, Martin, and Rebecca Cate. *Smuggler's Cove: Exotic Cocktails, Rum, and the Cult of Tiki.* Emeryville, CA: Ten Speed Press, 2016.

Chartier, Francois. *Taste Buds and Molecules: The Art and Science of Food, Wine, and Flavor.* New York: Houghton Mifflin Harcourt, 2012.

Chetiyawardana, Ryan. *Good Together: Drink & Feast with Mr. Lyan & Friends.* London: Frances Lincoln, 2017.

Cooper, Ron, and Chantal Martineau. *Finding Mezcal: A Journey into the Liquid Soul of Mexico, with 40 Cocktails.* Emeryville, CA: Ten Speed Press, 2018.

Craddock, Harry. *The Savoy Cocktail Book.* London: Pavilion, 2007.

Curtis, Wayne. *And a Bottle of Rum: A History of the New World in Ten Cocktails.* New York: Crown, 2006.

deBary, John. *Drink What You Want: The Subjective Guide to Making Objectively Delicious Cocktails.* London: Clarkson Potter, 2020.

DeGroff, Dale. *The Essential Cocktail: The Art of Mixing Perfect Drinks.* New York: Clarkson Potter, 2008.

—— *The New Craft of the Cocktail: Everything You Need to Think Like a Master Mixologist, with 500 Recipes.* New York: Clarkson Potter, 2020.

Dornenburg, Andrew, and Karen Page. *What to Drink with What You Eat: The Definitive Guide to Pairing Food with Wine, Beer, Spirits, Coffee, Tea—Even Water—Based on Expert Advice from America's Best Sommeliers.* New York: Bulfinch, 2006.

Embury, David A. *The Fine Art of Mixing Drinks.* New York: Mud Puddle Books, 2008.

Ensslin, Hugo. *Recipes for Mixed Drinks.* New York: Mud Puddle Books, 2009.

Haigh, Ted. *Vintage Spirits and Forgotten Cocktails: From the Alamagoozlum to the Zombie 100 Rediscovered Recipes and the Stories Behind Them.* Bloomington, IN: Quarry Books, 2009.

Jackson, Michael. *Whiskey: The Definitive World Guide.* London: Dorling Kindersley, 2005.

Kalkofen, Misty, and Kristen Amann. *Drinking Like Ladies: 75 Modern Cocktails from the World's Leading Female Bartenders.* Bloomington, IN: Quarry Books, 2018.

McGee, Harold. *On Food and Cooking: The Science and Lore of the Kitchen.* New York: Scribner, 2004.

Meehan, Jim. *Meehan's Bartender Manual.* Emeryville, CA: Ten Speed Press, 2017.

Mix, Ivy. *Spirits of Latin America: A Celebration of Culture & Cocktails, with 100 Recipes from Leyenda & Beyond.* Emeryville, CA: Ten Speed Press, 2020.

Morgenthaler, Jeffrey, and Martha Holmberg. *The Bar Book: Elements of Cocktail Technique.* San Francisco, CA: Chronicle Books, 2014.

Mustipher, Shannon. *Tiki: Modern Tropical Cocktails.* London: Rizzoli, 2019.

Myhrvold, Nathan, Chris Young, and Maxime Bilet. *Modernist Cuisine: The Art and Science of Cooking.* Bellevue, WA: The Cooking Lab, 2011.

Pacult, F. Paul. *Kindred Spirits 2.* Wallkill, NY: Spirit Journal, 2008.

Page, Karen, and Andrew Dornenburg. *The Flavor Bible: The Essential Guide to Culinary Creativity, Based on the Wisdom of America's Most Imaginative Chefs.* New York: Little, Brown, 2008.

Parsons, Brad Thomas. *Amaro: The Spirited World of Bittersweet, Herbal Liqueurs, with Cocktails, Recipes, and Formulas.* Emeryville, CA: Ten Speed Press, 2016.

—— *Bitters: A Spirited History of a Classic Cure-All, with Cocktails, Recipes, and Formulas.* Emeryville, CA: Ten Speed Press, 2011.

Petraske, Sasha, with Georgette Moger-Petraske. *Regarding Cocktails.* New York: Phaidon Press, 2016.

Regan, Gary. *The Bartender's Gin Compendium.* Bloomington, IN: Xlibris, 2009.

—— *The Joy of Mixology: The Consummate Guide to the Bartender's Craft.* Revised and updated edition. New York: Clarkson Potter, 2018.

Reiner, Julie, and Kaitlyn Goalen. *The Craft Cocktail Party: Delicious Drinks for Every Occasion.* New York: Grand Central Life & Style, 2015.

Robitschek, Leo. *The NoMad Cocktail Book.* Emeryville, CA: Ten Speed Press, 2019.

Simonson, Robert. *The Martini Cocktail: A Meditation on the World's Greatest Drink, with Recipes.* Emeryville, CA: Ten Speed Press, 2019.

Stewart, Amy. *The Drunken Botanist: The Plants That Create the World's Great Drinks.* Chapel Hill, NC: Algonquin Books, 2013.

Teague, Sother, and Robert Simonson. *I'm Just Here for the Drinks: A Guide to Spirits, Drinking and More Than 100 Extraordinary Cocktails.* New York: Media Lab Books, 2018.

Thomas, Jerry. *The Bar-Tender's Guide: How to Mix Drinks.* New York: Dick & Fitzgerald, 1862.

Wondrich, David. *Imbibe!* New York: Perigee, 2007.

—— *Punch: The Delights (and Dangers) of the Flowing Bowl.* New York: Perigee, 2010.

OUR FAVORITE BUSINESS BOOKS

Catmull, Ed. *Creativity, Inc.: Overcoming the Unseen Forces That Stand in the Way of True Inspiration.* New York: Random House, 2014.

Collins, Jim. *Good to Great: Why Some Companies Make the Leap and Others Don't.* New York: HarperBusiness, 2001.

Collins, Jim, and Jerry I. Porras. *Built to Last: Successful Habits of Visionary Companies.* New York: Collins Business, 2002.

Duckworth, Angela. *Grit: The Power of Passion and Perseverance.* New York: Scribner, 2018.

Gawande, Atul. *The Checklist Manifesto: How to Get Things Right.* London: Picador, 2011.

Gladwell, Malcolm. *Outliers: The Story of Success.* New York: Black Bay Books, 2011.

Kinni, Theodore. *Be Our Guest: Perfecting the Art of Customer Service.* Revised and updated edition. Glendale, CA: Disney Editions, 2011.

Stack, Jack. *The Great Game of Business, Expanded and Updated: The Only Sensible Way to Run a Company.* Redfern, NSW: Currency, 2013.

Wickman, Gino. *Traction: Get a Grip on Your Business.* Dallas, TX: BenBella Books, 2012.

ACKNOWLEDGMENTS

The content of this book is the collective work of a huge team, all of whom, in many ways, contribute to our approach. They are bartenders, servers, baristas, chefs, cooks, trainers, developers, prep ninjas, back servers, and barbacks, and the managers who lead and support them every single day.

We were deep into the writing of this book when the global pandemic hit. Within days the entire hospitality industry collapsed beneath us. Our guests were isolated at home, employees were sent away, and on March 15, 2020, we made the decision to close the doors to our bars indefinitely.

We are a people-led business. We value our team more than any other aspect of our company; they are what make us great. On that mid-March day—the Ides of March, no less—we laid off nearly all of the creative, passionate, talented, and damn-hard workers at Death & Co's three locations. At that time, we couldn't predict what would happen in the weeks and months to follow. It felt heartbreaking and hopeless, as if a desolate void lay ahead.

What did come next shouldn't have surprised us. During what seemed like an endless stretch of crisis, grief, and confusion, our community banded together. We made a bunch of cocktails at home, shared recipes over video conferences, planned new menus, and reminisced about brighter days. Friends, strangers, peers, and heroes offered their help and support. We kept writing this book. We worked. Slowly, we began to rebuild. Slowly, things began to get better.

It shouldn't have surprised us that our team was stronger than the turmoil we faced. That in spite of disaster and uncertainty, we all turned to connection. We do what we do because there are few things better than coming together over a drink. These acknowledgments honor the teams that were in place before the pandemic: a group of dedicated, brilliant, resilient professionals who make our company what it is. And to those who we've worked with in the past (or who are with us as this book is published), please know that we're incredibly grateful for your contributions.

At the mother ship, **Death & Co New York:** Alexander Ali, Kathryn Caine, Kayla Ferguson, Alex Frost, Joseph Gerbino, Andrew Hryniewicki, Galen Huggins, Shelby Hulse, Sam Johnson, Andreas Kaiafas, Alex Martin, Tiffany Nahm, Joshua Polina, Shannon Ponche, Jhevere Reynolds, Alix Russel, Javelle Taft, and Shannon Tebay.

At the sprightly sibling, **Death & Co Denver:** Matthew Albert, David Anderson, Jacob Bake, Margaret Behringer, Vanessa Bernal, Addison Bollaert, Jessica Coleman, Neil Dorschner, Kevin Dwyer, Grayson Fagan, Arlinda Fasliu, Jonathan Festinger, Jonathan Feuersanger, Kanayda Fierro, Tina Francis, Alegandro Galicia Hilton, Matthew Garcia, Gabriella Gonzalez, Aaron Griep, William Hieronymus, Sarah Hooks, Derrion Horn, Paul Jacobs, Donald Jenkins, Alex Jump, Kenneth Kebaara, Elijah Keller, Scott Key, Austin Knight, Kira Konstantinova, Jonathan Long, Dylan Lopez, Audrey Ludlam, Blake Manion, Antonio Marrone, Maximilian Martin, Kenneth Martinez Jr, Jonathan Mateer, Jonathan Merrill, Christopher Norton, George Nunez, Gianna Pachuilo, Everyn Phoenix, Willy Rosenthal, Caleb Russell, Margaret Sanders, Melisa Schmidt, Donald Sisneros, Nicholas Smedley, Phillip Smith, Reginald Smith, Ryan Smith, Liam Studdiford, Keely Sutherland, Jordan Tuzzeo, Elizabeth Vance, Kelly Waldo, Dagan Walton, Marvin Williams, Christopher Woerter, Brian Wyner. Our team in Denver receives immense support from our family at The Ramble Hotel; huge gratitude goes to Ryan Diggins, Andrew Guerra, Zack Fleming, and Tessa Harvey.

At our new baby, **Death & Co Los Angeles:** Jamal Arif, Shakirat Arije, Matthew Belanger, Cameron Brown, Joshua Chuandra, Mia de Guzman, Jacqueline Esbin, Thomas Eslinger, Raul Hernandez, Roxanne Hodge, Ashleigh Hopkins, Alyson Iwamoto, Michelle Jackson, John Lindsay, Nicholas Luna, Kevin Nguyen, Ethan O'Kane, Ana Palomares, Samuel Penton, Edwin Rios, Jonathan Salazar, Jennifer Sobel, Ryan Vermillon, Matthew Vogel, and Nina Wussow.

Many of our educational approaches to cocktails have been refined over the years thanks to our team at Proprietors LLC, the consulting and services wing of our company that designs, builds, opens, and operates bars and restaurants. Without their expertise, this book and our bars would be far less efficient: thank you to Jodie Calderon, Lauren Corriveau, Henry Foote, and Jordan Schwartz.

We're also lucky enough to work with a handful of individuals and agencies that are extensions of our team, and without whom so much of what we do would not be possible. Thank you, Nora Varcho, for being our voice via social media and so much more; Jenna Kaplan, for ensuring that our efforts are heard and seen in the press; Jeff Combs and the Craftwork team, for bringing the Death & Co Marketplace to life; Jade Howe, for translating our brand to retail; Matthew Goldman and the team at MFG, for driving new designs forward; and AAmp Studio, for translating our vision into beautiful and immersive physical spaces.

Keeping this group focused and thriving requires an incredible support network, and we're lucky to have a core leadership team that wakes up every day thinking about how to make our bars and businesses better: the national operations team, Michael Shain and Wes Hamilton; and our admin department who keeps the machines humming, Marie D'Antonio, Massiel Hurtado, and Chief Petting Officer, Oliver.

Getting to do what we do happens only because we've been given the opportunity by our investment community. This pool is made up of hundreds of investors—so we won't list all of you here—but we'd be remiss not to acknowledge all those who have contributed. Thank you for believing in us; thank you for supporting the Death & Co vision.

A special thank-you to our board of directors members, Bill Spurgeon and Leland O'Connor, who provide frequent and invaluable council. Likewise, thank you to our partners Ravi DeRossi and Craig Manzino for their support, guidance, advice, and friendship.

Turning a book from a bunch of jumbled ideas into something both coherent and beautiful takes a talented team, and we're so fortunate to get to work with the same people book after book. Thank you to Emily Timberlake for not only being the best editor in the biz, but for making a process that can be maddening so much fun; we relish your guidance (and cheeky comments) in tracked changes. Likewise, thank you to our long-standing friends Kate and Tim Tomkinson who, respectively, designed another beautiful book and gave life to our ideas through original illustrations. Our photographers, Dylan Ho and Jeni Afuso, are simply the best: You bring endless creativity and enthusiasm to every shoot; thank you for capturing our world so beautifully!

Thank you to the team at Ten Speed Press, who, on this third go-around, continues to be amazing partners in the long process of assembling a book. Julie Bennett, Ashley Pierce, Emma Campion, Betsy Stromberg, and Serena Sigona: your patience is saintly, your vision and commitment to quality unparalleled. And to the man behind the curtain, Aaron Wehner, thank you for continuing to believe in us (and draining our supply of IPAs). A special thanks to our copyeditor, Kristi Hein, and proofreader, Linda Bouchard, for saving us from embarrassing errors and asking the questions we didn't think to ask.

To our agents, Jonah Straus and David Black, thank you for keeping us focused and on track.

And finally, to our partners in life—Andrew Ashey, Rotem Raffe, Jenna Gerbino, Alejandro Guzman, and Shel Bourdon—your support, patience, feedback, and love keep us going.

—Alex, Nick, Dave, Devon, Tyson

INDEX

Text © 2021 by Alexander Day, Nick Fauchald, and David Kaplan
Photographs copyright © 2021 by Dylan James Ho and Jeni Afuso
Illustrations copyright © 2021 by Tim Tomkinson

Published in the United States by Ten Speed Press, an imprint of Random House,
a division of Penguin Random House LLC, New York.
www.tenspeed.com

Ten Speed Press and the Ten Speed Press colophon are registered trademarks
of Penguin Random House LLC.

Library of Congress Cataloging-in-Publication Data is on file with the publisher.

Hardcover ISBN: 978-1-9848-5841-2
eBook ISBN: 978-1-9848-5842-9

Printed in China

Acquiring editor: Julie Bennett | Developmental editor: Emily Timberlake
Production editor: Ashley Pierce | Editorial assistant: Want Chyi
Designer: Katherine Tomkinson
Production manager: Serena Sigona
Photo retoucher: Dylan James Ho
Copyeditor: Kristi Hein | Proofreader: Linda Bouchard | Indexer: Ken DellaPenta
Publicist: Kristin Casemore | Marketer: Andrea Portanova

10 9 8 7 6 5 4 3 2 1

First Edition